The Miyanmin
Human Ecology of a
Papua New Guinea Society

Studies in Cultural Anthropology, No. 9

Conrad Phillip Kottak, Series Editor

Professor of Anthropology
The University of Michigan

Other Titles in This Series

The Miyanmin
Human Ecology of a Papua New Guinea Society

by
George E.B. Morren, Jr.

UMI RESEARCH PRESS
Ann Arbor, Michigan

Produced and distributed by
UMI Research Press
an imprint of
University Microfilms International
A Xerox Information Resources Company
Ann Arbor, Michigan 48106

Library of Congress Cataloging in Publication Data

Morren, George E. B.
  The Miyanmin : human ecology of a Papua New Guinea
society.

   (Studies in cultural anthropology ; no. 9)
   Bibliography: p.
   Includes index.
   1. Miyanmin (Papua New Guinea people)   I. Title.
II. Series.
DU740.42.M66   1986   306'.0899912   85-20817
ISBN 0-8357-1558-2 (alk. paper)

Contents

List of Illustrations

Figures

Plates

Maps

Following page 305

List of Tables

Preface

As I prepared to write this prefatory note, I came across Roy Rappaport's preface to the new edition of *Pigs for the Ancestors* (1984) and was struck by several points. The first is that "Pigs" is an appropriate "lead" because it (or its precursors) started the train of thought and observation leading to this book. The second point is related to the first. In the new preface Rappaport reflects on the disagreements surrounding his original work. In particular, he targets anthropology's wastefulness in rejecting approaches before they have been fully explored and improved in the light of experience and criticism.

My view is that our early enthusiasm for "functional analysis" and "hard systems" was exaggerated rather than misplaced. This enthusiasm needed to be modified and shifted in the directions followed by adherents of other branches of the systems analytic arts. That fairly well describes the relationship between this book and my doctoral dissertation of 10 years ago. Some core ideas (such as the connections between hunting and movement and a "hard systems" model) remain, but in other respects I have pursued a "softer" path in order to reflect more realistically how things actually work in Miyanmin society. The two approaches are complementary, although perhaps only the latter is necessary once one is grounded in the systems perspective. This compromise also serves my desire to write a more widely focused ethnography.

Anthropology's strength *and* its weakness is that we demand virtuosity of our members; there are few teams, not many "schools," little replication and an excess of imagination, chauvinism, exaggeration, and polemic. There is also the trend toward specialization even within subdisciplines, only partly fostered by the Internal Revenue Service. Virtuosity and specialization together form a deadly combination. The watchword seems to be, "Don't look back."

This book is based on fieldwork done in Papua New Guinea, from December, 1967 to September, 1969 and from December, 1980 to June, 1981. The first of the two periods was supported by a fellowship and grant from the National Science Foundation, the second by funding from the Wenner-Gren Foundation for Anthropological Research and the Faculty Academic Study Program of Rutgers University. The latter (along with the Rutgers Research

Foundation) also supported the preparation of this book. In addition, in 1967 I was granted permission to enter the country and conduct research by the Administrator of the then Territory of Papua and New Guinea. The West Sepik district commissioner also sanctioned my project and offered advice. In 1980–81 my research was sponsored by the Department of Anthropology of the University of Papua New Guinea and permission to conduct the research was granted by the government of Sandoun (West Sepik) Province. The National Museum and Art Gallery sponsored a visit to the middle May River area to look into archaeological matters. I am grateful to all of these organizations and governments.

My principal and unpayable debt is to the Miyanmin people, especially to the residents of the Hak and upper May valleys, members of Kometen, Temseten, and Sokaten parishes. Above all else, they changed my life. From my first intrusion into their lives, people always received me with generosity, warmth, and a nurturing spirit—as well as with avid curiosity about my ways, possessions, and capabilities. On all too modest a scale, I was required to fulfill their needs and expectations as a responsible member of the community. This side of the relationship was revealed when a delegation approached me as I prepared to depart for home in 1969. Speaking for the group, the Luluai Beliap said, "Morren, when you leave we want to replace you with a doctor and a businessman."

In the late 1960s my home base was Ukdabip, a small hamlet of only six women's houses and a men's house on the Uk River several hours removed across a low divide from the airstrip site. Here I was able to experience social life intensely and only rarely with detachment. I learned of the "solidarity of the sibling group" from Alanharap and his younger brothers Monotap, Kwoifam, and Watiyap; about the roles and perspectives of women as well as the agricultural routine from Watkop and her daughter Kintememinap; about domestic strife from Ketotning and Amitap (who proved that a billet of firewood is a great equalizer); about grief, fear, and danger upon the death of Yungapsep; about the conflicts and contradictions of modernization from Sekerup and Amusep; and about reverence from Sawoiyap and the scope of valor from his younger brother Amit. I also found enduring friendship with Asuneng, Ikomtobal, Kwekiyap, and Tariyap.

My return in 1980—after an 11-year absence—celebrated both the reality of continuity and a multitude of changes. Though I felt as if I had never left, I was uneasy about the community's losses, innovations, and other surprises. I was met by more than a decade of fertility, growth, and mortality; an immense village around the airstrip where I now chose to base myself; a school with children speaking English and querying me about New York; and, finally, having the role of businessman thrust upon me. Friends and the children of late friends brought me up to date on events personal and public, sad and satisfying; and I picked up personally and professionally more or less where I had left off.

Because of the remoteness of Miyanmin country even today, I was dependent on the goodwill and assistance of the Australian Baptist Mission Society at Telefomin and the Missionary Aviation Fellowship in order to receive mail, supplies, and occasional treats. Mission folk and the Summer Institute of Linguistics workers studying Miyanmin and other Mountain Ok languages on Telefomin station were always generous and hospitable. I am especially grateful to Sister Elizabeth Crouch for her humanity and her patience in teaching me rudimentary medicine.

I am also indebted to Columbia University's anthropological community of the 1950s and 60s in which I spent both my undergraduate and graduate years. It was a remarkable group and program in terms of faculty, students, and atmosphere. I am particularly grateful to Marvin Harris for introducing me to anthropology and encouraging my growth, to A. P. Vayda for directing my interests and sponsoring my earlier research, to the late Paul Collins for fostering self-consciousness in philosophical matters, and to Alex Alland for a constructive and nurturing spirit.

Barry Craig taught me how to survive, if not prosper, in the bush and persuaded me (and many others) to do research in the Telefomin area. I am grateful for that but value his friendship even more. I am also indebted to present and former colleagues and collaborators who have shared their ideas, sensitivities, and references along the way. These include Mark Dornstreich, Richard Clemmer, Michael Little, Ken Hewitt, David Hyndman, Carmel Schrire, Bonnie McCay, Tom Rudel, and Pete Vayda. My secretary at Rutgers, June Needham, helped me get this project organized; and a lot of the typing was done by Debby Kantor, Joan Greene, and Nadya Silva. I created many of the graphics with Graphware's "Charts Unlimited." Maps 3 through 10 were drawn by Susan Naughton.

Finally, I am grateful to my wife, Janet Gardner, and to my son, Karl Debreczeny, for patiently suffering my absence in 1980–81. With Janet's arrival in the field in March I think my Miyanmin friends were convinced that I had really grown up.

1

People on the Move:
A History and Introduction

The story begins more than 12 generations ago. Fafaro of Sokaten and Wasano of Wameten were away from their home villages with separate sago-cutting parties where the Yuwa [May] River bends from west to north. Fafaro left to hunt and soon shot a wild pig. The wounded pig ran away and, because the *anat* arrow point did not part from the shaft as it was supposed to, the pig carried away the entire arrow.

While also hunting away from his group, Wasano saw the pig come to rest and die. He removed the arrow and stood and waited near a fallen tree. Fafaro, following the trail, soon appeared and discovered the pig. He immediately noticed that his arrow was missing and began searching. Noticing Wasano standing by the tree, he said, "I just shot a pig and have lost my arrow." Replied Wasano, "You shot and killed a pig alright, but I took your arrow."

Fafaro allowed Wasano to keep the arrow and offered him more. "I have a sister and now I have a pig. Let us go to my village." With Wasano's assistance, Fafaro bore the pig back to Noialbip, a hamlet on the northern fall of the range that encloses the upper Yuwa Valley. There the pig was dressed and cooked in a leaf oven. After the food from the oven was distributed, Wasano carried a share to his village on the Kokomo River.

Later Wasano brought his sister to Fafaro at Noialbip and Fafaro reciprocated by giving his sister to Wasano. Later still, Wasano's son Dukgena married Fafaro's daughter Mesek. As a result of this, Sokaten and Wameten joined together, pooled their taro stalks, and made gardens together on the Kokomo. When the gardens were mature they built a joint village called Dabwaibip.

Three generations later, Wameten and Sokaten were still living together on the May at Dabwaibip. Oiyap, a descendant of Fafaro and Wasano, was very old and, accordingly, he communed with the spirit world. Thus, he spoke to his line, "If you kill and divide me, taking my bones and wrapping them in *yom* bundles, your gardens will grow well."

So his son Sebandriyap and the rest of his line followed Oiyap's directions and clubbed him to death. New varieties of cane and pandanus sprang up where his blood fell. After his body had decomposed on the exposure platform, his bones were divided among men from all the eastern Miyanmin parishes including his own.

Later, Sebandriyap, his son Wemeyasep and their line carried these relics to the Nia [Frieda] River valley, then occupied by Miyanten, Togoten, Dariten, and Dabwariten. They moved to the east by way of a headwater tributary of the Yuwa and over the high divide that extends southward from Mekil [Mount Stolle]. Thence, they followed the Mikedam River to its junction with the Nia and made gardens. Later still they joined Dariten to make gardens further north on the Meleya River.

More years passed and Wemeyasep's line left the Niataman groups to move in small steps around the northwest slopes of Mekil. They made gardens at Amweblu Mountain, then at Mikmotaman, and then at Mikimtemtagan. There died Wemeyasep's father Sebandriyap, the son of Oiyap.

Then Sokaten-Wameten summoned Wemeyasep to rejoin the group and he and his line ascended Mekilgolim (the summit) to return to the main settlement at Ariyamobip. As he was still a young bachelor, he married shortly thereafter.

Exegesis

This story, part of the historical epic of two Miyanmin parishes, is being used currently to support a land claim. It also is a capsule ethnography, if you know what to look for.

The Miyanmin grow taro, hunt, and forage wild foods. People believe in spirits and an afterlife. They are highly mobile, both individually and in groups.

All people are equal and ennobled by unique names, although men are more equal than women. Friendship is as basic as the ties of blood and marriage, and one is readily converted to the other. An exchange of sisters creates an individual bond which launches a confederation embracing, perhaps, several hundred persons. Later, this union is reinforced by the marriage of double cross cousins, a common feature of the straight line genealogies of "big men" that order history. Big men are the sons of big men.

The old are separate as they begin their trek to the afterlife and sometimes rush to prepare for their task (as spirits) of ensuring the well-being of their fellows and descendants. All death is by violence, and its threat is a given. The bones of the ancestors are memorials; the spirits alone possess power.

Groups are in flux and motion, joined and separated, in one valley and out another in pursuit of plentiful game and fair land. Buildings and settlements are substantial but impermanent. Ties to place are in memory; and it is understood that in the modern world, memory of place is property.

The Problem of Movement

I have selected only a portion of the foregoing—the issue of individual and group mobility—for analysis in this book. I focus on this topic for two reasons. The first is that the Miyanmin are distinguished from many other New Guinea peoples by their mobility. Second (and possibly related to the first issue), mobility has not received the attention and understanding it requires from anthropologists and other observers of nonpastoral tribal peoples in New Guinea and elsewhere.

Mobility is often misunderstood. I am one of the anthropologists, previously thought to be apocryphal, who one morning awakened to a deserted village. My initial impulse was to take it personally. In his study of "bungled disaster relief," Waddel (1975, 1983) debunked the assumptions of disaster experts that the response of local people to the destruction of their food supply due to frost involved "fleeing" and "forced migration." He argued instead that most people were able to take refuge with long-distance trading partners according to a long-established pattern.

A patrol officer who visited the West and Landslip ranges in Miyanmin country in 1965 saw many old and abandoned village sites. He erroneously inferred that this was all that remained of a large population which had been extinguished by endemic warfare. In 1968, I chartered a light aircraft to take some air photos and to observe Miyanmin groups living on the middle May River. On the basis of the numerous settlements I saw from the air, I thought I had discovered perhaps 600 or 700 people on the Fiak River. When I later visited the valley I counted 157. I had been fooled by the fact that lower-altitude people establish and abandon settlements even faster than the familiar higher-altitude Miyanmin. I later found that the latter had a chauvinistic joke about it.

Perhaps because anthropologists observe a common prejudice that civilization equates with settled village life, we take for granted also a relationship between houses and domestic units in size and number, between settlements and more or less enduring local groups, and between the foregoing and the total population. In fact, none of these "rules of thumb" provides a basis for inferences about the Miyanmin.

The reasons are complex but revolve around these eight characteristics of Miyanmin population, settlement, and established ways of doing things: (1) the crude population density of the Miyanmin is low, less than eight persons per square kilometer (3 per square mile); (2) local groups have large territories, ranging from 36 to 197 square kilometers (14 to 76 square miles); (3) the size and arrangement of settlements vary; (4) groups occasionally fission, fuse, and confederate; (5) the overall settlement pattern of local groups is always changing; (6) families possess several houses in different locations and move among them; (7) effective group size diminishes with altitude, although the size of territories and the distance between settlements increase; and (8) in order to be sustained, major features of the subsistence pattern—specifically, the taro monoculture, hunting, and foraging—depend on mobility.

The reality confronting the ethnographer (or some other outsider with a need to understand these things) is that people move around a lot; and, although they do it in patterned ways, the patterns are very complex. Here again, understanding them involves knowing what to look for. In principle, and sometimes in practice too, scientists know what to look for by virtue of theory and method. If my identification of the research problem is valid, then we need a theory saying that movement is a key attribute of the experimental or field situation. I will propose such a theory later in this chapter, though first it is necessary to lay an intellectual and theoretical foundation. It should be obvious from my lead-in to the chapter that a substantial proportion of the ethnographic information I present is of a familiar type; what differs is the ecological perspective I adopt to deal with this information.

Ecology and Anthropology

Ecological anthropology tries to participate in two contradictory intellectual traditions, the social sciences and biology. Of particular relevance in the former case are political economy, evolutionism, and structural functionalism; in the latter, general ecology and evolutionary biology. A person undertaking a study of the interactions of people and the environment is thus faced with many choices of research strategy. Something needs to be said about the relationship between the two traditions in order to place the present study in context and to support my own methodological decisions.

The social sciences tradition is represented by the cultural ecology of Julian Steward, Carl Sauer, and their intellectual heirs. I contend that in anthropology, cultural ecology has had little to do with biological ecology. Instead, very early on the phrase "cultural ecology" was a euphemism that permitted anthropologists to employ a simplified Marxist framework. Steward could not cite his sources, but the linked concepts of "culture core" and "levels of sociocultural integration" are glosses for mode and organization of production. As Vayda and Rappaport (1968) have pointed out, Steward did not know very much biology and tended to equate the subject with genetics. (For that matter, he may not have known much about Marx!) He acquired his environmentalism from Sauer at Berkeley. Like Marx, Steward also excluded population from his framework. An heir of Steward's who can cite his sources,

Marvin Harris, has made his roots clear in the title of his book, *Cultural Materialism* (1979). I do not object to the use of Marxian concepts in anthropology. I merely wish to emphasize that cultural ecology and cultural materialism are not rooted in general ecology.

An alternative in anthropology developed out of the foregoing when cultural ecologists self-consciously turned to biology. This was done initially for environmental information, as in Conklin's (1957, 1961) early work on traditional agriculture. Scholars increasingly turned to biology for theory and method, as in Betty Meggers's (1954) attempt to use the "limiting factors" concept. This was facilitated by the sharing of certain intellectual and technical tools, e.g., the comparison of functionalism and ethnography to environmental systems and natural history approaches. Like biologists, cultural ecologists also tended to be materialists and positivists. Anthropologists had a lot to gain from ecology, a field that resembles anthropology in many ways. It embraces a broad range of problem topics and has been described as both a behavioral and a biological science, inherently multidisciplinary (Smith, 1966:5). It differs from anthropology, however, in having an integrating paradigm, the biological hierarchy and its associated concepts and rules of correspondence that permit observations belonging to different subfields or logical types to be (at least partly) related to each other. And despite the field's commitment to precision, generality, and the use of experimental procedures, one can still find works in ecology that more closely resemble ethnography, though theoretically informed, than anything else in the natural sciences. Ecologists have—with reasonable success—grappled with similar problems of making sense out of a tangle of naturalistic observations.

At the time cultural ecologists began to explore its usefulness, general ecology could be roughly divided into two segments, a division which still describes lines of controversy in the field. The first is synecology, an area concerned primarily with the ecosystem and community levels of the biological hierarchy. The ecology of Clements, Shelford, Allee, Dice, E. and H. Odum, Golley, and Margalief belongs in this category, which conceives of the field as the study of the structure and function of nature and pursues "hard systems" approaches. The second segment is autecology, concerned more with the species population and organismic levels. This emphasis is embraced by students as diverse as Wynne-Edwards, Deevey, Emlen, Calhoun, Slobodkin, and Colinveaux. These are the demographers and behaviorists of ecology, who conceive of the field as the study of what organisms and species actually do in their habitats.

The issues separating the two segments of the field reflect the divergent perspectives of "forest people" and "tree people" (to cite a well-known bromide). The autecologists say the synecologists don't know anything about trees, while the synecologists say the autecologists don't know the important things about trees. This kind of controversy should be familiar to anthropologists and other social scientists.

Beginning in the 1950s some cultural ecologists in anthropology turned to the synecologists. I have in mind the work of Barth (1959–60), Vayda (1961), Vayda, Leeds and Smith (1961), Geertz (1963), Lee (1969), Suttles (1960), Sweet (1960), Rappaport (1961, 1966, 1968), and Sahlins and Service (1960). The bibliographies of these works actually list one or another general ecology textbook, many of them works of systems ecology. Anthropologists were initially more interested in "self-regulation" (or equilibration), carrying capacity and limiting factors, elemental cycles, and energy flow than they were in predator–prey or successional studies (although the latter were equally prominent in ecology). This predisposition may be traced to Steward's translation of the nineteenth-century concept of production into "culture core," which placed the greatest emphasis on material culture and subsistence. However, it was also reasonably consistent with the trophic bias of many prominent community ecologists.

Thus, when I was preparing to enter the field in the 1960s, an established view in ecological anthropology and geography was that *the* limiting factor for human populations was nutritional energy. At that time I, too, was in the grip of a "calorific obsession" (Brookfield 1972:46). Such preoccupation with energy is seductive because it facilitates quantification—the integration of labor inputs, food outputs, and such physiological variables as energy expenditure and growth—and holds out the hope that generalizations can be drawn through precise comparisons. There was a proliferation of studies of food production and consumption by anthropologists and geographers in New Guinea (e.g., Salisbury 1962; Pospisil 1963; Brookfield 1962, 1964; Brookfield and Brown 1958, 1963; Lea 1964; Rappaport 1968; Watson 1965a, 1965b; Waddel 1972; Clark 1971) and in other world areas (e.g., Carneiro 1960; Allen 1965; Freeman 1955; Conklin 1951, 1959; Richards 1948, de Schlippe 1956). Many methodological and technical improvements were forthcoming, including Street's (1969) revision of the carrying capacity model, Boserup's (1965) model of intensification under population pressure, and more precise measurements of labor input and energy expenditure under field conditions (e.g., Thomas 1973). At the same time many of these excellent investigations of agricultural systems, land, work, production and consumption were deficient as studies of human adaptation, ultimately because of their calorific obsession.

As I—and others—have argued (Vayda and McCay 1975, 1977; Morren 1977) there are problems with the following four assumptions common in much of this work:

1. That energy is a limiting factor: there are situations (temporally and spatially defined) in which energy is limiting to groups or individuals in a society (e.g., Gross and Underwood 1971; the U.S. in the 1970s) or even in a region (e.g., the Arctic), but they must be specified rather than assumed (Slobodkin 1972:294).
2. That adaptation equates with energetic efficiency; as I have argued elsewhere (Morren 1977), in situations where energy is *not* limiting, there need only be some correspondence between input-output ratios (realistically defined) and worker-consumer ratios.
3. That the study of subsistence ecology (e.g., plant agriculture in predominantly agricultural societies) provides a sufficient description of how people survive; for example, most studies of energy flow and/or subsistence unrealistically restrict the *kinds* of inputs and outputs that are considered. Richard Lee's (1969) input-output analysis of !Kung-San hunting did not weigh such vital activities as movement from place to place, erection of shelters, and the like. Brookfield and Hart's (1971) typology of New Guinea subsistence systems, which applied Boserup's (1965) model of intensification, failed to include hunting, collecting, and pig husbandry.
4. That it is heuristically legitimate to treat small societies as "in harmony" with their natural environment. Thus, insufficient attention is paid to human behavioral and environmental change, including those changes, hazards, and problems caused by people, such as the decline in game animals resulting from optimal foraging (Martin 1983).

In an effort to transcend the calorific obsession, some students of tropical adaptation turned to "protein" as a limiting factor (e.g., Fonaroff 1965; Alland 1970; Meggers 1971; Morren 1974, 1977; Gross 1975). Alland has argued the case for this alternative assumption:

> in the cereal growing regions of the world protein and vitamin deficiencies were rare because unrefined grain is quite high in most of the necessary nutrients. But in tropical areas, particularly in those geographical zones in which grain crops do poorly and where the major [cultigens] are root crops such as the yam, sweet potato, manioc, and taro, protein scarcity becomes a severe problem. Populations lacking domestic animals for one reason or another must rely on hunting to fulfill protein requirements.... In most cases it is likely that such populations would be checked in part by Malthusian controls with protein, or more correctly, certain essential amino acids as the limiting factors. (Alland 1970:70–71).

Critics in both anthropology and ecology have raised serious questions about attempts to identify single limiting factors—be they energy, essential amino acids, or whatever—in studies of the adaptation of people or of other organisms (Vayda and McCay 1975, 1977; Colinveaux 1973). In criticizing synecologists, Paul Colinveaux has made a case that applies equally well to the work of many ecological anthropologists:

> They have conveyed the idea that all you had to do in your field studies was to go out and measure things until you found something that seemed to be limiting, and that you had then explained something significant. The chances were that you had done nothing of the sort. You may have come across some temporary condition in which an animal had bumped against some real limit, or even that the correlation with an apparent restraint was entirely fortuitous (Colinveaux 1973:276–77).

The criticisms and suggestions arising from this perspective can be summarized in the following seven points:

1. People and other organisms are simultaneously threatened by and exposed to many environmental conditions, problems, and hazards which vary in time, space, magnitude, and other dimensions.[1]
2. These problems include limiting and tolerance factors, disease and other biotic hazards, and "natural" disasters. Often overlooked, however, are anthropogenic problems and hazards, including those which have resulted from attempts to solve *other* problems in the past (Little and Morren 1976:6) and those of a political-economic character (Morren 1983a).
3. Indeed, absent in this discussion are useful definitions of "environmental problem." I have found four (of increasing specificity) to be valuable: (a) a change, which according to Bateson (1980) is "a difference that makes a difference"; (b) a factor that poses a threat to the survival of members of a group; (c) any factor contributing to higher levels of morbidity and mortality (Vayda and McCay 1975); and (d) any factor having a negative effect on the fecundity, speed of development, longevity, or spatial position of an organism (Maelzor 1965b).
4. Conditions said to prevail in broad regions are invoked to explain highly variable sociocultural patterns which may or may not include effective solutions to the conditions at issue. It is one thing to demonstrate that protein scarcity, lack of moisture, seismic risk, or some other condition is common in an area, another thing to demonstrate that it is a problem for people or other organisms in that area, and yet another thing to test the effectiveness of solutions to a demonstrable problem.
5. Related to the foregoing point, a solved problem is not a problem, the survival of an organism that is adapted to a particular condition is not

threatened by that condition (unless something else happens to interfere with its ability to respond or equilibrate).

6. In looking at how people and other organisms interact with their environment we must pay particular attention to the relationship between the characteristics of problems and the features of responses (Vayda and McCay 1975; Morren 1980, 1983a, 1983b). Because of this, the "objective" environment is of little interest. Rather, we must be concerned with the interaction of an environment with a specific group whose members have their own problems, needs, and capabilities.

7. The equilibrium-centered view of people–environment relations is static unless it is linked to a more dynamic view of how people respond to survival-threatening problems and hazards (Vayda and McCay 1975: 298–300, 302) that sees equilibration as only one of a variety of desirable features of systems. In this connection, equilibration refers to responses and mechanisms that attempt to achieve stability in relation to small, incremental, and regular changes. This is not to imply that equilibrium is always achieved (or maintained once achieved). An important qualification to enter at this point—and one to which I will return in the next chapter—is the difference between equilibrating behavior, on the one hand, and the achievement or maintenance of equilibrium (or stability), on the other hand. The former is a matter of observation, the latter of operations.

Despite these criticisms and suggestions, the concepts and methods of systems ecology have been particularly appropriate to the study of what were once relatively self-sufficient (although not stable) associations of people, plants and animals in small-scale, technologically simple societies. Given the prevalent preoccupation with production, equilibrium-based studies such as Roy Rappaport's *Pigs for the Ancestors* (1968, 1983) have helped us to ask new questions about how people deal with the more or less regular contingencies they face in a natural and social environment. The study of the Miyanmin presented in this book belongs to this genre as well: recognizing that a methodology has limitations does not provide grounds for abandoning it. Instead, I feel obliged to establish its scope and applicability and to say what it can and what it cannot do.

I agree that the kind of cybernetic or functional methods pursued here (discussed in chapter 2) are less suitable for studying survival-threatening change and irregular, unpredictable, or irreversible kinds of environmental and social variability. This includes the expansion and intensification of local systems, the flux of relations between groups, the evolution of complexity in social organization, and the consequences of rapid social and environmental change (Watts 1983:237f.). I will make some suggestions regarding the methods appropriate in these situations as I have made the attempt elsewhere in other analyses of Miyanmin field data (Morren 1977, 1980, 1984) and in studies of complex societies (Morren 1976, 1983a, 1983b). An equilibrium model does, however, provide a baseline for studying the kinds of changes mentioned; and I will return to some of these issues in other chapters.

A Taxonomy of Responses

The foregoing discussion of the development of ecological anthropology and its relation to the present study is not complete without a consideration of responses. In this regard, the corollary of a fixation on limiting factors and food has been the focus on technology, or "resource management strategies"— especially subsistence (for example, hunting, collecting, and agricultural techniques and technology). I have already alluded to the restricted vision of human life support that this entailed, particularly in energy flow and labor input-food output studies (Morren 1977). In my discussion of environmental problems I implied that studies of human adaptation must consider responses to a much wider spectrum of environmental conditions, problems, and hazards than those involving food or other resources.

My task is easier because responses are not problem-specific. And, as I have argued elsewhere (Little and Morren 1976), the entire spectrum of human behavioral responses having a direct effect on environmental interactions neatly fall into four categories:[2] movement, environmental modification, areal integration, and industrialization. I believe that these types are key features of the evolution of human societies.

Movement

Movement responses involve the internal movement of individual members and subgroups of a population within its territory. Movement is to be differentiated from migration, a demographic response involving changes in population membership. Opportunities and risks may be effectively controlled through the establishment and maintenance of territorial boundaries and the location of people in their habitats in relation to resources and hazards. Movement responses are patterned in space and time. They may be cyclical, for example, diurnal or seasonal. They are sometimes situational, occasioned by marriage, disease quarantine, or refuging in the face of disaster. In stratified societies social mobility involves movement responses as social "location" entails differential exposure to resources and hazards. Put another way, in egalitarian societies, local groups are stratified with respect to each other on the ground. The most intensive form of movement is warfare, which involves the attempt to extend or defend the space in which other activities are conducted. From the perspective of cultural evolution, hunter-gatherers are distinguished by the fact that their members "move around a lot" (Lee 1972), rather than by the fact that they hunt and gather. All humans hunt and gather, harvesting resources in relation to their needs. The key issue for people is access and exposure: how they make available in sufficient quantities the resources they need, or how they reduce hazards to tolerable levels. The stereotypical hunter-gatherer does it by moving.

Environmental Modification

Environmental modification responses involve changing the environment to make resources and hazards more predictable in time and space (i.e., they constitute a temporary reduction of entropy). This is the essence of agriculture, but it also characterizes hazard mitigation schemes that attempt to confine problems or eliminate them at their source. Acephalous, segmentary, horticultural, and pastoral peoples characteristically evinced a flexible pattern of movement and environmental modification strategies before they were incorporated into states.

Areal Integration

Areally integrating responses[3] involve patterned ways of marshaling the resources and capabilities of many communities to deal effectively with problems. They often entail a loss of local sovereignty and self-sufficiency, and accordingly, from the standpoint of the smallest units involved, are rarely voluntary or easily reversible. At issue is the cost to individuals and communities of participation in extensive networks of exchange and dependency which integrate wide and diverse areas for life support and hazard reduction. A typical cost is a loss of flexibility of movement and environmental modification responses (e.g., people are more sedentary, agriculture more permanent and specialized, people in other communities may control critical resources). Under an areally integrating regime, more commodities move than people. The political dimensions of areal integration are particularly important: power means control of the flow of a commodity through a particular node in the network. This is the strategy of the state where the use or threat of force is a feature of integration and performance, and "vertical" or social stratification succeeds the risks of geography.

Industrialization

Industrial responses involve the substitution for human labor of work from nonhuman animals and physical energy sources to carry out other kinds of responses. This assumes that they are available and that human somatic energy is limiting or cannot be marshaled in amounts sufficient for the task at hand.

Summary

This book is primarily a systems analysis of settlement and hunting strategies, of which movement responses are a prominent feature. These responses are, I argue, related to a variety of environmental contingencies including changes in the availability of meat, disease frequencies, and the intensity of interpopulation competition.

The book has three parts. The first, consisting of chapters 1 through 3, is introductory in that it is a theoretical prelude and establishes a research problem. It is intended to set things in motion intellectually and to present my central hypothesis. Chapter 2 concerns methodology (i.e., my logic of justification), and I discuss the study of hunting and systems analysis. Chapter 3 presents a hypothetical system relating kinds of movement to particular contingencies including those affecting hunting.

The second part of the book, consisting of chapters 4, 5, and 6, focuses on the material context of the environment and its uses. Chapter 4 studies the environment of the Miyanmin from the standpoint of the people: opportunities, problems, hazards, and perception. Chapter 5 is about extensive Miyanmin slash and mulch agriculture, the taro monoculture, pig husbandry, and variations and alternatives. Chapter 6 takes a look at game animals and how people interact with them.

The third part of this study, consisting of chapters 7 through 11, focuses on spatial organization, movement, and change. In chapter 7, I discuss individuals and groups, emphasizing the social dimensions of adaptation. In chapter 8, the religious aspects of social choice, decision making, and supralocal agencies are examined. Chapter 9 builds on the foregoing to describe how people actually move in the context of equilibration. Chapter 10 discusses changes of greater magnitude and escalatory responses, expansion, migration, and warfare. Chapter 11 is about the Miyanmin in the modern world, and how the new is based on the old.

2

Methodology

A Definition

Many social scientists use the term methodology more or less interchangeably with "techniques" or "procedures," as in the phrases "field techniques" and "laboratory procedures." While this is common in our field, according to philosophers of science it is at odds with the usage in the hard sciences and philosophy (Rudner 1966:4-5). More importantly, it doesn't contribute to clear thinking about the structure of our arguments. Ernest Nagel (1961:450) says that "methodological discussions" examine "a number of broad logical issues" such as whether or not explanations in the social sciences differ in form as well as in substance from those of the natural sciences. The term methodology is also taken to refer to the way rules of correspondence serve to link theory with experimental, technical, or operational matters. Thus, for Rudner (1966:5; emphasis his), "the methodology of a scientific discipline is not a matter of its transient techniques but of its *logic of justification.*"

Part of the problem is that, lacking any theory of our own, we have engaged in "terminological inflation"; what we call "theory" is methodology, what we call "methodology" is technique, and what we call "technique" is uncontrolled observation and note-taking. I have witnessed a conversation between anthropologists and a philosopher that illustrates this point. The philosopher said, "There is no theory in the social sciences." The anthropologists naively interpreted this to mean, "There is no *good* theory in anthropology or the social sciences," and disciplinary smugness permits no response. What the philosopher truly meant was that *there is no theory,* good or bad. What we label "anthropological theory" is either methodology, a hypothesis, or a "theory of the middle range," whatever that is.

For example, Marvin Harris's *Nature of Cultural Things* (1964) was neither a theory nor a technique. In proposing a hierarchical epistemology of the "things" that were to be the subject of an unarticulated theory, Harris engaged in a *methodological* exercise. In yet another work, Harris refers to the emic-etic distinction as involving alternative "research options" (1968:582), "approaches" (576), or "perspectives" (576). Again the referent is methodological.

For me, methodology is the hard look before the leap. It is how we think about our problem-topics in the light of whatever theories we have from the natural sciences, and the methodological discussions that have already been conducted for us, supplemented by the application of our own critical faculties. In this chapter I introduce systems approaches, take a closer look at hunting and its elements, discuss my central methodological tool—functional analysis—and examine some related methodologies.

A Metataxonomy of Systems Approaches

The word "system" is an umbrella term for a variety of ways of either viewing complex reality or designing approaches to deal with it. All systems approaches have in common the assumption, commonly referred to as the holistic perspective, that everything is or can be connected to everything else. A singular orienting idea is that the whole is different than (not greater than) the sum of its parts (Bateson 1980). These approaches encourage us to look at how things interact, interconnect, interrelate, or, in some sense, control each other. Systems approaches also share the idea that causality in nature is circular (or recursive) rather than lineal. Indeed, some advocates claim that this feature is the hallmark of future science.

Various systems approaches differ with respect to logical type, scale or unit of analysis, the kind of connections and currency selected, and other features. In other words, analysts or designers must make certain strategic or methodological decisions about the most appropriate way of solving their problems. We can look at some of these features in turn.

Logical Types

In order to think about complex reality, all human beings arrange their names for things and relationships into hierarchies of classes of greater inclusiveness or higher order. This is made explicit in science courses where we are taught, for example, that acceleration is different (higher) than velocity; or that a population consists of organisms and possesses its own emergent characteristics, or that in machines the bias set into a control device is of a higher level than the control issued by the device itself (Bateson 1980). People who are not scientists conceptualize the world in a similar way: plants and animals are of a higher logical type than dogs and trees. It is useful for us to look at systems or systems approaches in a similar way and I present herewith a metataxonomy of systems. This should help us to grasp the different senses in which the term "system" is used.

The first order system is *an arrangement of things in time and space.* Its exemplars are either precursors of or deviations from the "hard systems" approach. They may be relatively broad, vague, or qualitative, while emphasizing the holistic character of the approach. I have in mind our common use of terms such as "society," the "environment," the "global system" (politics) or the "world system" (economy), as well as more pragmatic or naturalistic approaches to particular situations such as the "new look" in general systems theory, or the "soft systems approach" (Naughton 1981). This is paralleled by A. P. Vayda's method of "progressive contextualization" (1984). It may also embrace logico-deductive systems such as grammars, kinship systems, and sciences.

The second order system is *a pattern of things interacting.* Here the emphasis is on objects and classes of objects that constitute the more visible aspects of the system. Possible examples include the ecosystem and community concepts in ecology as reflected in such attributes as the food chain, trophic pyramid, and measures of diversity. The concepts of social structure and institution belong here too.

The third type of system refers to *the pattern of interaction as an open sequence.* These interactions are presented as linear processes of cause and effect with discrete outcomes. Examples might be epidemiological patterns, a cropping system, or a MacHarg matrix (1969).

The fourth order system is *a closed sequence of interaction and control.* Here the focus is on processes involving feedback, particularly negative feedback, equilibration, or "self-regulation," and the maintenance of key system components within an appropriate range of values. Pertinent examples include energy flow and control models in ecology (Odum 1971), population control (Slobodkin 1961, Wynne-Edwards 1962), predator-prey models (Gause 1934), and certain functional analyses in ecological anthropology. Positive feedback or deviation amplification processes (Maruyama 1963) also belong here.

The fifth order system is *a sequence of escalatory and flexibility-restoring interactions.* Of interest are such system properties as resilience and the economics of flexibility with the goal of assuring the persistence of the system in the face of large and irregular changes in the task environment. Examples come from studies of adaptation and evolution in biology, ecological anthropology, and related fields.

Scale and Unit of Analysis

In building a systems model of some aspect of reality, the analyst has to both choose the unit of analysis and make a strategic choice among such desirable features of models as generality, precision, and realism that are otherwise in conflict (Levins 1968). One way of reducing the complexity of the real world is to construct a nested or hierarchical systems model in which smaller units are "nested" in larger units as subsystems. An example of this is the biological hierarchy. A human ecological analysis of people in a particular locale might examine individuals (as the basic unit of adaptation), families (as units of production and consumption), communities (as cooperative units in a social and economic sense), as well as local populations (in the ecological sense of fitting into a complex natural community), regional systems (from the perspective of trade and areal integration), and all of these imbedded in and influenced by even larger inclusive units with systemic properties.

Currency

Depending on problem-topic, variables selected, and level or scale of analysis, the systems analyst may choose from a wide array of kinds of interconnections or currencies. Examples of "currencies" are money, labor, energy, nutrients, quantities of goods or matter, people and other organisms, and the like. Of particular interest are kinds of relations such as feedback and linear control relations.

Systems approaches have been employed by scholars of varied disciplinary backgrounds and problem orientations.[1] Although these studies vary in quality, they testify to the attractiveness of the perspective (while exciting comment, criticism, and revision by adherents—see below).

In a wide-ranging and acerbic survey of the uses of systems analysis in the social and biological sciences, David Berlinski (1976) poses three main cautions to this enthusiasm. The first and most fundamental is that systems analysis is quintessentially qualitative in nature (60). This is similar to Bateson's view that "logic and quantity turn out to be inappropriate devices for describing organisms, their interactions, and their internal organization" (1978:15). The second is that the cultivation of quantitative data is often a symptom of theoretical inadequacy (77). The third caution is that mathematical modeling is justified only if analysts "start simply and use to the fullest the resources of theory" (83). Berlinski has particularly harsh words for the Meadows's "ineffable innocence" (83) and David Easton's "sheer linguistic enthusiasm" (125). He reserves singular praise for the biological sciences, particularly the Lotka-Volterra predator-prey models: "there is a kind of successful matching of ambitions to available mathematical models that is entirely rare elsewhere in the systems analytical arts" (180).

The success attributed by Berlinski to predator-prey models illustrates the methodological trade-off inherent in model building. According to Richard Levins (1966), it is not possible to be at once mathematically precise, general in scope, and realistic. The Lotka-Volterra model succeeds precisely because it eschews realism and thereby tells us only a little bit about complex reality in general. As Berlinski puts it, "Successful science is abstractive: of all that is of interest, only a fragment is susceptible to explanation, and only a fragment of that fragment to mathematical analysis" (85).

The Study of Hunting

When I initiated this research in the late 1960s, no one had presented a clear picture of the role of hunting in the subsistence of New Guinea peoples. Such study was undeveloped except for work focused on technology and ethnoscience. Many groups were reported to be enthusiastic about hunting, even those living in deforested habitats with little game. The enthusiasm of the Miyanmin for hunting, however, is fully warranted by the abundance of game, the level of hunting success, and the contribution of hunting to subsistence. Just as reported for other groups, Miyanmin hunting is "exciting" (Arnell 1960:7), a "pleasurable activity," "a sport, a game" (Bulmer 1968a:302), but it also contributes more than 70 percent of the meat consumed by the people. This contrasts with the way the cited authorities have characterized hunting in New Guinea as a "pure sideline" (Arnell, 1960) or as "providing . . . a small but significant component of animal protein to the diet" (Bulmer 1968).

The apparent uniqueness of the Miyanmin case is an artifact of the geographically and ethnographically biased sample available to Bulmer and Arnell in the 1960s, a factor Bulmer (1968a:303, 306) recognized. It is loaded in favor of high-altitude core groups of the eastern part of the New Guinea highlands and coastal and centrally organized riverine peoples. For the most part these are groups known for their dependence either on pig husbandry or fishing. It is also true that when these authorities were writing, almost no relevant research had been done on mid-altitude fringe groups such as the Miyanmin anywhere in New Guinea (Hyndman and Morren, n.d.).

Understanding also has been clouded by the technological bias built into categories such as "hunting," "agriculture," and the like. As will be illustrated in this book, a key feature of an equilibrating hunting and foraging strategy—one that strongly shapes the overall character of a society—is not chasing and killing animals, but rather movement and patterned shifts of location.

Lacking (or eschewing) theory, I take at least part of my lead from what is now a much richer body of ethnographic literature on hunting peoples in New Guinea. Productive as well as enthusiastic hunting is particularly characteristic of the mid-altitude fringe peoples. This is to say that they live in the foothills or lower montane zone, roughly from 500 to 1500 m (1500 to 4500 feet) above sea level *and* away from lowland and highland core centers of population pressure (Morren 1984; Hyndman and Morren n.d.). On the north slopes of the central cordillera of the island are the Sanio-Hiowe (Townsend 1969; Townsend et al.

1973), the Hewa (Steadman 1975), the Gadio Enga (Dornstreich 1973, 1977), the Kalam (Bulmer 1967, 1968b, 1968c; Bulmer and Tyler 1968; Bulmer and Menzies 1972-73; Bulmer et al. 1975; Majnep and Bulmer 1977). The south slopes of the range embrace the Papuan Plateau–Mount Bosavi Peoples (Schiefflin 1976, Kelly 1977, Dwyer 1982), the Anga–Kukukuku (Blackwood 1940; Godelier 1971; Herdt 1981, 1982), Dairibi (Wagner 1967) and several Mountain Ok groups related to the Miyanmin including the Wopkaimin (Hyndman 1979, 1982), Faiwolmin (Jones 1980) and Baktaman Faiwolmin (Barth 1975).

The similarities and differences of these groups support my methodological decision to focus on particular features of the environment in relation to human cultural patterns. These are the ecological problems of spacing, movement, predation, food and prey recognition, preference and selection, competition, habitat affinity, and equilibration, as well as a quintessentially human problem of escalating options, intensification, group dynamics, and martial violence.

All the groups cited appear to share a similar (though hardly identical) environmental setting. There is a broad similarity of floristic and faunal components in terms of specific identity, relative abundance and diversity, patchiness, and the relative absence of extreme hazards and limiting factors (possibly excepting malaria parasites). The agricultural environment appears to be very favorable for most groups, and all practice shifting cultivation (sometimes mixed with sago exploitation). All are dependent on hunting or inland fishing for animal foods. All live in dispersed settlements at least part of the time and move around a great deal. All are removed in varying degrees from regional centers characterized by higher population density and pressure.

In connection with the foregoing, a characteristic feature of these groups is low population density. It is one of the sufficient conditions for the persistence of the kind of system I describe in this book, since it helps to define the limits and boundaries of stability (Hollings and Goldberg 1971:225f.) beyond which a group's survival may be at issue and/or the system may be transformed into "something else." For example, at a later point I will argue that shifts from hunting of game animals to alternative forms of meat production (possibly including more intensive ones) result from a change in this boundary condition—that population expansion beyond a certain level, or concentration, due to external pressure brings about a steplike transformation of the system. This may entail the intensification of existing patterns, the adoption of new cultivars or domesticates, and increasing prominence of environmental modification strategies at the expense of movement ones.

The study of hunting has also been muddled by the variety of approaches that have been employed and the sometimes global claims that have been made by their practitioners. As in the conflict between "tree people" and "forest people" referred to in the first chapter, these approaches are not competitors. Instead, they are either closely related or pertain to different logical types. In order to make some (provisional) sense out of the field I can offer a metaclassification of the tasks of hunters, the task-goals of systems involving hunting strategies, and associated methodologies.

A Metataxonomy of Hunting Systems

The general task for a group of people practicing hunting or foraging is to maintain a satisfactory level of meat production in relation to its numbers, their needs and capabilities, and the characteristics of the natural and anthropogenic environment. However, the elements of this, including the larger patterns, pertain to at least five logical types and levels of analysis:

1. To get close enough to capture an animal
2. To have technology adequate to capture any animal encountered
3. To capture a sufficient quantity of animals to fulfill the overall task
4. To fulfill the overall task in the time and with the resources (and other inputs) allotted
5. To sustain the activity and its returns for a very long time in the face of unknown (and unknowable) changes.

The first two levels involve technical and essentially individual issues: knowledge (including ethnoscience), skill, practice and learning, and scheduling and other kinds of individual decisions. (Of course, there are social dimensions to the sharing of skills and kills, and the division of labor.) Arnell's survey (1960) and particularly Bulmer's work on classification, hunting tactics, and related sociocultural matters, are examples. The third and fourth levels are essentially social and are matters of control and equilibration (these are defined later in this chapter). Approaches to the study of hunting behavior that fit in here include Richard Lee's classic input-output analysis of !Kung Bushman (San) hunting (1969) and spatial organization (1972a), the work of the optimal foraging school (although this assignment needs closer examination, see below), studies of energy flow and control in human life-support systems (Bayliss-Smith 1977; Morren 1977; Little and Morren 1976; Odum 1971; Thomas 1973; Winterhalder et al. 1974), and the present analysis (see also Morren 1974, 1980). The fifth level involves major changes in the environment and escalatory responses to them, and how these are subsumed by the economics of flexibility (Bateson 1963, 1980; McCay 1981; Morren 1980, 1983a, 1983b; Slobodkin 1968; Waddell 1975).

The Miyanmin possess a complex strategy for the management and exploitation of their relationships with game animals. I use the term strategy to cut across levels of analysis such as those defined above in order to isolate a set of practices having a discrete outcome. As such, it may be part of a larger system isolated for study. In this usage, a given strategy may be seen to have cognitive, technological, economic, spatial, and other dimensions. Environmental management strategies involve practices that mitigate a problem or hazard. Abstractly, there is no useful distinction to be drawn between resource management and hazard management because a hazard is a "negative resource" (Burton and Hewitt 1974; Morren 1983a) in the same way that a tolerance factor is a negative limiting factor. Operationally, a resource management strategy is involved when the condition at issue is the availability of a material source. (Resource management strategies are discussed more formally later in the chapter.) A desirable outcome of such a strategy is both a sustained and satisfactory yield and the minimization of additive and fractionating costs. An additive cost is a conventional one such as the expenditure of time, energy, or money. According to the economics of flexibility, a fractionating cost is the loss of a faculty, the commitment of an existing potentiality for change (Bateson 1963). An equilibrium strategy is a set of practices that go directly to a quantity and correct for disturbances.

The Miyanmin strategy of hunting and settlement manages renewable game resources that are significant because they provide essential amino acids, lipids, iodine, and other essential nutritional elements. It is an equilibrium strategy because movement patterns and changes of settlement location seem to compensate for environmental changes that are potential problems to people. The supply of game can be a problem because the local abundance— and thus the availability of particular species—varies, in many cases decreasing due to human competition, predation, and habitat disruption. In the short run, the capture of game is costly to the extent that the time and energy required for hunting, or for other activities related to its management, is not available for other life-supporting activities. Management practices affecting game may also reduce options with regard to agriculture, intergroup politics, and modernization.

The Study of Equilibration

In this study I employ "functional analysis," a systems approach for studying "naturally" occurring control systems. According to Tustin (1952) there are at least two kinds of control systems, (1) open sequence or calibrated, and (2) closed or negative feedback. In open sequence control, all corrections for environmental variability are built in and the system cannot compensate for changes not anticipated in the original design or subsequent modifications. For example, you cannot vary the size of the cams in your automobile engine without rebuilding it, after which you are still left with a calibrated system.

Similarly, plants that set buds in the temperate spring in response to lengthening photoperiod may not be able to adjust to a cold spell. The closed, or negative feedback control system goes directly to the quantity to be controlled, corrects for all kinds of disturbances to that quantity regardless of their origin, and "feeds back" information on the degree of departure from the target condition. Functional analysis pertains to negative feedback systems.

It is an approach that A. P. Vayda and his associates (e.g., Roy Rappaport 1968; Paul Collins 1964; Collins and Vayda 1969) disseminated in ecological anthropology in the 1960s. Subsequently, functional analysis was the subject of criticism not only by outsiders (e.g., Friedman 1974; Watts 1983; Orlove 1977), but by its erstwhile practitioners (e.g., Vayda and McCay 1975, 1977; Vayda 1984). I outlined some of the issues involved, including general criticisms of systems ecology, in the first chapter where I also introduced my own position. Some of those points will now be elaborated.

Long-term stability is not a characteristic of natural or social systems. Nevertheless, when viewed as a dimension of behavior equilibration within broad domains of stability (Hollings and Goldberg 1971), stability can be observed and demonstrated within particular time frames. From the standpoint of the particular situation which we have isolated for study, the important issue is the magnitude and other characteristics of the change to which the organisms involved must adjust or adapt if they are to survive. Changes that are small, incremental, regular, cyclical, precedented, or predictable, and controlled in the past are the stuff of equilibration. One of the most notable features of our species is the ability to "routinize" change in time and space as we "muddle through" (Lindbloom 1959) the largest part of life's existential game. Following Tustin (1952), there are three rules for demonstrating (or accomplishing, in the operational sense) equilibration or feedback control:

> First, the required changes must be controllable by some physical means, a regulating organ. Second, the controlled quantity must be measurable, or at least comparable with some standard; in other words there must be a measuring device. Third, both regulation and measurement must be rapid enough for the job at hand.

Some changes, however, cannot be effectively dealt with by equilibration or equilibration alone. This is because of their larger magnitude (which may be the result of accumulating incremental changes), irregularity, novelty, unpredictability, or rapid development, or because the ability of organisms to equilibrate has been reduced by other conditions. Responses to changes of this nature may be escalatory and of themselves disruptive of equilibration to the extent that organisms are unable to go about their normal round or cope with succeeding changes. To cite extreme but instructive examples, consider the situation of people evacuated by authorities on short notice in the face of an impending disaster (who have had wrested from them the option of looking out for their own interests) or of long-term refugees removed from their usual range. This is the domain of the "economics of flexibility," which is concerned with the study of the allocation of finite capacities, alternatives, and potentialities rather than with the allocation of finite resources. It deals with the escalatory pattern of responses, their costs, and their effectiveness (including their effects on other responses).

As Vayda and McCay (1975) have argued, we need to be concerned with the responses of individuals as well as with those of groups of various kinds. While it is true that the "original" neofunctional school adopted the population as its unit of analysis (Orlove 1977:5), this assumption is not critical to functional analysis. The locus of equilibration, especially the muddling-through version, can be viewed as sometimes residing in individuals and at other times in groups—an empirical question (see chapter 7).

Thus, to suggest that ecological anthropologists "abandon an equilibrium centered view" (Vayda and McCay 1975) is the same as urging physiologists to cease studies of the metabolism of organisms under normal conditions in favor of looking exclusively at performance under extreme conditions. The only sensible position is that studies of the latter will be based in part on studies of the former; and the field, if not individual practitioners, would do well to do both.

Since this study was originally intended to realize the potential of functional analysis, I intend to hew to the program as it was disseminated in the 1960s. I will also take advantage of the criticisms and improvements promulgated since then, since the earlier version reflected the desire of some ecological and economic anthropologists to pursue a "hard systems" approach. The latter is now recognized not to have lived up to its early promise, and is seen by proponents (Bawden et al. 1981; Checkland 1979, 1981; Naughton 1981; Spedding 1979) as well as by critics (Berlinski 1976; Vayda and McCay 1975; Vayda 1984) to be of general heuristic value but unrealistic and of limited applicability. In particular, although the quantitative core of a "hard systems" analysis can describe the behavior of a system, it cannot explain how it works (Bunge 1977). I intend to try to do both.

In the original program, functional analysis was seen as both a mode of explanation and a methodological strategy. As a mode of explanation, functional analysis has been investigated by philosophers of science such as Ernest Nagel (1956), Carl Hempel (1959), Francesca Cancian (1960), and Paul Collins (1964; Collins and Vayda 1969), who have been concerned with its formal logical aspects. The conclusions of these studies have been to severely limit the scope of functional analysis (see below). With these considerations in mind I will turn briefly to a related methodology for the study of hunting in ecological anthropology, the optimal foraging approach.

Optimal Foraging: Functional Analysis in Thin Threads

Optimal foraging "theory" is a methodology based on models first developed in evolutionary ecology (e.g., MacArthur and Pianka 1966). As is demonstrated later in this chapter, similar models have appeared in the resource management field (e.g., Watt 1962, 1964a, 1964b, 1968) in the 1960s which may also be of use to ecological anthropologists. These models were themselves inspired by middle-range theory in economics, cost-benefit optimization approaches (Rapport and Turner 1977). Ecological anthropologists have used a series of related models to examine such problems as human territoriality (R. Dyson-Hudson and Smith 1978), spatial organization (Wilmsen 1973), and procurement and feeding strategies (Winterhalder and Smith 1981; Hawkes et al. 1982; Hames and Vickers 1982). The general approach has been criticized on a variety of grounds in economics (Simon 1968), ecology (Colinveaux 1973; Hollings & Goldberg 1971), evolutionary biology (Slobodkin 1968), and anthropology (McCay 1981; Martin 1983). Critics have pointed to unjustified theoretical claims, a lack of realism, weak conceptualization (including the optimization or maximization assumption itself), and even errors of quantification. As far as I know, the anthropological critiques remain largely unanswered.

The central "theorem" of the approach is that an animal will forage in such a way as to maximize its rate of net energy. It should be noted at the outset that this statement is an unverified hypothesis. It is not a deduction from natural law (as it has been represented), or an empirical generalization (Martin 1983:613). In addition, as stated—and especially when applied to human foragers—it is another expression of the "calorific obsession" discussed in chapter 1. This criticism has been recognized by Hames and Vickers (1982:358–59), at least indirectly. They defend the approach on the grounds that, since Darwinian fitness is difficult to measure in the short run, energy is an excellent general currency or indicator. I have made a similar argument in defending energy flow studies (Morren 1977) but without the (weak) linkage to fitness. (I argue that energy expenditure is a good measure of human activity and that input-output ratios are good indicators of change in certain system relations.) They go on to argue that any nutritional factor "necessary to an organism's fitness can be included in this model, either singly or in array" (359).

General indicators are of little use if the subject of an investigation is the situation of particular individuals and groups who face an array of conditions and problems arising from the ways in which they interact with their environment. Similarly, the pertinent issue in a field study of adaptation is survival rather than fitness. For this reason, as I argue later in this chapter, the resource management version of the optimization argument, exemplified by Watt's (1968) work, is a better guide to the analysis of hunting behavior.

Moreover, as far as I know, no anthropologists using the optimal foraging method have actually considered nutritional factors "in array." Finally, as I noted in the first chapter, there is a lot more to survival than coping with nutritional problems.

> The pressures of natural selection are pressures for survival, and survival may sometimes be more concerned with the efficient use of nutrients, ensuring that individuals mate, safe overwintering, or swift growth and dispersal, than with the efficient use, or even collection of, energy (Colinveaux 1973:296).

In addition, studies of nonhuman predators suggest that the most efficient are also the most specialized. Put another way, the cost of high efficiency is increased specialization, reduced flexibility, and possibly long-run maladaptation. There is no avoiding the fact that optimal foragers enter their research situation with the a priori assumption of the ascendancy of nutritional energy as a problem. Ironically, the more sophisticated biological practitioners of related approaches are concerned about environmental variability; and they recognize that to model real-life complexity is difficult (Wiens 1977).

Another criticism of optimal foraging studies in anthropology is that they tend to restrict themselves to harvesting and eating activities and to overlook responses involving changes of location, development of infrastructure (e.g., settlements), the defense or expansion of territory, the adoption or intensification of nonforaging subsistence practices, or other life-supporting activities that may directly influence the quantity and quality of the hunt (or, for that matter, the need for it). In essence, I accuse the proponents of the approach of carrying the technological bias described earlier in this chapter into their analyses, an error of logical typing.

Yet another general criticism of investigations employing the methodology is that the data base required is so large as to defy collection. Thus it is possible to pick apart the most ambitious, detailed, and successful studies of hunting behavior on the grounds that the required data on the biology and behavior of prey species is inadequate or nonexistent. As McCay (1981:365) points out, biologists and anthropologists are forced to use "informed guesswork" to fill in the blanks. Any intention to assess real environmental variability is automatically frustrated. For example, Hames and Vickers admit that "There have been few censuses that have sampled the species on which Amazonian hunters commonly depend" (1982:361).

I share their plight in large measure in this book. In my original analysis (Morren 1974), I did not have an accurate checklist of mammals in the Miyanmin area. I only realized how bad the situation was when I conducted my own trapping and collecting program in 1981, which even then only gave me data about a narrow period of time. I would have to propose (and defend) a test of "reasonableness" in assessing the quality of the data mustered by such an investigation and the strength of the conclusions drawn. What is really at issue in these studies is the illusion of precision (quantification) and generality (Darwinian selection theory) in the face of reality (and realism is a desirable feature of models in ethnology). Martin's (1983) critique has strongly argued the illusory nature of the quantification carried out in optimal foraging studies. In my own work I choose to "sacrifice" precision in order to analyze patterns and relationships and to thus better serve realism. Admittedly this also gets me out of a tight spot when it comes to assessing the quality of my own zoological data.

Bonnie McCay has pointed out that optimization models are "formalizations of functional arguments" (1981:365). What I think she means by this is that optimal foraging models refer to a type of control system. It is not, however, a functional or negative feedback system. Rather, the logic of the basic argument seems to involve an open sequence or calibrated type of control (see the discussion earlier in this chapter). This impression is reinforced by the failure of such models to incorporate a wide array of compensating mechanisms. This criticism pertains particularly to those models that do not take into account settlement and movement mechanisms, key features of hunting strategies, and hence fail to deal with the issue of sustainability of overall yields.

As a type of control system, optimal foraging models pertain to the third and fourth levels of analysis outlined earlier in this chapter (although I consider an alternate assignment below). Thus optimal foraging models share features with people-focused energy flow models (e.g., Little and Morren 1976, Morren 1977), as well as functional analyses of people–environment interactions (e.g., Rappaport, 1968; and the present work). All are concerned with the behavioral routine of people in relation to normal conditions, their established solutions to environmental conditions which, while they may have posed a threat to survival in the past, no longer do so. It is important to note the implied limitations of scope.

A more severe limitation is implied by McCay, who suggests a generic linkage between the optimal foraging approach and maximization/decision theory. When stripped of its tenuous connection with "fitness," that may be what is left: useful, actor-oriented, system-specific, and pertaining to the second level of my metaclassification of hunting tasks. The essential and original logic remains: the narrow utility of the input-output ratio as a measure of the state of a hunting system that consists of a variety of alternative meat procurement and production strategies. If you are hunting more and enjoying it less, it is time for a change!

Accordingly, I propose a more realistic and relativistic alternative "theorem" to that of the optimal foraging school presented earlier in this section: an animal ought to behave in such a way as to achieve a satisfactory balance between its capture of resources and its exposure to hazards and problems—including those resulting from the way it captures other resources and copes with other hazards. In the short run, this may take the form of minimizing risk, routinizing responses in various ways, including attempting to maximize returns for effort, and tending to adhere to routines even beyond the point at which they are adaptive. The warrant for this "theorem" is evolutionary theory:

1. "Selection chooses from among individuals those which are best adapted to avoid the hazards of life at that time and place" (Colinveaux 1973).
2. Environmental variability and other contingencies confer selective advantage to organisms that husband their flexibility (Bateson 1963).
3. Selection means staying in the existential game (Slobodkin 1968).

Thus, the index of a satisfactory balance is survival in its various degrees. The problem with this theorem, however, is that organisms are exposed to a wide array of conditions (resources and hazards) that vary in time, space, magnitude, predictability and other dimensions, and their responses to these can be characterized by highly variable capacities, tolerances, needs, constraints, contingencies, effects, and effectiveness. Neither "theorem" provides an optimal guide to the analyst interested in reducing complexity. This corresponds to the basic reality that people accept suboptimal solutions to their problems all the time.

Functional Analysis

In presenting the aims and structure of functional explanations I follow Collins's (1964) philosophical analysis. From the observer's standpoint, a functional system is an assemblage of variables that have been selected for study. This act of isolating the system partly determines its boundary conditions. The object of the ensuing exercise is to explain measurable changes in the values of the variables that the investigator has selected and assigned to the system.

Collins (1964:7) has identified the elements commonly possessed by functional systems:

> There is a range of states with specifiable limits within which the values of a given variable are maintained despite the action of factors tending to displace the variable from its specified range, and this maintaining of the variable within its range is effected by the compensating action of other parts of the system; or, if the variable is displaced from its range, it will be returned by the action of its compensating parts.

It is important to note at the outset that this passage may be taken both as a definition of equilibration and a description of a general program. A functional analysis based on it need not be static, synchronic, utopian, or concerned only with stability. Hence, it is not necessarily susceptible to the kinds of criticisms that have been leveled at the functionalism once practiced in social anthropology (see Leach 1951, including Firth's introduction). On the contrary, certain systems approaches provide powerful tools for studying real-world complexity.

Another philosopher, Cancian (1960:823f.), has taken up this problem in the social sciences and specified four ways by which change can be incorporated into the analysis of functional or negative feedback systems. The first is through the disappearance or destruction of the range variable (G) of the system through the exceeding of limits. The second involves the definition of a moving equilibrium or a stable rate of change. The third is the inclusion of changes in the values of the supporting variables (state coordinates). The fourth relates to changes in systems that are themselves subsystems of larger, more inclusive systems. Other possible ways of incorporating change into systems analysis include a consideration of processes involving positive feedback, such as deviation amplification (Maruyama 1963), and the kinds of systems used to describe adaptation in evolution by Bateson (1963) and Slobodkin (1968), referred to as the economics of flexibility.

Collins's definition also makes clear the necessity of framing functional analyses in terms of a range of states of measurable variables, the supporting variables or state coordinates that maintain a range variable or G (see also Cancian 1960:824). While anthropologists may suffer from a dearth of appropriate data and mathematical models, it is nevertheless useful to formalize our analyses and explicitly present the hypothesized relations between entities or variables. In this way, it is possible to verify the qualitative features of our systems, discover new or alternative relations, and manipulate the system. Indeed, according to Cancian (1960:824), the failure to formalize leads to inadequate analyses of both change and stability. As will be shown, the approach is also brutal in the sense that—lacking obvious rules of parsimony—variables and relations tend to proliferate.

A useful procedure for accomplishing formalization involves the use of a standard graphical notation for feedback systems such as can be found in many engineering textbooks (e.g., Harris 1961). Other standards, with more specialized operators, are also available and have been used by biologists and anthropologists (e.g., H.T. Odum 1971; Thomas 1971; Morren 1977). Mine is presented in figure 2-1. It will be used in this chapter with several examples, and later in the book to present my system.

There are many examples of functional hypotheses in anthropology. One employed by Collins (1963:3ff.) in his work was Murphy's (1957) sketch of the

Figure 2-1.   Graphical Standard for Feedback Control Systems

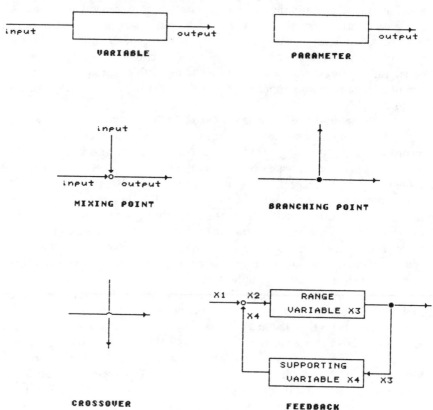

relationship between Mundurucu warfare and the social tension that was said to be provoked by conflicting descent and postmarital residence rules. Murphy characterized warfare as a "safety valve institution" among the Mundurucu which functioned to restore the integration and solidarity of the community when these were at low ebb. Collins showed how this unverified sketch could be formalized or "reconstructed," and I will borrow his treatment of Murphy's hypothesis to illustrate the application of my shorthand notation. I will also depart from it to show how an analysis can be pushed to raise new or different questions.

Murphy's barebones hypothesis is presented in figure 2-2(a). In this system the proposed variables are "Index of Social Cohesion" (X_2) and "Frequency of Warfare" (X_3). The methodology I propose, however, requires the specification of other kinds of variables. All systems must be placed in a material context, or environment, defining the boundary conditions (or what I refer to as the

Figure 2-2. Intergroup Hostility and Social Cohesion

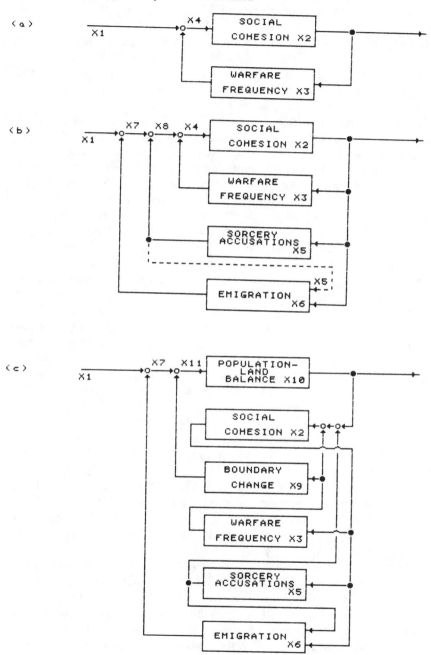

"parameters") of the system. These are the sources of disturbance known to the analyst. In the system under discussion (figure 2-2[a]), this is represented in general terms by X_1. In addition, all systems have outputs or environmental effects that influence other systems and subsystems at the same and different hierarchical levels. Here, this is represented by the arrow extending from X_2. Other variables result from operations at the mixing points (circles in the diagram), represented here by X_4, which is the result of "mixing" the environmental input (X_1) and warfare frequency (X_3).

When Murphy's sketch is set up this way, it invites elaboration and manipulation which lead to the generation of alternative hypotheses. A possible next step is to consider other cultural practices that may also function as "safety valve institutions" in connection with intragroup discord and social cohesion as in figure 2-2(b). Following Middleton and Winter (1963) and Marwick (1964), I then explore the regulatory functions of "sorcery accusations" (X_5) and emigration (X_6) in relation to social cohesion. The resulting additional hypotheses are that (1) the frequency of sorcery accusations is directly related to the "index of social cohesion"; (2) the frequency of emigration is directly related to "index of social cohesion"; (3) the latter relationship may be mediated by sorcery accusations (that motivate some, but not all, emigration); and (4) emigration, sorcery accusations, and intergroup warfare may increase social cohesion.

The next step is to propose other functions for the supporting variables (state coordinates) isolated above (X_3, X_5, X_6) in relation to alternate range variables (or G's). I do this in figure 2-2(c), where a new range variable, "population-land balance" (X_{10}) has been added along with the supporting variable "land gained or lost" (X_9). Note that while "index of social cohesion" is no longer a range variable, it now assumes the singular (though hypothetical) role of a measuring device in the system (Tustin 1952), comparable to the thermostat in a space heating/cooling system. Its task is possibly to measure changes in population pressure and to trigger mechanisms which may provide for its relief.

The "brutality" of the exercise arises from continuing to expand the system. I could, for example, interpose nutritional and health variables between "population-land balance" and "social cohesion," or build an agricultural subsystem, all of these components fitting readily into the proposed framework.

Rappaport's (1966, 1968) study of ritual and human ecology among the Tsembaga Maring of New Guinea illustrates this and many other points. It is a more successful attempt to formalize the analysis of a functional system than any of the studies cited, although it also presents several empirical and analytical problems. The present study is clearly inspired by Rappaport's.

In his explanatory sketch, Rappaport relates the operation of a long, 5- to

20-year ritual cycle of ceremonial acts, feasts, and wealth distributions to the regulation of the human population's relations with its subsistence and socio-political environment. Specifically, Rappaport proposes a functional system maintaining a balance between the size of the human population, the size of the domestic pig herd, and the amount of land under cultivation. Rappaport also claims for this system the additional functions of assuring an appropriate cultivation-fallow ratio, conserving primary forest, promoting efficient utilization of animal food sources, relieving population pressure, and controlling intergroup warfare.

Rappaport was able to achieve a certain level of success in his analysis, not because he verified his hypothetical system, but because he was able to reap the benefits of formalization. This harvest is represented by the string of proposed functions I cited. At the same time, the proliferation of variables and functions stands in the way of mathematical modeling and verification, particularly when a means of isolating a cross-section of the system for such treatment is lacking. When I applied my shorthand to Rappaport's array of variables and relations, I ended up with over 200 variables (including "mixing point" operations). The realism of Rappaport's system has offended at least one critic (MacArthur 1977), who correctly points to the difficulty of collecting the required data, but overlooks the qualitative nature of the analysis.

The lack of precision is justified by the latter as well as by the pioneering nature of the work. It should also be noted that Rappaport later took a portion of this system and data base and, using an energetic framework, demonstrated the systemic relationship between plant agriculture and pig husbandry (Rappaport 1971; see also Morren 1977). Rappaport's implied strategy seems to be consistent with Richard Levins's (1966) view, cited earlier, that it is not possible to be precise, general, and realistic in a single analytical bite.

Rappaport's study also points up the necessity to avoid rigid distinctions between, say, religious behavior and economic behavior, or between infrastructure, structure, and superstructure (cf. Harris 1979:52ff.). As I argued earlier, it has been shown to be more useful in a systems analytic framework to view strategies and systemic mechanisms as possessing economic, social, religious, and other dimensions. In my own analysis I opt for a narrower slice of reality than did Rappaport in the hope of gaining a degree of precision, but it will be shown that even the smallest bites are long in digestion.

Resource Management Strategies

As I indicated earlier, I have found the "resource managers" and students of predator-prey relations useful in shaping the way I think about hunters and their on-the-ground performance. This is tempered by specific reservations and qualifications, some paralleling my criticisms of the optimal foraging approach.

According to Watt (1968:57), there are at least two possible formulations of the optimal yield problem: one for (r-selected) species in which natural population regulation is density dependent, and the other for (k-selected) species in which population is regulated by climatic and other environmental factors. In the first case, in which population regulation is density-dependent, "The ideal harvesting regimen is that in which the sustained yield per unit time is exactly equal to the sustained productivity, less the remainder that must be left behind to sustain the yield" (Watt 1962:192–93; 1968:56ff.). Although elsewhere this (and its mathematical expression) is referred to as the solution to the "optimal yield" problem, it has little to do with the optimal foraging approach. Rather, it focuses on the interaction of features of the harvesting regime with characteristics of the species being harvested. Thus, among the resource management strategies Watt suggests for situations involving density dependent species are (1) changing the number and age distribution of individuals left in the population by changing mesh size of nets (for fish); (2) changing the legislation on hunting and bag limits (for wildlife); or (3) changing seeding density (for plants). These examples are not, of course, exhaustive, nor are they necessarily even accurate or cogent. This is because Watt and other "resource managers" have their own kinks and sources of unreality distinct from those of the optimal foragers. First, in the examples cited, the distinction between "R" and "K" strategists is not an exclusive one; rather, a given organism may be alternately one or the other, depending on the situation. Second, reproductive strategy is not the only characteristic of organisms that determines whether or not they will be seriously "over-harvested." Third, as is true with the optimal foraging approach, it is very difficult to get the required data on the biota, especially in the areas where we work.

These issues notwithstanding, while calling attention to the methodological importance of looking at the characteristics of prey species, the approach also goes to the heart of sustainability, one of the critical dimensions of hunting. A model based on Watt's two strategies may also be recast as a functional system. This is presented, initially, to exemplify the approach in figure 2-3. In a later chapter it will be used as a "subsystem" of a larger model of hunting and settlement.

In functional terms, Watt's first model postulates a system possessing a range variable: the ratio of yield to productivity, with an "optimal" value of one, which is maintained by a set of compensating mechanisms constituting a resource management strategy. These determine time, quantity, and quality (age, sex, weight) of harvested organisms whose summation is a yield. This also affects the structure of the population which, in interaction with environmental factors, determines productivity. Also implied is the necessity for a particular (equilibrating) resource management strategy to measure the state of the system by way of adjusting yield to productivity in compensation for the effects on productivity of both environmental effects and past harvesting.

Figure 2-3. Watt's Resource Management Strategy as a
Feedback System

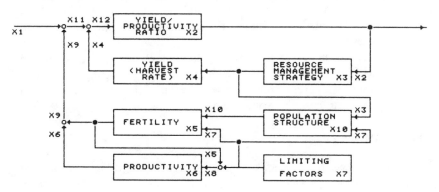

In Watt's second model, the harvesting strategy is aimed at minimizing waste resulting from natural mortality. This is because "any harvesting decreases productivity, because productivity is already as great as [the environment] will allow it to be" (1968:58).

Watt acknowledges the similarity of his models to the optimization approaches (1964a:409) that I have already criticized. Note, however, that the optimization assumption is unnecessary because I am not interested in evaluating a group of alternative strategies. Of interest is the nature of the strategies themselves, their outputs and their material constraints, their human demographic, economic, spatial, and nutritional limits, as well as their mechanisms. Unlike Watt, we are not faced with a multitude of resource management strategies having "fundamentally different effects in space and time [which] renders difficult comparative evaluation of long term effectiveness" (1964a:409–410). Rather, we are faced with a more limited set of strategies pursued by the Miyanmin who, judging by their persistence in the face of perturbations known and unknown, have performed them at a satisfactory level of effectiveness. Following Holling and Goldberg (1971), it need not be an efficient "system in an optimizing sense because the price paid for efficiency is a decreased resilience and a high probability of extinction" (225). In other words, if you take all of the bumps out of the road, you have to stay on the road. A reasonable long-term view of the Miyanmin situation is that for most of their history the ratio of yield to sustained productivity for the animals they hunt has been below the optimal or ideal level suggested by Watt. I will review some of the literature on predation in chapter 3.

Let me briefly summarize the useful aspects of Watt's view of resource management:

1. Different resource management strategies are required for each species because (a) some are subject to density control, others are subject to environmental control, and yet others are subject to both kinds of control at different times; and (b) the biotic potential of species varies.
2. Resource management strategies achieve their affects by (a) harvesting particular age-sex categories; (b) by limiting the harvest quantitatively; (c) by limiting the duration of the harvest; and/or (d) by limiting the interharvest time.

Hunting Systems

The Miyanmin system of managing their relationships with game animals is similar to those observed among hunter-gatherers (Moore 1957; Lee 1969, 1971; Lee and DeVore 1968), certain hunter-horticulturists (Siskind 1973; Carneiro 1960), true shifting cultivators (Allen 1965; Conklin 1961), and pastoral nomads (Sweet 1965; Gulliver 1955; Barth 1959-1960; Stenning 1957; Dyson-Hudson 1972) in that the most important strategies for regulating productivity and yield include human population shifts of various kinds. In their introduction to the *Man the Hunter* volume, Lee and DeVore (1968) describe the "nomadic style" of hunting peoples which applies to the Miyanmin: "We make two basic assumptions about hunters and gatherers: (1) they live in small groups and (2) they move around a lot."

The techno-economically inclined may object to my seemingly arbitrary lumping together of such diverse kinds of economies as hunter-gatherers, pastoralists, and shifting cultivators. As I argued in chapter 1, the established taxonomies have obscured similarities that are important for understanding the nature of human adaptations and, more behavioristically, how people respond to environmental problems. To reiterate the basic contrasts, I am particularly interested in societies that move people to patchily distributed resources, rather than those that modify the environment to concentrate resources near people, or integrate diverse habitats by bringing resources to the people.

In the short run, groups of people dependent on hunting who "move around a lot" maintain yields at satisfactory levels relative to the most harvestable fractions of prey populations. They achieve this by locating aggregates of people near the specialized natural or anthropogenic habitats of prey, thereby facilitating contact between them by redirecting human harvesting activity in space, and by allocating labor to hunting in proportion to need.

In the near term, productivity is assured by limiting the frequency and duration of the harvest in local areas, by geographically confining the environmental impact of other (nonhunting) activities, by creating disclimaxes and other kinds of artificial habitats that are attractive to prey or enhance their productivity, and by carrying out large-scale shifts of location.

In the long run and perhaps under the extreme circumstance of territorial restriction, population concentration, or other environmental stress (implying no possibility of movement at an acceptable cost), nonforaging meat production strategies and population regulation are possible.

In the next chapter I present a hypothetical systems model which relates hunting to patterns of movement. I will do this against a background of theory and empirical generalizations that have resulted from studies of nonhuman predation.

3

Hunting and Settlement: A Hypothesis

The Miyanmin are predators ecologically and, as I suggest in chapter 6, behave as predators at the individual level as hunters work to expand the space-time structure of their relationship with their prey. At the biotic community level, however, the Miyanmin do not look like predators because they are not subject to a conventional predator-prey oscillation. Except for certain brief periods in their recent history (to be described in chapters 7 and 10), the Miyanmin population has probably been growing. Those temporary declines seem to have been caused by intergroup competition and infectious disease.

There are perhaps five reasons for the absence of a predator-prey oscillation of the classic sort. First, the Miyanmin are omnivorous, though on a percentage basis they are virtual herbivores. Thus agriculture (and, at lower altitudes, sago collecting) is the bottom line. Second, their predation is characterized by many alternative prey species. Third, the Miyanmin do more than hunt and kill their prey; they kill trees and clear land, plant gardens and orchards, and change the environment in many ways that affect prey species (cf. Colinveaux 1973:399). Fourth, even as predators, the Miyanmin are unspecialized. Fifth, rather than allowing their absolute numbers to oscillate, the Miyanmin disperse and nucleate within the large territories they defend and expand, a simulation of an oscillatory pattern.

How they accomplish this will be the subject of later chapters. Why they do it, the systematic context, is the focus of this one.

Predation and Predator Behavior

Even critics of systems analysis and synecology have conceded the validity of the coupled oscillations model of predator-prey relations (e.g., Berlinsky 1976; Colinveaux 1973:397 ff.). The synecologists and autecologists nevertheless have alternative views of the study of predation. The former orientation has been summarized by Smith (1966:413) as follows: "predation is a highly complicated phenomenon which must be studied from a community and not an individual or prey viewpoint." Nevertheless, improvements in the systems analysis of predator-prey relationships have resulted from more individually and behaviorally focused field studies. These have elucidated such issues as how predators locate and select their prey, how they locate themselves, and how prey survive. The two approaches are complementary; and an ecological anthropologist would be well advised to combine them. I try to strike this balance in my discussion of prey characteristics and hunting behavior in chapter 6.

There are, nevertheless, significant barriers to a thoroughly satisfying systems analysis. The complexity to which Smith alludes makes it difficult to select important relationships as well as to quantify them. In his discussion of model building in population biology, Levins (1966) points out that precision, realism, and generality—otherwise desirable attributes of models—conflict with each other. If I were to practice precision in constructing a model of some narrow aspect of Miyanmin adaptation, I would end up saying very little about the Miyanmin and their faunal relations, although I might end up saying it fairly well. In fact, from a survey of the ecological literature on the subject, it is apparent that you can only do it well in the laboratory. Certainly no one in field ecology has conducted a precise study of a complex natural predator-prey relationship.

This problem has several sides. There is the empirical one—facing all natural scientists, including anthropologists—of not having a long run of observations. It is also difficult to make detailed observations of more than one or two species populations at a time. Most successful field studies of predator-prey relations get around these difficulties to only a limited extent. For example, Bartholomew and Hoel studied the reproductive behavior of the Alaska fur seal (1953) in order to establish a safe rate of commercial harvesting. "The population as a whole had to be censused each year to determine the rate of population increase. Details of reproduction, such as time and age of breeding, gestation period, number of young per litter, conditions suitable for breeding, and sex ratios most suitable for maximum production, had to be determined" (Benton and Werner, 1966:383). For similar purposes, I take many short-cuts in chapter 6 to provide inferences on such matters for many species. In the biological literature some of the best long runs of data on animal populations (particularly for predator species that also have handsome fur) come from commercial trapping records, sometimes used in combination with careful field observations (as in Errington 1943).

In a review article on studies of predation, Errington (1946) observed that

of the quantitative data bearing on predation pressures in vertebrate populations, only, as a rule, those small proportions resulting from investigation year after year on the same areas are likely to repay close study. Often too, an author's data may fit into a vastly broader scheme than his conclusions indicate.... (44)

Such broader schemes are my concern here. There are some studies that attempt to deal with "multiple" predator-prey relationships with some precision. I feel, however, that when ecologists use the adjective "multiple" in this connection they would actually benefit from the Miyanmin system of cardinal numbers, i.e., "one, two, three, plenty." When the relations between more than two or three species populations of predator or prey are involved, there is necessarily less precision, but greater realism. One example of this is the study by the Craigheads of hawk and owl predation on many prey species in Michigan (Craighead and Craighead 1969). Another example is the study by Pitelka and associates of predation by various owl and jaeger species in Alaska (1955). They studied three major predators, three minor predators, and one prey (the hapless lemming). The study is largely descriptive with semiquantative data concerning nesting and molting cycles and the peaks of predation for the various species (these articulate very nicely), predator weights, predator reproductive success, and the spatial aspects of predation. The field observation period was three summers. These two works appear to be representative of the best such studies to date, and the present analysis is comparable to them in many respects.

Such studies should be of particular interest to us, in contradistinction to more precise laboratory research, because they involve systems that are more progressive or mature (Margalief 1968), and which display greater stability as a direct consequence of complexity. The wild predator-prey oscillations and crashes characteristic of the simpler systems studied in the field (such as the well-known snowy owl case; Gross 1947), the laboratory (see below), or the computer (e.g., Garfinkel 1962; Meur et al. 1965) are absent. The criterion for progress or maturity is the extent to which such oscillations are absent, with the abundance of predator and prey maintained at a more or less constant level. This can be a result of community diversity, the complexity of trophic linkages, and the presence of buffers. I attribute such stability to the system of predation in which the Miyanmin participate.

I am defending myself in advance against the obvious criticism of my lack of mathematical precision. I've attempted in the foregoing review of ecological practice to deal with this, but the basic argument has been stated cogently by Margalef (1968:23–24):

> Almost everyone will agree that it would be difficult but theoretically possible, to write down the interactions between two species, or possibly three, according to the equations suggested by Volterra and Lotka. This can be done in the ordinary differential form, . . . or in the more fashionable cybernetic form. But it seems a hopeless task to deal with actual systems; first because they are too complex and second we need to know many parameters that are unknown. Thus we cannot use the magic formula "feed the data to a computer," the panacea of those who expect miracles from the feedback between man and machine. From the practical point of view of the average ecologist, it makes almost no sense to try to write down a system of equations . . . for all the inhabitants of a beech forest.

Students of predator-prey relations have isolated a number of types of responses in both predator and prey. The point of departure for this refinement was the mathematical model developed by Lotka (1925) and Volterra (1931, original 1926) which expressed the relationship between predator and prey in quantitative terms. These two students were apparently the first to hypothesize the existence of predator-prey oscillations. Gause (1934) showed in the laboratory that in a simple one predator–one prey situation the predator population could only be maintained in accordance with the predictions of the Lotka-Volterra model through immigration of prey. Further qualifications and elaborations to the model have ensued. The resulting model as described by Smith (1966:405) states

> that as predator populations increase, they will consume a progressively larger number of prey, until the prey populations begin to decline. As the prey diminishes, the predators are faced with less and less food, and they in turn decline. In time the number of predators will be so reduced by starvation that the reproduction of the prey will more than balance their loss through predation. The prey will then increase, followed shortly by an increase in predators. This cycle, or oscillation, may continue indefinitely. The prey is never quite destroyed by the predator; the predator never completely dies.

Now what does this have to do with the population of predators called Miyanmin? As I indicated earlier in this chapter, such an oscillation has not been characteristic of Miyanmin numbers. The point of the Lotka-Volterra model is that it specifies the terms of the problem, the things that are worth studying—although the scope of the model is much too restricted. The problem here is to explain why the Miyanmin and their prey do not appear to conform to the model predictions.

This problem is not unique or peculiar. Succeeding ecologists had research data that were similarly problematical. It is from the refinements and qualifications that they invented that my own analysis of Miyanmin-faunal relations can proceed. I have isolated 12 principles from relevant ecological literature and grouped them into two sets, one regarding the community level, the other the individual level.

Community Dynamics

1. A predator population cannot survive when the numbers of prey are low.
2. A self-sustaining predator-prey relationship can be maintained with immigration of the prey in an area or the dispersal of the predator.
3. The period of predator-prey oscillation is more dependent on the nature of prey dispersal and predator searching modalities (see MacArthur and Pianka 1966) and prey recovery time, than on the intensity of predation or harvesting itself.

4. Perpetuation of the system can be accomplished by altering the space-time structure, decreasing the density of predators and prey per unit of area; a greater number of individual colonies per predator population will assure the persistence of the system, "One tiger to a hill" (Errington 1946).
5. Mobility of predators enables concentration in areas of high prey density and the maintenance of continuous hunting pressure on prey in proportion to their numbers (Craighead & Craighead 1969:39).

Individual Behavior

6. Environmental discontinuity, such as strong topographic relief or dense cover, provides for relative inaccessibility of predator and prey, and thus expands the space time structure of the relationship (Timbergen 1960).
7. As the density of the prey increases, each predator may take more of the prey or take them sooner, this being the "functional response" (Holling 1959, 1961).
8. For vertebrate predators, the functional response is "compensatory," the harvesting curve is "S" shaped with the slope defined by the prey density level at which predators find it profitable to hunt, and the "threshold of security" (Errington 1946) the point on the curve below which it is in no longer profitable (MacArthur and Pianka 1966).
9. The predator response to reduced abundance of a particular prey population below the "threshold of security" may be buffered by the availability of alternate prey (Davis 1957) or the ability to move.
10. Such prey characteristics as food preference, use of cover, movement, activity, habits, size, strength, age and escape reaction, as well as density, will determine its relative ranking in the structure of predator food preferences.
11. The probability of a predator's being able to capture members of a particular prey species increases with its specialization, a prerequisite for oscillation (in this respect, human hunters are the most facultative of predators, with many alternate prey).
12. All hunts are not successful, fecundity is not constant, and sex differences are important (Colinveaux 1973:420).

Many of these principles have been stated in mathematical form in individual studies. This is important to the present analysis insofar as mathematical expressions verified in simple contexts provide part of the explanation of more complex situations (Holling 1961:181). The verbal form serves me better. Each principle can be related, in one way or another, to the details of the system, the analysis of which follows.

Presenting the System

Having a feeling for the deductive principles underlying the complexity of predation and being able to describe how it works are two different things. In attempting to resolve this I will observe the following outline. First, I have isolated 50 variables and parameters that I believe are important features of the system of predation by which the Miyanmin operate. This system, which presents only the equilibrational part of a larger process of response, is represented graphically in figure 3-1, and the variables themselves are operationally defined later in the chapter. This however, leaves the reader with the illusion of precision, imposing the requirement of equations as well as supporting data for the hypothetical system as a whole. For the reasons cited earlier, this is an impossible task and not even a useful one. The kinds of observations required exceed the capacity of any single investigator, even for short runs of time; and these observations would have to be repeated over a span of one or more decades and conducted in more than one local population simultaneously for purposes of replication and control. However, merely representing such a system graphically and cataloging its important components provides for a degree of realism that would not otherwise be possible. This degree of realism is absolutely necessary if some of the other stated objectives of this analysis, such as demonstrating the social dimension of human ecology, are to be realized.

The second main task is to show how the system works. This can be accomplished by making some explicit and, it is hoped, reasonable simplifying assumptions by way of reducing the number of variables and the range of values they might assume. Then some model predictions about smaller segments of the system will be made against which can be ranged data of varying quality which pertains to a number of time periods. In addition, I will demonstrate that there is a kind of oscillation.

This system describes the relationship between people and certain faunal components of the biotic community. Because the population of human predators is, for all practical purposes, a stable one, the focus here is on the causes and consequences of variations in the relative abundance of the various prey populations that people hunt. The system itself (as it pertains to the local population of humans as previously defined) has a number of equilibrating tasks, all generally concerned with sustaining the availability of meat. This is accomplished by maintaining the local abundance of certain prey populations, regulating the occasions for their exploitation, redistributing human population and activity in relation to seasonal and nonseasonal changes in faunal density, reducing competitive pressure from certain fauna, redirecting human harvesting in relation to the predator success or the threshold of security for particular prey or groups of prey, and maintaining an appropriate level of access to suitable prey habitats.

For my purposes, the regulated variable is the amount of meat produced on a per capita basis (X_1). There are several possible ways of accomplishing what Tustin (1952; see chapter 2) refers to as measurement or comparison to a standard in order for equilibration to be performed. The motivations of individual incidents of hunting, i.e., the decision to hunt, are various. Traditionally, some of it had the appearance of a closed sequence—for example, certain rituals call for the use or capture of particular animals (chapter 8). This appearance is reinforced by the seasonal nature of many rituals. On a more mundane level, people seek meat because they or family members desire it. A very common statement is "My child is crying for meat."

Pegged more closely to the level of this analysis, however, is the subjective perception of availability of game and hunting success. People are able to assess routinely the availability of particular game animals in their settlement area. Hence, I choose "hunting success" (X_2) as the principal "thermostat" in my system. First, this seems to be a likely pragmatic test of the state of the system even (or perhaps especially) from the standpoint of the hunter who also makes decisions about residential location. Second, it possesses generality insofar as it is linked to the "threshold of security" concept (Errington 1946; MacArthur and Pianka 1966) and other input-output measures employed by ecological anthropologists (see Lee 1969; Harris 1971). The "bias" (X_3) of this measuring device is set by seasonality and by situational factors affecting the ability of individuals and subgroups to hunt.

The most important dimensions of the regulatory mechanisms have been grouped into six phases, three nonseasonal, and three seasonal. The differentiation of the phases is not arbitrary. There are other possible ways of arranging the elements (or defining the variables, for that matter). Whatever the choices, each of the mechanisms isolated is fairly discrete. In the operation of the system, the three nonseasonal phases operate exclusively of each other, depending on the state of the system; and they succeed each other in a cyclical way. The two seasonal phases operate in a similar way with respect to each other, but also interact with some dimensions of the nonseasonal phases. The sixth phase can be viewed as a subphase or variant of one of the seasonal phases. The exclusive character of the phases is, in turn, an artifact of the exercises in classification of movement responses (chapter 9) and of faunal classes (chapter 6). This is so because two of the key dimensions of each phase consist of a movement strategy and an attribute of a faunal class. The six phases so identified are: I, Settlement Shift; II, Hamlet Shift; III, Settlement Cycle; IV, Dry Season Residence; Va, Rainy Season Residence; and Vb, Intergroup Visiting. I, II, and III are nonseasonal, and IV, Va and Vb are seasonally determined phases.

Figure 3-1. The System of Hunting and Settlement

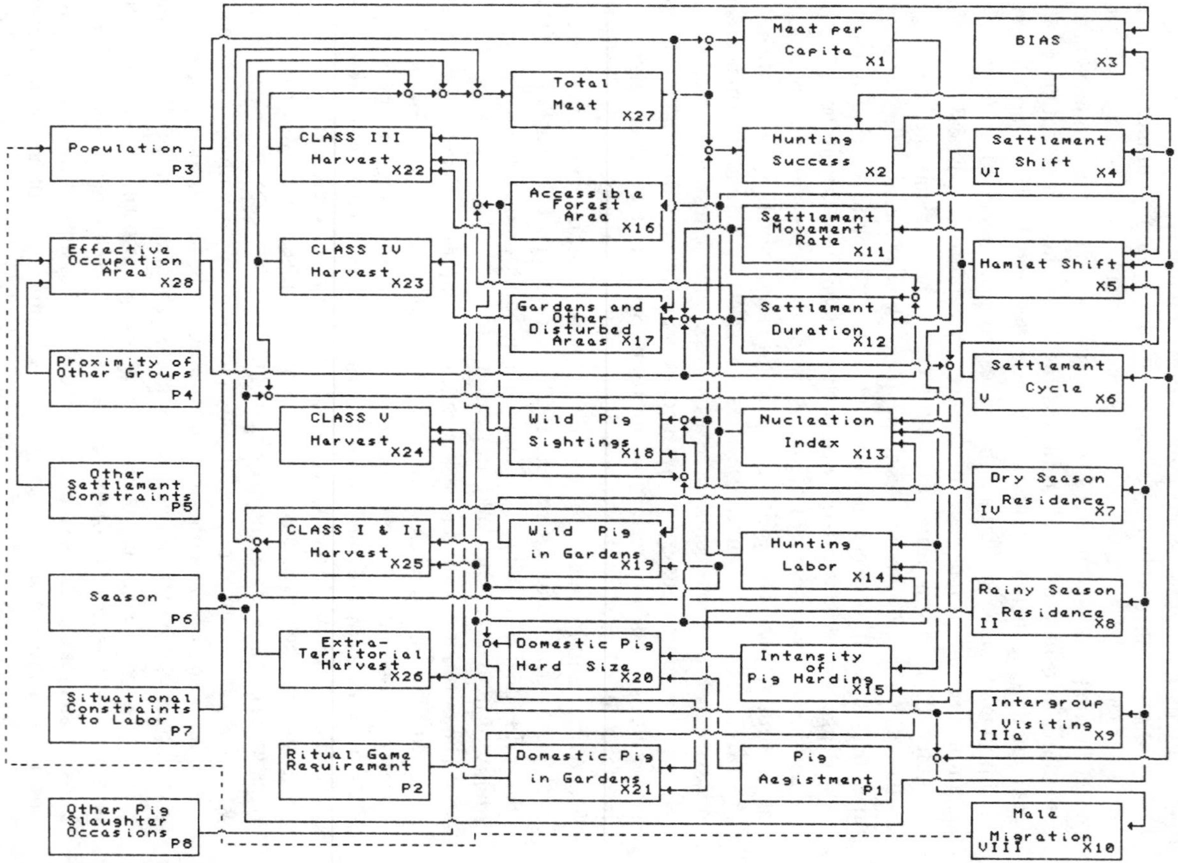

In chapters 9 and 10 I provide a richer picture of these movements through a discussion of the distinction between equilibrating and escalatory movements. The former involve adjustments to familiar recurrent, incremental environmental changes, both natural and anthropogenic ones. They are part of the hunting/predation system which is the principal focus of this study. Warfare, expansion, resettlement, and migration are escalatory in nature, although all are potentially reversible and/or equilibrating as well. These responses have been separated from the hunting/predation system because they involve responses to unusual (even novel), large, irregular changes.

To facilitate interpretation of figure 3-1, system variables are grouped by "kinds" from right to left as follows: movement, settlement and life support, human-faunal interface, and faunal classes. Ritual mechanisms are omitted in the interest of economy and because they are extensively discussed in chapter 8.

Connections to other levels or systems are suggested by the parameters isolated in figure 3-1. These parameters are inputs to the system, sources of disturbance, and/or they define its boundaries. With respect to system boundaries, the system under analysis displays a fairly high degree of "entitivity" (Dunn 1971) insofar as its exogenous links to systems of the same or higher level are few. This is the nature of the local population in tribal societies, where there is a high degree of economic encapsulation and sovereignty.

A preliminary understanding of the operation of the system portrayed in figure 3-1 can be acquired by cataloging the variables selected and reviewing their relationships and contingencies.

X_1　　"Meat per Capita" is the grams of meat produced per person; X_{27}/P_3.

X_2　　"Hunting Success" is the grams of meat procured per hour of hunting effort; X_{27}/X_{14}.

X_3　　"Bias" refers to factors that calibrate the "target" level of hunting success (as discussed earlier) and people's expectations of it. Seasonality (P_6) and situational factors affecting the ability of people to hunt (P_7) seem to be particularly important.

X_4　　"Settlement Shift" is a variable with two values. It is positive when a local population moves into a new occupation area. This occurs when the resources of the area currently occupied, particularly faunal resources, are depleted sufficiently to cause declining hunting success. Settlement shifts are constrained by the proximity of other groups and by environmental factors, including the potential for agriculture of a prospective occupation area.

X_5 "Hamlet Shift" also has two values. It is positive when a hamlet is abandoned and its inhabitants establish domiciles, including houses and gardens, in other hamlets. These may or may not be newly founded. I hypothesize that the ultimate cause of a hamlet shift or a series of them is declining hunting success (X_2), although the proximate cause is a death (see chapter 8). Hamlet shifts are influenced by nucleation (X_{13}) and the phase of the settlement cycle, and are the primary mechanisms for changes in the settlement pattern.

X_6 "Settlement Cycle" is another binary variable in a positive state when a settlement pattern reaches its maximum dispersal (X_{13}) and begins to drift in a given direction, usually with the grain of the land. It is also related to declining hunting success (X_2).

X_7 "Dry Season Residence" is a binary variable in a positive state when people concentrate on the pioneering side of the overall settlement. As a seasonal phase it interacts with and is limited by the three nonseasonal phases included in the system. It is tied to the local seasonal cycle and is probably triggered by seasonal changes in the distribution and availability of game animals, particularly wild pigs attracted by the fruits of certain forest trees.

X_8 "Rainy Season Residence" is the reciprocal of the foregoing. It is in a positive state when population is balanced throughout the settlement. The contingencies assigned to X_7 apply.

X_9 "Intergroup Visiting" is an alternative to X_8 and represents the number of people-days of activity outside home group boundaries. Adult men predominate, but male and female parish members and their families who reside elsewhere choose this time to visit their kin as well.

X_{10} "Male Migration" is not a major variable in the system but is included in the interest of realism, particularly because of its intimate relationship to X_9. A small number of men, both married and unmarried, find the hunting environment of the lowlands which they experience during visits to be overwhelmingly attractive.

X_{11} "Settlement Movement Rate" is the rate of unidirectional movement of the center of the settlement pattern after the settlement cycle phase (X_6) has been initiated.

X_{12} "Settlement Duration" indicates the years that a local population has occupied an area since the previous settlement shift. It is a function of the settlement movement rate (X_{11}) and limited by the size of the effective occupation area (X_{28}).

X_{13} "Nucleation Index" is the average of the distances between all hamlets of a given local population's settlement at a given point in time. It is a function of settlement duration (X_{12}). The lower limit on nucleation is set by garden invasions of domestic pigs (X_{21}), the upper limit (of dispersal) by garden invasions of wild pigs (X_{19}).

X_{14} "Hunting Labor" is a function of the perceived need for meat (or the desire to hunt) (X_1) and traditional ritual requirements (P_2). It is constrained, however, by other demands on labor (P_7), including agriculture.

X_{15} "Intensity of Pig Herding" is the ratio of domestic to wild pork in the meat harvest of a group: X_{24}/X_{23}. (Realistically, the dimensions of pig husbandry are more complex, and a focus on this subsystem might include such additional variables as the provision of fodder, confinement, the management of reproduction, and so on. I will consider some of these issues in the chapter on agriculture.) Intensification is related to declining availability of wild sources of meat which is, in turn, a function of overhunting and environmental disruption. Among the Miyanmin, failure to move due to modernization contingencies is the root cause.

X_{16} "Accessible Forest Area" is the amount of undisturbed primary or old secondary forest outside of the compass of the overall settlement pattern within a standard radius of 8 km (5 mi) of all hamlets. It is a function of nucleation (X_{13})—i.e., the more dispersal, the greater the area of accessible forest.

X_{17} "Gardens and Other Disturbed Areas" is the sum of the area within the compass of the settlement (including, but not limited to, active and abandoned gardens and second growth tracts) and the area of disturbance within the standard radius of 8 km (5 mi). (In other words, I assume that the entire area within the settlement is disturbed.) It is a function of nucleation (X_{13}) and the product of settlement duration and settlement movement ($X_{12}X_{11}$) subtracted from the occupation area (X_{28}).

X_{18} "Wild Pig Sighting" is the rate of reports of the presence of wild pigs (including evidence of their activity) within the territory of a local population. It is a function of wild pig invasions (X_{19}) in a rainy season phase (X_9) and of forest accessibility (X_{10}) and hunting labor (X_{14}) in a dry season phase (X_7).

X_{19} "Wild Pig in Gardens" is the frequency of incidents of wild pigs competing for garden produce per unit of time. It is a function of seasonality (P_6) and nucleation (X_9), it is higher in the dry season, and it is more likely under a dispersed regime.

X_{20} "Domestic Pig Herd Size" is the summation of the domestic pigs kept by the households of a local population. It is a function of "intensity" (X_{15}) both directly and indirectly, since under the traditional extensive husbandry regime a significant proportion of the stock were born in the wild (thus adding to domestic reproduction and acquisitions [P_1]). Numbers are reduced by the slaughter triggered by garden invasions (X_{21}) and other events (P_8).

X_{21} "Domestic Pigs in Gardens" is the frequency of reported garden invasions by village pigs per unit of time. It is a function of the size of the herd (X_{21}) and nucleation (X_{13}). All else being equal, the more compact the settlement pattern of residences and gardens, the greater the probability of garden invasions.

X_{22} "Class III Harvest" is the weight of the harvest of species in the class of reduced fauna. It is a function of duration of settlement (X_{12}), accessible forest (X_{16}), wild pig sightings (X_{18}), and tradition ritual requirements (P_2).

X_{23} "Class IV Harvest" is the weight of the harvest of species in the class of fostered fauna. It is a function of gardens and other disturbed areas (X_{17}).

X_{24} "Class V Harvest" is the weight of domestic animals, primarily pigs, slaughtered. It is determined by the rate of domestic pig garden invasions (X_{21}) and other pig slaughter occasions (P_8) of a less easily predicted kind, such as entertainment of visitors, concluding aegistments, and the maturity of individual animals.

X_{25} "Class I and II Harvest" is essentially a residual category embracing the harvest of rare, difficult, relict, or distantly located species and other animal foods that are harvested in small quantities. Some items here, however, are somewhat more common under a dispersed settlement regime (X_{13}) or were used in certain traditional rituals (P_2).

X_{26} "Extraterritorial Harvest" is the weight of meat originating outside of the territory of the local population and largely results from rainy season visits to other groups (X_9).

X_{27} "Total Meat" is the summation of the harvests of the various sources ($X_{22} + X_{23} + X_{24} + X_{25} + X_{26}$).

X_{28} "Effective Occupation Area" is the area occupied by a population during a particular settlement cycle. It is delimited topographically and politically.

Certain boundary factors of the system are referred to as parameters designated by P and a subscript. These parameters define links between the hypothetical system and its larger context, including other systems not analyzed in this study.

P_1 "Pig Aegistment" is an arrangement whereby the owner of a pig boards it with a member of another local group, with both parties sharing the product when the pig is deemed ready for slaughter.

P_2 "Ritual Game Requirement" represents the traditional rituals which require the capture of particular game animals in connection with initiation, mourning, and curing. The types of game include wild pig, cassowary and certain marsupials.

P_3 "Population" is the number of people residing within the boundaries of the territory controlled by the local population. For illustrative purposes, I have included only one significant input to it from the system, male migration (X_{10}).

P_4 "Proximity of Other Groups" is a significant political constraint on decisions to shift to a new occupation area or to place a residential and gardening complex within an established occupation area. A local population with prior use of a boundary zone can inhibit another local population's inappropriate or incompatible uses of the corresponding boundary zone.

P_5 "Other Settlement Constraints" is a catchall for miscellaneous accidents of topography and hazard and resource distribution that reduce the usefulness of parts of an area. Agricultural factors loom large here.

P_6 "Season," which for analytical purposes has been divided into two parts: a "dry season" and a "wet season." These appear to be significantly related to reproductive and other biological rhythms in plants and animals. The rainy season commences at the time of the austral spring and is the time when many fauna reproduce. The dry season, which is merely less rainy than the wet, occupies the June to December period.

P_7 "Situational Constraints to Labor" involves a variety of factors affecting individuals and subgroups and their ability to hunt. Diurnal movements and associated activities involve both patterned and idiosyncratic decisions regarding the focus of labor. Members of families broken by either death or the absence of other members tend to drop out of hunting.

P_8 "Other Pig Slaughter Occasions" is another catchall for indeterminate decisions to slaughter domestic pigs. Such reasons include the maturity of an animal and/or the desire to offer more than minimal hospitality to a favored visitor.

There are also 14 mixing points which, strictly speaking, are also variables. In order to reduce clutter and enhance legibility, variable names for them have been omitted. It is assumed that the operations they represent will be self-evident.

The Operation of the System

This account begins with a description of the nonseasonal phases of the system and then moves on to describe the seasonal ones. As described in chapter 10, the Miyanmin occupy an area of high but irregular relief, with the landscape transected by mountains of variable altitude and cross-section and normally placid small rivers. In the southern higher-altitude areas the grain of the land is east-west; but further north it is more varied, with major river valleys, such as the Sepik, the May, and the August gradually turning to a north-south orientation. This geographic variability interacts with historically determined political boundaries to produce a jigsaw puzzle of group territories that are idiosyncratic in size, shape, and distribution of the main features which render a particular area suitable or unsuitable for human occupation and use. I do not attempt to account for the full range of geopolitical idiosyncrasies as they might affect the operation of this system. These must be recognized, however, as they affect the unfolding of different phases of the system, especially duration and direction of movement.

The basic unit of territory for the purposes of this study is the "occupation area," a pristine or recovered and topographically distinct area such as a divide between two small rivers. Both sides of a typical divide will be exploited at some point in the cycle. For any particular local population it is important to know the set of best or likely occupation areas and their spatial relationship. For a particular settlement cycle of a local population, it is also important to know about the characteristics of the area presently occupied and the possible optional occupation areas for the next settlement cycle.

First Phase

A particular settlement cycle starts when a local population carries out a "settlement shift" into a new occupation area. The ultimate cause of a shift will have been the proximity of a topographic or political boundary. During this early phase, settlement will be nucleated, with the majority of the population occupying a long house/dance house. In a short time at least one more large nucleated hamlet and associated gardens will be established on the other side of the divide. The ratio of accessible deep forest to disturbed vegetation may range from roughly 1:1 to 2:1, depending on the distance entailed in the shift (hence the relative location of the previous occupation area). In higher-altitude areas the distances involved are not great; and, as a result, the proportions of the two types of vegetation are fairly even. During this phase of settlement the harvest of "reduced" (Class III) fauna—including wild pigs—is moderate or high, while the harvest of fostered (Class IV) animals and the slaughter of domesticated pigs (Class V) are low.

Second Phase

The second phase of settlement proceeds with fluctuating hunting success due to the early impact of human settlement and hunting, particularly on Class III animals. Progressively more and smaller hamlets are established by means of "hamlet shifts," and these are more dispersed. This compensates for short-run fluctuations in hunting success. While the harvest of Class III fauna declines, the slack may be taken up by the slaughter of domestic pigs. This is triggered by increased garden invasions of a growing population of village pigs when the settlement is nucleated and the distance between hamlets and gardens is small. As dispersal of hamlets proceeds and the distance between hamlets and gardens increases, the rate of domestic pig slaughter triggered by garden invasions diminishes. At the same time, the exposure of gardens to wild pigs (particularly in the rainy season) is enhanced and the wild pig harvest approaches its highest annual level. The harvest of fostered (Class IV) animals increases slowly. Progressively, the success of wild pigs as competitors for garden produce sets a limit on denucleation so that in time (two to four years) simple dispersal as a mechanism for increasing access to deep forest can no longer be practiced in order to maintain the level of hunting success.

Third Phase

Under such circumstances the chain of hamlets must move in one direction and maintain approximately the same degree of nucleation. This compensates for fluctuating hunting success and marks the third phase in which the rate of movement is sufficient to maintain the ratio between deep forest and disturbed vegetation. Note, however, that the absolute extent of disturbance is increasing. The harvest of "reduced" (Class III) fauna is further diminished, the harvest of fostered fauna (Class V)—at least half of which occurs in gardens and is accomplished at very low cost in terms of hunting effort—will be increasing, and the slaughter of domestic pigs will proceed at only a moderate level. This kind of compensatory movement continues until the amount of accessible deep forest comes to be constrained more and more by geographical or political boundaries, and the absolute supply of game to be found is diminished. Hence, a settlement shift is triggered and a new cycle initiated.

Dry Season Phase

The seasonal phases of the system interact with the nonseasonal phase described in the foregoing. These involve the movement of individuals and families rather than hamlet shifts. Dry season residence involves the concentration of active men of the 15 to 45 age group in hamlets that permit direct access to deep forest. On the one hand, this facilitates hunting prey species of undisturbed forest areas that are in greatest abundance during this period, including wild pigs and other "reduced" fauna that have been protected from settlement effects by natural barriers. On the other hand, the harvesting of fostered and domestic fauna is reduced. As it interacts with the nonseasonal phases, the function of the latter in maintaining a large area of accessible deep forest is most critical.

Rainy Season Residence and Visiting

In the rainy season phase of the system, involving a distinctive pattern of residence, visiting, and hunting expeditions, the local harvest is focused on fauna characteristically found (or most easily hunted) in zones of disturbed vegetation and gardens. Included here are wild pigs taken in lesser abundance and at greater cost than in the dry season (but facilitated by garden invasions), fostered fauna such as certain rats, possums, and bandicoots, and bird hunting (which is not otherwise classified) because tree climbing and hide construction is easier in secondary forest. According to informants, the motivation for extraterritorial expeditions is the low level of hunting success at home, particularly with respect to wild pigs. Thus, in the south during this period many young men, including married men, part from their groups to hunt further north in the middle May River area for several months. They return home bearing a full load, some 50 or 60 pounds of dressed smoked pork and other meat. As this phase interacts with the nonseasonal phases, the function of the latter in maintaining access to areas of disturbed vegetation (including nonmovable capital such as economic trees and the favored habitats of certain fauna) is most important.

Change in the System

This model focuses on equilibration. Although the picture conveyed is not static, the overall argument emphasizes a pattern of relationships between people and fauna which has persisted. As was stated earlier in this chapter, the boundaries of the system, hence the limits on stability, are defined by the variables called parameters. Some of these have a narrow range of action on the system, mainly affecting selected components, establishing a range of values for some, and triggering others by mediating events outside the system. Also, some of the parameters—like the biotic potential of specific mammalian populations—are "hidden" in the faunal and movement classifications on which so much of this analysis hinges. Beyond these considerations there is a set of parameters that affects the system as a whole. These are primarily attributes of population and territory that have been isolated, including the size of the human population (P_3). These parameters can also be seen as variables in other systems that, for quite practical reasons, it has been impossible to analyze here. If is granted that such movements as expansion and migration (described in chapter 10) are likely mechanisms for relieving relative population pressures, then it should be possible to consider the effects of changes in population or in population density in the region on the operation of this system.

A parsimonious way of looking at the matter is to examine system change through the adoption or loss of phases. This is the same as saying that the addition of phases to the system is a form of intensification (as that term has been applied to changes in agricultural systems by Boserup [1965] and—in New Guinea—Clark [1966], Brookfield and Hart [1971], Brookfield [1972] and others). As new phases are adopted, particularly in the sphere of environmental modification, movement spheres are permanently lost and groups become more sedentary.

I do not have enough information for a detailed discussion of the most extensive version of the system under analysis, that of the most northern *sanakai* Miyanmin groups (which are the smallest and live at the lowest altitude). Among these groups the horticultural base is somewhat smaller and less reliable so that there is greater dependence on natural stands of sago. Settlements are more dispersed, hamlets smaller, local lineages more prominent, and small segments more mobile. Fish and wild pig are exploited intensively, and the smaller mammals seem less prominent. Movements— including settlement shifts—are over greater distances, are more frequent, and apparently have a very short settlement cycle. On the basis of this information, a system with only two phases (or one combining two nonseasonal phases with two seasonal phases) could be hypothesized. In this connection, the account of Kome attempts to settle in this area, presented in chapter 10, are particularly revealing. In this more extensive system, I hypothesize that long houses are built more frequently, with the *Ita* held more frequently as a rainy season event. The shifting and occupation of small dispersed hamlets is, on the other hand, a dry season strategy.

The version of the system analyzed here, pertaining to the large high-altitude *am-nakai* Miyanmin groups, is the intensive or progressive form. Predatory warfare is an example of the addition of a phase to the system. This occurs under circumstances, albeit temporary, that suggest positive changes in key parameters. These circumstances will be described in a somewhat different context in chapter 10. The detailed argument has been presented elsewhere (Dornstreich and Morren 1974), but can be summarized appropriately here.

Cannibalism is a feature of warfare throughout the Mountain Ok area and, at the time of pacification, the Miyanmin had gained an unusually fearsome reputation. It is useful to distinguish between expansive warfare, a movement strategy discussed in chapter 10, and predatory warfare, a subsistence activity that resembles intergroup visiting and may intensify in a situation involving extreme food stress.

The process of adopting a predatory warfare phase was initiated by the expansion of the Telefolmin peoples in which they were attempting to move out of environments that were heavily disrupted and depleted of game. In the eastern Miyanmin area, the consequence of Telefolmin pressure was that a number of Miyanmin local groups came to be concentrated in refuge on the middle May River with the groups already living there. The latter included Sokaten, Wameten, and Mabweten and the refugee groups were Kometen and Temseten. The ecological consequences of this can be inferred from informants' statements. In the area in which the groups concentrated, game declined rapidly and the ability of people to compensate for this by activating the familiar settlement and movement mechanisms was restricted in terms of the parameters that have been specified: size of population, size of occupation area, and proximity of local groups. Perhaps the necessities of defense imposed limits on dispersal as well. Some intra-Miyanmin population displacements (chapter 10) ensued, but the tempo of armed conflict, at first against the Telefolmin people to the south, was greatly increased. With the movement of Miyanmin goups to the north, the foothill peoples on both sides of the lower May River were increasingly subjected to Miyanmin raids. Initially this raiding may have been initiated in retaliation for attacks on small Miyanmin hunting parties venturing out of their own territory in search of game. However, this pay-back ideology was soon lost. According to Miyanmin informants, the quest for human flesh became an end in itself, a phase in a very complex system balancing a local human population with the rest of the faunal community.

The key to an argument about the value of this process is that the level of cannibalism would not have to be high in order for it to make as large a contribution to the Miyanmin diet as that of even the most important source of high-quality protein, the wild pig. Under normal conditions the Miyanmin obtain some 23 grams of protein/capita/week from pork, most of it wild. If the Kome parish group, numbering some 159 people, benefited from the human flesh resulting from the killing of only some 30 adults per year, the figure for pork would be equalled. Such a level of cannibalistic activity is apparently realistic for only a few periods in recent Miyanmin history, but, as is discussed in a later section, these were probably periods when Miyanmin hunting output was extremely low.

This interpretation of Miyanmin cannibalism has ethnographic parallels. Colin Simpson's (1953) reference to the Miyanmin as the "Kukukuku of the West" points the way. Beatrice Blackwood (1940), an early ethnographer of the Kukukuku, paints a very similar picture of the cannibalism practiced by that group.

> I feel convinced that in the case of the Kukukuku, protein shortage is, if not the only, at least a powerful, contributory cause of cannibalism, the concomitant of the fighting and raiding that has made these natives the terror of all their neighbors. They told me themselves that they regard the bodies of their enemies—men, women, and children alike—simply as meat, and while they usually find some excuse for a raid other than the necessity of replenishing their larder, they consider it very wasteful not to utilize in that way any spoils that may result. There seems to be no magico-religious or other sanction behind their cannibalism, such as the idea that the strength of a brave enemy passes into them with his flesh (114–15).

Predatory warfare apparently possessed the same expeditionary character which I have attributed to hunting trips to the north during normal (or postcontact) times. Informants' descriptions of their participation in such raids evoked an image of commonplace hunting expeditions, including the return trip with *bilum* loads of meat. It was not unusual for young men to spend several months at a time away from home, living in small bush hamlets in the territory of a host parish in the north in order to raid the villages of May River groups.

The few Miyanmin raids that can be documented in calendric terms from patrol reports are southern ones occurring in the dry or at the beginning of the rainy season, including a 1954 raid in the Eliptaman Valley reported by Jones (1954), and large scale raids on the Atbalmin in November and again in late December, 1956, as reported by Ron Neville (1956). I do not believe that this defensive warfare in the south was seasonal. Raids in the north seem to have occurred most frequently at the height of the rainy season because Miyanmin raiding parties characteristically rode rafts down the May River to get at their prey.

It should be possible to talk about further progressive changes in the system under analysis—the kinds of systemic changes resulting from higher parametric stresses respecting both population and territory. One might ask if the Telefolmin system were not, in fact, an even more intensive form or variant of the same system. The question is not relevant to the prospect for change among the Miyanmin, for as long as the lower-altitude area functions as a population sink, no such stresses are likely. Modernization may have already nullified this, however, as certain sites are attractive due to the services and opportunities they appear to represent. The question is more relevant to the ecological history of the Telefolmin peoples themselves. If we assume that some 300 years ago the Telefolmin system of resource management was essentially similar to that of the high-altitude Miyanmin, then the trajectory of change among them can be outlined. For one thing, the Telefolmin of that time had no such effective population sink, no direction of easy expansion or ready migration. This would help to account for their fairly rapid growth of population (chapter 10), with the system having to operate with lower success levels in support of larger populations.

The component of the system undergoing the greatest elaboration and intensification was the pig husbandry sector, with the phases having to do with reduced fauna withering away. From the standpoint of the way the system came to be structured, the most significant feature of the pig husbandry strategy has to do with the expansion and intensification of horticulture and the progressive cultivation of the sweet potato (a feature that further distinguishes the Telefolmin from the Miyanmin), all concerned with providing fodder for pigs. The positive feedback or "vicious circle" side of intensification has been recognized in similar contexts. Chaplin (1969) speaks of the domestication of animals in the ancient Near East: "To be a successful cultivator... one had to virtually exterminate the game. It is perhaps at this stage that the most valuable species were brought into captivity" (239). Based upon a superficial acquaintance with the situation of the Telefolmin, the phases of the system that seem to remain are two seasonal ones—one dispersed and one nucleated—plus one nonseasonal phase providing for the management of the herd. The dispersed phase might be further subdivided, with one strategy involving local dispersal in small garden hamlets and the other having to do with long-range visiting and intergardening.

Having presented the foregoing argument about the Telefolmin and the evolution of their resource management strategy, I am provoked by several points that bear on Watson's "Ipomoean Revolution" argument (1964a, 1965b) and criticisms of it (see especially Brookfield and White, 1969). By and large, I am in sympathy with the arguments of the latter critics concerning the nonrevolutionary character of subsistence change in New Guinea. I agree that population expansion has been proceeding for much longer than the 300 years proposed by Watson, but at a fairly slow rate. Moreover, the sweet potato is precisely the kind of variation which will be widely adopted when it will confer an advantage in terms of sustaining population growth for commensurate inputs of labor. The same is true of intensive forms of pig husbandry. Thus if I were to advocate "revolutionary activity," I would have to argue for a "Susian Revolution," with the sweet potato being an important component of the transformation (Morren 1977). As Brookfield and White (1968:45) and their collaborators seem to recognize, a factor limiting human population in the high mountain interior of New Guinea is not likely to be met by the introduction of a starchy vegetable, especially one notably lacking in many essential amino acids unless staple vegetable crops have been effectively destroyed by a pathogen (chapter 5).

As will be discussed in later chapters, some Miyanmin groups are traversing similar ground as they attempt to reconcile the old with the new. Larger and potentially more permanent settlements are aggregating around airstrips. This has resulted in resource shortages which are only partly mitigated by the use of dispersed hamlets, intensified pig husbandry, increased sweet potato production, and other innovations and modern advantages. An alternative most often discussed among the highly mobile groups in the north is to shift the airstrips, keeping them in step with settlement changes that are viewed by the people as necessary to their life-style and well-being.

In the next chapter the environmental context of my research problem will be examined in order to establish the broad interactional matrix in which the Miyanmin move, farm, and hunt. It is particularly important to focus on a human-centered environment of problems and opportunities that arise from the way in which these people interact with their environment in this time and place. We are much less concerned with an "objective" environment described for its own sake. Thus, all movement acts or strategies that are not directly concerned with hunting, and responses (including movement responses) are not problem-specific.

4

The Human Environment

The basic unit of analysis for this study is the interaction between the Miyanmin and their environment. The features of the environment that are of concern here are those which are relevant to the situation of people at a particular time and place. Features of the environment that are anthropogenic, human artifacts, are also of concern. Thus, the human environment is the product of the relations and interrelations among the characteristics, capacities, and acts of the people and the features of the living and nonliving world in which they live.

The activities and movements of people may produce hazards as well as resources. Characteristics of the "objective" environment that pose only a potential threat to people, or did so in the past, may have been wholly or partially mitigated by them through the routinization of their responses. Such "solved" problems do indeed reemerge as threats when responses to other changes interfere with their ability to sustain an otherwise established routine. Or the routinization of some problem responses may inhibit the ability to respond to others. Some survival-threatening problems are directly caused by other people. Finally, the way in which people perceive changes and classify features of their environment (or their relationship to them) is an intrinsic part of the routinization of their adaptive activities and movements. Perception (and its linguistic dimension) particularly affects the ability of people to respond in the presence of novel or unusual changes.

Thus, social and environmental change can be viewed as a unified process, and the environment of concern may be seen as as much of a product of history as is society. This chapter begins by placing the Miyanmin in geographical and cultural-historical perspective. The "objective" environment is then examined before a picture of a human environment in operational, cognitive, and interactional terms is presented.

Location and Cultural History

The headwaters of New Guinea's largest rivers, the northward flowing Idenberg and Sepik and the southward flowing Strickland and Fly, all originate in the high mountains near the geographic center of the island. This area also marks a significant biogeographical and cultural break. This is the home of the Mountain Ok (Healey 1964; Craig 1969) or "Min"[1] peoples. The region is part of the 1500 mile (930 km) central cordillera of New Guinea that includes peaks exceeding 5300 m (16,000 ft) in altitude. In the Mountain Ok region peaks to 4300 m (13000 ft) exist in the Star Mountains, 3000 m (9000 ft) in the Donner range, and 3700 m (11,000 ft) in the Hindenburgs. The topography of the area is characterized by broken ranges and one of the 11 great intermontane valley systems of New Guinea.[2] The central valley is the Ifitaman (in legend the original home valley of the Telefolmin people) which, as part of the Sibil-Ifitaman-Teken complex, is an important regional, demographic, and cultural center. Today, it is also the location of the area's principal administrative center, the Telefomin District Office. In Ifitaman the valley floor, consisting of a large alluvial fan, is at approximately 1900 m (5000 ft) above sea level (ASL).

On the northern fall of the central range in this area, beginning with the crest of the Donner and Thurnwald ranges, there is a gradual descent through lower montane and foothill zones to the lowlands of the Sepik plains. This descent is characterized by mountains of decreasing altitude, then low divides, then relatively flat land and wide, meandering rivers. The high mountain country here is drained principally by the May and August rivers, major tributaries of the Sepik which local people call *Teken*, as well as by the smaller Hak River which is fed by the northern face of the Donners and the south slope of the eastern Thurnwalds. Part of the northern fall of the Thurnwalds, as well as the west and south slopes of Mount Stolle (which the Miyanmin call *Mekil*), feed the May. The vast area stretching from the Donner and Thurnwald ranges in the south to the May Hills and the West Range in the north is the home of the Miyanmin. For the most part, it is an area of steep, rugged topography, continuous rainforest, high rainfall, and relatively few people.

The name Miyanmin (or Mianmin, according to official usage) originally belonged to a now-extinct local group, but was assigned generically to an entire ethnolinguistic group or "tribe" by the Telefolmin people of the Ifitaman and Eliptaman to the north. According to my own informants, the word *miyan* means acorn, hence Miyanmin means "acorn children." Gardner (1981) believes that it derives from the Telefol for "dog." Indeed, the Miyanmin never had a name for themselves as a group, although group terms of extralocal import do exist (chapter 7). During the early contact period the name Miyanmin was communicated by helpful Telefolmin to various white visitors. It became "official," and the Miyanmin have accepted it as their name in the modern world.

Properly speaking, the people and the area upon which this study focuses is East Mianmin, a census and electoral division of Telefomin District, West Sepik (Sandoun) Province, Papua New Guinea. In the 1960s, when I first entered the field, East Mianmin also designated the portion of the greater Miyanmin area that was not classified as restricted by the Australian administration. The relevant contrast was with West Mianmin, which remained restricted until the early 1970s because it was considered to be uncontrolled. An additional portion of Miyanmin territory is administered from May River Patrol Post, part of Ambunti District of the East Sepik Province. In West Mianmin some Miyanmin people, including a few who had had virtually no contact in the 1960s, live in areas on the Wagarabe and Idam Rivers that were nominally administered by the Green River patrol post. Today, there is a new patrol post and airstrip named Yapsiei on the upper August River which administers much of West Mianmin.

The data presented here are based on intensive residence and study with groups in the Hak-Uk Valley between the Donner and Thurnwald ranges in 1968–69 and 1980–81. For comparative purposes, I also made long visits of up to a month's duration to all the other East Mianmin groups that I enumerate and describe in chapter 7. I will cite and identify pertinent observations from them when appropriate. Since my initial fieldwork, Donald Gardner (1981) has conducted social anthropological research among several West Mianmin groups.

Miyanmin (or Mianmin) is also the name assigned by linguists to the language spoken by the people of the area. Miyanmin is a member of Alan Healey's *Ok Family* of languages (Healey 1964; also called the Telefomin family by Wurm 1964). According to Wurm, although it has not been assigned to it, Ok has ancient connections to the East New Guinea Stock.

Miyanmin shares membership in the *Mountain Ok Subfamily* (Healey 1964) with languages of several close neighbors (map 1), Telefol to the south and east, and Tifal spoken by the Atbalmin to the southwest. Immediately to the north are the lower May River peoples, Iwam speakers, and, on the Idam and August rivers, speakers of Abau, all members of the *Upper Sepik Family* (Laycock 1965a, 1965b). None of the languages cited are mutually intelligible with Miyanmin, but people in border areas are often bilingual in Telefol and possibly other languages.

When I initially joined the Miyanmin in 1968, only the Telefolmin of Ifitaman, Oksapmin[3] of Teken, and the Ngalum of Sibil (in the western Star Mountains area of what was then Dutch New Guinea) of the Mountain Ok had been studied by anthropologists at all. The Healeys commenced their linguistic research on Telefomin in the early 1960s (A. Healey 1962). With their own data, as well as that gathered by other Summer Institute of Linguistics workers who had preceded anthropologists into many Mountain Ok groups, they gave us the first look at the region as a whole (A. Healey 1964). Barry Craig's interest was the art of the Telefolmin, and ultimately of the entire upper Sepik region (1967, 1968, 1969). Ruth Craig's concern was social organization (1969). B. A. L. Cranstone (1968) visited Telefomin and Tifalmin briefly to record and collect art and material culture. In addition, Telefomin rated a mention in the works of several less professional visitors: Stuart Campbell (1938), the pilot for a prospecting group; Ivan Champion (1966) and J. L. Taylor (1939), who participated in early administration exploration patrols; P. J. Quinlaven (1954), who helped prosecute Telefolmin rebels (and attributed their acts to a myth); and Colin Simpson (1954), a journalist. Arnold Perey, worked in Oksapmin from 1966–67 and ultimately focussed on world view (1973). In addition, a Dutch research team that included the anthropologist J. Pouwer (1964, 1966) and the agronomist J. J. Reynders (1962) surveyed the Ngalum peoples of the Ok Sibil in the western Star Mountains in the late 1950s.

Before I had left the field in 1969, Fredrik Barth (1971, 1975) had commenced his study of the Baktaman Faiwolmin, and Wilson Wheatcroft (1975) had begun his work among the Tifalmin. Since that time there has been a virtual flood of research on this area. In the center, the Telefolmin have also been studied by Jorgensen (1981a, 1981b) and Brumbaugh (1980, 1981). Brumbaugh has also recently worked at Feranmin. Among high-altitude fringe peoples, in addition to Perey's work in Oksapmin (see also Weeks, ed. 1981), Poole (1981, 1982) has worked in Bimin, and Berkovitch (1982) in Atbalmin. For the mid-altitude fringe peoples of the north slope, in addition to my own work (Morren 1974, 1977, 1980, 1981a, 1984) and Gardner's (1980, 1981a 1983) on the Miyanmin, Moylan (1979) has worked among the Ninataman Telefolmin. On the south slope, Hyndman (1979, 1982, 1984a, 1984b) has worked among the Wopkaimin and Jones (1980) among the Faiwolmin. There is now sufficient information on the various peoples of the Mountain Ok area to begin to piece together a coherent regional picture from various perspectives.

Elsewhere (Morren 1984, Hyndman and Morren n.d.) it has been argued that Mountain Ok is an appropriate label for a unit that has more than cultural or linguistic importance. The term *sphere* was adopted to refer to an expanding, segmentary, reticulated aggregate of local groups that not only share a common historic, cultural, and linguistic tradition, but are also strongly influenced by a core population at the geographic center of their region. According to this definition, Ifitaman is a center and the Telefolmin, Tifalmin, and Feranmin living there constitute the core. (Oksapmin and Sibil may constitute second centers in the sphere.) The Miyanmin, by virtue of location and low population density, are one of several fringe groups that, while remote from the center and contesting frontiers with groups belonging to other spheres, are nevertheless influenced by changes originating in core groups.

The position of the Miyanmin in a regional interactive sphere of diverse peoples says as much about their ecological situation as do the features of the objective environment with which they interact. The former will be considered in some detail—particularly regional patterns of expansion and warfare and their local consequences—in chapter 10 (see also Morren 1984). Until pacification took hold in the early contact period, the threat and fact of resource competition and displacement loomed very large in the lives of all Miyanmin, even those not directly occupying or attempting to control frontiers.

Although this chapter examines the natural environment, it is particularly concerned with features that are important because they affect people's situations: actual or potential problems, hazards, and resources arising from the way they interact with the environment. The flux of people's perceptions and the cognized environment will also be discussed (Rappaport 1968, 1984).

Across the expanse of their territory the majority of Miyanmin dwell in lower-montane forest with a smaller number occupying lowland rainforest. In some areas, group territories extend into mid- and upper-montane zones. A given person may exploit any of these zones, from lowlands to upper montane, at some time.

Hence, for the Miyanmin the forest community of plants and animals is an important feature of the natural environment. In the southern part of Miyanmin country (where I carried out most of my research), human settlements were located in the altitudinal range between 850 m (2500 ft) and 650 m (4000 ft) ASL. In this range people had ready access to two fairly distinct zones: below 1000 m (3000 ft) was the lower-montane forest of oak, and mixed composition; and above that mark, was the mid-montane forest of beech and conifer.

The Miyanmin use forest flora for building and craft materials, firewood, and some vegetable foods. These kinds of resources present problems mainly in the context of unusual concentrations of people, something that has become characteristic of modernization. The faunal component is extremely important as the principal source of animal foods. Under most circumstances, game is abundant and diverse, and the Miyanmin get their meat supply from hunting wild pig, cassowary, rodents, marsupials, and birds. Meat may occasionally be scarce for some individuals and groups. (Animals and hunting are discussed in chapter 6.)

The forest also produces an exceptional environment for agriculture, which is centered on the cultivation of *Colocasia* taro. The most significant agronomic factor is high rainfall. Agricultural land has become a problem in the same way that forest resources have become scarce, i.e., when people concentrate in refuge or in response to modernization. There are some important, though relatively infrequent, hazards to agriculture, such as drought and plant pathogens. Labor scarcity due to death or labor mobility also disrupts domestic subsistence, although this is tempered by kinship and egalitarianism. (Agriculture is discussed in greater detail in chapter 5.)

Disease-causing parasites are another important component of the Miyanmin environment. Malaria, filariasis, yaws, and a number of respiratory and gastrointestinal diseases have probably always been present. The range of some endemic diseases such as malaria may have been extended by contact and pacification. Influenza and other viral diseases, tuberculosis, and leprosy have been directly or remotely introduced. Yet others, such as yaws, have been rapidly eliminated. In common with many other groups in New Guinea, the Miyanmin population declined during the early contact period. At least partly related to the foregoing, underpopulation is a survival issue that people have recognized. This is particularly true of the shortage of women in some groups (chapter 7).

The Physical Environment

The mid-altitude zone pertains typologically to the area between 500 m (1500 ft) and 1500 m (4500 ft). Topographically, it ranges from foothills to auxiliary ranges and lower slopes of the central cordillera. The zone embraces areas with some of the highest rainfall in New Guinea, with regimes of low seasonality characteristic (Brookfield and Hart 1971:9–13). It is geologically unstable. It is also rich in wild food resources, both animal and vegetable. Many original New Guinea domesticates, economic trees, and nonmammalian fauna are unusually abundant in the zone, which also provides a very favorable environment for agriculture.

Climate and Weather

Both the general seasonal conditions of the Southwest Pacific area and highly localized factors bring about the seasonal pattern of rainfall in the East Mianmin area. Within it, rainfall seems to vary in abundance from place to place. Brookfield and Hart (1971:9) have clearly described the pattern:

> ...the maximum [rainfall] tends to lie between December and late March, February being most commonly the wettest month. Minimum rainfall usually occurs between May and August. Mid-August maxima are recorded only where sharp uplift of the southwesterlies occurs.

How this pattern is expressed in the upper Sepik can be seen in figure 4-1. Here I have plotted my own limited observations from the Uk River along with the mean monthly rainfall from the two nearest official stations, Telefomin and Green River. Telefomin lies to the south at approximately 1660 m (5000 ft) ASL in high mountain country. It participates along with East Mianmin in the August maxima associated with the uplift of the prevailing southeasterly winds. Green River is in relatively flat terrain and the August maxima is thus absent. The rainfall pattern of the Miyanmin area north of the Ulame and Fiak Rivers converges with this pattern. For the present, it is important to note that the annual distribution of cloud cover, closely correlated to the rainfall regime, may have an influence on vegetation and crops. In addition, the reproduction of certain mammals coincides with the main period of maximum rainfall, say January to March (see chapter 6).

The mean annual rainfall for both Telefomin and Green River is approximately 340 mm (135 in). The total rainfall recorded for the year August, 1968 through July, 1969 at my "station" on the Uk River was approximately 465 mm (185 in). This was probably not a typical year in the area; my recorded total of 206 mm (82 in) for the January to April period exceeds the estimated mean for that period and area (Brookfield and Hart 1966, map 6) by 50 mm (20 in). I recorded 50 mm (20 in) of rain for a single month (March, 1969) when the Uk River was in full flood twice, threatening my house both times. This did not happen at all the previous year, including March, 1968 when I was just establishing myself among the Miyanmin.

Figure 4-1. Monthly Rainfall

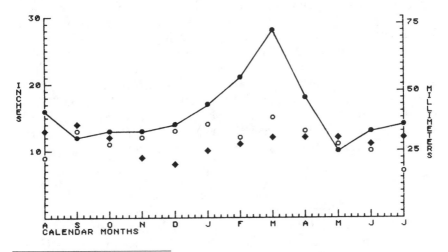

● Uk River, August, 1968–July, 1969
◆ Telefomin, 1963
○ Green River, 1963

SOURCE: Brookfield and Hart 1966

Temperature in the area is moderate and daily minima and maxima vary little: the modal minimum was 68 degrees Fahrenheit, the maximum 84. The absolute range I recorded was 64 to 87. Climatic hazards to human life and to agriculture exist but occur infrequently. Unusually high rainfall contributes to flooding of riverside settlements, can imperil people attempting to walk to gardens, and result in erosion and falling trees. Because all Miyanmin live below 1200 m (4000 ft), frost is unknown. Droughts, however, have occurred; and taro is particularly vulnerable if the period of reduced rainfall is prolonged.

With incomplete rainfall and climatic data I can only speculate about relationships with agriculture and other aspects of the life-support system. The overall climate is strongly favorable to agriculture. Heavy rainfall and high humidity go together but it is their diurnal distribution that is most important. In my area, at least, most days are clear and free of rainfall, a situation that is more typical of high intermontane valleys. Most of the rainfall is at night. This produces near optimal growing conditions. I speculate that the breadth of the Hak-Uk Valley, enclosed by ridges of 2000 to 3000 m (6000 to 9000 ft) and with only a low divide between the two rivers, replicates some of the conditions that have made many of the major intermontane valleys of New Guinea so favorable to human life.

I have no basis for assessing the affects of seasonality on agriculture, although I attempt to look at hunting in these terms elsewhere (Morren 1980) and in chapter 6. The people recognize seasonal patterns in relation to vegetation, the distribution of game, and their own hunting activity.

When people plan their daily work, they can usually tell what the day is going to be like. Though people rise from sleep at dawn, the day's real work normally does not commence until around 10 in the morning. Most people wait around their houses eating, talking, and doing light work until the early morning hours have passed without a shower. In that case the relative humidity will continue to fall steadily through the day until the expected late afternoon shower ushers in the heavy nightly rain. And people will have dispersed to gardens or forest, leaving the hamlet essentially deserted. It is, of course, not possible to count the times you get caught in the rain away from shelter or count yourself lucky to be in one. A day that is rainy from the outset will see a majority of people staying home.

Topography, Geology, and Soils

In the land of the the more southerly Miyanmin groups, the terrain is rugged and broken with serrated ridges of metamorphic rock. The slopes of valley walls rise from between 700 m (2100 ft) and 1000 m (3000 ft) at the riverbed to 2000 m (6000 ft) to 3000 m (9000 ft) at the peaks and ridges of the larger mountains. The slope surface is complicated by the drainage capacity required to handle the runoff of heavy rainfall. There are numerous small spurs that project from the main structures and, more importantly for Miyanmin agriculture, many fairly squat low divides separating the secondary rivers and streams of the drainage. The lower quarter of mountainsides, with an average slope of approximately 20 degrees, also has natural terraces or benches and hollows between spurs that provide extensive tracts of flat or gently sloping ground. These sites are favored for cultivation because soil and moisture conditions are excellent, humus, litter and other nutrient sources from further up the slope are trapped, and moisture is retained, thus countering to some degree the drying effect of clearing.

The area is geologically diverse but can be roughly characterized. Metamorphic rocks, particularly siltstones, mudstones, and "rotten" shales, predominate from the Mittag Mountains to the Thurnwald range. As a consequence, this area is relatively unstable—erosion, landslips, and landslide scars are common. Agriculture is a frequent cause. Brookfield and Hart (1971:37) find "abundant evidence that mass movements are the greatest erosional hazard in cultivated areas, that slope failure occurs much less under forest than on denuded slopes, and that within the forest such movements are augmented or initiated in many cases by tree fall" (see also Bik 1967; Ruxton 1967). This association between agriculture and mass movement is supported in our area by a comparison of the Elip and Hak valleys. In the 1960s the two valleys were the locale for agriculture in support of 1700 and 200 people, respectively. The Elip has been ravaged; and on the ground, large areas resemble abandoned Appalachian coal fields due to landslips which have exposed the underlying shales. Aerial photographs reveal many such sites in the valley. Though I believe that the geology of the Hak Valley is similar, this phenomenon is totally absent.

North of the Thurnwald range, in the upper May Valley which includes the southern and western slopes of Mount Stolle, metamorphic rocks predominate: granites, volcanic pebble conglomerates, and shales. Mass movement is unlikely here in any event and many of the little rivers on the middle slopes of these mountains have been scoured out of "living rock." The foothills area of the middle May Valley north of Mountain Gate is limestone country.

I did not collect soil samples and no studies have been conducted in my area. Standard sources (e.g., Brookfield and Hart 1971: Fig. 1:10A) indicate that soils of the area are regosols and lithosols, with podzolics coming in south of Telefomin and in the Sepik basin west and north of Miyanmin country. Regosols and lithosols are young soils that result from recent erosion and weathering. They are azonal, lack well-developed soil characteristics, and are typical of mountainous areas (Bridges 1970:79f.). Podzolics characteristically develop under oak and beech forests and are more mature, though leached (Bridges 1970: 50). Alluvials, resulting from recent erosion from siltstone, are patchily distributed in the area. There are extensive tracts of consolidated alluvium at the bases of steeper valleys, remnants of ancient riverbeds that form the natural terraces or benches favored for taro cultivation. In general, the alluvium and the brown podzolics are significant to agriculture.

Vegetation and Altitude

The forest of the southern half of East Mianmin consists of lower-montane oak, and mixed rainforest with two arboreal strata and, above 650 m (4000 ft), mid-montane beech and conifer forest with three strata. Some common trees and plants of the lower-montane forest that I have collected[4] are listed in table 4-1. Particularly characteristic of the 20- to 25-meter canopy of the lower-montane forest are the oaks, *Castanopsis, Lithocarpus*, and *Pasania*, the *Elaeocarps*, and certain *Lauraceae*, which set fruit that are attractive to pigs and other game animals. As far as I know, *Araucaria* "hoop pine" and/or "klinki pine" are absent. Because Johns (1982:323f.) suggests that *Araucaria* forest is seral in nature, its absence may be related to the relatively minor scale of the disturbance accompanying traditional agriculture in the area, particularly the limited size of man-made patches. Pandanus species, in both tree and liana form, seem unusually common possibly due to high rainfall.

Characteristic species of the higher mid-montane forest are *Elaeocarpus, Nothofagus* (beeches, especially as a successional plant), and *Podocarpus* (conifers) (Womersley 1978:10; Johns 1982:324f.). Other notable features include the abundance of ferns, mosses and lichens, and climbing bamboo (rattan) in disturbed areas.

Miyanmin living on the middle May River north of Mount Stolle interact primarily with lowland rainforest. This type is almost a residual category in terms of its diversity, mixed composition, and the absence of characteristic dominants. From the standpoint of people, the most important features are extreme patchiness and scattered distribution of resources. Forest trees tend to be buttressed with very high dense canopies, hence the relatively sparse undergrowth and openness. Pure stands of fresh water sago (*Metroxylon sago*) are probably the single most important floral resource in the lowlands.

As indicated earlier, the mid-altitude zone is very rich in wild vegetable food resources. The Miyanmin and other peoples of the zone (see, Dornstreich 1973, 1977; Hyndman 1979, 1982) are able to exploit wild tubers, trees for nuts, fruits, and leaves, grasses for their stems and tender inflorescenses, ferns for tender leaf tops, gingers for roots and leaves, fungi, wild pandanus, herbs, palms for tender immature stems and inflorescenses, lianas for fruit, and vines and creepers for leaves and fruits. Pandanus,

Table 4-1.   Some Trees and Other Plants
of the Local Lower Montane Forest

CANOPY

Castanopsis* accuminatissima	Myristica hollrungii
Lithocarpus* schlecteri	fatua
rufo-villosus	Bischofia javanica
Pasania* sp.	Ficus variegata
Elaeocarpus* sp.	virens
Sloania* forbesii	Galbulimima belgraveana
nymanii	Alphitonia macrocarpa
Litsea* opaka	Carpodetus arboreus
elliptica	Octomeles sumatrana
polyantha	Endiandra hooglandii
engleriana	Pometia sp.
globosa	Alstonia sp.
Cryptocarya* densiflora	Chisocheto trichocladus
Cananga odorata	Podocarpus nerrifolius
Pimeledendron sp.	Syzygium plumeum
Semecarpus sp.	Glochidion sp.
Gnetum gnemon	

SUB-CANOPY and CLIMBERS

Myristica* subalulata	Prunus sp.
Eleocarpus* sp.	Haplolobus corynocarpa
Schefflera* bougainvilleana	floribundus

* Genera considered major or dominants by botanists

Table 4-1. (continued)

filipes

elliptica

Rhododendron* macgregoriae

Ficus pungens

adelpha

macrorrhyncha

warsa

Artocarpus urieseanus

Conandrium polyanthum

Garcinia assugu

Cinnamomum frodinii

eugenoliferum

acuminatus

Endospermum molluccanum

Clematis* pickeringii

Rubus moluccanus

Psychotria beccarii

Lasianthus papuanus

Macaranga warburgiana ?

Sauravia calyptrata

Wendlandia paniculata

Ardisia subaceps

Laportia sp.

Microcos tetrosperma

COLONIZERS, YOUNG SECONDARY, EDGES & GAPS

Cyathea spp.

Cytandra wariana

Pipturus argentus

Geunsia cumingiana

Abelmoschus moschatus

Cypholophus macrocephalus

Selaginella liverina

latifolia

Pangium edule

Clematis pickeringii

Breynia cernua

Piper gibbilimbum

Ficus arfakensis

Callicarpa longifolia

Lindsaea obfusa

Impatiens sp.

Tapeinocheilos sp.

Aphanamixis macrocalyx

Melastoma offine

malabathricum

Rungia, the pit-pits, and sugar cane are among the original New Guinea domesticates centered in the zone. The range of most other domesticates includes the zone. Even sago, the wild staple of many lowland areas, occurs in the mid-altitude zone as a domesticate up to 1000 m (3000 ft). The wild fauna of the zone are surveyed in another chapter. For now it is enough to indicate that the mid-altitude zone is superior to higher altitudes with respect to most classes of forest products including vegetable foods, craft and building materials, frogs, reptiles, birds, and bats. Higher altitudes appear to be superior only in the diversity of rodent and marsupial species and a greater prevalence of the larger sized possums, kangaroos, and rats (Hyndman 1982:226f.). The mammalian fauna of the mid-altitude zone are nevertheless rich and, given low human densities, the potential for hunting is great.

An important feature of any ecosystem inhabited by people is the nature and scope of disturbance regimes that result from their activities, and the extent to which they represent problems and opportunities. In an earlier section on the geology of the area I invited attention to one extreme in the Eliptaman, agriculturally related deforestation leading to mass movements, and noted that this kind and scale of event is rare in the Hak-Uk Valley. Less extreme forms of erosion are, however, common features of agriculture; and small incidents of sheet erosion of garden sites adjacent to small rivers are particularly prone to occur during the rainier part of the year. Old village sites and traditional hunting camp sites present a distinctive picture of disclimax. Anthropogenic grasslands are, however, totally absent from Miyanmin settlement areas in the lower-montane zone. Forest succession on garden land is the norm. Seral communities are important to people and are socially recognized (see below and chapter 6). Moreover, Miyanmin agricultural practices are conservational in the sense of fostering a regular forest fallow on agricultural tracts that may be used again according to a relatively long cycle (see chapter 5).

The Operational Environment

The most important aspect of the distribution of these biogeographical, topographic, soil, and human disturbance features is how they describe the context for critical human activities including food procurement, the exploitation of nonfood resources, and routinizing responses to other nonresource issues. Several recent studies of societies of the mid-altitude fringe have attempted to identify "resource areas" (Dornstreich 1973, 1977) or "biotopes" (Hyndman 19779, 1983), specialized microenvironments whose most distinctive features are human resource utilization patterns. They may also be characterized by natural and anthropogenic features, and frequently conform to the emic environmental categories of the people.

Dornstreich (1973, 1977) identifies 15 "resource areas" for the Gadio Enga; and Hyndman (1979, 1983) defines 11 "biotopes" for the Wopkaimin. I don't think that the approach has been thoroughly worked out, and am particularly dissatisfied with the subsistence bias implied. Thus, I elect to use the term "microenvironment" instead of Dornstreich's or Hyndman's terminology. A comparison of Miyanmin microenvironments with those attributed to the Gadio and the Wopkaimin is presented in table 4-2. Although the patterns of use and exploitation are of interest, even more significant are the disturbance regimes associated with each. In the table, Miyanmin microenvironments are arranged in order of decreasing human disturbance, with the currently occupied hamlet representing maximum sustained disturbance and the various pristine forest types away from settlement areas representing a minimum. Disturbance regimes are discussed in greater detail in later chapters. Here, some of the environmental and interactional qualities associated by the Miyanmin with each microenvironment can be briefly explained.

The *hamlet* is, for residents and visitors alike, a repository of virtues, life support and security, the quintessential payoff of sociality. A person's residential choice is determined by close consanguinity or affinity (see chapter 7, where I discuss hamlets and other units of population in detail). Here children are born to woman and socialized by family and community. And the dead are mourned, commemorated, and beseeched for aid and direction in consensual decision making. Labor is exchanged and group activities organized. Food is concentrated, prepared, shared, and dispersed. In an uncertain and violent world, hamlets are less unsecure than other places, though they are hardly invulnerable. Food, shelter, security, and hospitality are the basic prerequisites of survival.

Among the higher-altitude *am-nakai* Miyanmin, hamlets are ephemeral as physical places, but they endure as likely associations of people. According to Gardner (1982), even the latter is not an expected feature among the more mobile and "anarchistic" lower-altitude *sa-nakai* Miyanmin.

The Miyanmin choose locations because of proximity to agricultural, hunting, and other resources; and specific sites are selected and prepared with due regard for safety (e.g., defense, flood, mass movement, tree falls). Agricultural capital in such long-term propositions as pandanus and sago orchards is typically invested near a current hamlet. Although there are no "door gardens" as such (cf. Hyndman, 1982:244), small amounts of traditional and introduced economic trees are planted near the houses. These include breadfruit, citrus, and coconut, *Rungia*, as well as useful crops such as tobacco, *Xanthosoma* taro, banana, and *amaranthus*, and ornamentals such as *coleus*, and *cordyline*. Because hamlets are also the domiciles of domestic pigs, young trees as well as other useful plants must be fenced to protect them.

Table 4-2. The Identification of Microenvironments
Miyanmin Compared with Gadio (Dornstreich 1973)
and Wopkaimin (Hyndman 1979)

GADIO ENGA (resource area)	WOPKAIMIN (biotope)	MIYANMIN (microenvironment)
1. Hamlet Site: Current	(7) Hamlet in Use	1. Current Hamlet
2. Hamlet Site: Abandoned	(9b)Abandoned Hamlet	2. Abandoned Hamlet
3. Living Site: Current		3. Settlement Area
4. Living Site: Abandoned	(9c)Abandoned Hamlet	4. Garden
5. Garden: In Production	(6) Gardens in Use	5. Plantation
6. Garden: Abandoned	(9a)Abandoned Gardens	6. Old Field
7. Forest Tree Stands		
8. Sago Swamps	(8) Pandanus Orchards	
9. Sago Stands	(2) Sago Grove	
10. Stream or River:Low Alt.	(1) Ok Tedi River	7. Edge & Stream
11. Stream or River:High Alt.		
12. Stream Bank	(4) Streams or Banks	8. Lowlands
13. Rainforest	(3) Foothill Rainforest	
	(5) Mid-Montane Forest	9. Lower-Montane Forest
		10. Mid- & Upper-Montane Forest
	(10)Moss Forest	
	(11)Upper-Montane Forest	

NOTE: Numbers in first and middle columns are those of the authors cited.

Newly established hamlets are likely to be on the edge or, at lower altitudes, even in the midst of productive taro gardens. Domestic dogs are residents also, and have a variety of uses (chapter 6). House rats, *Rattus ruber* (in occupied houses) and *Melomys rufescens* (in empty houses), are resources and pests. Occupied hamlets represent maximum disturbance because they tend to be virtually denuded of natural vegetation with all except edible fruit-bearing trees felled and a central plaza scraped and leached down to an even clay surface. They are also the centers of noise, smoke, and other potential disruptive factors; and disturbance ripples outward from the hamlets of a settlement area.

Abandoned hamlets continue to be visited as long as they are within reasonable travelling distance in order to exploit old investments such as oil pandanus orchards and breadfruit. Due to the extent of human modification of hamlet sites, forest seres do not inevitably ensue when a settlement is abandoned. Groundcover typical of this disclimax are *Selaginella liverina* and *S. latifolia*, and they served me as a clue to old living sites (chapter 9). Other colonizing plants are desirable resources and targets of foraging (Dornstreich 1973:125), including certain ferns and grasses, feral curcurbits, bamboos, and fish poison vine. As a result, they may serve as convenient and safe camps for small groups of people a day or more from home who are hunting, harvesting, or collecting craft material and otherwise taking advantage of features of an abandoned settlement area.

Settlement area refers to a space defined by the constellation of hamlets of a local population (chapter 3) and the diurnal pattern of routine activities and movements of people. Strictly speaking, it is a "higher-order unit" in that it includes current and recently abandoned hamlets and living sites, gardens, plantations, old fields and tracts of primary forest that are immediately accessible. It is useful as a unit of resource management, disturbance, degradation, and successional communities of plants and animals.

The *garden* is the focus of approximately half of Miyanmin labor and the location of more than 90 percent of the food consumed. The majority of gardens are dominated by *Colocasia* taro. Indeed, a virtual monoculture is involved. I analyze Miyanmin agriculture in chapter 5.

Plantation refers to a concentration of economic trees planted to gain the long-term usage of a desirable food item or raw material. Among the high-altitude Miyanmin, the most important tree crop is oil pandanus (*P. conoidus*) which is valued as a source of a lipid-rich red sauce. Teenage boys start the plantations that will supply them in their maturity and plantations are common in the vicinity of current and abandoned living areas. Sago is a secondary crop planted for its starch and, due to its scarcity in modern settlements, increasingly for roofing material. Sago is out of its natural range at 1000 m (3000 ft) and all plantings are derived from shoots carried up from lower altitudes.

The *old field* of a recently abandoned garden quickly gives rise to a forest succession. In the earliest phase it continues as a source of vegetable foods, mainly greens such as fern tips, pumpkin tips, and pit-pit, but the site quickly becomes an excellent place to hunt such game animals as *Phallanger orientalis*, which seems to favor the leaves of young trees and vines, and the hornbill that likes to make its nest in hollow standing trees. Secondary forest is also an excellent source of the small timbers used in house construction.

Edges and streams is seemingly a residual category but the operational reality is that people interact with both most frequently while in transit and opportunistically identify resources that may be exploited at another time. For most of the year stream beds are convenient tracks to and from gardens and between hamlets; and their use exposes the traveller to fish and eels in shallow pools, frogs and tadpoles, and the tracks of game animals large and small. Similarly, the terrestrial traveller is constantly exposed to change with edges between, say, garden and forest being the most common example. Sightings of flowering or fruiting trees such as *Schefflera spp.* and *Ficus spp.* are welcome, and the trees are marked for possible use as the site of a bird hide or a nocturnal mammal ambush.

The *lowlands* is, for most higher-altitude Miyanmin a "nice place to visit" on a seasonal basis and, for some, an alternative place to live (chapter 9). Partly due to the sparseness of the human population, and partly due to physical environmental differences, hunting and fishing are particularly favorable. Wild pigs are abundant and the conditions for hunting them are particularly favorable (chapter 6). Exotic game animals such as crocodiles, "standard" large cassowaries, and certain possums desired for their colorful pelts, and desired palm species used for bows, arrow points, and foreshafts are also available.

The *lower-montane forest* has already been described in this chapter. This is the forest in which the higher-altitude Miyanmin pass most of their time and, as indicated earlier, an environment particularly favorable for gathering wild plant foods, collecting frogs and reptiles, and hunting birds and bats. In undisturbed areas, small forest mammals, both terrestrial and arboreal, are abundant enough to warrant hunting; but areas of secondary forest *(old field)* and mid- and upper-montane forest receive comparable attention from hunters.

The *mid- and upper-montane forest* is accessible for hunting from the settlement areas of most of the higher-altitude Miyanmin groups in the Donner and Thurnwald ranges and on Mount Stolle. As indicated earlier, this microenvironment is particularly important for the hunting of small mammals and the dwarf cassowary (chapter 6).

The Cognized Environment

The Miyanmin version of the culture-nature dichotomy is the distinction between the "house" (*am*) and "forest" (*sa* or *sesa*) habitats, summarized in figure 4-2. *Am* implies culture, domesticity, security, and sociality; and embraces the place types of "villages" or "hamlets" (*bip*), "gardens" (*ban*), and "secondary forest" (*mon*). *Sa* implies "nature," wildness, danger, and anarchy. It seems that, in using the same terminology for both, the Miyanmin rank and evaluate environmental zones and places and the people living in them in a

Figure 4-2.   The Physical and Moral Dimensions of a Place:
Miyanmin Classification of Cultural and Natural
Things

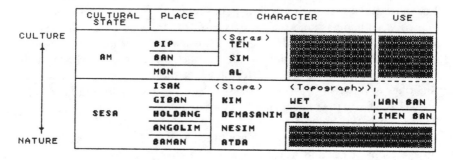

moralistic way. Thus, there are two kinds of Miyanmin. There are the *am-nakai* "house people" of the larger, higher-altitude groups of the south, the Hak, upper May, San and upper August River valleys. And there are the *sa-nakai* "bush people" of the small, low-altitude groups on the middle May River, the West and Landslip Ranges and the Wagarabi-middle August River area. The former view the latter as "hicks" who speak poorly and are uncultured, unsocialized, and discordant.

Consistent with the foregoing, people of the mid-altitude zone view the lowlands tropical rainforest (*giban*) as a poor and difficult, even dangerous, place to live full-time, but enjoy visits of no more than a few months duration that allow hunting and the gathering of valuable craft materials. While hunting is good, gardening is difficult and health a recognized problem. Informants are able to precisely specify trees, vines, palms, mammals, birds, and other biota that are distinctive to this and other zones.

Types of gardens include the predominant "taro garden" (*imen ban*), the "sweet potato garden" (*wan ban*), and oil pandanus and sago groves. The secondary seres produced by agriculture (*mon*) are further classified as "recently harvested" (*mon ten*), "abandoned" (*mon sin*) with tree ferns and wild banana characteristic, and older secondary (*mon al*) forest succession. Particular tracts are also classified as to their potential uses based on topography, higher well-drained sites suitable for sweet potato (*wet*) and lower, flat, moist sites at the bottom of slopes and hollows that are most suitable for *Colocasia* taro (*dak*).

In addition to the *giban* lowlands tropical rainforest type, the Miyanmin also classify the lower-montane forest (*isak*) which includes the foothills, montane forest (*holdang*) which refers to the forested upper slopes and headwater areas, moss forest (*angolim*) typical of high slope and ridge areas here, and alpine grassland (*baman*) which, as far as I know, is found only atop

Mount Stolle in the East Mianmin area. *Isak* is recognized as their ideal range, though *holdang* possesses certain admirable qualities such as the variety of mammals that may be hunted there (chapter 6). There is also a subsidiary classification of slope. *Kim* is flat ground, *demasanim* gentle slope, *nesim* moderate slope, and *atda* steeply sloping ground.

Although it is not included in the larger scheme presented in figure 4-2, the Miyanmin also classify the domain of soils (*debal*) according to provenance and uses. Agricultural soils include "leaf meat" humus (*uk dim*) and sandy alluvial soil (*nenim*). Others are the grey shale-sand-clay aggregate used for hearths (*geim*), red-yellow earth (*bitbit*), clay (*gang*), and house dust (*bitim*).

The Miyanmin have a detailed and complex classification scheme to encompass the specifics of the natural, as well as the social, world. This topic will be treated in chapter 6, where some sense will be made out of ethnozoological terminology.

Having taken a detailed look at the physical and sociocultural dimensions of the environment, some of the most critical linkages and interactions in the complex pattern that relates the Miyanmin to their material environment can now be summarized:

1. Territorial control (sovereignty and settlement pattern) in relation to environmental degradation, resource competition, and meat availability in particular
2. Altitude and, for some individuals, nutrition in relation to disease and population structure
3. Labor in relation to food production, both agriculture and hunting
4. Local group flexibility and self-sufficiency.

These linkages turn out to be critical both to our appreciation of the long-established or "traditional" adaptation of the Miyanmin, and to an understanding of the dynamics of modernization. The main body of this work is aimed at examining these linkages in some detail.

5

Agriculture in Context

Along with hunting and movement, horticulture is a basic part of the Miyanmin life-support system, an element in a complex adaptive routine that reduces uncertainty and risk in relation to normal variation in the environment. Miyanmin agriculture is not so demanding as to prevent the pursuit of a variety of other life-supporting activities. It permits a broad range of locational, social, and technical options in relation to food and other kinds of resources and hazards. The "seeds" of intensification and technological change are present. It is part of an overall subsistence strategy that can deliver a high quality and healthful diet under most circumstances and on a self-sufficient basis. It is also satisfying in terms of the people's subjective evaluation. Though rare, crop failures have occurred.

Notwithstanding possible virtues, Miyanmin agriculture does not measure up to conventional and regional standards. It is neither intensive nor productive on a land-yield basis, nor is it efficient on a labor or energy basis. Indeed, it is an effective monoculture and possibly subject to familiar kinds of vulnerabilities. By New Guinea highland standards, the Miyanmin are indifferent pig herders. Yet, even if all of these declarations were to stand, it could still be argued that Miyanmin agriculture need not be more intensive, productive, diverse, pig-centered, or efficient in the context in which the Miyanmin have lived up until recently.

Typologically, the Miyanmin are "true shifting cultivators" (see Conklin 1961). However, although their "shifts" are equilibrating responses, in most cases they are not related to agricultural contingencies. On a strictly technical basis, Miyanmin agriculture has some unusual features. David Hyndman (1979) has labeled the pattern shared by the Wopkaimin, Miyanmin and certain other Mountain Ok groups as "slash and mulch" because of the absence of a general burn. According to Brookfield and Hart's (1971) definitions, Miyanmin agriculture is a "low intensity" system of the "swidden type," "depending on prolonged natural regeneration between periods of cultivation" (105). Although the Miyanmin exploit many wild plants, cultigens provide 90 percent of the vegetable food consumed by the higher-altitude southern groups. The situation among lower-altitude *sa-nakai* groups in the north is that as much as 50 percent of all vegetable food consumed is wild, with sago heading the list. Also with these groups, cultivation practices are somewhat less extensive than those described here.

A Metataxonomy of Agricultural Systems

Using the analytical approach introduced in chapter 2, I can specify the senses in which the term "agricultural system" may be applied to make sense out of my observations.

The general task of any group engaging in agriculture is to achieve a satisfactory level of living by this means (or by means of agriculture in combination with other activities) in relation to its numbers, their needs and capabilities, and the characteristics of the natural, anthropogenic, and sociocultural environment.

This entails perhaps six specific tasks. The first is to have sufficient land of appropriate quality; and the second is to possess adequate technology, plant and animal stock, the means to control natural factors, and the knowledge to make use of them. The third need is to regulate population, labor, and other inputs which include—but are not limited to—family (or unit) organization and structure, and substitutes for labor. The fourth is to determine an appropriate quantity and mix of crops and other activities including the regulation of production. The fifth is to maintain productivity and the returns from labor and other inputs at satisfactory levels; and, finally, the sixth task is to husband options in order to sustain the pattern and to survive.

In this chapter I focus particularly on matters relating to agricultural technology and knowledge, labor and other inputs to agriculture, production and the mix of crops and other subsistence activities, and the sustaining of the agricultural sector. The issue of the qualities of agricultural land was examined in chapter 4. The quantity of land and other territorial issues will be studied in chapters 7, 9 and 10.

Agricultural Technology

Cultigens

Miyanmin horticulture is dominated by taro (*Colocasia esculenta*). Overwhelmingly the carbohydrate staple taro constitutes more than 90 percent of all garden plantings and it produces a proportionate amount of food by weight (table 5-1). Taro is not only well adapted to the area's high rainfall regime and high soil moisture content, it demands these conditions.

Table 5-1. Garden Food Harvest for Two-Week Period in 1968 for an
Average Population Unit of 18 Adults and 10 Children

Commodity	Weight kg.	Edible %	Value Energy kcal.	Protein (gms)	Fat (gms)	Proportion of Diet by weight	by energy
Colocasia	574,764	100	614,997	8,621	575	.886	.958
Musa	9,080	65	6,492	71	12	.014	.010
Pandanus	11,350	40	7,627	168	636	.018	.012
Greens	34,844	95	8,607	1,324	132	.054	.013
Pangium edule	1,589	30	776	2	0	.002	.002
Chalote	11,804	68	2,809	89	16	.018	.004
Cucumber	4,540	68	370	22	5	.007	.001
Bean	568	80	100	6	23	.001	.000
Total	648,539		641,780	10,303	1,398	1.000	1.000

Indeed, in order to maintain moisture levels in newly planted gardens, clearing is not completed (as far as it goes) until after the young taro plants are well established. The Miyanmin possess and designate with terminal taxa at least 50 varieties subsumed under the primarily taxon *imen*. With two exceptions, all of the varieties called *imen* refer to *Colocasia* taro; the exceptions are one *Allocasia* taro variety that appears to be traditional, and one *Xanthasoma* taro, a recent introduction. All other tuberous vegetables or edible roots, wild and cultivated, are covered by a separate primary taxon, *wan*. Included are two long-established sweet potato (*Ipomoea batatas*) varieties and at least 10 new ones acquired in the 1970s, two kinds of manioc (*Manihot spp.*), one of which is claimed to be traditional, and three varieties of wild yam (*Dioscorea spp.*).

In addition, there are six traditional varieties (or subspecies) of banana (*Musa paradisiaca, Musa spp.*) and at least four newly introduced ones, all covered by the primary term *som*. Many other native cultigens are also grown, including traditional green vegetables such as beans (*mil*), "spinach" or slimy abika (*amol*), amaranth (*kabi*), highland and lowland pit-pit (*dup; Saccarum edule, S. sp.*), several gourds (*gemang*; Curcurbitaceae) exploited for their leaves, with fruits providing the traditional male genital covering, and sugar cane (*kwet; Saccarum officinarum*). Tobacco (*fut*), considered by the people to be a traditional plant, is grown for local consumption. Similarly, a small yellow tree tomato is long established. The list of exotic introduced cultigens is ever expanding. In the 1960s, pumpkins, cucumbers, maize, papaya, and pineapple were present. More have been added since then, including tomatoes and new bean varieties. Established economic trees include breadfruit, many named varieties of *marita,* or oil pandanus (*em; Pandanus conoidus*), and sago (*Metroxylon sago*) which must be carefully tended to be successful up to a maximum altitude of approximately 1350 m (4000 ft) above sea level. Within the past 10 years, tree and other perennial crops with supposed commercial potential have also been introduced, including chile peppers, lemons, nonhybrid oranges (by the writer), and coffee.

Tools

Steel axes are demonstrably more efficient than stone in agricultural work (Sharp 1953; Salisbury 1962; Hames 1979:219). With this in mind, I questioned older people about their introduction (see chapter 11) and also attempted to obtain a picture of the differential use of new and traditional tools.

Only a rough equation can be drawn between them. The traditional stone adze (*bankli*) was primarily a man's implement, used in woodworking, felling trees in agriculture, and in collecting building materials and fuel. It was part of a man's daily adornment, carried slung in the cane belt at the bearer's haunch. The modern steel quarter axe with locally made handle is a direct substitute for the stone adze, though it is handled differently and is not suitable for all of the same tasks. Women may borrow and handle adzes and axes, but they rarely carry them. Although ownership of steel axes was universal by the late 1960s, stone adzes were still a common sight hanging in people's houses.

The traditional woman's implement was the small bladed hand-hoe (*bankli unang*). It was carried in her *bilum,* itself part of woman's adornment, along with other utensils for routine work, and would be used for surface clearing of gardens in uprooting small shrubs, creepers, and roots. The trade machete (or *busnaip*) is the modern substitute, but it is both more and less than an equivalent. On the one hand, it is a superior cutting tool to the traditional hoe, useful for downing small trees and for woodworking, as well as for attacking light vegetation. On the other hand, it is not a digging tool that can help uproot and lever things out of the ground. Men carry the *busnaip* mainly in modern chores, track work, patrols, or when gathering craft and building materials. In the 1960s it seemed that most *busnaip* were the possessions of women and men borrowed them as needed. Today they are a common part of a man's tool kit as well.

Another common traditional tool is the bamboo knife/spatula (*yang*), part of a woman's kit. It is used in the garden for cleaning taro corms as they are harvested and for separating them from leaf stalks. At home it is used for grating taro for cake dough. A man may also use it when he performs these tasks, particularly when sponsoring a feast, which obliges him to provide large amounts of taro and firewood. The division of labor tends to go by the board under these circumstances (see below). Small knives with four-inch blades are the modern substitute for some tasks (e.g., in the garden) but are not appropriate for others such as taro grating.

The digging stick belongs in a separate class because, while it is the Melanesian agricultural implement par excellence (Barrau 1958:9), among the Miyanmin it is a simple ad hoc fabrication and not a long-lasting "capital good." Barrau presented an array of six digging sticks (1958:10, Fig. 5) showing their development from simple, slightly pointed ones to full-blown wooden spades. If this is taken as a "scale," the Miyanmin variant drops off the simple end. It is a blunt pole of about five cm (2 in) in diameter which a woman fabricates on the garden site and which she is likely to abandon when planting is completed on the site.

Two other traditional men's utensils—daggers and chisels—were manufactured from cassowary femurs. The dagger was a stabbing weapon, carried (like the adze) tucked in the bearer's cane belt. It was also a puncturing tool applied to animal carcasses, tree barks, palm spathes, and the like. In the sixties I saw them used most frequently in house building to make lashing holes in bark used for floors and wall linings. Bone implements have a point but not a sharp edge. Cutting is done with a bamboo sliver or with a flint or chert chopper. The latter is also useful for the low relief decorations on wooden war shields and drums. Bone chisels, similar to daggers in appearance, are also male utensils used in the preparation of such foods as oil pandanus (to remove the interior fruit pulp) and in woodworking. These bone tools have been slowly displaced by machetes and other large knives, at least in the Hak Valley, and it is possible that a decline in the number of cassowaries taken in the hunt is a factor. The traditional rat's-jaw graver (*no ban*), used by men to carve fine decorative relief and barbs for arrows, have become less functional as people have ingeniously developed steel arrow points for virtually all purposes (chapter 6).

Division of Labor

Flexibility is characteristic of the sexual division of labor, and I have observed men and women performing virtually all agricultural tasks (though perhaps not with equal frequency). Nevertheless, tasks can be stereotypically ascribed to each sex. Woman's tasks include surface clearing, planting, harvesting, carrying produce, and routine food preparation. Men perform the heavy clearing, felling or defoliating of trees on the garden plot, and removing the heavy debris to the margins. In the higher-altitude Miyanmin groups, weeding is a family affair. Half of a given household's gardens can be weeded, albeit on a crash basis, in little more than a week of heavy labor. Gardner (1981) reports that among the low-altitude Miyanmin of the August River, weeding is exclusively women's work. I attribute this difference to significantly divergent settlement strategies characterizing the situations of the two kinds of groups (chapters 7 and 9). In practice, women spend more than half (65 percent) of their working time in agricultural labor and men spend an almost comparable proportion of their time on clearing, planting, and weeding activities (table 5-2).

Modernization has affected both sexes. Steel axes have speeded up the typical male task of tree felling, and bush knives have expedited the process of surface cleaning which is usually woman's work. According to informants, modern implements have not increased agricultural production, (i.e., more gardens), but have increased the amount of time that people can devote to other activities, including hunting and work in the modern sector. The attractiveness to men of contract labor, however, has tended to shift the burden of subsistence onto women, at least in the short run (see below and chapter 11).

ASSUME 9.5 men
8.2 women
(18 adults)

Table 5-2. Labor Expended in Life-Supporting Activities by Sex for Two-Week Period in 1968

Activity	Men hours	%	Women hours	%	Total
Construction	1,872	69	858	31	2,730
Travel	2,028	67	1,014	33	3,042
Horticulture	3,432	46	3,978	54	7,410
Harvest	1,170	26	3,354	74	4,524
Collecting	156	17	780	83	936
Hunting	3,978	100	0	0	3,978
Ritual	182	72	72	28	254
Food Prepar.	2,496	43	3,300	57	5,876
Total	15,314	53	13,356*	47	28,750

4.42 hr/man day 4.46 hr/woman day
ANNUALIZED! (See table 5-3)

* Women's total labor is underestimated due to exclusion of pig tending, crafts production, housekeeping, child care, routine food preparation, and similar activities that are difficult to pick up with the methods employed or else are by-products of primary activities.

Construction: Assembling materials and constructing buildings; men cut and transport timber and carry out heavy construction including laying of roof; women gather leaves for roof, cane and vines for lashing, and clay conglomerate for hearth.

Travel: Movement between hamlets or settlements involving absence from residence of a day or more.

Horticulture: Clearing, planting and weeding.

Harvest: (Married women and single men) Picking crops in garden, cleaning, sorting, separating food and planting stock, collecting firewood; bagging, bundling and transporting to residential hamlet; (Married) men harvest taro for large feasts or to prepare for a dual residence move, also most *marita* pandanus and some firewood.

Collecting: Cropping wild plant, miscellaneous animal foods, and craft materials; edible leaves, buds, fruits, berries, tubers, bulbs and fungi; small mammals, insects and grubs, land crabs, frogs; bark products, palm and pandanus fronds, canes, bamboos and vines; often combined with horticulture.

Hunting: Searching, stalking and killing medium- and large-sized mammals, birds, aquatic life forms such as fish and eels; constructing and setting hides, blinds, traps, and dams.

Ritual: Traditional male cult activities, mortuary and curing rituals as well as modern church and mission activities including bush schools.

Food Preparation: Large-scale leaf oven cookery and associated tasks; men do rail splitting, hot stone placement, pig butchery, pandanus sauce preparation, dough kneading, and wild meat apportionment; and women, taro peeling and grating, leaf collecting, leaf bundle preparation, oven fabrication, vegetable foods and domestic pork apportionment.

Cultivation Methods

Miyanmin cultivation methods are conservative, if not conservational, and are well suited to minimizing irreversible changes and ensuring a forest fallow.

The gardening sequence begins with the selection of a site possessing the kinds of features described in the previous chapter. Typically, the options are weighed by an older man whose judgment is respected and emulated by the people who reside with him. More than likely, he will have had an important role in larger settlement decisions already implemented (chapter 9). Nevertheless, according to the consensual form, there is considerable discussion within the community,

> a great deal of conversation and fussing in dyads and small groups, whereby pressures to open a new garden build up. The final overt move must be made by a senior man, but they are highly sensitive to the opinions of their wives and juniors and unwilling to clarify disagreements and impose a showdown.... (Barth 1975:31f.).

An elder's move comes as an apparent surprise and produces a bandwagon effect. Among the Miyanmin this process creates the appearance of a communal garden because of its precipitate nature, the need for further discussion and coordination, and labor sharing. As with Faiwolmin, it contrasts with decision making that occurs in a ritual context (chapter 8). Thus the siting of one garden on a tract is normally followed by others.

The mechanical task of clearing to rid the site of unwanted vegetation and open it to light can be accomplished by a husband and wife working together, or by a larger party. In removing small to moderate-sized trees, one or more men work upslope partially cutting through the boles. Simultaneously, others (men or women) clear low vegetation, shrubs, saplings, and creepers. Then the planting of taro begins. When the highest part of the tract has been reached in this fashion, one or two of the larger trees are felled in such a way as to complete the felling of the others on the site like a field of dominos. The foliage is then removed and piled up along the margins of the garden or in gulleys that are not cultivated, and the trunks are left where they fell. The young taro plants are often established before clearing is completed, and the site will not be fully exposed to sun and rain for up to a month longer (cf. Schieffelin 1975). In addition, there is no general burn, and the original forest seed bank is left intact.

Planting begins as soon as some small portion of the site has been cleared. Planting stock is accumulated steadily at all times because it results from the routine harvest of taros from other gardens. The stock consists principally of the leaf stalks and connected corm tops; cormlets and suckers may be planted as well. Several days' worth are accumulated at home and then brought to the new garden. There, all are sorted by variety, with like being planted together.

Planting involves driving a blunt digging stick into the forest litter and humus to a depth of 7–10 cm (3 or 4 in). The ground around the planting hole is loosened by rotating the stick. The stick is then withdrawn and one large or two smaller stalks or suckers selected. The two-leaf stem segments of a particular stalk are pulled apart with a "squeak." Then the planting material is placed in the hole, the soil firmed about it with the stick or the planter's foot. About 60 cm (2 ft) separate each planting.

The largest trees on the site that formed the canopy of the primary or old secondary forest being cleared are left untouched as the planting proceeds. The garden is almost as dark as the original forest floor while the young plants are setting their first leaves. This is considered to be a critical period in the cycle because if the clearing advances too quickly, the garden can be damaged by too rapid drying. As the young plants are observed to take hold, more light can be admitted. It is sufficient to build a fire amongst the roots of the largest trees in order to stun and defoliate them. Most seem to recover and later help reestablish the forest on the site. Depending on exposure, some of the edge vegetation may also be cleared to admit the morning or afternoon sun. If this process has been appropriately orchestrated, the surface of the garden will be entirely covered with taro leaves by the time the garden is exposed to full sunlight; and, in combination with the mulch on the ground, this will preserve soil moisture, prevent erosion, and inhibit the growth of weeds.

At the beginning of this chapter I said that Miyanmin agriculture did not measure up to regional standards. I have in mind the cultivation practices that have been reported for other parts of New Guinea, particularly the intensive agriculture of the high valleys of the eastern and western spheres. Against this standard (cataloged by Brookfield and Hart 1971:94–124) the list of negatives for Miyanmin agriculture is long: there is no tillage, deep holing, mounding, ditching, composting, soil placement, reclamation, irrigation, or active control of fallow cover. Fences are only built in gardens in unusual circumstances. Yet, it should be said that, although Miyanmin agriculture lacks these features of land and labor intensivity, it is nevertheless technically demanding. Perhaps more important, it is inherently flexible in that there are several directions in which people can go if their situations demand a change.

Some crop segregation is practiced for food plants other than taro, or in special gardens. Within a taro-dominated garden, subsidiary crops are planted in selected patches of the site that possess special soil, drainage, topographic, light, or other characteristics such as the presence of dead standing timber or rotting logs (see Brookfield and Hart 1971:102). Leafy succulent *abika* type vegetables are planted against rotting logs, sugar cane and pit-pit in small moist depressions that catch runoff, curcurbits at the well-lit margins away from taro, banana near the edges of natural benches, papaya where people have enjoyed a casual snack, and beans among the roots of small dead trees left standing for the plant to climb on.

Some gardens have a small amount of sweet potato, planted in the best-drained patch on the site because it demands relatively dry conditions. This modest crop is planted because it is relatively fast growing and will begin to yield within four to five months. It is a stand-by, particularly intended to support the family during weeding (which occurs in the last half of the taro growing period). This provision is necessary because, in accordance with the dual residence pattern (chapter 9), the immature garden(s) requiring weeding are at some distance from the household's producing gardens.

In this sense, sweet potato is considered by the Miyanmin to be something of a hard-times food, though they do not call it "pig food" the way many other New Guineans do (normally Miyanmin pigs eat cooked taro). In the 1970s, production of sweet potato was dramatically expanded (see below). For the Miyanmin and many other Melanesians, however, sweet potato contributes to the flexibility I invoked earlier. Among its virtues is the fact that it will grow quickly on somewhat more marginal soils, at higher altitudes and lower soil temperatures; and its abundance can be expanded rapidly because planting stock, consisting of vine slips, is inexhaustible.

Pig Husbandry

Traditional Miyanmin pig husbandry can be classified as "extensive." It is only marginally related to horticulture, although it is more closely tied to hunting. In the 1960s almost two-thirds of the pigs I censused originated as wild piglets captured in the course of hunting.

Domestic sows are fecund but people consider the business of pig breeding to be risky. All male piglets are castrated by cauterization of the testes when very young (at the same time that the tails of all piglets are amputated). Accordingly, village sows depend for their impregnation on adventuring with wild boars in the bush. According to informants, the major risk occurs when pregnant sows come to term and are allowed to go to the bush to bear their young. Their owners must keep track of them because they are prone to become feral at this time. Moreover, piglets are removed from the sow soon after birth and, not permitted to nurse, must be hand-fed cooked taro which is sometimes premasticated. They must become imprinted on the woman caring for them rather than on a sow in order to be well domesticated; and they quickly learn their names and various commands. I have no concrete data, but apparently piglet mortality is high at this stage for both (semi-) domestically bred and captured animals.

Traditionally, the domestic pig herd was never large by New Guinea standards. That of Kome parish reached an apparent peak of approximately 40 towards the end of my first field work period in 1969. This small size is attributable to a several factors. First, there are the breeding, capture, and survival contingencies just cited. Second are the mechanisms that trigger the slaughter of domestic pigs. One of the most important is the rule and practice whereby the owner of a pig determined to be a habitual garden invader is obliged to slaughter it upon the complaint of an aggrieved garden owner. Although it is not part of the rule, the wife of the pig owner may also be subject to lesser physical sanctions. The pig must be seen and identified in the act or in circumstances clearly supporting the presumption. In fact, it is permissible but hostile for a garden owner to summarily kill the offending animal. This mostly occurs between parties who are already feuding. It is socially disruptive and wasteful from both a subsistence and a gustatorial standpoint because the rancorous (ex-)pig owner often refuses to see the pig dressed and cooked. Rather, it is left to rot. The potential for conflict in such a situation is buffered by the fact that everyone is an interested party. As indicated in chapter 3, the frequency of pig slaughter triggered in this way is related to the degree of nucleation or dispersal of the settlement pattern.

Pigs are also slaughtered in connection with sickness, the visit of a prestigious person, or when the animal is mature. They also had traditional importance in the payment of compensation for land (chapter 10), in death payments to affines, in certain types of marriages, and in trade for such capital goods as finished stone adze blades. It should be emphasized that pigs have no particular role in marriage, exchange, or prestige. I have never seen more than three or four pigs slaughtered at one time; and informants' descriptions of events that they considered to be unusually impressive indicate an upper limit of approximately eight pigs.

New Guinea pigs are small in comparison to American or European swine. My butchered weights from a small sample average 43 kg (95 lb) for domestic and 46 kg (102 lb) for wild pigs. Individual domestic pigs achieve larger sizes than wild pigs, however. The largest domestic pig weighed 132 kg (290 lb).

As will be discussed in the next section, with the decline of wild pig and other game in the Hak Valley in the 1970s, attempts have been made not only to increase the size of the pig herd but also to adopt more intensive husbandry methods. A functional boar has been kept for several years, and a few families have built piggeries separate from their family houses where pigs would traditionally be kept. Others have built larger houses. Moreover, sweet potato cultivation has increased significantly over former levels and some of this produce is feeding a larger pig herd that may now approach 80 in number.

Labor and the Issue of Efficiency

Miyanmin agriculture also fails to measure up in terms of labor efficiency, but this is misleading as a reflection on their adaptation. In table 5-3, I present estimates of labor, energy expenditure, and proportion of effort for a variety of routine life-supporting activities. These estimates are based on work diaries containing daily entries for every adult sleeping in my base hamlet during two separate two-week periods. I also conducted time and motion studies for stereotyped tasks such as planting and harvesting in order to estimate activity levels and establish associated temporal patterns of activity such as walking, carrying, and the like. Having established a facsimile of the daily activity pattern, I employed the energy expenditure values published by Norgan and associates (1974) to estimate daily energy expenditure for the study population. These calculations were then projected onto an annual time frame to facilitate comparison with other data bases (see, e.g., Morren 1977; Little and Morren 1976).

These calculations show that horticulture is the most demanding pursuit, absorbing almost 28 percent of human somatic energy allocated to work. The proportion rises to 37 percent if the harvest and transportation phases are included. Comparison to other data bases shows, however, that the Miyanmin expend less effort on agriculture than some other well-known peoples of montane New Guinea such as the Maring (Rappaport 1968, 1971) and the Enga (Waddell 1972). According to my own analysis of their only partly comparable data (see Morren 1977), the comparable proportions for the Maring are 45 and 73 percent, and for the Enga 39 and 64 percent. The explanation for this difference is that approximately 27 per cent of Maring production and 64 percent of Enga production is pig feed, whereas Miyanmin pigs are given only 16 percent of garden production in the form of scraps, peelings, and (cooked) undersize taros (see below).

Miyanmin agricultural labor efficiency is low. Combining the production estimates of table 5-1 with the labor inputs of table 5-2, the energetic efficiency of agriculture is 7.5. A roughly comparable figure for the Maring is 18 and for the Enga 16.2. The relative inefficiency of Miyanmin agriculture is partially attributable to the demands of upland taro. Perhaps the most significant of these is single cropping. Taro is a luxury crop, more demanding of soil qualities than sweet potato, yams, or cassava. It grows best in the moist forest environment which translates into higher labor requirements. In compensation, it is more valuable nutritionally than most other root crops, with a starch form that is more readily absorbed and a higher amino acid content.

The Taro Monoculture

The Mountain Ok have been widely identified as "taro people" (Watson 1977; Brown 1978), a view that corresponds to the preferences of people in many, though not all, groups and to the fact that in the mid-altitude fringe areas of the region taro cultivation is a virtual monoculture. Technical differences account for very little of the variability observed in the agricultural systems of

Table 5-3. Estimated Labor and Energy Expenditure and Proportion of
Effort in Routine Activities

Annual Projection for Community with
Average Population 9.5 Men, 8.2 Women, and 10 Children

Activity	Labor (people-hours)	Energy Exp. (million kcal.)	Proportion
A. Movement [a]			
1. Settlement/ Construction	2,730	0.7	13.0
2. Travel	3.042	1.2	22.2
B. Environmental Modification [b]			
3. Horticulture	7,410	1.4 $(189 \, kcal/h)$	27.8
C. Cropping			
4. Harvest [c]	4,524	0.5	9.3
5. Collecting [d]	936	0.1	1.8
6. Hunting	3,978	0.7	13.0
D. Food Preparation & Exchange			
7. Ritual	254	0.1	1.8
8. Cook & Feast [c]	5,876	0.6	11.1
Total	28,750	5.4	100.0

a. Warfare suppressed since early 1960s; aspects of intergroup political activity aggregated in 2 and 8.
b. Little time is expended directly on pig herding; it is imbedded in other activities.
c. Some fuel wood collection is picked up in 4 and 8.
d. Underreported; produce typically contributes to snacks away from residence.

the area. Local garden differentiation according to crop composition is more significant. Although the "infield-outfield" system comparable to that found in the centers of the eastern and western spheres is absent from the Mountain Ok, the Ngalum in the Ok Sibil (Reynders 1962:56–59), the Bimin (Poole 1976:266), and the Oksapmin (Perey 1973:37–45) separate taro from sweet potato gardens. Moreover, sweet potato rather than taro is the staple for these high-altitude fringe peoples. Among mid-altitude fringe peoples such as the Miyanmin, the Wopkaimin of the south slope (Hyndman 1982:242), and Faiwolmin (Barth 1975:30), for whom taro is the subsistence staple, undifferentiated garden plots are planted in taro. Sweet potato is either absent or is a marginal subsidiary crop.

It is conventional wisdom among advocates of appropriate and alternative technology in modern agriculture that polyculture is more adaptive than monoculture. As Wortman and Cummings (1978) point out, monoculture is not as common as polyculture in traditional farming. This may be a valid observation but not a rule. The key dimension is not just the diversity of crops cultivated by traditional cultivators, but the diversity of the larger systems in which they participate. Particularly important is the element of risk arising from the interaction between cropping pattern and the larger system. Mountain Ok gardeners have a range of means at their disposal for minimizing or at least reducing risk. All else being equal, monoculture is more risky than polyculture. All else is rarely equal, however. There is a distinction among Mountain Ok peoples between monocultural patterns of high flexibility and low risk in the mid-altitude fringe and those associated with diminished flexibility and high risk exemplified by the agriculture of the Telefolmin of the Ifitaman regional center. My discussion of the viability of taro monoculture therefore focuses on the nature of agronomic problems and hazards and the subsistence alternatives available to the peoples of the mid-altitude fringe.

Current arguments about the alleged maladaptiveness of monocultures focus on three interrelated elements: (1) simplification of the ecosystem, (2) loss of biological variability, and (3) general vulnerability of the food supply. It should be emphasized that these are variables rather than discrete elements, and that it is possible to find alternatives in traditional monocultures that mitigate the risks and hazards entailed.

All agricultural systems simplify the natural ecosystem. However, some do this more than others and some produce more irreversible effects than others. Even permanent agriculture need not produce irreversible effects if it is practiced conservatively on appropriate sites. The problems that arise in the context of either permanent or shifting agriculture problems include monocultural disasters when the site is inappropriate, marginal, and easily degraded. On a cross-cultural basis, shifting cultivators tend toward monoculture.

Loss of biological variability is mainly associated with the modern use of hybrid varieties. The problem with hybrids is twofold: they show only limited expression of the total genetic variability of a particular plant species, and they tend to be adopted wholesale with one or two hybrid varieties replacing a multitude of established nonhybrid varieties. Taro monocultures of the mid-altitude fringe tend to an exceedingly large number of stable varieties—the Wopkaimin (Hyndman 1979) and the Oksapmin (Cape 1981:155) recognize over 100 cultivars and the Miyanmin have over 50. These cultivars have evolved and proliferated through uncontrolled breeding and cultural trials. The tendency toward many varieties of taro arguably affords these agro-ecosystems some protection from loss due to pests and pathogens (Gagne 1982:232).

The vulnerability of a single staple food plant such as taro to disaster from pest, blight, or climatic changes is not only related to the state of the variable elements discussed in the foregoing. It is also affected by the established capacity of the agriculturist to exploit other crops and subsistence resources to buffer both the ecosystem and life-support system. Marginal, low flexibility, high-risk monoculture is vulnerable to the stereotypical monoculture disaster even under routine conditions. Thus the vulnerability of Irish potato farmers in the 1840s arose, not from the monoculture per se, but from the fact that many had no effective agricultural or subsistence alternatives when the blight struck. Indeed, under the colonial regime, potato cultivation on marginal land was the end point of a long series of adjustments to conquest and the alienation of prime land. Arguably, the Irish peasantry had used the last agricultural option available to them. The modern practitioner of high-yield, capital-intensive, mechanized agriculture is similarly less flexible in that his large debt load makes a switch to other crops and production techniques extremely difficult.

The high flexibility-low risk taro monoculture of the Miyanmin and other Mountain Ok peoples is vulnerable to disaster, but it assumes a different form and magnitude than the Irish famine. In particular, with sweet potato as an option not yet exercised by many, possible disasters in the future could be of shorter duration and lesser magnitude, and could be partially reversible. Thus, long-term or chronic famine of the classic sort might be avoided.

Flowers and associates (1982) present polyculture as a variable feature of swidden or shifting agriculture rather than as a constant. This contrasts with the generally held view, propounded by Geertz (1963:7), that diversity of cultivated species is the sine qua non of swidden agriculture.

In their study of four societies of the dry Certado region of central Brazil, Flowers's team found a general tendency to plant single crop plots in swiddens with each group apparently emphasizing a different crop. It should be noted, however, that in no case did any group seem to practice a monoculture. Two groups derived more than 60 percent of their food from rice, two others gained

Plate 1. Opening a Leaf Oven

Plate 2. Apportioning the Contents of a Leaf Oven

This includes taro cake and pork. Every member of the local population gets a share whether or not they are present for the feast.

approximately 40 percent from manioc, and one of the latter gained a comparable amount from rice as well. According to the authors the situation of Certado groups does appear to contrast strongly with that of tropical forest Indians, where much greater diversity is seen to prevail. It also seems to be the case that low crop diversity among the Certado groups is at least partly due to the effects of contact: territorial loss, population increase, new crops and techniques, opportunities for cash sales, and the like.

The mid-altitude taro monoculture of the Miyanmin and other Mountain Ok groups contrasts even more vividly with the "rain forest metaphor" of an idealized polyculture popularized by Geertz (1963). Of their cultivated foods, the Miyanmin gain approximately 89 percent by weight and 96 percent on an energy basis from taro. Other vegetables or groups of vegetables such as leafy greens, pandanus, bananas, pumpkins, sugar cane, and beans (in descending order) provide from five to less than one percent by weight in the Miyanmin diet.

The mid-altitude fringe taro monoculture also contrasts with the agricultural pattern both of the central Ifitaman groups such as the Telefolmin, Urapmin, and Tifalmin and of the high-altitude fringe groups east and west of Ifitaman such as the Ngalum speakers (Sibilmin), the Atbalmin, and the Bimin, who all grow significant amounts of sweet potato in addition to taro.

The lack of diversity apparent in Miyanmin agriculture is relieved by considerable flexibility in the exploitation of a wide variety of alternative wild and domesticated foods, and by the fact that taro is locally represented by such a large number of varieties. Although neither sago nor sweet potato turned up in my samples in the 1960s, both were observed among high-altitude Miyanmin groups. In the 1970s and 80s some Miyanmin have significantly increased their production of sweet potatoes in response to a variety of factors (see below).

The relatively flexible monoculture of the mid-altitude fringe nevertheless entails risks including those associated with new and recently appearing plant diseases and pests and climatic hazards that have also occurred in the past. Taro is always subject to low-level infestation by specialized insect pests and corm rot. Corm rot seems to be due to excessive moisture and high soil temperature. According to Don Gardner (1981), it is particularly prevalent among low-altitude groups of Miyanmin living on the August River. The Wopkaimin associate corm rot with lower elevations and have only begun to cultivate taro regularly below 1200 m since the initiation of the Ok Tedi mining scheme. Small local losses also result from invasions by domestic and wild pigs that appear to enjoy the garden milieu more than the taro itself. In New Guinea 75 percent of the major pests of taro are territorial and have a long generation time because gardens are surrounded by naturalized and/or derelict plants near new gardens, thus creating a stable habitat (Gagne 1982:233).

Various Mountain Ok groups, including some Miyanmin, have recently been afflicted with taro leaf blight *Phytophthora colocasiae* (Pearson and Thistleton 1981) which seems to inhibit corm growth. A combination of this pathogen and dasheen mosaic virus totally destroyed the taro stock of several small Miyanmin groups on the right May River in 1981 and gave rise to a localized famine.

In the distant past, taro monocultures were probably universal in the higher rainfall mid-altitude fringe and highland areas of New Guinea. Their transformation and replacement was contingent, not on disaster, but the need to expand the capacity to produce pig fodder. The choice was sweet potato, a crop that permits cultivation to be extended into areas, especially higher altitudes, that would otherwise be marginal or absolutely unfavorable for taro growth. Disastrous failures of taro (which lead to the wholesale adoption of sweet potato) occurred in the lowlands of the Solomon Islands in the 1940s (Oliver 1955; Connell 1978a and 1978b; Mitchell 1976; Packard 1975; Scheffler 1965), but similar disasters (with similar results) have not been reported for the Mountain Ok.

Crop Mix and Production Levels

Anyone who practices agriculture must decide how much of what commodity to plant. Neither an "aggregate," or cultural, explanation nor an idiosyncratic situational one is adequate to explain the variations in abundance of the significant cultigens from community to community or even from family to family. In montane New Guinea, as indicated above, more often than not the choice is between taro and sweet potato. Values partly "set the bias" of the system and the Miyanmin say that "taro is our bones." It is the desire and conscious target of all Miyanmin in the *am-nakai* communities of the mid-altitude zone to control and grow enough so that they and their families might subsist on taro. At an individual level, however, taro and the means to realize the ideal are limited. There are two aspects of this issue; and, in order to make some sense out of it, I will compartmentalize them to a degree. One aspect has to do with the fact that the amount of taro planting stock is limited, partly by convention. This will be examined in the next section. The other is more broadly situational, related to the availability of labor, land, and other capital, especially in the context of modernization. This will be studied later in this chapter.

A Domestic Production System

First let us look at the matter of planting stock so that we can tentatively isolate the control system which determines production levels of taro under normal conditions. It was indicated earlier that the principal planting stock consists of the stalks of mature taro plants. The number of stalks available for planting depends on the harvesting of large corms and the small natural increase represented by cormlets and suckers. Stalks are owned by families and individuals and represent their most important domestic capital.

Here we confront one of several of Marshall Sahlins's departures from realism in his model of the "domestic mode of production" (1972). According to Sahlins, "the main run of primitive economies, agricultural as well as preagricultural, seem not to realize their own economic capacities. Labor power is underused, technological means are not fully engaged, natural resources are left untapped (41)." Cultural means exist for curtailing the working life of the individual, and only fractional use is made of labor in such societies; people could work longer and harder than they do (51 ff.). Land is underutilized and underexploited (42 ff.). Higher populations densities could be supported in some areas. Most important to Sahlins, a significant number of families in a community "chronically" fail to meet their own nutritional requirements from household production. Their deficits are made up by other families that [chronically?] produce surpluses (73 ff.). The principal cause of this marginal performance on the part of the tribal agriculturist is the "dominant production institution" in such societies, the family or "domestic mode of production." "The household is to the tribal economy as the manor to the Medieval economy. . . . each is the dominant production institution of its time" (76).

Sahlins believes that the only social unit in tribal societies whose food production activities we can examine systematically is the domestic unit. Other suprafamilial units that may be formed from time to time are unimportant and have little power to affect the productive performance of families. For the time being, it is sufficient for me to point out that my overall analysis of Miyanmin resource management tends to negate Sahlin's conclusions. First, in its preoccupation with agricultural production, Sahlins's argument is a victim of the "calorific obsession"; tribal people do not live by plants alone. Second, although Miyanmin agriculture is a domestic matter, it is strongly influenced by the dynamics of the settlement and hunting system presented in this book. This system is organized at a suprafamilial level, the units involved endure, they deflect family labor in patterned ways, and they possess "independent social realization." But this is merely a peripheral argument in the present context. Of more immediate concern is that Sahlins's vision of families *qua* families and as units of production is static

Plate 3. Preparing Taro Dough for "Pandanus Pizza"
The steamed *marita* pandanus on the right is mixed with water
and the thick red sauce is then squeezed onto the cake.

and unrealistic. In particular, he fails to take into account the familial developmental cycle and how it affects production.

Sahlins examined data on family production from a variety of sources and concluded that "an interesting percentage of households chronically fail to provide their own customary livelihood" (74). A little earlier, he noted that the domestic differences seem to be distributed as a normal curve around the point of *per capita* subsistence" (73). The latter proposition seems to mean that, while some families may not be self-sufficient, communities do manage to balance their books. If this is so, then we have to take a closer look at the underproducing families and the factors that may be responsible for this.

Sahlins correctly identifies at least two of the key variables in this determination—variations in household composition, or "Chayanov's rule" (87 ff.), and stage of the familial developmental cycle (88)—the two being partly related. He nevertheless seems to suggest, in his use of the word "chronically," that the same families that are underproductive at one time always have been and always will be. It is unclear why Sahlins did not pick up on his own lead, i.e., the link between productivity and the developmental cycle.

The basics of the situation are that many newly founded nuclear families start their careers as undercapitalized production units with escalating per capita demands (i.e., children) on their inadequate production facilities. Within a few years, however, families begin to achieve a reasonable degree of self-sufficiency and even become surplus producers, enjoying a long period of high production before slipping into the underproduction of old age. Of course, this is the normal pattern within which a variety of situational factors may operate (see below). Over the span of its existence as a unit, the production of a family is likely to more or less equal its requirements, and there will be less deviation from this level of performance in a given sample than there would be in a shorter period of observation (e.g., a year, or the few weeks characteristic of most attempts by rural social scientists to measure production). What this implies, contrary to Sahlins's conclusion, is that the domestic mode of production will not work unless it is nested in a "community" mode of production and distribution, a suprafamilial unit that organizes the distribution of household surpluses, sees to the capitalization of new households, and controls other life-supporting activities and strategies such as hunting and the location of settlements. In summary, households may strive for self-sufficiency, achieve it over a span of time, and regularly produce surpluses at some point in their careers. However, the basic, encapsulated, self-sufficient unit in tribal societies in the short run is some kind of local and territorial population.

Among the Miyanmin, young families at the beginning of the familial developmental cycle are limited not only by the availability of labor and the demands of young children but also by their stock of planting material, the taro stalks described earlier. People actually begin their agricultural careers in childhood when both boys and girls are given planting stock and the responsibility for a small portion of their family's gardens. Their stock slowly expands through natural increase and grants from kin. Men and women bring their stock to their marriages, and continue to expand it in the ways described until they achieve an appropriate level. Then they will cease acquiring stock and may even discard "natural increase." Once this has occurred, the domestic production system is set: it is what is referred to in chapter 2 as a control system of the "closed sequence" type. As such, once it is established for a given domestic unit, it is quite unresponsive to environmental changes. If a young or middle-aged man goes off on contract labor for the normal term of two years, he must really work hard to get back into this production system. When a person, male or female, dies, his stock is uprooted and burned (chapter 8).

The advantage of a control system is that, in a pattern of continuous nonseasonal cultivation, agriculturists need not keep track of their planting: what you plant today is essentially determined by what you harvested (and ate) yesterday, and, assuming no major problems, the system should run smoothly without significant oscillations. Thus, the agriculturist can pay attention to the more critical and less routine aspects of the enterprise such as settlement and site selection, and to nonagricultural issues.

Why Grow (More) Sweet Potato?

In an agricultural system dominated in the aggregate by taro, many individuals nevertheless choose to grow significant quantities of sweet potato. Among the Miyanmin, this is most apparent in the context of modernization, but the option to grow sweet potato has existed for at least 300 years in New Guinea, it has been important to other Mountain Ok groups for a long time, and I observed a small number of Miyanmin families growing moderate quantities in the 1960s and more families growing greater amounts in the 1980s.

Gaining answers to the question of why people change basic features of their subsistence economy is not a simple exercise. For one thing, the issue can be viewed on an individual or on a group basis. (The two are not unrelated, but are nevertheless different.) Also, there are several hypothetical formulations and empirical observations in anthropology and related fields that attempt to explain agricultural changes and differences in general and in particular.

The development of increased sweet potato production I have observed among certain Miyanmin groups since the late 1960s is worth examining more closely for the light it may shed on these theories and observations. In the end, I offer eight explanations for my basic observation, explanations that often pertain to different levels and are therefore complementary rather than exclusive. My operational point in offering this multitude is that an examination of agricultural change cannot be limited to plant agriculture on the supply side and immediate human nutritional needs on the demand side. Rather, it must look more broadly at the domestic economy, at the agricultural or food sector, and—in many circumstances—at the wider political-economic system, including the penetration of villages by the cash economy. For the sake of brevity I label these explanations land and resource scarcity (which is the reciprocal of population pressure), reduction of game, intensification of pig husbandry, commerce, favorable environmental conditions, new cultivars, (pre)adaptation to taro disease, and situationally determined inequality.

Land and Resource Scarcity

One of the most widely applied hypotheses is Boserup's (1965) model of agrarian change in relation to population pressure. Her model has been applied, albeit in my opinion simplistically, to Melanesia by Brookfield and Hart (1971). Boserup essentially turned Malthus's doctrine (that food production limits population) on its head. According to Boserup, agricultural technology and related practices respond to population increase and concentration by increasing output. She feels that, by and large, the relatively low population densities observed in traditional societies are due, not to limitations imposed by agriculture, but to other nonsubsistence problems.

Certain relevant hypotheses of the classical economists are also worthy of examination. According to Boserup (1965:12), the classical economists envisaged two mechanisms for increasing aggregate agricultural production, expansion at the margins of un(der)utilized land, and intensification of cultivation of existing lands. She argues that this view is ethnocentric, arising particularly from ignorance of the facts of shifting cultivation in which the distinction between fields and uncultivated land is blurred. She chooses to emphasize cropping frequency and to identify a continuum of land-use types from truly virgin land, "through land cropped at shorter and shorter intervals, to that part of the territory in which a crop is sown as soon as the previous one has been harvested" (12). The advantage of Boserup's approach is not only that it treats intensification as a continuous variable, but that it allows us to place agriculture in a systematic framework in which the environment is part of the system, at least some of its features are man-made, and a wider variety of human activities are included in the analysis.

In attempting to overturn Malthus, however, Boserup may have been guilty of promulgating a false dichotomy of mutually exclusive alternatives. There can be no doubt that food production and supply can severely limit population, and that intensification under population pressure is not inevitable. The operation of "Malthusian checks," as well as less extreme population control factors, has been observed repeatedly. Both positions are realistic possibilities associated with different situations. Apparent conflicts are resolvable only within a systems framework which looks at the dynamic interplay between people and their environment. As is argued in the introductory chapter of this study, people confronting an environmental problem can deal with it in two basic ways: they can change how they interact with the environment, or they can change themselves demographically (or they can do both).

Among the Miyanmin of the Hak Valley, land and resource scarcity is the result of unusual population concentration and duration of settlement. The general implications of this summary will not be entirely clear until chapter 11, but the specifics can be presented here.

An airstrip construction project that originated and was fully initiated solely by local people commenced in the early 1960s. At that time the people also built what was by Miyanmin standards a large village of eight substantial "family" houses not only to shelter the workforce but to ensure access to the benefits that were expected to soon follow. Some were forthcoming (although meager at first) and also intermittent, so that this village was effectively abandoned by its owners soon after the airstrip became operational in 1967 (Morren 1981). There had been some gardening in the immediate area of the village, but most of it was confined to the airstrip site itself, an ancient riverbed now raised some 50 meters above the Hak River.

By the time I started living with the Miyanmin in 1968, the large village near the airstrip was completely disused and much of the nearby gardening was not subsistence-oriented, but was an expression of optimism for *bisnis,* containing substantial plantings of pineapple, Cavendish banana, and other newly disseminated vegetables such as tomato. At that time, except for the airstrip tract itself, gardening was forbidden south of the Hak because this zone was then reserved for hunting. Kometen (Timelmin) habitation sites, actually a string of small hamlets, were ranged along the divide to the north between the Hak and Uk rivers and in the latter valley, and Temsapmin was continuing its drift from the San Valley (see map 10).

A new settlement around the airstrip was started in the mid-1970s, encouraged by the relocation of the aid post from the San and the building and opening of a government primary school in 1974. Once again, a large labor force was gathered, and in the long run, the school has been powerfully attractive. People from various Miyanmin groups, as well as aliens, have moved to the Mianmin Airstrip vicinity. When I flew into the area late in 1980, I viewed the immense village that had sprung up around the airstrip with horrific fascination. I soon took the opportunity to survey it on the ground

Plate 4. A Garden Clearing in the Forest

Plate 5. Planting a New Garden
To make a planting hole, the digging stick is wielded with great
force. Taro stalks are in the foreground.

and I counted 58 family houses (or their modern idiosyncratic equivalents) and nine men's houses, as well as a large number of public buildings.

More will be said about this complex in the final chapter. For the present, it is important to note that in mid-1981 it could shelter more than 400 people; and after six or more years of growth (depending on when one starts to count), it was putting considerable pressure on agricultural and other kinds of environmental resources. This is the case despite the fact that, for a variety of reasons, the daily roll of residents only rarely reached the 400-person range.

The 60 or so potential resident families require food as well as shelter and all but the superannuated maintain gardens in the vicinity. Thus the pressure on prime agricultural lands (i.e., those most suitable for taro cultivation), as well as on game animals and craft and building materials, has been accelerating. As indicated earlier, taro ground is newly cleared old secondary forest in the 1000- to 1500-meter altitudinal range, on poorly drained or otherwise moist sites that possess a rich store of nutrients in decaying organic matter. It should also be no more than an hour's walk from the habitation site.

As these sites have tended to be used up and are only renewed on a 12+ year fallow cycle, people have had to exercise other options. These options include investing more effort in less convenient locations and spending less time in the vicinity of the airstrip, shortening fallows, and planting more sweet potato and cassava. Increasingly, lineages of the land-holding parishes have begun to assert cultivation and hunting rights that, in the 1960s, were only discussed in the abstract. This has contributed to enlarged and uncharacteristic social differentiation, though it is not yet institutionalized (see the discussion of situationally determined inequality below). People have also begun to plant more sago, primarily for roofing material to replace the special forest tree leaves which have become scarce rather than as a food source.

Game Reduction and Intensification of Pig Husbandry

Game animals, wild pigs, marsupials, cassowaries, and other birds continue to be an important source of animal food for all Miyanmin, but the people living around the airstrip have experienced a progressive decline in their availability. The impact of human activity on game animals is considered in detail in chapter 6 and only some of the relevant facts will be summarized here.

Wild pigs are now considered to be totally absent in this part of the Hak Valley (a proposition which I find doubtful, but which is a subjective indication of the relative magnitude of the problem); and none were taken during my time in the field in 1980–81. The prime mechanism for this animal's virtual disappearance has most probably been overhunting rather than habitat disruption. Indeed, the growing prominence of sweet potato might otherwise be expected to attract wild pig. Turning this around, I also argue that the decline of wild pig has created conditions favoring the expansion of sweet potato cultivation.

Impacts on other game are harder to assess. Dwarf cassowary (*Cassowarius bennettii*) are occasionally sighted and people attribute their persistence to the creature's great mobility and range. Village and garden rats (*Rattus ruber, Melomys rufescens*), the garden-raiding gray possum (*Phallanger gymnotis*), the edge-dwelling bandicoot (*Echimipera kalubu*), and perhaps other animals have been unaffected or even fostered by the creation of habitats favorable to them. True forest-dwelling species of rats, possums, and other marsupials have become scarcer around the airstrip settlement. A more subtle effect is that due to the new kinds of attractions there, men are less inclined to hunt at great distances from home, further contributing to the impoverishment of the wild animal foods harvest.

An apparent response to the reduction in game (and its contribution to the human diet) has been an intensification of pig husbandry. As I have noted elsewhere (Morren 1977), when Brookfield and Hart (1971) undertook to apply Boserup's model to agricultural intensification in New Guinea, they omitted a realistic consideration of the role of pig husbandry. In so doing, they overlooked Boserup's own discussion of the influence of livestock fodder production on agricultural intensification (1965:36–37, 85–86). In my earlier paper I emphasized this connection in carrying out a comparative analysis of energy flow paths in three New Guinea life-support systems. It would be an error of logical typing to construe my present argument as a recantation of that earlier position, which involved fairly abstract statements. I still hold that there is a general and direct relationship between the degree of intensification of pig husbandry and the character of agriculture. My instant argument is a situational analysis of a particular case.

A summary of field data from the 1960s indicates that the pig-to-people ratio was 0.1:1. Data from 1980–81 show that in the settlement around the airstrip the ratio has doubled to approximately 0.19:1. This ratio is still low in comparison to that reported for other montane New Guinea peoples such as the Maring, with a range of from 0.3:1 to 0.8:1 (Rappaport 1968), and the Raiapu Enga, with 2.3:1 (Waddell 1972).

Commerce

Another classical economist we can look to for improvements to Boserup's model is Adam Smith. According to Smith's *The Wealth of Nations* (1775; cited in Jacobs 1969:44–45), the most highly developed agriculture is found in countries with the most highly developed urban-industrial patterns, rather than in countries with primarily agricultural economies; and, within a given country, the most productive agriculture is to be found near cities. This raises an issue of some generality which is that there is more to population pressure than "more people." Specifically, Smith's observations suggest the existence of something which we might provisionally refer to as "induced population pressure," in which people experience the same symptoms of, say, undernutrition and high mortality, but the causes of their condition are political-economic ones—the costs of areal integration, rather than the weight of their own numbers, create the problem. The airstrip-based settlement described earlier in this chapter can usefully be viewed as an "incipient city" in Jacobs's sense of developing a dynamic of its own consisting of new pursuits, new jobs, commerce, and the beginnings of a multiplier effect.

There are relatively few jobs that can be identified as such, including church pastor, aid post orderly, grass cutter, shopkeeper, anthropological field assistant, and schoolteacher. Only the latter is full-time and thus almost completely removed from subsistence production. Nevertheless, for the time being at least, this complex is peculiar to this place alone and *kaukau* production is "new work" in Jacobs's terms.

One of the elements of the modernization package people developed and implemented here in the 1960s (see chapter 11) was the desire for *bisnis*. As I indicated a moment ago, the earliest manifestation of this was in modest plantations of newly diffused pineapple and Cavendish banana. This effort failed for lack of a market and reliable transportation, but the fruits themselves were firmly established in local subsistence. Subsequently, with the encouragement of government agricultural agents, export-oriented crops such as coffee and chiles were tried. These also failed.

Until approximately 1980, *bisnis* was confined to casual sales of small amounts of fruit to the mission through the agency of the MAF pilot. In 1980 an expatriate volunteer *ditiman* arranged several larger sales to the Ok Tedi and Frieda mining camps and to the Oksapmin Cooperative. Although this was irregular, it helped to define a market. I was able to extend this effort and regularize it to the extent of a standing order from the Frieda Camp for several hundred kilos of fruit and vegetables twice a month. By the time I left the field in 1981, the income from this was up to 300 kina per month. The single largest commodity by weight in this commerce was the sweet potato, which suggests that even if commerce was not yet a stimulus to expanded production, it might be in the future.

Favorable Environmental Conditions

In the course of my 1968–69 field work I noticed the scarcity of sweet potato because initially I preferred it to taro and later liked it as a change of pace. Hence, I badgered my neighbors to sell me some *kaukau*. As I described earlier, I also carried out a more objective measurement of production by weighing food brought back to my hamlet during sample periods. Sweet potato did not turn up in my sample, although it was "present." When I pressed for an explanation, my informants advised me that growing conditions were not favorable on the Uk River side of the divide where we were living, but that more sweet potato was grown on the Hak side to the south.

It was further explained that sweet potato grew best in dry, sandy, and/or well-drained soils with river banks of old alluvium likely sites. As a "young" river lying in a relatively deep cut for much of its course, the Uk provided few appropriate places of the sort that are usually located on the inside of meanders or on old raised riverbeds. During this period, a young family decided to make a sweet potato garden on such a site nearby (indeed it was the former location of the same hamlet which had been destroyed by a flood). The field was modest in size, only a quarter-acre in extent, and had to be heavily fenced to bar village pigs from it. It conformed in most respects to the characteristics I described earlier. I was also advised that after its harvest the tract would be planted in *marita* pandanus, a common pattern in the area.

In 1980–81 I took up residence at the airstrip village in the Hak Valley. Almost immediately I was inundated with sweet potatoes by optimistic vendors. Subsequent measurement indicated that sweet potato constituted almost 25 percent of production. As the general argument in this chapter indicates, this is not attributable exclusively to more favorable environmental conditions. Nevertheless, as a larger, more mature river, the Hak's valley is broader, providing more space for a meandering and sinuous course with suitable land for sweet potato cultivation at almost every bend. In addition, there are broad flat terraces of consolidated alluvium, segments of the ancient riverbed that also provide suitable ground.

New Plant Varieties

In the 1960s I recorded the names and descriptions of 45 *Colocasia* taro varieties, all grouped under the higher-order taxon *imen.* All other root and tuberous vegetables were grouped under the taxon *wan,* including two varieties of cassava, several wild yams, and only three varieties of sweet potato.

The "modern period," starting with the mass jailing in Wewak on the north coast in 1959 (Morren 1981; see also chapter 11), has offered the Miyanmin many opportunities to travel within Papua New Guinea, including visits to Rabaul, Bougainville, and Mount Hagen for contract labor and, to a lesser extent, mission educational activities. And from the beginning, Miyanmin "tourists" have returned home not only with clothing and trade goods, but with plant materials, seed packets, ornamental cuttings, banana varieties, a few new taros, and at least 12 new sweet potato varieties, mostly from the highlands to the east. One innovator described his experience with a new variety he had obtained, "In Hagen they grow like this [indicates object about the size of a hen's egg], but here they grow like this [indicates object the size of a soccer ball]." And most of the new varieties indeed do very well. Of course, this is diffusion though the mechanism and opportunity is an aspect of modernization.

(Pre)Adaptation to Taro Disease

Strictly speaking, there is no such thing as a preadaptation, since there is no way to respond to a change that has not yet occurred. Nevertheless, as is argued earlier, some groups—through chance or other systematic factors—have options at their disposal that prepare them for a novel change, and that is the sense in which I use the term "preadaptation" here. As stated earlier in this chapter, the Irish potato blight and famine of the 1840s (Woodham-Smith 1962; Regan 1983) is the example always cited of the risk of monoculture or overdependence on a single crop. Although the historical circumstances behind and situational factors surrounding the Miyanmin taro monoculture are very different, the resulting risk is comparable in that the staple is vulnerable to biotic hazards (plant diseases and blights or pests). Taro is so vulnerable that it has been eliminated in other parts of the country such as Bougainville.

The Miyanmin recognize several insect pests of taro and, as discussed earlier in the section on monoculture, at least three kinds of diseases. These are corm rot, leaf and stalk fungus, and a severe disease that has only recently appeared in the gardens of several communities. Corm rot (*imenkok*) is endemic, but is of low intensity throughout the Miyanmin area. According to informants, some varieties may be more subject to it than others; and it may also be associated with plants left overlong in the ground. It normally affects only the base of the corm and the diseased portion may be cut out and the stalk salvaged as seed material.

Leaf and stalk fungus, *Phytopthora colocasiae,* became established throughout the Mountain Ok area in the late 1970s. It is apparently transmitted through contact between plants, exposure to a contaminated medium such as a *bilum* or storage place, or by rain splashes. It seems not to kill the plant outright but damages mature leaves and stalks and reduces productivity.

The third disease has been tentatively identified by scientists of the Department of Primary Industry as dasheen mosaic virus. It is extremely contagious, kills entire plants while rendering the corms inedible, and rapidly spreads through the entire sock of an affected community.

In 1980–81, this disease ravaged the crops of four small Miyanmin groups on the right May River, quite distant from the Mianmin Airstrip. Three of them totally lost their crop and planting stock and have become famine areas, while the fourth lost part of its crop before the disease appeared to die out. People have resorted to exploiting emergency plant foods such as sago, "tulip," and the like. They have undertaken to plant sweet potato and cassava on a crash basis while also attempting to obtain planting stock from unaffected neighboring groups in order to reestablish their staple. In this low-altitude area, planting of sweet potato and cassava is said to be unsuccessful due to marauding wild pigs. Sweet potato is, nevertheless, a likely element in a larger "bundle" of responses. Accordingly, although this disease has not turned up in the gardens of southern Miyanmin groups (reportedly some diseased plants have been identified in Eliptaman, the Telefolmin valley immediately to the south), the increase in sweet potato cultivation observed in the Hak Valley represents a degree of preparedness in relation to this hazard. And while no informants made the connection, people are aware of the plight of the right May groups, are anxious about the potential threat it represents, and have received advice on possible countermeasures from a volunteer *didiman.*

Situationally Determined Inequality

Due to particular circumstances that prevent their pursuit of "normal" subsistence production, some individuals and families opt to grow sweet potato to fill significant gaps in their life-support system, an escalatory response. These circumstances may pertain to limited capital or labor. Situationally determined inequality and associated responses are potentially reversible and temporary, distinguishing the phenomenon from social stratification. Indeed, some manifestations of it are aspects of the life-cycle or the familial developmental cycle rather than ascribed and permanent features of a person's life. This is not to deny the possible historical roots of social stratification in circumstances in which situationally determined inequality becomes permanent as part of some larger, irreversible transformation.

So, among the Miyanmin at least, we are concerned with circumstances under which certain individuals become less equal than others, at least temporarily. Such people include the newly married who—as is discussed earlier—are undercapitalized with respect to taro planting stock, widowers, members of single-parent households, the elderly, perennial bachelors, "foreign" schoolchildren and their guardians, and the families of contract laborers. All but the first are essentially limited by the factor of labor. Land scarcity is at issue in that some find it expedient to shorten the fallow by clearing relatively young second growth sweet potato and cassava with appropriate crops for this and other marginal practices. Only the last two categories are related to modernization. Nevertheless, increased resource pressure and "privatization" of resources and income is a likely outcome, and is already apparent among the Telefolmin (chapter 11).

6

Hunting and Faunal Resources

Hunting is a very visible feature of Miyanmin living; and the pattern of relationships between people and game animals influences many aspects of their culture and adaptation. The wild fauna are abundant and varied here although, because of its insular nature, New Guinea and Austronesia generally display less faunal diversity than other tropical areas (see Harrison 1959, 1960; Menzies 1979:3; MacArthur and Wilson 1967).

I collected faunal material over several field seasons in order to obtain biological identifications[1] that might yield scientific information and facilitate the assessment of faunal resources and their exploitation by humans. I obtained a fairly comprehensive collection of mammals and a more restricted sample[2] of frogs and lizards, and submitted these to biologists. I attempted to classify birds myself by using the keys provided by Rand and Gilliard (1967), and, later, Diamond (1972) and Beehler (1978). Unfortunately I was not able to attend similarly to fish, snakes, or insects. Table 6-1 is a partial list of vertebrate fauna.

In addition to *Homo sapiens*, placental mammals are represented in my collections by the feral pig, rodents (7 genera, at least 9 confirmed species), and bats (at least 4 species). Marsupials are represented by wallaby and tree kangaroo (4 species), cuscus, ringtail and other possum (12 species), dasyurid (3 species), and bandicoot (3 species). There is one monotreme, an echidna. In addition, reptiles are represented by various lizards (at least 11 species), the crocodile, frog (at least 12 species), turtle (2 named varieties) and snake (at least 12 named varieties). The diverse bird life is most striking and includes more than 150 named varieties, including dwarf and "standard" cassowary, perhaps 11 bird-of-paradise species, crown pigeon, cockatoo, and hornbill. In some areas catfish and eel (2 named varieties) are plentiful; and insects, having varied relations with people, are very numerous indeed.

Although exploitation of wild fauna is more significant in this subsistence economy, some domesticated or tamed animals are also kept. In fact, the Miyanmin, like many other New Guinea peoples, like young animals and enjoy keeping pets even though these will ultimately be converted into

Table 6-1.   Partial Ethno-Biological Checklist of Vertebrates and
Miyanmin Terminal Taxa

A.   Mammals

Biological Classification	Miyanmin Classification
MONOTREMES	
Echidnas	
Zaglossus bruijni	no yakel
MARSUPIALS	
Dasyurids	
Myoictes melas?	tangtangibo
Murexia longicauda	tangtangibo hom
Antechinus melanurus	temiyap
"small marsupial mouse"	bibi
Bandicoots	
Echimipera kalubu	aiyal
Perorhyctes raffrayana	duwin
Echimipera clara	kiyok
Phallangers	
Phallanger orientalis m.	ibim
f.	ariken
gymnotis	kwiyam
vestitus	aatol
carmelitae	"
maculatus m.	tekep derakeme
f.	tekep gaong
albino	tekep nema
atremaculatus/rufoniger	tekep aaul
Pseudocheirus corrinnae	kiyong
forbesi	tifon
cupreus	nenem
Dactylopsila trivigata	kwidiaim
Petaurus breviceps	befagum
Distoechurus pennatus	mamaenabu
Kangaroos	
Dendrolagus dorianus	debarim
goodfellowi	yema
Dorcopsis vanheurni	sumul
hageni	sumul aoiyabu
RODENTS	
Hyomys goliath	afut
Uromys anak?	debam
caudimaculatus	kwateribo
sp.?	sobim
Xenuromys barbatus	bobol
Rattus ruber	aanuk
Melomys rufescens	abul
var. ?	abul sombo

Biological Classification	Miyanmin Classification
levipes	briazu
var. ?	briazu dowan
lorentzi	temeya
Pogonomys sp.	idam
"tiny forest rat"	titiyabu
Hydromys chrisogaster	aiyam

BATS

Dobsonia sp.	wan ketap
Pteropus sp.?	sewi
Nyctimene sp.	timinim wafume
Paranyctimene raptor?	uleulelabu
?	tiktenunimin

PIGS

Sus scrofa	el
(wild)	el halap

DOGS

Canis familiaris	til
(wild)	til sa til

B. Frogs

Hyla arfakiana	map bobliman
angiana	wisi
modica	dindin
eucnemis	ankal
Rana grisea	waip
	imegit
jimiensis	akimen
Xenobatrochus obesus	ngongol
Metropostira ocellata	kwekwi
Ceratobatrochus sp.?	sawa
"Small tree frog"?	bowan
Nyctimystes sp.?	tarip
?	dengdeng

C. Reptiles

Goniocephalus dilophus	tim sanglom
modestus	yaria
	melawe
Emoia pallidiceps	metok
sp.	montim
sp.?	makatim
Dasia smaragdinum	odok
Gekko vittatus	berebo
Gymnodactylus sp.?	alom
"primary drum-skin lizard"	sebaribo
"secondary drum-skin lizard"	meribo

Table 6-1. (continued)

Biological Classification	Miyanmin Classification
?	gwe
?	menenfaiya
?	ta
Crocodiles	
Crocodylus sp.?	tim senabe

D. Birds

Cassowaries	
Casuarius bennettii?	kobol
casuarius?	waniki
Grebes	
Podiceps novaehollandiae?	wan iwal
Herons	
?	edawe
Hawks & Eagles	
Hernicpernis longicauda?	tolim
?	fifil drobumin
Brush Turkeys	
Tallegalla sp.?	gowan
sp.?	senga
Aepypodia arfakianua ?	akwil
Megapodius freycinet?	winim
Pheasant & Quail	
Turnix maculosa?	bringwen
Rails	
Porphyrio porphyrio?	gimai
Sandpipers	
?	bungkak
Pigeons	
Ducala zocae ?	anening
Gymnophaps albertsii?	homone
Megaloprepia magnifica ?	kiruan
Reinwartoena reinwardtsi?	miyun
Goura victoria?	wobadiya
?	wowoliya
?	kubiyami
Parrots	
Psittrichas fulgidas?	abou
Ptillinopus superbus?	afwel
sp.?	bri

Biological Classification	Miyanmin Classification
ornatus?	saria
coronulatus?	uwen
?	daiglo
Psittacella sp.?	imet
Trichoglossus sp.?	kataribom
sp.?	kel
Domicella lory?	kwesu
Micropsitta sp.?	mangman
bruijnii?	sabwem
Cocatua galerita?	nema
Alisterus sp.?	nesin
Opopsita diopthalma?	rititin
Pseudeos fuscata?	seriawariya
Probosciger atterimus?	samdan
Charmosyna papou?	su
josephinae?	titin
Oreopsittacus arfakis?	uletitin

Cuckoos
?   nobo

Barn Owls
Tyto sp.?   krokobe

Owls
Ninox theomacha?   shroiabunim
?   souwan

Frogmouths
Podargus sp.?   moniai

Swifts
?   dekdek
?   drikim

Kingfishers
Halycon sp.?   konok
Tansptera galatea?   arifaiyom
Melidora sp.?   mamtap
Clytoceyx rex?   tofak
?   monongol

Hornbills
Aceros plicatus?   saiyon
     kwairon

Cuckoo-Shrikes
Coracena sp.?   bunel

Thrushes
?   brit

Table 6-1. (continued)

Biological Classification	Miyanmin Classification
Flycatchers	
Rhipidura sp.?	brimen
sp.?	bripsapsapen
sp.?	brisesa
?	dida
?	dirak
?	dorap
Heteromiyias abbespecularis?	getako
Machaerirhynchus sp.?	gidak
Peltops montannus?	gweron
?	motemin
Microeca griseoceps?	nemantip
Poecilodryas sp.?	tetubangkana
Wren Warblers	
Clytomyias insignis?	serere
?	sangsangim
Warblers	
Malarus sp.?	mekalwan
?	diyapmet
?	nimnim
Whistlers	
Pachycephala sp.?	dorap
sp.?	finfun
?	gwanim
?	gwekgwek
Shrikes	
Lanius schack?	alifabiyou
Wood Swallows	
Artamus sp.?	dokdok
Butcherbirds	
Cracticus cassicus?	aboye
Drongos	
Dicrurus sp.?	tantaribo
Birds of Paradise	
Paradisaea ragianna?	abiya
apoda?	wau
minor?	bimal
Epimachus sp.?	afwet
sp.?	bgobgo
Lophorina superba?	awem
Loriae loriae?	bingam
Parotia carolae?	gwadibo
Diphyllodea magnificus?	komonsan
Astrapia stephanie?	krosol
Cicinnurus regius?	nono
"female of one or more spp."?	emeyabu

Biological Classification	Miyanmin Classification
Bowerbirds	
Aituroedus sp.?	awit
?	defugam
Chlamydera cerviniventris?	fagan
lauterbachi?	siyo
?	wongwong
Honeyeaters	
Myzomela sp.?	nitnet
?	troktrok
Meliphaga sp.? m.	tabrak
f.	duran
Melidectes sp.?	tina
Flowerpeckers	
?	kekenma
White-Eyes	
Zosterops sp.?	arifep

human biomass and fuel. Pigs are kept, most after being captured in the wild as piglets, but with some being the issue of matings between village sows and feral boars (chapter 5). Traditionally all domestic boars were castrated, but this has been changing due to modernization pressures. Young cassowary of both species are also tamed whenever there is an opportunity to do so. Cockatoo and hornbill young and certain marsupial young are also kept from time to time, but more as an avocation than a serious subsistence activity.

Virtually all of the fauna listed are exploited at some time, and I have observed most of them in people's diets. The productivity of wild mammals for people is particularly significant and so this discussion will focus on them. Nevertheless, the importance of small nutritional inputs from many and varied sources—bird, fish, reptile, insect—cannot be overlooked (see Dornstreich and Morren 1974; Dwyer 1974, n.d.) and will be examined later.

A Description of Hunting

The most notable feature of Miyanmin hunting is that a lot of male labor is invested in it. Certainly no other activity is so diligently and regularly pursued; other tasks such as garden clearing, house building, and the like are nothing more than interludes between periods of intensive hunting. Consistent with the fact that it produces the major protein component of the diet, hunting is enthusiastically performed, competitive, individualistic and one of the prime foci of the local status hierarchy. Until traditional religion was eclipsed by Christianity and modernization, hunting (along with warfare and gardening) was the focus of ritual attention and belief. Group welfare is associated with an abundance of game. Hence, according to traditional religious tenets, ancestral spirits who are responsible for the general welfare are also involved in helping the living to a successful hunt (chapter 8).

The most time-consuming, individualistic, and prestigious hunting activity is the search—putting the hunter in proximity to the quarry (see also Dwyer 1974). The intellectual side of hunting is oriented toward this, the quest, rather than toward the kill itself or the elaboration of killing technology (weapons). Many full days of hunting effort involve a man, alone or with a dog, moving through the forest looking for direct or indirect evidence of the recent presence of game and, most importantly, investigating potential feeding sites. Unless a man is acting in response to reports, such as that of a garden invasion by a wild pig, his search is often quite generalized and it is not unusual for him to cover 16 to 24 km (10 to 15 mi) in a day, through rough, untracked, and steep terrain. A man searches the ground for spoor, food remains, feces, wallows, nests, and disturbances indicating a burrow. The trunks of standing trees are examined for claw marks. Tracks may be followed and feces examined for information about the immediate diet and feeding place of the animal. Fruit-bearing trees and shrubs are also sought out and those close to fruiting are noted for such future action as the building of a ground blind or arboreal hide, or a moonlit ambush. At the same time the stalker is alert to movement in the undergrowth and the canopy of the forest, listens for calls, and is ready to be distracted long enough to stalk a single lizard or small bird. This phase of the hunting process has been labelled "scanning" by Laughlin (1966:306–7) and "searching mode" by the animal behaviorist Timbergen (1960).

I have observed kills and had others described to me soon after their accomplishment that appear to have been a matter of luck: the hunter, wandering aimlessly through the forest, stumbled over or flushed an animal which, after recovering his composure, he shot or clubbed to death. This is, however, a superficial impression. For one thing, the hunter chooses an area to search and, in a general way, has expectations about the kinds of animals that belong there. Thus, he may have chosen to stalk within or on the fringes of a settlement hoping to pick up a wild pig. Moreover, once a choice has been made, a hunter's knowledge of plant and animal associations, habitat preferences, feeding habits, and landscape will shape his course. He will examine habitats that he has visited before or that are similar to others visited many times before. Thus almost any Miyanmin can cite the names of fruiting trees most important for locating a particular animal. (Some of this information is presented in table 6-2.) They are like good poker players, well aware of the probabilities associated with the different biotic associations dealt to them. Thus a single informant was able to recite, virtually without repeating himself, the vernacular names of 80 different trees, along with their particular uses—including the fauna (if any) that might be found feeding on their fruits, leaves, or buds.

Table 6-2. Miyanmin View of Food Preferences of Selected Terrestrial
and Arboreal Game Animals

| ANIMAL | | FOOD SOURCE | | |
Vernacular	Scientific	Vernacular	Scientific	Notes
kobol	Casuarius bennettii	biyal	Palmae	palm fruit
el-halap	Sus scrofa	ulep	Pangium edule	fruit eaten on ground
		wem	Ficus spp.	
no-kwiyam	Phallanger gymnotis	beral	Cyclosorus sp.	fern tips
wan-afwel	Ptilinopus sp.	gomo	Litsea sp.	dove; ripe tree berries
no-sanuk	Rattus ruber	imen	Colocasia esculenta	cultiva- ted taro
no-temeya	Melomys lorentzi	boliyam	Gnetum sp.	small tree fruit
no-kwateribo	Uromys caudimaculatus	frim	Palmae	palm fruit
noial	Echimipera kalubu	tiyop	Ficus sp.	fruit on aerial roots
		wan	Dioscerea sp.	wild yam

The way this kind of information is structured, or perhaps more properly, the way the hunter structures his or her choices, is a necessary part of the present account. Accordingly, in the next section the nature of taxonomies, both "scientific" and "folk," will be discussed in order to provide a foundation for an interpretation of some Miyanmin practices.

The Nature of Taxonomies

In science, taxonomies are not merely conventional (or convenient) pigeonholes into which the otherwise disorderly phenomena of a domain of nature may be stuffed. Rather, they are expressions of theory regarding the behavior and material character of the things being classified. Moreover, their relevance is their usefulness in predicting previously undiscovered phenomena and anticipating succeeding theories and experimental or practical results. In this sense scientific taxonomies are maps of segments of the empirical world and the scientist consciously designs experiments in accordance with them.

I argue that "folk" taxonomies[3] have a similar character. While most people (folk) do not practice science in their daily lives (in the sense of consciously subjecting theories to rigorous tests), their behavior in relation to the material world is nevertheless being tested continuously by changes and problems large and small. To the extent that a taxonomy can be shown to coincide with a delimited set of behaviors having effects in the material world—effects that directly bear on the survival of members of a group—the taxonomy itself is being tested, though without volition. In other words, the taxonomy is an attribute of this segment of the behavior stream. It is part of an adaptive strategy, and all the attributes of it have developed and changed together. Mystical theories and assumptions about the world that are often the concomitants of such taxonomies are not relevant to this problem because the test consists of the payoffs and environmental effects of the strategies. Of course the same thing can happen in science when the assumptions or theories embedded in a taxonomy may ultimately prove to be erroneous while the regularities established by it are true.[4]

From the standpoint of the individual adhering to some variant of his group's adaptational behavior pattern, a taxonomy is a map of the empirical world. As Bulmer and Tyler have observed (in relation to Karam frog taxonomy),

> It provides a framework for storing and communicating information which enables [the people] to go at the right time to the right locations and search the most likely host plants to enjoy fair prospects of success in collecting a meal: and to know when calls are worth following up, and when not (1968:378).

Of course, the individual applying such a taxonomy is not just "cognizing," but is using a strategy which may or may not be appropriate or successful in each instance. Direct personal experiences in life situations are part of the learning schedules of all individuals, but behavior in response to those situations which are new to the individual tend to be formed in accordance with the map. In the long run this is the test to which all taxonomies and their associated strategies are subjected. I also expect to find some concordance between language and behavior on this level.

Approaches to the problem of ethno-taxonomies that compare them with the extant scientific taxonomies, or concern themselves with testing native biological knowledge and theory against scientifically generated knowledge and theory, beg the question of the nature of these taxonomies. It is not just the fact that the theory of evolution is not a part of native cosmology that would render such an approach to faunal taxonomy unreasonable (see Bulmer and Tyler 1968:335, 377). A scientific taxonomy and the full scope of

Western scientific knowledge would serve a person poorly in a tropical forest unless he were on a grant. Even then, an evolutionary taxonomy and the information ordered by it doesn't help the field anthropologist studying the interaction of people and the faunal community. The oft-noted consistency (Diamond 1966, 1972:90) between lower-order folk taxa and the species of the biologist cannot be explained by appealing to the "intention" (Bulmer and Tyler 1968:375) of the person applying the taxonomy when this cannot be reliably retrieved. An "observer orientation" leads to the hypothesis that lower-order folk taxa of the zoological domain may correspond more closely to what are called "ecological species" (Huxley 1964:270). Ecological species involve ad hoc, but not arbitrary, discriminations on the part of a biologist formulating them, and are sometimes reducible to biological species or subspecies. The discrimination is made on the basis of the occupation by an assumed Mendelian population of a particular ecological niche in a specific geographic area.

Consider the classic taxonomic problem, "When does a robin cease to be a robin and become something else?" There are several possible answers to this question, depending on the assumptions adopted. If the criteria of morphological species are applied, one kind of answer will result, but it won't be that relevant to the issues at hand. The criterion attached to the ecological species concept is more to the point but is still logically connected to evolutionary theory. It seems that the best analogy, perhaps a homology, is Timbergen's (1960) "specific search image" concept, which directs us to answer the question from the standpoint of a predator feeding on robins.

The hypothesis underlying the "specific search image" concept is that predators are capable of learning certain characteristics of their prey, particularly those which would facilitate locating and/or capturing the prey. Some biologists employ a "calorific" reinforcement paradigm: "Predators with the ability to learn may change their diet to reflect the relative energy reward values associated with different prey species" (McNaughton and Wolf 1973:258). Aside from giving the picture a cognitive slant that is relevant to my argument, the methodology does not differ markedly from MacArthur and Pianka's (1966; see chapter 2). From this perspective, a robin ceases to be a robin when it can no longer be identified and hunted like a robin. Is there any experimental evidence from behavioral psychology, preferably based on work with predators, to support the notion of an "energy reward"? Or is it the case that predators will lunge at anything that moves, large or small?

Linguistic approaches to ethno-taxonomy formulate questions about the morpho-syntactic and formal semantic status of the terms involved and attempt to deal with perception working from this level, but these do not help too much in formulating questions about adaptation (except insofar as they direct our attention to a "problem"). An apt analogy is the interface between molecular and population biology. The point is that the speech patterns of a linguistic community do not exist in a void any more than the molecules carrying the genetic code. Some attributes assume their formal character as a result of the experience of the individual speaker, including socialization and the past adaptive and continuing experience of members of the group.

Information discussed in later chapters shows that Miyanmin local groups possess very large group territories in relation to their numbers. Due to the very low population densities of these groups, only a fraction of their territories will ever be exploited for horticulture, disturbance is minimal, and diversity is high. Thus all group territories embrace large tracts of undisturbed primary forest, smaller areas of second growth in various stages of succession (but no grassland), and considerable ecological zonation from the standpoint of altitudinal range, topography, and drainage (chapter 4). Over the greater Miyanmin area biotic associations range from riverine in the north to montane in the south. Hence, from direct individual experience (and socially transmitted learning) most Miyanmin are familiar with a wider range of plants and animals—and diverse associations—than is characteristic of many groups (or linguistic communities) of similar size (ca. 2000) elsewhere in New Guinea. Opportunities for exploitation of this range are very great indeed.[5] Accordingly, the Miyanmin "problem of information storage and retrieval" in this domain is unusually great.

Miyanmin higher-order faunal taxonomy, which is presented in table 6-3, corresponds to important behavioral categories; that is, it is more felicitous to give them behavioral glosses than ones keyed to kinds of animals or their characteristics. In a real sense, they are relationship terms and they relate to the kind of behavior characteristic of the relationship between people and the fauna concerned. The terms discussed have in particular to do with the acquisition and consumption of the prey.

Faunal Taxonomy and the Food Quest

I have isolated two cross-cutting taxonomies that circumscribe the zoological domain. In accordance with the foregoing argument, I characterize them behaviorally, calling them respectively "quest" and "consumption" taxonomies. In this section I argue that the two taxonomies taken together constitute an important mechanism for managing options in the resource management sphere in addition to serving as an "information storage and communications" system.

The quest taxonomy conforms closely to Western scientific notions of biological taxonomy because it is hierarchical and binomial in most respects.[6]

This taxonomy is presented in table 6-3, which lists 10 primary taxa encompassing the domain of potentially edible creatures, along with their "simple" animal glosses for purposes of identification and more detailed behavioral glosses respecting both search and kill modes.[7]

In normal speech these nouns are usually combined with secondary, and in some cases tertiary, terms to form sets, e.g., /noial/=bandicoot (*Echimipera kalubu*), /map-ngongol/=a frog (*Xenobatrachus sp.*), and /no-tekep-asul/= a "spotted" cuscus with a particularly valued pillage (*Phallanger atrimaculatus*). The morphological characteristics of the fauna probably have more to do with the discriminations made on the level of secondary or tertiary taxa than on the higher level under discussion. For example, in species of commonly hunted mammals and birds displaying extreme sexual dimorphism, each sex form will have a different terminal term. In other words, terminal taxa are "specific search images" in Timbergen's (1960) terms.[8] On the primary level the discriminations that seem to be implicit relate to characteristics of habitat and search modalities for putting the hunter within killing range of the quarry. As Loughlin notes, "Getting close to an animal represents the major investment of the primitive hunter and explains the extensive attention given to childhood programming and to the location of game" (1966:309). Given a limited but effective killing technology, two kinds of bows with a variety of specialized arrows, various snare and trap designs, and ad hoc clubs (to be discussed later in this chapter), the greater payoff comes from intellectual activity aimed at "delivering" the hunter, rather than the killing stroke (the "stalking phase" in Laughlin's terms [308–9]).

The consumption taxonomy presented in table 6-4 has a very different character: three primary taxa encompass the entire faunal domain, there is no way to apply "animal identification" glosses, and the behavioral glosses have to do with food preferences, taboos, and prejudices or aversions. In isolation, the categories are ethnographic curiosities, more examples of irrational or uneconomic attitudes toward food resources. Many of the reported examples of this apparent irrationality—implying, as they do, that local people are misusing their resource base and that "First Worlders" could do better—have been reexamined from an ecological standpoint and positive adaptive values hypothesized for them.[9] This is yet another case.

At issue are the Miyanmin categories *awem*, meaning "sacred" or "taboo," and *misiyam*, meaning "bad." An obvious approach is to look at some of the restricted or unsavory species piecemeal and seek some "objective" rationale for as many individual creatures as possible. The *awem* animals are not too difficult in this respect. For one thing, they are eaten by someone. Their role in the symbolism of sex and age ranking in the male initiation cycle is described in chapter 8.

More troublesome are members of the *misiyam* category, particularly the

Table 6-3. Miyanmin Zoological Quest Categories with Behavioral
Glosses

Taxon	Actor Type	Search Mode	Kill Mode
/el/	men	One or two pick up spoor of animals in deep forest or garden area and stalk in a loop until it can be assumed to be at rest.	Ambush-drive, large group forms line towards which quarry is driven. Shoot at close range (and/or climb tree). Capture young and place in custody of women.
	women/ children	A group formed to drive animal under control of men. Raise tamed young.	
/kobol/	men	Locate current feeding place and build blind on ground in proximity to it.	Wait in blind during day for animal to feed and shoot from ambush. Capture young and lure adult by mimicking young. Club to death.
"cassowaries"	women	Raise & tame captive young.	Blow to head.
/aning/	men/ boys	Search favored aquatic habitats; pools, undercut boulders, upper creeks during high water, etc.	Fish may be shot opportunely (stalked) or stunned with rotenone poison (from Derris sp.) in still water, sometimes created by damming. Eels flushed from hiding place in deep water and driven to ambush in shallows where shot. Conical basket traps used for fish by most northern groups.
/wan/ "birds & bats"	men	Search for appropriate trees where fruiting is imminent or locate bathing pool. Build hide within ten feet of ambush site, lure with calls.	Stalk and shoot opportunistically in low vegetation. Wait in blind at dawn or late in day and shoot until arrows expended.
		Locate nest site of larger bird (as a hollow tree).	Beset in nest or chop down tree and capture or kill.
/no/ "various small mammals"	men	Search for current nocturnal feeding site or diurnal nesting place (sometimes with dog). Fruit may be set as lure.	Ambush at feeding site at night when moonlight permits; stalk and shoot opportunistically or beset in or flush from nest during day.
	women	Dog taken to garden or foraging site and allowed to search.	Dog flushes small mammals which are beset or chased and beaten to death.
/map/ "frogs &"	women	Go to area of known domain of animal and search sometimes using return calls to locate (for frogs).	Catch by hand, (tadpoles netted) or kill with club; may also be kept alive and killed by cooking.

"turtles"	men	Turtles (common at low altitudes) found during general stalking/fishing.	Capture by hand, killed during cooking.
/inap/	women	"Look surprised and scream."	Kill with stick.
"snakes"	men	"Look surprised," or search in known habitats (such as natural cane stands for pythons).	Kill with stick or (pythons) capture by hand and shield head.
/tim/ "lizards"	men/ boys	Search on sunny day (particularly following extended cloudy period) for animal sunning on exposed trees and rocks.	Shoot directly or drive with thrown missiles into range and shoot or chase and club to death.
/kuruan/ "various insects & crabs"	women/ children	Most are searched for in microhabitats associated with particular stage of garden succession. Children hunt others systematically.	Exposed with cutting/digging tools and taken by hand. Children shoot with toy bows and arrows.
/til/ "dogs"	men	Almost mythic wild dogs occur in areas remote from human habitation and not hunted systematically. Village dogs trained and used in deep forest hunting.	None taken.
	women	Village dogs are true domesticates; women most concerned with care and use in high-altitude zone.	Occasionally beaten to death with a club.

animals related to or resembling edible creatures. Questioning informants does not help to negate the element of irrationality. For example, there is the case of the dog. The common village dog *til* is considered *misiyam* although the wild dog *til-satil* is *awem*. The latter is so rare in any event that I was only able to find one very old man who claimed to have eaten it. The unfitness of the village dog is attributed to the fact that it eats feces, including human feces. The same explanation is applied to the common village rat *no-sanuk* (*Rattus ruber*) which men consider inedible, but which is eaten by women and children in fair quantity. When it is shown that village pigs also eat feces, the inconsistency is admitted but irresolvable. An objective view might be that a hunting people, dependent on dogs, would do well *not* to kill and eat them any more than use their bows as firewood. But the Miyanmin claim that their dogs are "useless" (this claim is analyzed later), and the issue at the moment is supposed to be rationality. Similarly, we might argue that the inconsistent point of view concerning the village rat has the effect of directing a regular and significant increment of high-quality protein to women and children who need

Table 6-4.   Miyanmin Zoological Consumption Categories

Taxon	Associated Consumption Behavior
/kuruan/*	All food of animal origin the consumption of which is without restriction.
/awem/#	Ritually restricted animal food.
/misiyam/+	Animals and animal products considered unfit for human consumption without supernatural implications.

* The word /kuruan/ also appears in the quest taxonomy, table 7-2 as the name of a residual but coherent group of small fauna.
# See chapter 8 for details concerning ritually restricted foods.
+ The common earthworm is the most prominent here, in its own right, for its implications in the food chains of other "bad" animals, or by analogy.

it the most. But this too has nothing to do with consciousness because it is not recognized.

There are certain insects, reptiles, and molluscs that can be shown to be inedible because of specific poisonous or noxious elements, but these cases are just as difficult to pinpoint. For one thing, it is not easy for an ethnographer to collect such animals, as he is dependent on the aid of the very people who carry the food prejudices being investigated. They do not normally hunt and kill the animals involved and in some instances they may not bring themselves to do so.

In the field I publicized a list of the animals I was interested in adding to my collection of frogs and lizards. Those which people normally catch and eat were no problem at all. In fact it was recreational for me to go frog hunting with a group of young women from the hamlet where I made my home. But with the list narrowed in this way, I could do little more than mention my interest in more "exotic" fauna from time to time.

One day a young male acquaintance came to tell me that he and some friends had found a *tim-brebo* (*Gekko vittatus*). I was already acquainted with this common lizard as well as Miyanmin attitudes toward it. While I was relaxing in my house one evening before I was truly interested in the topic, one dropped at my feet. It is a medium-sized lizard, perhaps 30 to 40 mm, from nose tip to tail point, with pink skin and golden eyes. I knew that the Miyanmin found it disgusting just to talk about this animal. I discovered this when, while questioning an older informant, a 12-year-old boy asked us to stop talking about the *brebo* because it made him sick.

I urged the fellow who had come to tell me about the lizard to go back and capture it while I laid out my preservation equipment. Without further elucidation, he said that I'd better come myself. So I followed him to an old house that was being torn down. Four other young men were standing around, one gripping a small bird bow and pronged arrow more or less in readiness. They pointed to the lizard lying motionless on a roof beam a few feet above our heads. I urged the armed man to shoot it. He drew his bow, took aim and then relaxed saying, "Ugh, I can't do it" (or words to that effect). I took the bow and managed to get off a near-perfect shot for my purposes, with the prongs of the arrow bracketing the lizard's neck and embedding themselves firmly in the beam. It was a simple matter to free the arrow with the lizard wedged, squirming, between the prongs. I inspected it at close range and then looked at my companions who visibly paled. I ended up chasing five young men across the village, brandishing the lizard on the end of the arrow. And I didn't even have to pay for it before I pickled it to be sent to Fred Parker in Daru.

While this anecdote indicates the strength of the sentiments involved, the incident did not contribute greatly to my understanding of the aversion. With the collection available for identification I was able to ascertain that there was nothing toxic or dangerous about the animal and that other New Guineans eat it (Fred Parker, Personal Communication). The only fragmentary "ecological" explanation I might venture on this level would call attention to the gekko's niche as an insectivore and the connection of this with roof preservation, but this doesn't satisfy the lust of an unreconstructed "systems monger." In other words, although I wouldn't utterly reject the "just so" stories offered, the piecemeal approach does not strike me as being too fruitful. Moreover, it is likely that any successful search for logical (e.g., rational) consistency will be the analyst's own delusion. It is perhaps more credible to show that a particular behavioral routine is associated with a larger pattern of sentiments and perceptions that have equilibrational effects.

This is illustrated, albeit speculatively, in table 6-5, where the two taxonomies have been combined in an observation matrix correlating quest and consumption taxa in terms of numbers of secondary taxa. When the data are presented in this way, an interesting pattern emerges involving the allocation of hunting and collecting labor by men and women. The matrix summarizes the relative rank of the animals with respect to the advantages expected from hunting members of each class. The *awem* and *misiyam* taxa mark the categories of fauna with the lowest payoffs. And animals in highly ranked taxa are most worth hunting systematically, are primarily the focus of male activity, and bear the fewest negative weights. It is also suggestive that the largest animals, plus the small but very abundant ones, rank very high. On the other hand the lower-ranking fauna are worth exploiting only sporadically or as an adjunct to other activities, are more the focus of hunting by women or children, and bear the largest proportion of negative weights.[10] When looked

Table 6-5.   Quest and Consumptions Categories Correlated by Number
of Secondary Taxa (Frequencies Based on 1968-69 Collections)

'Quest' Taxon	Total Secondary Taxa	/kuruan/	/awen/	/nisiyan/
/el/	2	2	0	0
/kobol/	2	2	0	0
/no/	21	17	3	1
/wan/	46	35	8	3
/inap/	12	9	1	2
/map/	7	5	1	1
/tin/	11	6	2	3
/aning/	7	3	4	0
/til/	2	0	1	1
/kuruan/	6	6	0	0

at in this way, Miyanmin faunal taxonomy is an important attribute of prey
selection and resource management.

Woman the Hunter

The Miyanmin claim that hunting, like warfare, is the exclusive male sphere, a
common statement by and about hunting peoples. Earlier in chapter 2 and at
the beginning of this chapter, I presented a male-oriented characterization of
hunting as a "game" and as a nearly full-time activity of men. Claims
concerning woman's preeminence in the gardens are not as strong.

The male stereotype is belied by the substantial contribution of animal
foods women make to the diet of the group. It is true that their pattern of
hunting or collecting of game is different from that of men. As is noted in the
previous section, most of this is secondary to gardening and foraging of wild
vegetable foods and other materials, and less time is spent at it. Moreover, the
fauna taken by women tend to be creatures of village, garden, edge, and
second growth: small rat (*Melomys spp., Rattus ruber*), certain possum
(*Dactylopsila trivigata*), bandicoot (*Echimipera kalubu*), frog, land crab and
various insects and their larvae are more representative of the woman's bag.
They are also the items least visible to the observer of subsistence activity.
Women and children tend to consume them away from the village with only
an occasional surplus returned to the various hamlets (there to be seen,

weighed, or counted by the ethnographer). I was able to get a limited amount of data on the small mammal harvest only by offering to buy people's garbage at a standard price independent of the size, rarity, or attractiveness of animal kinds.

This can be made more concrete by focusing on *no* mammals taken during one representative three-week period: 12 women killed 65 small mammals, as compared with only 51 reported killed by 28 men. It is true that, in terms of the weight of meat produced, the male contribution is greater but so is their expenditure of labor for hunting these animals. The distribution by species and sex of hunter is displayed in table 6-6.

As indicated in chapter 5, the division of labor by sex in most spheres is flexible. Miyanmin men do not have as strong a view of their prerogatives as that reported for other New Guinea peoples. For example, in *am-nakai* groups, married men spend as much time weeding gardens as their wives. The widely reported taboo on women handling bows and arrows is absent among the Miyanmin. On a long walk women often carry their husband's weapons while he carries an infant on his shoulders. Men tell condescending stories about women hunting small mammals with bow and arrow or going into bird hides with their husbands.

Table 6-6.   Hunting Returns of *No* Mammals for Three Weeks in February, 1969, by Sex of Hunter and Kill Modes

Species	Sample Size	M.	F.	Dog	Hand/ Stick	Bow & Arrow	No Data
Zaglossus bruijni	1	-	-	-	-	-	1
Myoictis melas	2	-	1	1	1	-	1
Dendrolagus spp.	2	2	0	0	0	2	-
Dorcopsis vanheurni	1	1	0	0	0	1	-
Phalanger orientalis	4	3	1	1	1	3	-
P. gymnotis	7	1	4	4	2	1	2
Dactylopsila trivirgata	1	0	1	1	1	0	-
Hyomys goliath	1	1	0	0	0	1	-
Uromys caudimaculatus	3	3	0	1	0	3	-
U. sp.?	2	0	2	2	0	0	-
Echimipera kalubu	35	24	6	6	3	24	5
Melomys spp.	38*	15	23	30	28	10	0
Rattus ruber	28*	1	27	19	23	4	0
TOTALS	125	51	65	65	59	49	9

* Despite their large numbers these small rats are probably more underrepresented than any other species.

Use of Dogs

The craven, starved, mangy, noisy New Guinea dog is a prominent inhabitant of every Miyanmin settlement. It is a persistent scavenger and thief and is frequently beaten especially at (human) mealtimes. It is also battered by the village pigs with which it competes for garbage rather than affection. The Miyanmin of the middle elevations claim that their dogs are useless in the hunt; and for a long time I accepted this opinion at face value. A number of facts and observations finally led me to question the statement, or at least my interpretation of it.

When men talk about hunting in this regard, they mean hunting the most important game animal, the wild pig. The data presented in table 6-6 show that dogs figured in 52 per cent of the kills of *no* mammals and that in this respect they are mainly (though not exclusively) the hunting tool of women. These observations are reinforced by some anecdotes.

During my first rainy season with the Miyanmin the oldest man in my hamlet was visited by his little brother, a man in his forties who was residing uxorilocally with Hoten on the Usake River. He brought on his visit five of the fattest, sleekest, sauciest New Guinea dogs you would ever hope to see. People came from nearby hamlets just to look at them, and I was told in very positive terms that these were real hunting dogs. Working as a pack they were capable of running down, surrounding, and immobilizing a wild pig long enough for a group of hunters to approach and shoot it. The problem was that persistent attempts in my area to employ them in this fashion failed. They apparently can only operate in the more open gallery forest or flatter topography characteristic of the lowlands, such as in the middle May-Usake River area.

Given the sorry state of the dogs in my area and their poor public repute, I was always surprised at the joy which greeted a litter of puppies. "After all, what do they need more of these things for?" The following is the pattern I discovered.

Each family tends to maintain one dog, usually a bitch, with each hamlet having only one male dog. It is—and this is hard to believe—even skinnier and mangier than the rest. It is nothing more than an ambulatory penis, maintained just this side of death's door for one purpose. Whenever a bitch is in heat he services her. Once the bitch has her pups she is ready to do her job. This is to go hunting at night and bring her prey back to her pups in the hamlet, something she would not otherwise do. The women of the household confiscate her bag. Hence, the value of puppies.

Hunting Technology

All killing weapons are employed at close range. This obviously applies to the variety of digging and walking sticks and other pieces of wood employed as bludgeons in almost half the cases tabulated in table 6-5. It may not seem as obvious for archery, but the most effective fire is delivered within a range of around three or four m (approximately 10 ft).

Three reasons can be cited for this. First, the long bow *anok* used to kill large animals such as pig, kangaroo, cassowary, and people, is not an accurate long-range weapon, especially in combination with relatively heavy unflesched arrows. According to Longman and Walrond (1967:292), "The length of a bow should be proportional to the arrow to be used with it, and also to its own weight; a short bow will give a sharper cast than a long one, but to shoot a 29-inch arrow out of a short bow would be dangerous to the bow." Accordingly, the advantage of a long bow is the acceleration—and thus the force—it can impart to a heavy projectile. Second is the density of vegetation, especially in second growth where much of the hunting is conducted. As Bicchieri (1969:67) has noted, "Visual contact with the prey is difficult because the density of the forest precludes it." Third, stalking and firing at long range is not only impractical but is dangerous with wild pigs. Older, more experienced hunters in an ambush drive withhold their fire until the careening pig is almost on top of them before delivering a single blow with a heavy broadbladed arrow. Younger, less cool hunters are prone to fire prematurely and inaccurately. They often miss completely, but sometimes wound the pig and render it very dangerous. When an effective blow is delivered other hunters rush to deliver other arrows at very close range. The atmosphere enveloping a successful or nearly successful pig hunt is one of tension and excitement, with many people actually shaking after the action has passed. It is combat and, due to the similarity of the subjective experience, the Miyanmin use the word in referring to it (cf. Gardner 1981, who translates it, inaccurately I believe, as *war*).

Arrows can be cast accurately under awkward circumstances. During a hunt for *no* mammals we discovered a pair of cuscus (*Phallanger orientalis*), the dark brown male *aliken* and the buff colored female *ibim*, feeding high in two adjacent trees in an old second growth tract. A young man shinnied up another tree to a point some 30 feet off the ground and, holding on with his feet, shot the *aliken* behind the ear with a barbed palmwood pointed arrow at a range of four or five meters (15 feet or so). To get the *ibim*, the tree in which it fed was downed and after a short chase it was seized by the tail, spitting like an angry cat, and clubbed over the head with a hunk of wood picked up on the spot. The young it carried was taken as a pet but it escaped from our camp during the night.

The technology of bird hunting is noteworthy. A hide or blind is a prominent feature. It may be constructed on the ground near a feeding or bathing place, or high in the trees near a feeding site. In the trees, the construction technique is particularly demanding. At from 6 to 30 m (20 to 100 ft) off the ground, two trees, one of them fruiting, are warped together. To accomplish this people use a tackle of heavy cane of up to four parts, with the falls leading around the trunks of the two trees (the Miyanmin, of course, do not have blocks). As soon as the trees have been drawn closely together, the cane falls are stopped off and used as the base of the shooting platform. A rough floor is laid and a dome-shaped framework of widely spaced poles built over it. This frame is thatched with ferns to produce an opaque screen. The hide is then ready.

A special bow and arrows set is used in conjunction with the blind. The bow *(gemanok)* is a short one, approximately half the length of a long bow. The accompanying arrows *(gem)*, a set of between 20 and 30, have short thin shafts and are mostly pronged, though several arrows with single bamboo blades are included in the set for the occasional large bird that may come to feed. Typically, two men use the blind early in the morning and late in the day. They fasten their weapons to a length of cane secured to the blind, climb the trunk of the tree using the lianas growing on it, and then haul their weapons up after them.

They sit in the hide with weapons at the ready and one man attempts to call the birds. The Miyanmin claim the ability to lure more than 50 species of birds and readily identify those which cannot be lured. Calls of specific birds heard in the vicinity may be made and answered, or many calls may be made in a string in order to, as they say, give the impression that a lot of birds have already come to feed. The hunters shoot as soon as the first bird alights within range. The fern covering provides an adequate screen without interfering with the shot. An arrow is slowly poked through the screen as the bow is drawn, and the birds seem not to notice even when a hit is scored and a bird is borne flapping down to the ground by the weight of the arrow. The men continue shooting until all of their arrows are expended or the birds cease to feed. Then, descending from the blind, they collect their bag and retrieve their arrows. Most birds are dressed and eaten on the spot, so that, as with the collecting activities of women, it is difficult to measure the payoff from bird hunting back at the village. The only times I ever saw birds taken in this fashion brought back to the hamlet involved visitors from other parishes who were obliged to share the bag with their hosts.

By the late 1970s shotguns and other introduced items were common in Miyanmin communities. The impact on hunting has not been as great as might be inferred. For one thing, the number of shotguns permitted to a community by authorities is limited to two, procedures and cost make them difficult to maintain or replace, and ammunition is expensive relative to the nominal cash budgets of villagers. For another, people aver that archery is superior to firearms in many hunting applications and that the introduction of new arrow technology has been at least as significant. Today, everyone has steel-pointed arrows, heavy broad-bladed pig arrows and small-pronged arrows for lesser game.

A frequently overlooked dimension of modernization is that technological progress as conventionally defined may be fostered, not through the introduction of superior finished goods, but rather by establishing junkheaps! When people return from contract labor or even a visit to the small administrative center at Telefomin they bring scrap metal and sometimes finished arrow points if they have managed to gain access to a shop with a grinding wheel. Barrel hoops, umbrella ribs, automobile leaf springs, coat hangers, and construction rods are common sources. This is in addition to the store goods, transistor radios, clothing, flashlights, lanterns, and modest hords of currency (or passbooks) also brought home.

A principal effect of steel-pointed arrows in pig hunting is to reduce the need for accuracy. Formerly, a killing blow with a bamboo point required a shot under the shoulder to the pig's heart or vascular region which would cause the animal to bleed to death. That is still desirable, but a head shot with a steel point can shatter the cranium. People say that this is more devastating than a shotgun.

Shotguns are useful for hunting birds, particularly terrestrial ones such as cassowary, bush turkey, and quail. This closely parallels the use of shotguns by our own recreational hunters and the case says something about "appropriate technology."

Characteristics of Game Animals

As Raymond Chaplin has noted, "Man's exploitation of a wild population is governed by his needs, his technical skill, and *the biology and behavior of the animal population*" (1969:234; emphasis mine). Our appreciation of the role of settlement pattern, movement, and hunting technique in successful hunting requires an understanding of the fauna and their characteristics. Yet the required information is relatively sparse. Most studies of New Guinea mammals are taxonomic. Information on habitat, reproduction, food preference, and other behavioral characteristics is patchy. Although this situation has improved somewhat since I first became interested in the problem (see particularly Dwyer's work), my knowledge of the lives of animals is incomplete and my inferences are limited and speculative in some cases (see Bulmer 1969:303).

Five kinds of information and data have been used for the analysis which follows:

1. My own observations. These consist of trapping records involving mainly rodents, collection records for variously sized samples of most mammals, and dissection records of reproductive status also mainly for rodents. The reservation here is that I am an admitted "handbook" field and laboratory biologist.

2. The reports of Miyanmin informants and assistants. As Bulmer's pioneering work has shown (1968:621ff; Bulmer and Tyler 1968:346; Majnep and Bulmer 1977), these kinds of data beg to be verified in detail and are often both accurate and relevant to the work of anthropologists and biologists (see also Rand and Gilliard 1970:19).

3. Scientific studies of the same mammals (e.g., Dwyer 1975; Hyndman 1982) or related ones of Australia and New Guinea (e.g., Cremer 1969; Calaby 1966; Brongersma 1958; Bennett 1860; Frith 1969; Griffiths 1947; Guiler 1958; Hitchcock 1964; Laurie 1952; Mayr 1932; Mohr 1947, 1956; Ride 1970; Tate 1951, 1952; Taylor et al. 1973, 1982; Troughton 1967a, 1967b; Van Deusen 1960, 1966, 1971, 1972; Van Deusen et al. 1969). The former need not be accepted as "definitive" in the absence of replication. The latter must be used with care, or merely as "background" because the adaptations of even closely related mammals differ in significant ways.

4. Pertinent studies from other world areas make a more general contribution, addressing questions about tropical plant and animal associations, the interaction of agriculture and wildlife, people-animal competition, and the like (e.g., Cook 1959; Ellerman 1966; Harrison 1955, 1957, 1958, 1962a, 1962b, 1962c; Harrison et al. 1950; Hartman 1952; Kauie 1966; Sakagami 1961; Tevis 1956).

5. Personal communications from mammalogists and others who are familiar with New Guinea fauna.

These restrictions are acceptable in that the objective here is not to summarize what is known about these animals but rather to extract the factors that are useful in isolating a system and defining variables. The immediate task is to classify the interactions of people and fauna using pertinent informations about human activity and the characteristics of the animals. The effects of human activities on animals and people's strategies appropriate to their exploitation and management are of particular interest (see N. Dyson-Hudson 1971:24–26 for a similar approach).

It would be ideal to build population models of the wild and domesticated fauna for any type of exploitation or resource management regime if there were sufficient information about the animals and the people in question. Chaplin (1969) presents a straightforward example of the kind of thinking required:

The amount of time required to capture an animal is not proportionate to its size; thus in its quest for food man tends to exert a choice for the largest ungulates available that are consistent with his needs, abilities, and his efforts. Depending on relative abundance however the same quantity of meat may be more easily obtained from several animals of a smaller species. Further some animals can survive much higher cropping rates than others (236–37).

Similarly, we can recognize other considerations on the game or prey side of the relationship. According to Timbergen (1960),

> The many variables that make up the odds than an animal will be captured by a predator—the prey risk—is determined in part by the availability of food and cover to the prey, its movements, activity, habits, size, strength, age and escape reactions. . . . [T]here is a strong interaction between predation and cover. Prey that occupy secure habitats with good cover are much less vulnerable to predation. . . . (111–12).

The interaction of people and fauna can be examined analytically as the result of people's social, behavioral, and spatial characteristics (discussed in later chapters), and the characteristics of the fauna. In reviewing field data and other sources of information on faunal characteristics, I have paid particular attention to feeding and nesting habits, diurnal and nocturnal activity patterning, migrality,[11] sociality, fecundity, density, mobility, and seasonality. The latter, which can involve cyclical changes in abundance of game, habitat selection, food preference, and breeding, appears to be particularly important and therefore merits detailed discussion.

Seasonality

Seasonality is a complex phenomenon of debatable implications for the study of human behavior and adaptation in the humid tropics (Morren 1979, 1981b; Gardner 1981). It is often taken to refer to the natural environmental flux determined by the movement of the earth relative to the sun: variation in rainfall, cloud, solar radiation, and temperature. This in turn patterns such biotic phenomena as leaf fall, flowering, fruiting, and primary production of plants, as well as changes in activity pattern, abundance, habitat preference, location, reproduction, and growth of animals. Seasonal changes in the humid tropics, "Where Winter Never Comes" (Bates 1952), may not be apparent to a visitor familiar only with temperate patterns that are different in kind and degree.

Seasonality also has cultural dimensions, directly as an expression of environmental seasonality in the human component of an ecosystem, and indirectly as an effect of other environmentally influenced cultural patterns. When the members of a society explicitly classify seasons, or have other terms with seasonlike glosses for parts of a cycle as do the Miyanmin, they are employing a shorthand label for an environmental interaction pattern or resource management strategy. At least one anthropologist, Colin Turnbull, has claimed (fallaciously, I believe) that the pattern of seasonal shifts of hunting strategy among the Mbuti pygmies is entirely a sociocultural phenomenon (1968). More realistically (and closer to home), Peter Dwyer (1982:180) has attributed seasonal shifts of hunting focus and technique among the Etolo of Papua New Guinea to the labor requirements of agriculture and sago collecting, rather than to a seasonally variable characteristic of wildlife. Nevertheless, the possibility of more direct seasonal influences in New Guinea needs to be closely examined.

The seasonal climatic regime in New Guinea and in the Miyanmin area, along with some of the seasonal characteristics of vegetation and human activity, were described earlier in chapter 4. It is appropriate here to review evidence of the expression of seasonality in the faunal community. I should say at the outset that the evidence is fragmentary but suggestive.

Several published studies and my own field data point to a fairly distinct breeding season for a wide range of animals. This seems to coincide with the rainy season, with breeding reaching a peak at the time of the austral spring. Rand and Gilliard (1967:18) report one such study of birds conducted in southeast New Guinea. Although there was considerable variability among species, most conformed to the pattern described: a peak in breeding can be observed during the period August to November. John Baker (1929:109–14) conducted a study in the New Hebrides which selected one species from each of three faunal groups, a bird (*Zosterops vatensis*, a frugivorous "white eye" dove), a lizard (*Lygosoma kordanum*), and a mammal (*Pteropus geddiei*, a fruit bat). The bird and lizard fit the pattern reported by Rand and Gilliard very well. The bat, however, reaches a breeding peak in January to February. Baker generalizes, "the greatest amount of conception takes place in all three species when the days are getting longer or very soon afterwards (114)."

In reporting the results of the best and most useful research on the biology and behavior of New Guinea mammals to date, Peter Dwyer (1975:35) finds "some correlation between reproduction and the wet season" for certain species of rodents, several of which are also present in my area. Although grassland *Rattus* and *Melomys* breed throughout the year, breeding is reduced during the dry season. In contrast, rainforest species cease breeding entirely during the dry season. In the foothills of the East Mianmin area the identical "grassland species" studied by Dwyer are garden and village species (since there are no grasslands), specifically, *Rattus ruber* and *Melomys rufescens*. The relevant forest species is *Melomys levipes*. The pattern of my own observations, based on the examination of 94 small rats, is similar to Dwyer's. Unfortunately, neither Dwyer nor I were able to get an entire year's run of observations; Dwyer's embraces the period March to December, 1972, my own, January to May, 1981. In addition, I found the breeding pattern of rainforest marsupials to be even more distinct, restricted to the period January to March.

The human pattern of seasonal movement, described in chapter 9, appears to be linked to changes in hunting focus which are, in turn, related to seasonal changes in the local abundance or accessibility of game animals, particularly the wild pig. To summarize, one season is the period of deep forest hunting, keyed to the driest part of the year from approximately June to December, when certain trees are fruiting and the location of pigs and some other game is more predictable. The other season involves a more diffused pattern of hunting and long-range expeditions keyed to the rainiest part of the year from December to June, when wild pigs are discovered in gardens or are sought in lower-altitude zones. During this period, people in general and hunters in particular are more dispersed both within and without their settlement areas and group territories. Again, Dwyer provides some insights. He finds that among the Rofaifo Siane hunting effort is greater in the dry than in the wet season and also during clear rather than rainy conditions. He also finds return for effort greater in the dry season, with the best hunting on wet days in the dry season (Dwyer 1974:215).

Faunal Interaction Classes

As indicated earlier, the aim of this chapter is to classify the fauna according to how they interact with people. The framework for this has five classes of animals defined primarily by the linked criteria of accessibility, local abundance, and the variable impact upon them of human activity. Its implementation, which involves using information on the various animals, will support the isolation of certain variables in the system presented in chapter 3 (which hypothesizes that particular supporting variables involving patterns of movement are linked to the state of particular classes of animals).

The interaction classes and the species assigned to them should not be read as discrete or absolute. Rather, a species is roughly placed along a continuum from relative scarcity and difficulty to abundance and predictability. Thus, where a particular creature belongs on the continuum probably varies in time in a particular place and from place to place under different social and environmental conditions. In other words, there may be something fairly specific to Miyanmin patterns of environmental use; or the situation of the local population in the Hak Valley in 1968 may make the abundance of a particular species population radically different from that seen in, say, 1978. Hence the assignment of a species to a class is imprecise and temporary, based as it is on a consideration of the characteristics of the organism as it interacted with the human activity patterns I observed in the late 1960s. I discuss these effects at the end of chapter 9 under the rubrics of horticulture, village and settlement, and hunting.

Note also that this approach is similar to and compatible with the "resource area" (Dornstreich 1974) or "biotope" (Hyndman 1979, 1982) approaches that have been used to study other hunting peoples of the highland fringe of New Guinea. These approaches (discussed in chapter 4) attempt to isolate microhabitats or broader zones that also correlate with significant human use patterns. They may be operationally differentiated on the basis of habitat association and altitude, focal resource, and/or human control and disruption.

The five classes of animals are:

1. *Rare and difficult* animals are never abundant or accessible in the domains of particular Miyanmin groups, are difficult to observe or catch, and are not hunted systematically.

2. *Relict and removed* animals are rapidly depleted (and reproduce slowly), or are located in zones and areas fairly distant from customary human settlement (e.g., the upper slopes of high mountains). While they may be desired and hunted systematically from time to time, to do so requires temporary long-distance movement.

3. *Reduced* animals are hunted systematically and intensively and, possibly due to the initial abundance of pristine populations in forests or higher reproduction rates, take longer to be depleted in local areas than Class 2 animals. They may also be disrupted by human activity unrelated to hunting. In my judgment the Miyanmin are more likely to eliminate animals by overhunting and disturbance than by habitat destruction.

4. *Fostered (commensal) and tolerant* animals maintain or increase their local abundance due to high fertility, or habitat and food preferences that are appropriate in the presence of human activity, even though they are hunted systematically.

5. *Domesticated* animals are concentrated in human settlements in varying numbers above a minimum. There, they reproduce at least part of the time and are maintained independently of local limiting factors, though limited by human labor inputs.

A selected set of animals, including but not limited to mammals, are assigned to interaction classes in table 6-7.

Rare and Difficult

Although this set of animals was assembled on entirely different grounds, they all are carnivorous/insectivorous. Hence, their relative scarcity makes (thermodynamic) sense in terms of their position in the food web.

The echidna, *Zaglossus bruijni*, is a less specialized relative of the Australian spiny anteater, and feeds on insects, worms, and larvae in soils and rotting wood. All authorities (e.g., Van Deusen 1972:15; Bulmer 1968:304; Griffiths 1968; Anderson and Jones 1967:370; Ziegler 1972:5) and Miyanmin

Table 6-7.   Selected Animal Species by Interaction Class

Class	Species
I. Rare and Difficult	Zaglossus bruijni Myoictes melas Antechinus melanurus Petaurus breviceps Distoechurus pennatus Hydromys chrisogaster Canis familiaris (wild)
II. Relict and Removed	Perorhyctes raffrayana Echimipera clara Phallanger vestitus P. carmelitae P. atremaculatus Pseudochirus corinnae P. cupreus P. forbesi Dendrolagus dorianus D. goodfellowi Dorcopsis vanheurni D. hageni Hyomys goliath Uromys sp. ? Xenuromys barbatus Casusarius casuarius
III. Reduced	P. maculatus Uromys caudimaculatus Melomys lorentzi Pogonomys sp. Sus scrofa (wild) Casuarius bennettii
IV. Fostered	Echimipera kalubu Dactylopsila trivigata Phallanger orientalis P. gymnotis Rattus ruber Melomys rufescens M. levipes
V. Domesticated	Sus scrofa Canis familiaris

informants rate it as uncommon. People may excavate its burrow after discovery by a dog, or more rarely find it abroad in undisturbed forest. Virtually defenseless against people, it is killed with a club or by forcing an arrow prong through the snout to the brain.

Two of the Dasyurids taken in my area are described by Ziegler as "captured only rarely" (*Myoictes*) (1972) or "scarce" (1982:869) and "sparsely distributed" (*Antechinus*) (1972) or "moderately abundant" (1982:869). Both are small, anatomically unspecialized, nocturnal, scansorial insectivores. They do not particularly lend themselves to being lured with baits or trapped using conventional or traditional methods, but they may be taken at feeding places such as crab grounds. I took only one in a trap baited with the fruit of the wild tulip tree (*Gnetum sp.*). Neither is hunted systematically although people will take them opportunistically, for example, when they are found in tree nests during a search for something else. Indeed, they are regarded by the people as fearless, even aggressive creatures, humorously described as "hunting the hunter," fighting back, and killing forest rats of the same or larger size.

Petaurus, the "sugar glider," and the similar but nongliding *Distoechurus* "feather tail" are small Phallangerids (possums) which are also insectivorous, scarce, and captured most commonly in their nests. Winter (1966:530) calls *Petaurus* an "avian predator" and Troughton (1967a:97,101), credits it with the ability to take small rats by pouncing on them from the air and nipping their necks. Another authority, Harrison (1962a:54), claims that *Petaurus* is largely frugivorous. My own experience in attempting to keep one was that it preferred large spiders and beetle larvae and disdained all fruit and vegetables. Either animal may be captured in its nest by day or taken on the ground by a dog at night.

Hydromys is a "medium-sized" fully aquatic water rat with webbed feet. It feeds on crabs, insects and other invertebrates and occasional fish and frogs. According to Menzes (1979:52) it is widespread and common though "rarely seen." Curiously, after 20 trap nights using frogs for bait at waterside sites, I caught one in the forest in a trap baited with sweet potato.

Wild dogs are now very rare in New Guinea. In the 1960s I knew of only one elderly man who claimed to have eaten their flesh. More recently several people have reported hearing their distinctive howls while hunting high on Mount Stolle. I have only seen and heard them myself at the Beijer River Preserve.

Relict and Removed

Few of the animals assigned to this category are scarce in an absolute sense. Rather, they live in zones and areas away from the settlements in the Hak Valley I studied most intensively that are at about 1000m (3000 ft) ASL. Many are common elsewhere. Hence, they are either lowland species (e.g., *Echimipera clara*, certain members of the *Phallanger maculatus* "group," the "standard" cassowary) or are fauna of the mid- to upper-montane zone (the ringtails and kangaroos). The former are accessible to Miyanmin groups living on the middle May River, while the latter must be sought on the slopes of large mountains far from where most people live, such as the Donners or Stolle. The "spotted phallangers" are particularly sought after because their ornately marked fur is valued as sing-sing finery. All are, of course, edible and the kangaroos and the big cassowary are particularly meaty. *Phallanger maculatus* and certain large rodents (*Uromys spp.*) were present in the Hak Valley in the 1960s but are now said to be all but extinct locally.

The phallangers, ringtails, and tree kangaroos are usually discovered and beset in the trees where they rest during the day. Terrestrial kangaroos such as *Dorcopsis spp.* must be stalked or driven, sometimes with the assistance of dogs. Typically, cassowaries are taken from ground hides placed near feeding places or lured with simulated chick calls.

Reduced

The members of this class dwell in rain forest and hill forest up to at least 1500m (4500 ft) ASL, the normal occupation zone for the Miyanmin of the southeast part of their domain. They are particularly desirable game animals, are hunted frequently, and also serve as a rough index of the duration of a given settlement since they decline in number through overhunting (pigs, cassowaries) or habitat disruption ("giant" rat, striped possum, "long-footed" *Melomys*). Contrary to the established literature, the latter, *Melomys lorentzi*, is not "sparsely distributed . . . in open to moderately dense forested areas" (Zeigler 1972:22) and is sympatric with other members of the genus such as *M. levipes* (c.f. Menzes 1979:36). Instead, as a "common" animal of the forest, *M. lorentzi* is probably sensitive to disruption of its habitat. It is, however, abundant and easily found in forests away from gardens and readily taken near its favorite food source, the fruit of *Gnetum sp.* I trapped 12 using either this bait or wild pandanus at sites that were not far (less than one hour, uphill) from the Mianmin Airstrip and village. When a particular tract is disturbed, this rodent is replaced by several other sympatric rodent species (see below).

Because of their size and cultural and nutritional significance, wild pig and cassowary merit separate and more detailed discussion than other members of the *reduced* group.

Wild Pigs. The New Guinea pig, sometimes assigned the subspecific or varietal designation *Sus scrofa papuensis*, is the regional representative of the "true pig" which is distributed, mostly as a domesticate, from Western Europe to China, Japan, India, and Malaysia (Burton 1962:211). It is presumed to have been present in the New Guinea highlands for at least five to six thousand years and possibly as long as ten thousand years (Golson and Hughes 1976; White 1972:142,147; Swadling 1981:44). I would suspect that its earliest presence in the highlands was as a feral animal, although it undoubtedly landed on the coast as a domesticate.

The biology and behavior of pigs as feral (or wild)[12] animals has received only limited attention from specialists. I have reviewed studies of wild pig (*Sus scrofa*) populations from several areas of the world but none from New Guinea (Australia: Tisdell 1982; Pullar 1950, 1953; the U.S.: Wood and Barrett 1979, Wood and Lynn 1977). Notwithstanding limited field research, a number of authorities feel confident enough to generalize about them. In other words, there is a "party line" regarding wild pigs and their behavior (a line I intend to criticize) which will now be described.

Wild pigs (according to this "party line") are terrestrial and omnivorous, eating "anything, animal or plant, that comes their way" (Burton 1962:211). They keep to thick cover, favoring the forest edge or disturbed forest, mixed ecological zones, long grass, scrub, dense reed beds, and secondary forest, rather than deep primary forest (Bulmer 1968a:313; Burton 1962:211). They spend most of their time rooting in the ground for bulbs, roots, insects, and small animals they may find, or they browse on green foliage. As Bulmer asserts "even as a feral beast it appears . . . to be largely symbiotic with man . . . , for man is a prime creator of the pigs' favored habitats and human cultivations provide the richest source of favored food." "The effect of tillage is to insert into the environment patches of concentrated luxuriance which few herbivores can resist" (Chaplin 1969:239).

I have three basic criticisms of this characterization. First, it doesn't conform to my informants' accounts of pig behavior and the rhythm of movement and hunting activity I observed (discussed in chapters 3 and 9 and below). Second, it is inconsistent with accounts of "pig management systems" in other parts of New Guinea in which abundant pig populations can be at least partially supported on natural vegetation or nongarden produce like sago (see Hughes 1970). Third, I am not prepared to assume that, all else being equal, pigs will necessarily favor garden produce over other foods.

My informants say that the wild foods pigs favor, at least in the southern lower-montane zone, are the fruit of such forest trees as *Pasania sp.* and *Leca sp.* which they eat off the ground. These are only abundant seasonally in the drier part of the year between June and August and possibly again in December and January (the actual rhythm of flowering and fruiting of vegetation in New Guinea is not well documented; see Morren 1980a). Pigs seem to prefer such wild foods to garden taro, which is more or less constantly abundant year-round. Thus hunters find wild pigs during the dry season within and on the fringes of primary and old secondary forest. It is only during the rainier part of the year, when these wild foods are not available, that the wild pigs resort to garden produce such as taro. Even at that, garden taro may be pretty far down the list of pigs' food preferences. According to Miyanmin informants, pigs don't like raw taro and when domestic pigs are given taro it is always cooked. My own observations of the aftermath of garden invasions by wild pigs are consistent with this characterization. Although an extensive area may be uprooted, surprisingly little taro is actually eaten; the corms have been merely gnawed at, perhaps without gusto. The situation of sweet potato growers in relation to wild pigs for other parts of New Guinea is possibly quite different because their staple crop makes excellent and carefree pig fodder. Clearly, in order to deal with this kind of problem we have to look at the entire range of wild and cultivated plant foods available in an area for pigs to eat. I would thus qualify Brookfield and White's (1968:47) statement that pigs "may prefer sweet potatoes, but they will happily live on taro, coconuts, and other foods."

As I have argued elsewhere (Morren 1977; Hyndman and Morren n.d.), New Guinea wild pigs become truly commensal with people in montane New Guinea only when, where, and if sweet potato cultivation intensifies and begins to replace taro as the human staple and agricultural dominant. More than likely, this occurred in connection with a "Susian Revolution" when pig husbandry was intensified in response to a long-term decline in wild pig and other game. In the work cited I applied this hypothesis to the problem of prehistoric agricultural change in the highlands. It also appears to describe the situation of the Miyanmin of the Hak Valley in the 1980s where a large settlement has now existed for approximately 20 years. Here, wild pigs are scarce, and the Miyanmin are growing an uncharacteristically large volume of sweet potato and experimenting with more intensive pig husbandry (see chapter 5).

Pigs are apparently wide ranging rather than confined to small home ranges as many of the animals I have already described appear to be. They are said to possess a "weak social structure" (as compared to sheep and goats) (Chaplin 1969:239) but they normally appear in "family parties" or "sounders" (Burton 1962:211) consisting of an adult male, one or more sows, and the young of the latter. I have a feeling that this pattern varies with certain environmental parameters. Pigs occur up to 1700m (5000ft) ASL in New Guinea (Bulmer 1968a) and may go even higher. Their distribution, however, depends on habitat favorableness, which varies inversely with altitude.

It seems that pigs are more numerous and likely to occur in groups in the lower-altitude flood plain forest and more sparse and solitary in the deep forest of higher-altitude zones. Thus, the only time I have "stumbled over" wild pigs, outside of systematic hunting with "experts" or very close to human settlements, is on the lower reaches of some of the major tributaries of the Sepik (the May and August rivers) and the middle Sepik itself. In the area where I spent most of my time, at 650 to 1300m (2000 to 4000ft) ASL, I saw wild pigs only when hunting or in the singular circumstance of a wild boar accompanying a domestic sow back to her village. In the extreme south of the Miyanmin range, single kills of wild pigs (or a sow and several young) are the rule, whereas in the northern lower-altitude area multiple kills are common. In both areas, however, abnormal concentrations of wild pigs may, in the appropriate season, be affected by the establishment of human settlements.

In addition, pigs are reported to breed continuously, with three to twelve piglets per litter, and to have a short generational period (i.e., they mature quickly). Hide's study of domestic pigs in New Guinea (1981:462–68) notes the possibility of a "natural" seasonality of breeding, with a peak of farrowing in the wetter December-to-April period, but is inconclusive because pigs are rigorously managed by their owners who may be selecting the period in relation to the availability of fodder.

Wild pigs are intelligent and wary, difficult to stalk and capable of great ferocity when disturbed, particularly when wounded. Although diurnal, they tend to be active mainly early in the morning or late in the day (Tisdell 1982:394). They are quick of foot and, more often than not, evade stalkers and escape from hunters waiting in ambush. As the largest land animal in New Guinea, aside from people, the pig is also one of the most desirable to hunt. In addition, piglets captured very young are easily tamed, and hand-raised animals, particularly sows and castrated boars, are docile and easy to handle even when fully grown (see chapter 4).

The most common pig hunting tactic among the Miyanmin is the ambush and the ambush drive. Pigs are occasionally taken by individual stalking as well as by luring and trapping.

Most hunts are a response to reports of pigs in a neighborhood. In the rainy season reports often originate in a garden owner's discovery of an invasion with produce uprooted and eaten. Of course, village pigs are capable of and prone to engage in similar acts, but the Miyanmin say that they differentiate between domestic and wild pigs on the basis of the area of the garden damaged and the inferred route of entry. Wild pigs are presumed to enter from the forest side and feed in that area of the garden, whereas domestic pigs are thought to enter on the side of the garden exposed to nearby hamlets.

When the report of a wild pig is received, word for men to assemble is yodeled from hamlet to hamlet. Meanwhile, one or two experienced men will undertake to track the pig. They attempt to pick up its trail at or near the point where its activities were first discovered to determine either its habitual resting place or the point at which it has turned in its tracks. It is on the basis of such assumptions that the experienced stalker will at some point decide to veer off

Plate 6. Shooting at a Wild Pig at the Edge of a Village
Tobacco at right grows beside a house.

the pig's trail and start to slowly work around in a circle. If, during the course of this movement the tracks of the pig are picked up again and are still moving off, then another encircling movement will be attempted. If it can be carried out without discovering the pig's tracks, then it is inferred that the pig has come to rest and will remain so.[13]

The stalkers return to the assembly place of the hunting party and report to the waiting men. Considerable discussion ensues regarding the tactical dispositions appropriate to the situation. When a consensus is reached, the party of ambushers moves off to take up their positions. Shortly afterwards, a party of drivers, consisting of women and older children and led by one or two men, also moves off. Once they have reached a point more or less on the same contour as the pig is presumed to be, they proceed towards it, making a lot of noise, mostly through vocalization. The ambush party takes up a similar position on the other side of the pig, away from the drivers. Men are spaced some 6 to 12 m (20 to 40 ft) apart in the ambush line, waiting with their bows at the ready while also prepared in advance with a personal route of escape. Men often place themselves close to a climbable tree.

If the drive is successful the pig can be heard as it breaks through the low vegetation, grunting and snuffling. If it appears from this that the pig is off the center of the ambush line the men on the flank can sometimes turn it to improve the likelihood of a clean shot at close range. Normally the line itself is not shifted in this situation, but individuals may move in cover to improve their position. The pig seems not to be alert to the threat even when it is close enough to be seen, but instead is bent on escaping the drivers. It is just as likely as not to run directly towards a motionless archer. As described previously, the experienced hunter withholds his fire until minimum range, hoping to deliver a disabling or even killing blow in the vicinity of the heart. I describe the tragic consequences of a nondisabling wound in chapter 8. Otherwise, it is not unusual for a badly wounded pig to be dealt the coup de grace within a short distance of the initial blow, although longer chases do occur.

The pig "belongs" to the hunter delivering the first effective shot; he assumes responsibility for its preparation, contributes the major portion of taro to be cooked with it, and sees to the equitable distribution of cooked meat and taro throughout the local population. He will often carry the undressed carcass of the pig back to the hamlet unassisted.

In the drier part of the year wild pig reports result from a much more wide-ranging pattern of scanning, tracking, and stalking in deep forest. Particular attention is paid to fruiting trees such as those cited earlier. When a feeding site is discovered (depending on its remoteness from settlements), it may take several days before a party of hunters ventures out to exploit it. The prime tactic in deep forest hunting is the encircling drive and the chase, rather than the ambush, with a well-briefed party of hunters attempting to move in on an active feeding site from several directions. Initial contact with a feeding pig will put it to flight, and the hunters are dependent on their speed, mobility, and knowledge of the terrain to surround the pig and take advantage of the momentum of its initial flight. I was never in on the kill in such a hunt because I couldn't keep up with it; I frequently didn't see the main party of hunters for the rest of the day because the chase carried them far beyond the limits of my endurance.

Tempering these idealized accounts is the fact that most such drives are unsuccessful; the pig does not fall so easily into the grip of waiting or encircling men. My own rough tally indicates that only one such hunt in eight or ten pays off. This is because the chain of action and inference I described earlier is a fragile one, and the pig is a shy and elusive animal.

Other hunting tactics are applied less frequently but with occasional success. During the rainy season (when wild pigs are more active within the settlement), opportunities for individual stalking kills occur but success is as much a matter of luck as of skill. In such circumstances, with a pig sighted near or even in a hamlet, the first problem is to make sure your quarry is not a neighbor's domestic pig.

Once, while sitting with an informant in his wife's house in an otherwise deserted hamlet, I saw two ordinary looking pigs come trotting into the hamlet square. I thought nothing of it and did not alert my companion. It was some time before he happened to glance out the door himself. Then it was an instance of the classic double take as he evaluated the situation. Apparently he had either recognized one of the pigs as a "stranger," or else had automatically checked the one true mark of a wild pig (its possession of a tail), or both. (To facilitate correct decisions in such instances the Miyanmin routinely amputate the tails of all domestic pigs in infancy.) There was a moment's indecision on his part as I became aware that something was the matter. I watched him slowly move to the back wall of the house and, again hesitatingly, take the only bow there, a light bird blind bow *(gemanok)*, along with a correspondingly light bamboo bladed arrow. He returned to the shadow beside the door and watched as the two pigs eventually moved between two houses and out of the hamlet. He had, meanwhile, communicated to me, in a very few words, the fact that a wild boar was with a domestic sow. I quietly followed him out of the house in a state of suppressed excitement. I remained on the edge of the hamlet as he set off into the scrub to stalk the pig. He returned in a short time with a broken arrow for his trouble and an oath for the fact that his long bow and hunting arrows were in the men's house.

The necessity of making a sure identification is obvious because the mischance of shooting a neighbor's pig leads to sorrow and anger. Yet the necessity of stalking close enough to a distantly seen pig to check out its hind quarters does not put the hunter in the most favorable position for a killing shot. Moreover, stalking or encircling a wild boar accompanying a domestic sow sometimes leads to the wrong pig being shot in the heat and confusion of the chase, since both pigs will flee.

I have heard of people staking out a sow in estrus in the bush to lure a wild boar to an ambush. People occasionally build a pig trap with a sharp bamboo blade into a fence put up for the purpose in gardens, but I don't think they have great expectations of success. The one trial of this tactic carried out while I was in the field was a qualified success. A wild pig was killed but the builder of the trap did not visit the site until several weeks later.

Cassowary. Rand and Gilliard (1967) describe the cassowary as one of the largest indigenous game animals of New Guinea. The cassowary of hill and montane forest which embraces the Hak Valley is *Casuarius bennetti*, the "Dwarf Cassowary," which in adult form is little more than a meter (approximately 3.5 ft) tall. It is a diurnal creature, occupies a terrestrial niche, and is important to the Miyanmin as a game animal and as a tamed semidomesticate.

The main food of the cassowary is "The fruit that falls in the forest and litters the ground under the trees throughout the year.... [It is] swallowed whole, surprisingly large fruit being accommodated in the bird's wide gape" (Rand and Gilliard 1967:21–22). They apparently eat some animals as well, including insects, fish, lizards, frogs, and crustacea (Rutgers 1970:2,5; Wallace 1962 [1869]:305). Rand and Gilliard (1967:25) attribute the small size of this species to the smaller size of the fruit found in the montane zone. They feed and move about the forest, sometimes in groups, during the day, but are extremely shy and retiring and are seldom seen by the casual intruder. They make nests in a depression in the ground with a few leaves and may lay three to eight large eggs. The monogamous male of a pair does the incubating, which lasts some 49 to 52 days. When newly hatched, the young are tan with darker stripes and it takes perhaps two years to acquire black adult plumage.

The cassowary is probably capable of considerable movement and can swim even the largest water barriers (Rand and Gilliard 1967:25; Rutgers 1970:5). It moves quickly and is reputed to be a dangerous fighter using its large clawed feet (Rutgers 1970:2). According to Miyanmin informants, it is never found very close to human settlements.

By the 1980s, cassowaries had been reduced by hunting pressure in the Hak Valley but, unlike wild pigs, are still seen and taken because, according to informants, they are replaced by birds from unaffected areas. The Miyanmin most commonly hunt the cassowary from a ground blind placed near a lavishly fruiting forest tree which has already been regularly visited by the birds. Chicks are frequently taken in season for taming and their capture may also allow the parent bird to be lured by mimicking the call of the young. The cassowary can be stalked and chased but these tactics are mainly used when the birds are discovered by pig hunters.

Captured young are placed in the care of women who train them to respond to calls and accept human food. The animals are fed cooked taro and allowed to forage in the village, forest, and garden as they accompany women in their daily round and are sheltered at night in small basketlike coops beside their owners' houses. Slaughter occurs before they lose their immature brown plumage. Unlike some New Guinea peoples (see Bulmer 1967) the Miyanmin do not cite the physical dangers of temperamental adult birds. Rather, they point out that as a bird approaches maturity its natural affinity for wild foods will overcome its training and it will run away. Hence the early slaughter.

Fostered

Fostered or commensal animals share a liking for habitats created by people, possibly including a preference for cultigens and also an affinity for edge effects (Peterson 1981). They must also be able to tolerate the hustle and bustle of human settlements created by people, pigs, and dogs, and their well-trampled hinterlands. The bandicoot common to the area, the exclusively terrestrial *Echimipera kalubu*, is a creature of edges, gaps, late gardens, and early regrowth. It has a taste for garden produce such as banana and food scraps (Audy 1947), as well as wild yams and the fruit of certain second growth *Ficus*; an ambush can be baited with the former and established at the latter. The arboreal *Dactylopsila trivigata* (Rand 1937) and *Phallanger orientalis*, as well as the terrestrial and scansorial *Phallanger gymnotis*, are animals of second growth, though the latter may also raid gardens. The distribution of *P. gymnotis* may also be influenced by the availability of suitable nest sites; it appears to prefer burrows in dry clay and consolidated alluvium although it reportedly will also make a home in a hollow tree. All three are commonly taken in multiples of two or more, usually mating pairs and young or larger groups.

My assignment of *Dactylopsila* to this category is somewhat arbitrary since, in the absence of a large sample (five from 1981, one from the late 1960s), its characteristics present a mixed pattern. On the one hand, it is largely insectivorous, possessing an elongated fourth digit for extracting larvae from timber and strong rodentlike incisors for tearing bark and wood. It might be grouped with the other "rare" insectivores. On the other hand, since people produce a lot of dead standing timber, its abundance seems to be encouraged. Women were involved in the capture of my entire sample in edges and abandoned gardens, with the downing of a hollow tree being the most common method of capture.

The scenario for capturing *P. orientalis* is similar. One or two animals are discovered during the day sleeping in the trees in secondary growth by men or women on "other business." The young tree is easily chopped down and the animal caught by the tail and clubbed to death. Alternatively, a man may shinny up a small adjacent tree and shoot the sluggish possum with bow and arrow. A common clue to the presence of a variety of possums, but particularly *P. gymnotis*, is the observation of claw marks on timber. Their very frequency may suggest the proximity of a nest or burrow. This can be sought and, when found, excavated or the entrance invested. One burrow I investigated ultimately yielded six *P. gymnotis* possum as well as several *Pogonomys* rat over a period of weeks. Possums may also be surprised in the open on the ground and run down by man and dog.

Melomys levipes is a rat of edges and gaps. I took all of mine in patches of primary and secondary forest near or between gardens or on the forest edge of gardens. In contrast, *Melomys rufescens* is a rat of "weedy" and "grassy" gardens including recently abandoned ones, also occasionally of abandoned villages and houses, and according to Dwyer (1978), of *Miscanthus* grasslands elsewhere in the highlands. The Miyanmin also differentiate a secondary variety of *M. rufescens* found at waterside sites and said to live on flotsam. According to Lidecker and Ziegler (1968), *M. rufescens* "seems to be adapting to the steadily increasing encroachment of human disturbance." I would speculate that it also has some systematic relationship with increasing prevalence of the sweet potato.

Finally, as is the case with other "taro peoples" of the Telefomin area (Menzies 1979:30), *Rattus ruber* is the village rat and also a common inhabitant of producing and recently harvested taro gardens. According to the people, its overwhelming food preference is for fresh moist raw taro, a curious specialization given this aroid's high oxalic acid content. I started my trapping early in 1981 in new regrowth near my house, an area reputed to be teeming with *R. ruber*. Indeed, every day I saw bits and scraps of the creature along foot paths, the result of nocturnal hunting by village dogs. Employing raw sweet potato laced with peanut oil for bait (following the advice of knowledgeable zoologists), I reaped a modest harvest of *M. rufescens*. My records show that as long as I persisted in baiting with sweet potato I did not catch my first *ruber* until the second month of the study. Only in the fourth month did my local assistants persuade me to try raw taro and the results were dramatic; 19 of the animals trapped were taken in the last month of my program.

I believe that the association between *R. ruber* and *Colocasia* taro is so strong that it might usefully serve as an "index fossil" for investigations of prehistoric agricultural change in the New Guinea highlands. Thus, a shift from taro cultivation to sweet potato would be marked in faunal remains by an increase in *M. rufescens* and a reduction in *R. ruber*. In contemporary sweet potato growing areas such as Siane (Dwyer 1978) *R. ruber* may become a relict inhabitant of cane stands between agricultural tracts and the tree lines.

In the Miyanmin area, due to the variety and patchiness of the environment partly created by people, there is a great degree of "close packing" of rodent species. Four or five species are sympatric: *M. lorentzi* in primary forest, *M. levipes* in second growth, edges and pandanus groves, *M. rufescens* in gardens, grassy areas, and waterside places, *R. ruber* of village and garden, and possibly *Pogonomys sp.* of second growth. I trapped some of all of these species within a few hundred meters of each other in seemingly predictable and replicable microhabitats. I should add that small rats such as these are nutritionally important especially to women and children because they are abundant and always available.

Domesticated

Strictly speaking the only true domesticates kept by the Miyanmin are pigs, dogs, and chickens. Since the 1960s repeated attempts have been made by mission and agricultural extension workers to establish a chicken flock but its main success has been as a "Canine Nutrition Improvement Program." Dogs were discussed earlier in this chapter in connection with hunting. Wild pigs were also described earlier in this chapter in the section concerned with reduced fauna and domesticated pigs in chapter 5 in the context of agriculture. It is important to emphasize here that domesticated pigs are merely a subgroup of the inclusive pig population of the region, part of the same breeding pool as wild pigs, sharing portions of a habitat, and probably varying in number more or less in relation to each other as people respond to reductions in wild pig and other game by expanding or intensifying husbandry.

Discussion

Recent studies of the interaction of people and animals in New Guinea suggest that although the methods pursued here have wide applicability, conclusions are specific, local, and strongly influenced by field techniques. For example, Hyndman's research among the Wopkaimin, another Mountain Ok society located far to the south under the Star Mountains, presents interesting similarities and contrasts. Like the Miyanmin, Wopkaimin practice low-intensity taro-based agriculture, control large territories, and exploit diverse natural resources along altitudinal and anthropogenic gradients (Hyndman 1979, 1982). Their wild plant and animal inventory is quite similar to that of the Miyanmin of the Hak Valley. Possibly because of differences in altitude of settlement and regional climate, however, a number of the phallangerids

Hyndman associates with abandoned gardens are actually removed from Miyanmin gardening and settlement areas.

Dwyer's work among the Rofaifo Siane of the eastern highlands perhaps illustrates the point about field technique. He reports (1978) difficulty trapping *Melomys rufescens* with most of his collections resulting from hand catching or bow and arrow hunting, but he had no difficulty trapping *Rattus ruber*. In contrast, using Dwyer's own traps as well as other types, I successfully trapped *M. rufescens* and failed totally with *R. ruber* until I changed baits, a small point until it is recognized that skewed trapping returns produced divergent inferences that are difficult to distinguish from real systematic differences.

Hence, most investigators who write about New Guinea mammals caution that there is insufficient data on which to generalize about habitat, distribution, food preferences, sympatry, reproduction, behavior, and the like. The quantity and quality of relevant field studies is improving; but there is as yet insufficient information to allow us to more than speculate about patterns that have some generality, such as Dwyer's suggestion that *M. rufescens* and *R. ruber* increase in abundance in direct relationship to human disturbance, or my own concerning the association of taro and *R. ruber*.

The wider applicability of the approach can be illustrated with other kinds of animals I have not dealt with in detail. This is feasible because, while they are very different biologically from the mammals I focused on, they bear similar relationships to people. Some are important enough in the human diet to merit at least passing discussion.

The most important of the nonmammalian sources of meat is the cassowary. Other avifauna are more difficult to assess. In terms of my own unsystematic observations, few are seriously affected because, in relation to their abundance and the dispersal of human activity, relatively few are taken and only meager portions of their habitats are seriously disturbed. Even the various birds of paradise, valued as decorations and for use in minor trading, are not affected to a significant degree, possibly due to the absence of significant trade. Certain ground-nesting birds, such as the bush turkey (*Aepypoedius arfakianus*?, *akwil*) may be affected by egg collecting but this activity is also sporadic and diffused. On the other hand, certain small birds (which are absent from zones of natural climax vegetation) are attracted by gardens and other disturbed areas that people create (Bulmer 1968a:314).

When it comes to the smaller, less visible exploited creatures, including frogs, lizards, and insects, it is still possible to generalize about the consequences of human activity, but difficult to particularize about the direct relationship of quantitative changes in faunal abundance to specific acts. One faunal group can serve to indicate the possibilities here. Among the lizards (Parker, Personal Communication), small basking skinks (*Emoia spp.*)

multiply in gardens and secondary growth; arboreal species preferring sun (such as *Dasia smaragdinum*) are commonly found basking on dead standing trees in gardens and clearings, and the gekko (*Gekko vittatus*) is commonly found in old houses, banana plants, sago, and pandanus. Certain leaf mold dwellers of the forest floor that need no moisture and avoid sun will be eliminated from cleared areas. Arboreal species that depend on vegetation such as *Vavanus prasinus* are affected by deforestation (Menzies, Personal Communication). Other lizards (such as goannas) that do not depend on vegetation are not much affected except by opportunistic hunting which occurs most intensively near human settlements.

7

People, Groups, and the Organization of Responses

In the first chapter it was argued that movement was a distinctive and important type of response. This also provided the basis for an alternative approach to social organization. In this and the following three chapters I focus on how movements occur rather than merely describing them as in the model in chapter 3.

These four chapters will sketch out the kinds of movements that occur, and differentiate them on the basis of their material effects, contingencies, constraints, and the kinds of units or groups that are involved. Part of the question of how movements occur is the contingent nature of social groups themselves—the issue of why certain groups emerge and/or why individuals form and join groups. We will also have to understand something about Miyanmin social organization and marriage, as well as their religious beliefs and practices (chapter 8). This is because responses and strategies have social and religious dimensions. Note, however, that I do not argue that all aspects of religion and social organization (conventionally described) are related to adaptive behavior.

Processes involving expansion and warfare have been advancing for a long time and have had significant long-term and cumulative effects. Because their identification supports my overall analysis here and elsewhere (Morren 1984; Hyndman and Morren n.d.), I present and discuss ethnohistoric information on large-scale movements in chapter 10. At the end of chapter 9 I focus on the environmental effects of human settlements and the activities that they organize and concentrate, because these are the most important results of different kinds of movements. This also provides a link to the assessment of the relationships between people and the animals they hunt carried out earlier in chapter 6.

The Human Ecology of the Social

The social issue in human ecology is that people sometimes respond to problems and changes as individuals and at other times as members of groups. Put another way, people often use their membership in groups to solve problems and cope with change. Moreover, one cannot talk about equilibration without identifying the pertinent unit of action. The process of responding "may involve shifts in the unit of response [and hence, also changes in measurement bias of the system or "rules of equilibration"] as from individuals to groups of various kinds and degrees of inclusiveness and back to individuals" (Vayda and McCay 1975). This preliminary statement should help to define the social dimension of adaptive responses.

Consistent with the economics of flexibility approach, I see two ways to approach the problem. One is by asking questions about individuals and their actions; the other is from the standpoint of groups and their characteristics and actions vis-à-vis other groups and individuals. The two are intertwined.

The first case concerns the circumstances under which individuals subordinate their interests to the group's, the advantages accruing, the costs incurred, and the ways in which they may reverse the action or features of it. The second concerns the characteristics of the established and ad hoc groups that sometimes successfully recruit members or are otherwise renewed, sustained, or expanded in a patterned way, and at other times decline, disintegrate, or lose members. When the cells of a group are subgroups they relate to the inclusive group as individuals do. The linkages between them are characterized by marriage, mobility, migration, exchange, alliance, ideological similarities, cooperative demonstrations, competition, and conflict.

People come to join specific groups by virtue of birth, through socialization, by following a leader, as a result of coercion, and by exercising options learned, invented, or otherwise acquired. Similarly, small groups come to form or join larger more inclusive ones through sharing space, membership, resources, problems, solutions, perceptions, or competitors and adversaries. People tend to exercise available options according to their individual character and capacity, perception of the magnitude and duration of changes in their circumstances *and* in relation to such features of optional responses as their difficulty, effectiveness, and reversibility.

Groups attempt to maintain their membership by means of population "policy," recruitment and initiation practices, and social control, including the shaping of perception and the regulation of emigration. Social success is marked by immigration and recruitment, and adaptational success by natural and social increase. The appropriate reciprocals—the markers of decline—pertain as well.

The structural-functional approach to sociopolitical organization (which combines "ideal type" and "jural rules" methodology) still pervades sociocultural anthropology and political science even as it is shown to be incapable of making sense out of people's behavior in Western and non-Western societies. A typical example comes from studies of the New Guinea highlands. "The father-son-brother ideology of male group relationship is, for the most part, common and comprises the basis of descent theory in highlands society" (Brown 1978:148). The problem is that a theory explaining a variable by appealing to a constant is no theory at all.

To begin, I can only present my claim that if one starts by examining the behavior of ordinary people it can be shown that in all societies it deviates from the manifest institutional model in regular ways. In this regard, certain critiques and modifications of the segmentary model have been instructive. These have tended to show that, not only do New Guinea highland societies deviate from the "classic" model (Barnes 1962; Vayda and Cook 1964), but segmentary organization is alive and well in stereotypically hierarchical Western states (Gerlach and Hine 1970, 1973; Toffler 1971).

If we look at things from the standpoint of the behavior of individuals rather than of aggregates, we can range societies along a continuum. One extreme is represented by the Hobbesian "war of all against all," the ultimate in individual flexibility characterized by the "scrambling behavior" of schoolyard and land-rush, with groups formed only as temporary ad hoc expedients. The other extreme is represented by the monolithic, centralized, hierarchical totalitarian state in which individual behavior is rigorously controlled and the queue is the norm. All societies fall somewhere in between these extremes that otherwise have no empirical existence except possibly in the minds of "structural-functionalists" such as Thomas Hobbes and Hannah Arendt. My point is that, to varying degrees, all societies involve elements of segmentation and hierarchy, and that these are in constant flux.

The dimensions of nonhierarchical forms of organization are segmentation, decentralization, reticulation, and multipenetration (Gerlach and Hine 1979, 1973). I emphasize that these are variables. The use of the ideology of descent to institutionalize segmentary organization, as in lineage systems, is merely one variant and a variable at that. Segmentary organization (wherever found) is characteristic of situations involving growth, expansion, and innovation. It is an adaptive form of organization because it minimizes the consequences of the failure of an individual cell to larger, more inclusive units.

Another perspective on segmentary organization can be derived from Hirschman's (1971) model of *Exit, Voice and Loyalty*. In this approach, members of a group are viewed as having two options when the performance of an organization is in flux: exit, or quitting the group, and voice, or staying in the group and participating in corrective action. The issue for any group is the balance of the two, for if exit prevails the group cannot (will not) persist. Segmentary societies are characterized, I believe, by the relative coexistence of exit and voice. This is achieved in such societies in part by inculcating *loyalty*, a mode of inhibiting exit. Loyalty is an issue in any group in which the objective price of joining is low; among the Miyanmin, not only are most people born into their groups but others may join with few constraints and all can readily join other groups. This is axiomatic to the extent that it is also projected onto the behavior of ancestral spirits: they too have the option of joining another group's ancestral spirits and in doing so exact a high price from the living (chapter 8).

Gardner's (1981) description of the extreme mobility of members of *sa-nakai* Miyanmin groups realizes this possibility. The way that the *am-nakai* groups mitigate it, however, is to induce loyalty by means of more rigorous initiation rites and institutionalizing voice in rituals that are initiated in the face of random changes. This discussion and application of Hirschman's scheme is expanded in chapter 9 because the balance between exit and voice is at the core of the operation of the movement strategies analyzed there.

In emphasizing the difficulty of applying the jural approach, students of Melanesian social organization have repeatedly shown that local groups are genealogically complex, and extremely variable (or flexible) in the application of supposed rules determining membership. They have tended to deal with the muddle by modifying the jural approach to somehow accommodate this complexity (e.g., the conceptualization of the parish—Hogbin and Wedgewood 1953). It has been suggested that rules emerge or come to be more rigorously enforced in the context of pressure on resources (e.g., Meggitt 1965) and modernization (which, of course, may amount to the same thing). This suggestion is useful precisely because it emphasizes the social dimension of coping with environmental problems. It is still regarded as desirable to identify socially realized groups and isolate rules however dishonored. My pragmatic decision is to follow both tracks, the ecological one previously described, and the modified jural one to the extent that it facilitates basic ethnographic reporting and provides names for aggregates of people I need to discuss.

Even this latter task is logically complex. There are at least four levels of understanding involved, a metataxonomy of groups: (1) assemblies of particular people at a specific time and place engaging in certain activities and movements; (2) the name of the particular assemblage and its associated range(s), settlement(s), and environmental effects; (3) the particular kind of assemblage, its taxonomic level, and ascribed limits, capacities and competencies; and (4) the reticulate and hierarchical linkages between groups and kinds and within larger inclusive groups.

Miyanmin Groups

According to my criteria, the Miyanmin are at the high flexibility end of the social continuum because hierarchy is absent: segmentation is high, leadership is egalitarian and highly specialized as to competence, and individual networks that cut across the boundaries of large territorial groups are significant. The Miyanmin contrast with certain core groups of the New Guinea highlands in which the beginnings of hierarchy can be observed side by side with segmentary organization, and hence "stronger" institutionalization is contradicted by inherent flexibility. To a lesser degree this contrast exists between the *sa-nakai* Miyanmin of the lowlands and the *am-nakai* Miyanmin of the foothill and lower-montane zone; the former are "scramblers" and the latter are (relatively speaking) "queuers."

Thus also from a jural standpoint it is difficult to define and describe a structure for the Miyanmin in the sense of an elegant, replicable pattern of groups, subgroups, institutional linkages, rules, and hierarchy. There is organization nevertheless in patterned social relations, behavior and, above all, movement. Miyanmin informants do not help, either with a conscious ideal model of their society, or with unambiguous statements about their individual affiliations and loyalties. The metafeatures of their segmentary organization are more diagnostic: variability in "shape" from place to place, flexibility in the locational options of individuals, and what Gardner (another student of the Miyanmin) refers to as "weak institutionalization" (1981:42–44). For me, this means simply (relative) absence of hierarchy. Ultimately, I conclude that Miyanmin social organization is a patterned "adhocracy" (Toffler 1971:124ff). This implies that the only way to grasp features of particular groups is by starting with the ad hoc of what people actually do.

Even an ecological anthropologist has to know what to call the groups with which his subjects affiliate. Lacking place and group names would make it impossible to carry out the stereotypical first task of field research, censusing and mapping. I worked intensively with informants to penetrate the topic, walking from hamlet to hamlet to map houses and record the names of their occupants, filling out genealogies, ordering kin terms like roof leaves, and gathering group terms as varied as shards of broken pottery of unknown provenance. Accordingly, I start with a survey of the terms I found in use.[1]

I have assembled a list of seven terms or synonym sets that belong to the group domain. As I indicated earlier, without even considering the variability and ambiguity of Miyanmin usage, the task of making sense out of these terms is logically complicated. As Bateson has observed, "the map is not the territory, and the name is not the thing named" (1980:32). The elements of the muddle include the levels of understanding and range of applicability outlined above, as well as people's usage and apparent meaning. In attempting to translate group terms, informant/interpreters can provide allusions, examples, and implications, but in most cases cannot provide referential definitions. The ethnographer attempts to chart usage by observing the contexts in which the terms are used and establishing the general "shape" of their reference (figure 7-1). In light of the foregoing, the ethnographer can then select among the terms, including apparent synonyms, and decide what to call things observed on the ground. This is known as "getting on with it!" I will first run through the available corpus and discuss terms at the level of apparent meaning. I will then return to some of them that I have selected as operational units and describe their substantive characteristics. The latter task will occupy the bulk of this chapter.

Mit

According to my "map," *mit* is a generic embracing many kinds of assemblages of things and people. I translate it as "gathering." For example, *eimen mit* is a "pile of taro." Its proper use as a group term is in the form *naka mit* (see also Gardner 1981:95). Gardner, however, translates it as "base," "origin," and "kind." One usage I observed, *naka mit sum* (*sum* = large), is applied to what I call the parish, but the word *ten* is more consistently applied (see below). Gardner believes that the use of *mit* to apply to any group that occupies land justifies translating it as "parish" even though only one group in his area of West Mianmin, Kari, resembles the *am-nakai* groups of the east I call "parishes." Indeed, at one point he refers to Kari as consisting of a "set of *mit*." And at another he admits that use of the term "parish" for *sa-nakai mit* is problematic because there is no corporate basis for land ownership. Gardner's pragmatic decision to employ *mit* to refer to the highly variable, mobile, and unstable *sa-nakai* groups (excluding Kari) is understandable. He is mistaken, however, in applying it to *am-nakai* groups and equating it with "parish." It is perhaps more suitable for relatively independent parish segments that may also equate to lineages or hamlets (see below).

Sel

Sel is a male-focused group term. In common usage it is coupled with a noun as a suffix to refer to a male core associated with the referent (see *-tamansel*, below). It is also used with lineage names as in *omara morupsel*, the members

Figure 7-1.   A Map of Miyanmin Group Terminology

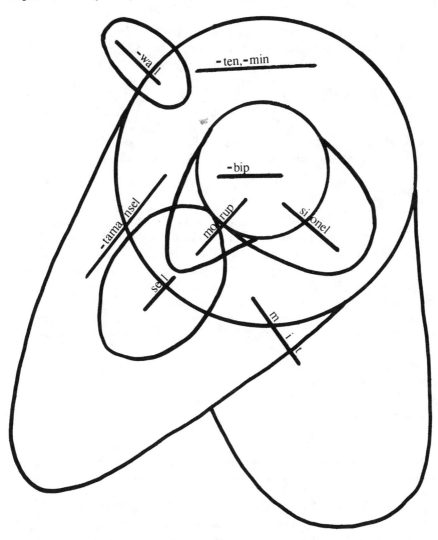

of *omara* lineage. It may be linked with male kinship terms as in *aensel*, male matrikin of the A2 generation, or even the male generic *nakai*. The latter usage is illustrated in an admonition contained in a conversation I recorded, "You cannot get angry with that woman. She has a lot of *nakasel* [male supporters]."

Wal

I translate *wal* as "kind," marking a metaclass. It is commonly used with male and female kin terms as in *biyemwal* ("women of the A2 generation" or "the mother-kind") and *faningwal* ("the ancestors"). It can also be used to designate animal-kinds at the level of terminal taxa. There are many seemingly idiomatic usages. For example, *hek* is the kin term for eldest (contrasting with elder) brother; *hekwal* means "village elders." It can also be used to emphasize one's own singularity as in the following scene. Getirap's wife Watkop calls out to a sound in the night, "What's that?" From outside, her husband replies, *Getirap wal nitaba* ("It's Getirap, that's who!").

Ten, Min

Ten and *min* translate as "children" or "descendants." They are commonly used to mark the parish as in *Kometen* and *Timelmin*. The two examples refer to the same parish group; and I believe that the former is the traditional Miyanmin usage while the latter is Telefolmin usage now widely adopted as "official" in the district. *Ten* also marks other ethnolinguistic groups such as *Kelefoten* "Telefolmin" and *Nemayeten* "Atbalmin." *Ten* can be used broadly to refer to an ad hoc assemblage; e.g., *naka teno* is the cry relayed from hamlet to hamlet to gather men for a pig drive. Apparently the *ten* parish group has little social reality among the *sa-nakai* of the west which I believe partly explains the difference between Gardner's (1981) terminology and my own (see below and previous discussion of *mit*).

Morupsel, Meletan

These synonyms designate the patrilineal lineage which also carries the name of a big man *(kamok)* of the recent past. Each is chartered by a genealogy which, after four or so generations, becomes a straight line list of *kamok*. Oral tradition is ordered by these genealogies. The legend which opened chapter 1 is an example. *Am-nakai* parishes tend to have four lineages each. Thus, the contemporary Kometen lineages are named *Omara, Drifup, Berabesep-Baran*, and *Druban*, all prominent big men two or three generations ago. The lineage also is the core of residential units (see below).

Tamansel

This is the composite term for a "valley group," as in *Haktamansel*, "the people of the Hak River Valley." Later in this chapter I introduce it as a unit of analysis because, among the *am-nakai* at least, it often is a significant supra-parochial group.

Bip

This is the hamlet or residential village. Under a dispersed regime (chapter 9), a given hamlet is identified with a particular *morup* (lineage) and a leader or elder of it. The actual residential group, however, consists of lineage members, and their affines and matrikin, at least part of the time.

The Corporate Attributes of the Parish

A parish has many corporate attributes, but the most readily diagnostic one distinguishing it from other parishes is the possession of special buildings which have important ceremonial and secular uses. These buildings also serve, along with the ceremonies performed in them, as indices of some of the kinds of movement discussed in chapter 8.

Both subsistence and nonsubsistence parish resources nominally belong to all de facto members of the parish. In practice virtually any friendly Miyanmin visitor can gain temporary access to parish resources by citing a concrete or hypothetical relationship with a member of the host parish. Environmental diversity in the eastern Miyanmin area (chapter 4) encourages visiting for trade or the collection of raw materials.

Particular parishes are known for their possession of important resources or the manufacture of articles with them. Sokaten, which characteristically occupies a somewhat higher altitudinal range (on the slopes of Mount Stolle) than other eastern Miyanmin parishes, is known for the "black palm" used in the manufacture of bows. Wameten is known for two varieties of cane, one used for arrow shafts, the other for belts and arrow bindings. Mabweten, on the Fiak River in the 1960s, provides a special palmwood for making barbed arrow points from the Aki River area it occupied until pacification. Stone for adzes was collected from a quarry on one of the headwater tributaries of the Usake River originally captured from the *Yanfa* people and now controlled by Hoten. Raw materials may be collected without compensation, but finished manufactured articles are bought or bartered.

The only word in the Miyanmin language which even begins to gloss with my (and other outsiders') use of the name Miyanmin (which is the Telefol name for them) is *alwal*, which means roughly "vegetable food-group." The implication is one of minimal hospitality to be accorded to friendly nonforeign outsiders, the provision of cooked taro. A nonparish member who desires to hunt or gather raw materials such as those noted must be accompanied by a host parish member, someone with whom he has an established relationship.

Parish territorial boundaries are spoken of in a permanent and exclusive way, but the politics of boundaries is quite different. The movement of parishes within their own territories is subject to a number of constraints from neighboring parishes through the maintenance of buffer zones to prevent mutual ecological interference. In the past, boundaries changed through the acquisition by force or granting of small tracts of land between normally friendly parishes with compensation paid for fixed assets such as pandanus, breadfruit, and sago. These matters will be discussed in greater detail below and in chapter 9 and 10.

In the eastern Miyanmin area, displayed in map 3, there are presently eight *named*[2] parishes that range in population from 53 to 185 (table 7-11).[3] These parishes claim territories ranging from 36 to 197 square km (14 to 76 square mi),[4] with population densities ranging from 1.7 to 22 per square km (0.69 to 8.5 persons per square mi). The total population of the eight parishes is 915, occupying a total land area estimated to be 810 square km (313 square mi). Thus, the raw population density for the east Miyanmin, a group that may be treated as a unit for the purpose of studying internal migration and areal integration, is 7.5 per square km (2.9 persons per square mi). An important characteristic of this unit, bearing on questions raised in succeeding chapters, is that the most populous groups with the smallest territories are in the higher altitude south, while the smallest groups with the largest territories are in the lower altitude north and west.

Age and Sex Composition

There are at least two ways of talking about the data on age and sex composition shown in figures 7-2 through 7-4. Because the overall sample, shown in raw numbers in figure 7-4c, is reasonably large, some statements can be made about past and future population in the eastern Miyanmin area. This area, in other words, can be viewed for a number of purposes as a population unit. Another way of looking at the same data is to examine the population structure of local groups, both parishes and local populations (see below). The parish and local population profiles will reflect their idiosyncratic histories, their relations with other groups, and the like. This kind of breakdown is exemplified in figure 7-4a, c and g as percentages of each population and in figure 7-5 in the section on the "local population."

The age-sex composition of my eastern Miyanmin sample, a composite of five of the eight parishes which make up this unit, is shown in figure 7-3. This sample totals 592, including 306 males and 286 females. It is a very young population with 42.5 percent under 15 years of age. Only 13.0 percent of the population is over 40.

The problem of estimating ages in remote populations should lead us to accept these figures with caution. My methods were partly subjective and

Figure 7-2. Population Pyramids for Five East Miyanmin Groups
(1969)

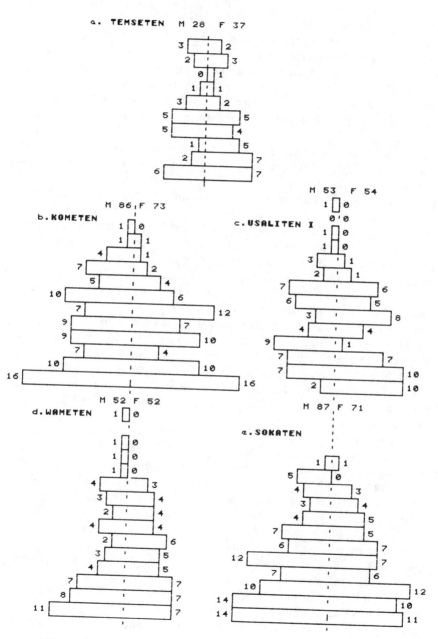

impressionistic. The Miyanmin helped me in objectifying my observations because the criteria of relative age is built into their kinship terminology. Thus the birth order of sets of siblings can be established and comparisons made between such sets using the usual subjective criteria of appearance and social age. In addition, birth records are available in government census material for some parishes going back as far as 1963. The records of the Child and Maternal Welfare Clinic of the Australian Baptist Mission Society at Telefomin provided very precise data for a smaller segment of the population going back to 1966, and independent estimates of the ages of some older children.

I conducted my census and assembled the raw data in the following manner. In 1968 I accompanied a routine government census patrol in order to make use of the "line-up" at assembly places. I was able to compile fairly complete censuses for all of the East Mianmin parishes except Boblikten, where attendance was poor, and Hoten, which is censused from Ambunti. I was also able to census a non-East Mianmin parish, Mabweten, at this time. I compared my record with the cumulative one employed by the patrol officer and copied down birth, death, marriage, and migration notes made by previous patrols and "bracketed" age estimates that diverged greatly from my own. Subsequently, I was able to make more extended follow-up visits to four eastern Miyanmin parishes and Mabweten, spending two to four weeks residing in each (in addition to Kome parish, which was my permanent base). At those times through greater familiarity, I was able to revise many of my original estimates of individual age, recording the names and ages of adults and children I met in the course of a day's work independently of my census. I also collected more detailed information on migration and intermarriage from informants, along with standard sociological data, and identified persons in different parishes who had been captured from enemy groups. I have included in my sample only those eastern Miyanmin parishes I revisited.[5]

I believe that my least reliable ages pertain to the over-40 segment of the population, and that the ages of women are skewed in the direction of overestimation. Howell's work (1979) has sensitized me to the possible sources of error, but I have resisted the temptation to "rework" the data as originally recorded to allow for the problems cited by Howell. As it is, the overall age pyramid looks like a reasonable one.

There are three attributes of the eastern Miyanmin population pyramid, figures 7-3 and 7-4f, that bear on my later discussion: the effects of contact (particularly epidemics), the sex-ratio, and counter effects.

One difficulty in discussing the effects of disease on the Miyanmin population is that, although I have a fairly clear picture of the spectrum of mortality risks that existed while I was in the field, the precontact picture is not at all clear. During the period of my fieldwork, the main cause of death for

Figure 7-3. Population Pyramid for Five-Parish East Miyanmin Sample (1969)

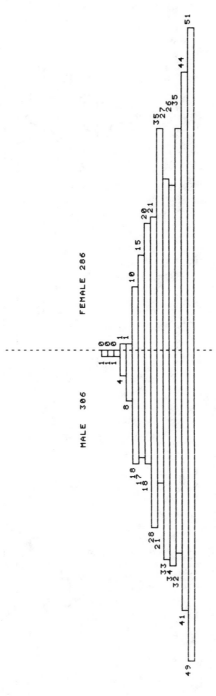

Figure 7-4. Percent Age-Sex Composition for Certain Miyanmin Population Units (1969)

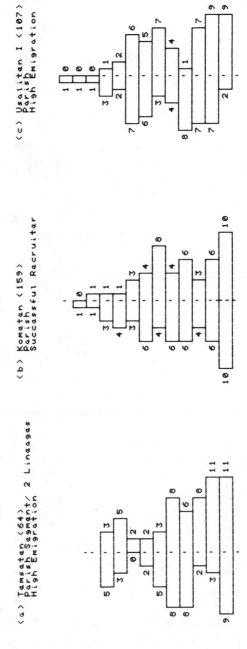

(a) Temsoten <64>
Parish Segment/ 2 Lineages
High Emigration

(b) Kometen <159>
Parish
Successful Recruiter

(c) Usoliten I <107>
Parish
High Emigration

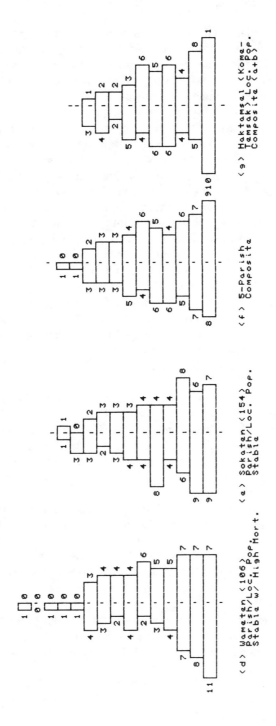

(d) Wametan <106>
Parish/Loc.Pop.
Stabla w/High Mort.

(a) Sokaten <154>
Parish/Loc.Pop.
Stabla

(f) 5-Parish
Composita

(g) Haktamsal <Komal-
Tamsak> Loc.Pop.
Composita <a+b>

adults was pneumonia, usually following a more mild viral upper respiratory infection. The main risk for children was infantile diarrhea, probably connected with malaria, with upper respiratory infections being less of a problem. Malaria is endemic, but no adults suffer from it chronically. Dysentery has never become established in the Miyanmin population, although people often return with it from the government station (including the "Hospital"). I believe that the failure of dysentery to become established is due to the low population density and established sanitary and hygiene practices. Human feces are deposited away from habitation sites in places that are visited only for that purpose, and people bathe regularly. Ringworm (*tinea*) affects some people in the south, is much more common in the north, and is thought by the Miyanmin to have entered the area through contact with the population of the lower May River (captured women transmitting it to their children), among whom it is endemic. Ringworm itself is not an acute condition but, in children at least, it seems to be associated with a susceptibility to conditions such as impetigo and tropical ulcer.

Precontact endemic diseases included yaws (completely eliminated by early government patrols), and malaria (this possibly spreading to higher-altitude areas in the south after pacification). In addition, many people suffered from iodine deficiency, with goiter and cretinism common in children. This has only recently been subject to treatment by Western medicine under existing conditions. It is not clear what kind of risks are involved in iodine deficiency, but it seems to me that women would be more affected than men because of the iodine given up to the fetus in pregnancy. The effect is cumulative: first-borns are less likely to be cretinous than later children because of the iodine they get from their mothers. The supply of maternal iodine is increasingly depleted by subsequent pregnancies.

The probable effects of contact can be seen in the over-15 portion of the population pyramids, although differing somewhat from parish to parish, especially as to chronology. Based on oral accounts, there were two main epidemics, both involving upper respiratory diseases and their complications (including septicemia as well as pneumonia), one in the early 1940s and another in the first decade of sustained contact in the 1950s. Both of these are apparent in the population pyramids, and the later of the two epidemics (or some other factor associated with contact) seems to have been accompanied by lowered fertility or higher infant mortality. In a census patrol to the Eliptaman Telefolmin immediately to the south of the Miyanmin, Patrol Officer Booth (1957) reported an excess of deaths (111) to births (73) and attributed high mortality to an influenza epidemic which occurred in August, 1956. The neighboring Miyanmin most likely suffered identical effects at this time.

Figure 7-3 shows an excess of males over females, 306 to 286. Until the age of 20 (when women are beginning their reproductive careers) there is no imbalance. It begins around the age of 35 or 40. The main causes of the imbalance are the risks of childbearing, including the pregnancy-iodine deficiency linkage which acts to increase susceptibility to infectious diseases. Women might therefore have been even more susceptible than men to upper respiratory infections.

The Miyanmin attempt to cope with mortality risks in several ways. Anxiety about sickness and death was common in the 1960s and traditionally there were numerous curing rituals, including large public ones (see chapter 8). Sickness is associated with sorcery; and in the 1960s there was widespread belief in the notion that the enemy was seeking a numerical advantage. Accordingly, various forms of recruitment from outside the parish were practiced before pacification, including the capture of both male and female children. In fact, from four to seven percent of the various parishes consist of captured people. Other practices tending to counter these problems include men marrying later in life than women, and the rapid remarriage of widows. All of these practices will be discussed in greater detail later in this chapter.

Although epidemics of upper respiratory diseases continued in the 1960s, some groups also gained access to Western modes of treatment (especially in the most southern groups), and children began the process of acquiring a partial immunity to a broad spectrum of viruses. The demographic evidence from this period suggests that some kind of adaptation was taking place. The three youngest cohorts of the population pyramid display the pattern of a stable population in which birth rates and death rates are both high; while the older portion of the pyramid exhibits features of a situation in which birth rates have been low (or infant mortality has been high) and the death rate has been high (see Heer, 1968:82). Health and health care markedly improved in the 1970s for some Miyanmin groups. Children born in the 1960s who grew up with exotic viruses now enter adulthood with sufficient immunity to prevent the deadly pneumonia epidemics observed in the 1960s. Fertility improved and infant mortality has declined. Nevertheless, several new communicable diseases—filiaviasis and leprosy—have appeared.

The individual parish pyramids shown in figures 7-2 and 7-4(a,b,c,d, and e) tell somewhat different stories. They manifest relatively stable populations (b,d,e), one which has been sapped by emigration of mature (30+ years) males and families (a), and a population which has lost young (20+ years) and mature males to migration and has recruited a large number of mature males from other parishes (c). The background is provided in the section of chapter 9 on expansion and migration. Figure 7-4(g) shows the demographic effect of (and perhaps one of the bases for) the maintenance of a special relationship between two parishes. The resulting composite (of a and b) population is a

Plate 7.   A Widower and His Infant Daughter
He has become a full-time gardener since his wife's death.

more balanced and stable one, similar in structure to figure 7-4(f), the pyramid for the total sample. The magnification of the "squeeze" in the 10- to 15-year cohort, displayed by all the populations in the sample, is due to the fact that Kometen and Temseten have had the longest sustained and most intimate contact with whites in the area. For example, the majority of men sent to jail for four years in 1956 for participating in a raid on the Atbalmin people were from these groups (Morren 1981, 1984; see also chapters 10 and 11). The special relationship between Kometen and Temseten parishes is described in detail in the section on the "local population" below.

Genealogical Composition

The parish looks like a cognatic unit in terms of genealogical composition, but descent is not the idiom for talking about membership in the group. In other words, the Miyanmin do not possess a cognatic "structure" in the same sense that the Mae Enga, by Barnes's (1967:39) reckoning, do not possess an agnatic "structure." It is rather a matter of residence and recruitment with individual parishes, as corporate entities, acting to conserve and expand their populations through endogamy, reciprocal interparish marriages, invitations for outsiders to contract uxorilocal marriages, or the taking of captives in war.

In most parishes more than half of all residents are born into the parish with both parents as full parish members. Most of the remaining residents are likely to have had at least one parent who was a parish member by birth. The exception to this pattern, Hoten, the most northern of the eastern Miyanmin parishes, involves a population at least half of whom are immigrants (see chapter 10). All other parishes possess only a small fraction of people with no immediate parish antecedents. Kome parish, for which I have the most detailed data, appears to be typical enough, falling into the mid-range of intact parishes that have neither been depleted by emigration nor greatly augmented by immigration. If a resident is defined as a person who exploits parish resources at least half the year or a person who is part of a household unit which does so, fully 52 percent of all residents of Kometen parish have two Kome parents (table 7-1). Residents possessing one Kome parent make up an additional 40 percent. Only 8 percent of parish residents have no Kome parent at all.

If the frequencies for adults and children are compared, these proportions appear to be relatively stable ones over time. The two population fractions make up 60 percent and 40 percent of the total population, respectively. The parental affiliation percentages for adult and child residents with two and with one Kome parent (k percentages in table 7-1 and 7-2) are similar to their proportions in the total population. The only significant difference between adults and children is in the "no Kome" parents category,

Table 7-1. Affiliation of Kome Parish Residents (1968)

Kome Residents with n Kome Parents

Population Fraction	n=2				n=1				n=0					
	f.	Percentages R	K	T	f.	Percentages R	K	T	f.	Percentages R	K	T	f.	Per-cent
Adult 15 yrs.	46	48.0	55.4	29.0	38	39.5	59.3	24.0	12	12.5	100.0	8.0	96	60.0
Children < 15 yrs.	37	58.7	44.6	23.0	26	41.3	40.7	16.0	0	0.0	0.0	0.0	63	40.0
Totals	83	///	100.0	52.0	64	///	100.0	40.0	12	///	100.0	8.0	159	100.0

Chi-Squared = 8.75   d.f. = 2 $p < 0.01$

Table 7-2. Kome Residents with One Kome Parent and Sex of Kome Parent (1968)

Population Fraction	Male (Father) Percentages					Female (Mother) Percentages					Total Population	
	f.	R	K	T1	T2	f.	R	K	T1	T2	f.	Percent
Adult 15 yrs.	32	84.3	61.5	50.0	20.0	6	15.8	50.0	9.5	4.0	38	59.3
Children < 15 yrs.	20	77.0	38.5	31.0	13.0	6	23.1	50.0	9.5	4.0	26	40.7
Totals	52	///	100.0	81	33.0	12	///	100.0	19.0	8.0	64	100.0

T1 : % of all residents

T2 : % of all residents with one Kome parent

Chi-Squared = 0.16   d.f. = 1   p. <0.70   phi = .09

NOTE: In tables 7-1, 7-2, and 7-3 proportions have been calculated for both rows (R) and columns (K). This permits the sample to be stratified horizontally and vertically.

where all observations pertain to the adult portion of the population. This is expectable—most are men and women who have married into the group.

In view of the imbalance between the sexes in individual parishes and the overall sample, the recruitment of females from outside the parish is particularly important. The effects of female recruitment on parish composition are apparent: 81 percent of the Kome residents with only one Kome parent (or 32 percent of all residents) had non-Kome mothers (table 7-2). Most of these residents (51 percent, or 16 percent of all residents) had mothers from Temseten (table 7-3), a parish closely aligned with Kometen in a special relationship. Another large fraction (36 percent, 11 percent of all residents) had mothers who had been captured from enemy groups. Only a small fraction of Kometen residents, seven percent, had non-Kome fathers. Here again, most of these were from Temseten (table 7-3),

Of those Kome residents with no Kome parents (table 7-4), 83 percent are in-marrying or captured women. The two males in this group, two young men with estimated ages of 17 and 20 (in 1969), were both captured as small children in the course of Miyanmin forays against May River groups.

People who have one or more non-Kome antecedents suffer no disabilities, but rather exercise the same privileges as any other resident of the same sex and age. This may be due to the absence of significant intragroup resource competition (described below) and the open land tenure situation. There are few assets that are worth inheriting, including "real property." Even with respect to the scarcest good of all, women, there seems to be no disability. The eldest of two male captives was given a young bride by her brothers in 1969 and the younger married a widow in 1980. The only resentment the first instance engendered was among village women who identified with the bride's desire to have more say in the matter. Of course, people with one or more non-Kome parents are also denied the benefits of association with mother's or father's kin if bilocality cannot be maintained (see discussion of dual residence in chapter 9). The importance attached to affines is reflected in the acts of certain men married to captured women, following the Australian administration's initial attempts at pacification. In 1955, two such men from Boblikten parish in the Thurnwald range attempted to establish friendly relations with their Atbalmin "affines." Unfortunately, the "prodigal sons-in-law" along with two other companions were converted to "fatted calves" when they reached an Atbalmen village, and this led to a coordinated raid on the perpetrators by six eastern Miyanmin parishes (chapter 11). Sixteen Atbalmin were killed, and over 20 Miyanmin went to jail.

In any event, such practical disabilities only last a generation. Thus an informant whose mother was an (Eliptaman) Telefolmin woman told me that, although he could accompany a raid into the Elip River Valley, burn villages,

Table 7-3. Parish Affiliation of Non-Kome Parent (1968)

Kome Parent	Parish of Non-Kome Parent	Adult f.	Adult Percentages R	K	T	Child f.	Child Percentages R	K	T	Total f.	%
A. Father	Tenseten	15	55.6	46.9	29.0	12	44.5	60.0	23.0	27	51.0
	Sokaten	0	0.0	0.0	0.0	2	100.0	10.0	4.0	2	4.0
	Waneten	3	100.0	9.4	6.0	0	0.0	0.0	0.0	3	6.0
	Mabweten	2	100.0	6.3	4.0	0	0.0	0.0	0.0	2	4.0
	Enemy Groups										
	Kelefoten	3	100.0	9.4	6.0	0	0.0	0.0	0.0	3	6.0
	Nemayeten	6	60.0	18.8	12.0	4	40.0	20.0	8.0	10	20.0
	May River	3	60.0	9.4	6.0	2	40.0	10.0	4.0	5	10.0
	TOTAL	32			62.0	20			38.0	52	

Chi-Squared = 8.62   d.f. = 6   p.< 0.20

Kome Parent	Parish of Non-Kome Parent	Adult f.	Adult Percentages R	K	T	Child f.	Child Percentages R	K	T	Total f.	%
B. Mother	Tenseten	4	40.0	66.7	33.0	6	60.0	100.0	50.0	10	83.0
	Waneten	1	100.0	16.7	8.0	0	0.0	0.0	0.0	1	8.0
	Mabweten	1	100.0	16.7	8.0	0	0.0	0.0	0.0	1	8.0
	TOTAL	6			50.0	6			50.0	12	

Chi-Squared = 2.4   d.f.= 2   p.< 0.5

NOTE: In tables 7-1, 7-2, and 7-3 proportions have been calculated for both rows (R) and columns (K). This permits the sample to be stratified horizontally and vertically.

Table 7-4. Affiliation and Marriage Mode of Kome Residents with No Kome Parents (1968)

Affiliation	Males		Females		Status
	f.	%	f.	%	
Tenseten	0	0	4	33.0	Married in
Sokaten	0	0	2	17.0	Married in
Nenayeten	0*	0	3	25.0	Captured, married
May River	2	17	1	8.0	Captured, females and 1 male married
Total	2	17	10	83.0	

Chi-Squared = 7.2   d.f. = 3   p. < 0.05

* One additional male and two additional females were returned to Atbalmin by the administration in the late 1950s.

and destroy gardens, he couldn't kill his matrikin nor could he eat them. He said, "It would be like eating my own leg." But this disability does not extend to his children.

The positive side to being the issue of or a party to an exogamous marriage is that one often has a greater role in interparish politics, an enhanced position in interparish visiting (see below) as the focus of hospitality which is also extended to one's companions, and wider, though rarely exercised, residential options.

Marriage

Much of the foregoing discussion has turned on marriage, e.g., the cognatic appearance of the parish as an attribute of parish endogamy. The parish is highly endogamous, with only 20 to 40 percent of all marriages in particular parishes being exogamous. This variable frequency depends on the presence or absence of a close relationship between particular parishes which will be described below. This can more readily be seen by examining the details of marriage among the Miyanmin.

The minimal definition of marriage that I find useful is "cohabitation without public outcry." My familiarity with many marriages in the sample I describe statistically leads me to view the institution as relatively open, with few rules universally or even widely observed to provide a formal foundation for legitimacy. There are instances of matchmaking, careful negotiation, adherence to the ideal of sister exchange, public ceremony, and lineage exogamy, but in the majority of marriages, the (parish) endogamous ones, only lineage exogamy comes close to being unexcepted.

If we take the cases assembled in *Pigs, Pearlshells, and Women* (Glasse and Meggitt 1969) as a sample of New Guinea marriage custom, the Miyanmin are atypical. There are no "pigs and pearlshells," i.e., no bride price. The Miyanmin are familiar with, and bemused by, the practice of bride price by their Telefolmin neighbors to the south (see Ruth Craig 1969). This familiarity serves only to confirm their stereotype of the Telefolmin as stingy (among a long list of other negative attributes). Polygyny is limited to two wives at a time and is relatively infrequent. Divorce among the *am-nakai* groups is recognized, but most marriages are dissolved only by the death of one partner. Gardner (1981:128), however, finds a high frequency of divorce among the *sa-nakai* groups of the west and describes wife-killing as a substitute for divorce. There are instances within the parish of levirate, sororate and apparent widow inheritance, all idiosyncratic and balanced (in terms of their resemblance to practices widely reported for New Guinea) by instances of stepdaughter marriage, marriage with a classificatory sister, elopement, matrimonial rape, and true marriage by abduction. None of these,

Plate 8.   A Boy Listens to His Father

Plate 9.   The Same Boy Learns from His Matrikin
He spent half his time with this person growing up. Here, they
are working on the roof of a new men's house.

however, is frequent enough to be "reportable." Individualism, friendship, openness, durability and the absence of formal sanctions seem to be the salient characteristics of intraparish marriage among the Miyanmin. As will be described later, interparish marriages are the antithesis of this: formal, fraught with mistrust, with sanctions applied as one of the most important expressions of interparish politics.

There is a relationship between lineage exogamy (the classification of kin) and the lineage pattern, on the one hand, and the material on-the-ground articulation of settlement, people, and components of the environment, on the other hand. This articulation is described in detail in a later section. Here I focus on the rules and their immediate ramifications in the sphere of marriage. The rules of lineage exogamy are incest taboos and concern with bilateral kin. These are stated in terms of the siblingship of age-mates in father's and mother's agnatic lineages.

As I describe in the sections on hamlets below and dual residence in chapter 9, a child spends approximately half the time living in a hamlet consisting largely of father's agnates and the other half in a hamlet identified with mother's lineage. In effect, the rules of lineage exogamy involve an incest taboo imposed upon the opposite sex co-residents with whom one grows up in the two kinds of hamlets. The two apparent violations of the bilateral rule known to me involved persons in prohibited categories who had not shared residence in this fashion until after puberty. On the other hand, in discussing marital opportunities with young bachelors, I have heard young women not standing in a prohibited category to the speaker rejected from consideration because they were "too much like a sister," e.g., they had grown up in close proximity to each other. Of course, the term of address used by a man to a young woman whom he is courting is *nenge*, the kin term for "little sister." This could be an inconsistency or an assurance of honorable intentions. Another possible inconsistency involves "captured" wives. Such women are typically captured as children, raised in their captors' family, then married by them or given to a younger brother. Of course, in this respect they are more like daughters than sisters!

Given the dual residence pattern, with small dispersed hamlets limiting the exposure of nonprohibited persons to each other, courtship and marriage have a somewhat cyclical character keyed to the flux of the overall settlement pattern. Consistent opportunity goes with nucleation, e.g., the maintenance of a long house/dance house or a larger hamlet or tight cluster of hamlets (see below and chapter 3). Young bachelors are mobile and footloose at times with reasonable excuses or opportunities to loiter for several days around a hamlet not their own. There are more marriages during the nucleated phase at the beginning of a settlement cycle than during a comparable period of the later dispersed phase.

One reason for this is that building a dance house and holding a festival, while associated with the general well-being of the parish (see below), are focused on the set of youngest married people in the parish. The interior of the dance house/long house (*itam*) consists of a large central dance floor with a raised sleeping platform and hearths around the four walls. There are 15 hearths, each assigned to one of the youngest married couples. The festival is also a time of relative sexual license and marriages follow dalliances in the bush close to the *itam*.

The ensuing pattern of residence, with more heterogeneous groups of people sharing the long house and large hamlets, also mixes single people who have not previously shared residence. The associated work patterns encourage courtship as well, particularly the kinds of work requiring overnight bush expeditions away from settlements. These include foraging, distant clearing operations in areas to be settled in the future, or visits back to old habitation sites to harvest pandanus. The close accommodations of one or two crude bush houses in a small clearing is romantic as well as convenient; chaperonage, while official, is not always effective before the fact. Under such circumstances, girls are as aggressive as boys in inviting intimacy of some kind, although this often is no more than holding hands in the dark.

One thing leads to another, however, and "public outcry" could conceivably enter the picture. When both man and woman are of the same parish, and both are willing, "outcry" is possible but unlikely. Young women, who are said (by men) to be more aggressive in courtship than young men (or more interested in marriage), have a good chance of having their choice sustained (or even helped a little) if their parents are alive. Fathers dote on daughters and view sons-in-law as old age insurance ("someone to hunt for me"). A go-between, typically a girl's mother's brother, may be used to develop enthusiasm in the young man's family sufficient to ensure his agreement too. The ideal of sister exchange, realized in more than half of all first marriages (43 percent of all intraparish marriages, table 7-5) doesn't interfere with the Miyanmin version of the "storybook marriage." Such an arrangement may be constructed by the go-between, or two unrelated young men or even women may try to set it up in advance of the go-between's activity. Strong ties of friendship (even solidarity) within particular age-sex groups are parish-wide or wider and brothers-in-law should be good friends (as witness the story of Waisano that started this book).

An additional dimension is the visible solidarity of women. Women, as well as men, have common interests in congenial affines and in limiting their variety. The fewer sets of affines shared by a group of siblings, the fewer the conflicts in establishing individual dual residence patterns that are in step. This permits maximum contact between siblings and, with respect to men, is the basis for identifying particular hamlets with particular lineages (see

Table 7-5. Kome Wife Acquisition (1968)

Method	Intraparish				Interparish			
	f.	Percentages			f.	Percentages		
		R	K	T		R	K	T
Sister Exchange	9	69.3	42.9	26.0	4	30.8	30.8	12.0
Gift	6	85.8	28.6	18.0	1	14.3	7.7	3.0
Capture*	3	75.0	14.3	9.0	1	25.0	7.7	3.0
Residence	0	0.0	0.0	0.0	4	100.0	30.8	12.0
Widow Remarriage	3	100.0	14.3	9.0	0	0.0	0.0	0.0
Elopement	0	0.0	0.0	0.0	2	100.0	15.4	6.0
Delayed Reciprocity	0	0.0	0.0	0.0	1	100.0	7.7	3.0
TOTAL	21			62.0	13			29.0

Chi-Squared = 15.46   d.f.= 6   p.< 0.02

* Marriage with a captured woman is classified as inter- or intraparish depending on the parish into which she was adopted after capture.

NOTE: This table shows the frequency distribution of methods of wife acquisition for all contemporary intra- and interparish marriages of Kome residents. Proportions have been calculated for the rows (R) and the columns (K) and for the total marriage sample (T). The row proportions stratify the sample by marriage method, the column proportions by political context.

below). In theory, polygynists in my sample have "solved" it. In all but one case, at least one of the two wives was a "free" woman lacking close agnates; in two cases captured women were involved.

There is a four- or five-year difference in age between husbands and wives, with men marrying between the ages of 20 and 25 and women in their late teens (these ages are increasing in the modern period). Women and their parents are interested in assessing the potential of young men. Also, their assumption of adult initiation grade of *dil* (chapter 8) was a traditional prerequisite to marriage. At the same time, young women express an aversion to marriage with "old" men, especially widowers with children. Only a few first marriages are of this nature and they tend to begin with "outcry," or worse, and to be short.

Thus the "storybook marriage" is not universal. For one thing, sister exchange is not always practical, but the pattern is sufficiently flexible for almost a third of first (intraparish) marriages to be unbacked or a "gift" (28 percent of all contemporary Kome interparish marriages in table 7-5). For another, a girl with one or both parents dead may be in a fix. If her father is widowed and she is the youngest or sole unmarried daughter, she may be "bound" by her father to take care of him until he dies. As one elderly friend told me, "If they want to marry my daughter they can give me some old woman to take care of me." A girl who is the ward of her brothers may find herself given against her will to one of their pals, in fact beaten into submitting to the marriage. In this situation young women find considerable support among other women. I observed one incident of mass intersexual "war" that continued for a week or so, with many beatings and minor (with antibiotics available in the anthropologist's kit) arrow wounds and firewood contusions. A girl who runs away can hide in the bush and receive food covertly from other women or take food from gardens at night. Without a guardian, however, the would-be husband is free to stalk her, catch, and rape her. Pregnancy is what finally makes her "settle down." If she flees to another parish she may be leaping into the "fire" of even greater coercion and lack of security, although she may have won on principle. Finally, as Gardner (1981:125) also has reported, old women may not only threaten but kill the children of their sons and daughters if the latter marry against their wishes.

There is an optional wedding ceremony employed only rarely. In this ceremony, the bride roasts a sufficient quantity ot taro to feed those present. The bride's mother's brother, who may have served as a go-between, then takes one of the cooked corms, breaks it in two parts, and presents these to the bride and groom.

In the majority of intraparish marriages, residence is bilocal, part of the pattern of dual residence described in chapter 9. Because of this virtual universality (table 7-6), those intraparish marriages which are classified as

Plate 10. Young Sokaten Maidens

The solidarity of women is manifested in gatherings, work sharing, assistance at parturition, and occasional mass resistance to male authority.

Plate 11. Women Make the Clay Hearth of a New Men's House
It will be cured with a carefully tended fire.

unbacked ("gift" and "widow remarriage" in table 7-5) involve de facto bride service. Earlier, I noted the expectations of a father-in-law regarding his daughter's husband. Cooperation in horticulture, hunting, and other tasks goes along with periodic residence with one's affines (from either a married man's or a married woman's point of view). It amounts to bride service in practice. Widows are never backed with a sister, but relations with affines follow the general pattern of bilocality/dual residence.

As we shall see, "outcry" is more characteristic of interparish marriages, because these are characterized by more extensive negotiation, an insistence that marriages be backed, less contact and cooperation between affines, and correspondingly more distrust and discord (sometimes perennial outcry).

Table 7-5 compares intra- and interparish marriages with respect to the mode of wife acquisition for all contemporary Kome marriages. The typical mode for backing marriages between parishes is also sister exchange, but uxorilocality is a frequent option, with delayed reciprocity agreed to only occasionally. But interparish marriages are almost always backed as the table indicates. The few exceptions (also discussed in more detail later) are the result of the postcontact loss of parish sovereignty. For example, a young Kome man who eloped with *two* girls from Sokaten kept the women and his skin intact. One reason for the insistence on backing marriages between parishes is that bilocality is not always practical, so that the bride service benefit does not hold. The contrast between intra- and interparish marriages with respect to postmarital residence (table 7-6) is just as striking and holds even for marriages between Kometen and Temseten where bilocality would be a practical possibility because of settlement pattern cooperation. Instead, two separate hamlets are maintained in close proximity to each other, one Kome, and one Temse, in which many of the participants in marriages between these two parishes reside for part of the year.

Marriage is considered to be the natural state for all adults. The division of labor between men and women, while flexible (chapter 5), is only part of the story. The range of necessary activities, and the amount of time which must be devoted to them, means that only married couples can achieve any degree of self-sufficiency and maintain a normal standard of living. The situation of widowers, especially those with children, sheds light on this. A widower becomes almost a full-time gardener, making only a token contribution to local meat production. At that, the garden production of widowers is barely adequate, and they cannot continue to support the pigs formerly cared for by their wives.

Most people want to be married, with some 61 percent of the adult (over 15 years old) fraction of the Kome population achieving it at the time of my census (table 7-7). The imbalance between the sexes, previously described, is partly compensated for by the disparity in age at marriage. The eleven

Table 7-6. Contemporary (1960s) Marriages of Kome Men (1968)

(Including Nonresidents, Affiliation of Wife, and Postmarital Residence)

Affiliation of Wife	f.	%	Bilocal				Virilocal				Uxorilocal			
			f.	R	K	T	f.	R	K	T	f.	R	K	T
Kometen	21	53.0	17	81.0	100	43.0	3	14.3	21.5	8.0	1	4.8	11.2	3.0
Temseten	4	10.0	0	0.0	0.0	0.0	4	100.0	28.6	10.0	0	0.0	0.0	0.0
Sokaten	2	10.0	0	0.0	0.0	0.0	2	100.0	14.3	5.0	0	0.0	0.0	0.0
Mabweten	1	3.0	0	0.0	0.0	0.0	1	100.0	7.2	3.0	0	0.0	0.0	0.0
Hoten	6	15.0	0	0.0	0.0	0.0	0	0.0	0.0	0.0	6	100.0	66.6	15.0
Wameten	2	10.0	0	0.0	0.0	0.0	0	0.0	0.0	0.0	2	100.0	22.3	5.0
Enemy Group	4	10.0	0	0.0	0.0	0.0	4	100.0	28.6	10.0	0	0.0	0.0	0.0
TOTAL	40		17				14				9			

Chi-Squared = 60.80   d.f. = 10 $p < 0.001$

NOTE: This table shows the frequency distribution of group affiliation of the wives of Kome men at the time of the survey. Proportions have been calculated for the rows (R) and the columns (K), as well as for the total sample (T). The row proportions stratify the sample by the wife's group affiliation, the column proportions by postmarital residence mode.

unmarried women in my sample represent one very old widow, one very recent widow, and almost the entire 15- to 20-year-old female cohort (figure 7-1b). On the other hand, the 49 percent of all males who are presently unmarried represent a substantial portion of the 15- to 20- and the 20- to 25-year male cohorts, plus five widowers and two confirmed bachelors. I have already described the contribution of the fertility of captured women to the Kome population. Several informants stated independently that they had participated in a series of Atbalmin raids explicitly (and successfully) to get a wife.[5] They had previously been unsuccessful in contracting a regular marriage because of the recognized shortage of women.

A more detailed breakdown of marital status and history is provided by tables 7-8 (for men) and 7-9 (for women). Here the contrast between men and women is heightened: a quarter of the women as against half the men without mates, twice as many widowers as widows, a third of the men and two-thirds of the women married to only one person, twice as many widows remarried as widowers. This also points to the remarkable stability of marriage, the fact that most people will have only one mate throughout their lives (table 7-10). In the 1960s I found that among the present residents of Kome parish, there had been only one divorce (the permanent return of a woman to her family after an extended period of sanctioned cohabitation). I also recorded one case of annulment in which a confirmed bachelor was given a women and did not like the state of marriage. Divorce is reportedly more frequent in West Mianmin (Gardner 1981) and is more common now in the east.

Polygyny was similarly infrequent in the 1960s: the five instances in Kome parish are unusually high for Miyanmin groups known to me. There were no contemporary polygynists at Sokaten; one at Temseten, two at Usaliten I, four at Mabweten (a noneastern Miyanmin group which I censused), and and three at Wameten. As previously noted, polygyny is limited to two wives at a time, and the prevailing sentiment among Miyanmin men and women is that two wives is one too many. Gardner (1981) reports a contrary statement, that three are less trouble than two. There is almost always discord in polygynous households. Although each wife is entitled to her own hearth and door, wives otherwise share the same unpartitioned house. Discord often centers on sex or work and (young) polygynous males are advised (by older polygynous men) to practice discretion and evenhandedness (if that's the term) in sexual matters. One young polygynist with two young wives (unusual in itself), was the subject of a lot of jibes ("stone cock") and gossip ("too busy to hunt"). The sleep of his hamlet-mates was often disturbed because he liked to make love to one wife while the other was asleep nearby. She would awaken and attack her husband and co-wife, on one occasion scooping up hot ashes from a hearth and dumping them on them.

Table 7-7. Kome Parish Marriage Rates (1968)

Status	Men				Women				Total	
	f.	Percentages			f.	Percentages			f.	%
		R	K	T		R	K	T		
Married	27	45.8	51.0	28.0	32	54.3	74.5	33.0	59	61.0
Single	26	70.3	49.0	27.0	11	29.8	25.6	11.0	37	39.0
Row TOTAL	53			55.0	43			45.0	96	

Chi-Squared = 4.56   d.f. = 1   p.< 0.05

NOTE: This table shows the frequency distribution of marriage among men and women residents of Kome parish. Proportions have been calculated for the rows (R), the columns (K), and for the total sample (T). The row proportions stratify the sample by marital status, the columns by sex.

Co-wives do not garden together and never attend each other in the parturition hut. Today, polygyny has virtually disappeared in the east.

Plural marriages were not associated with high social status of the husband as they are in some societies. Of the five polygynists residing in Kometen, only one would score high in a status ranking as the traditional shaman and government appointed *tultul.*

The subjective side of marriage is that the husband is always dominant. He may beat his wife for minor reasons, and she, according to the rules (not honored by all women by any means), may only strike the ground beside him in return. But husbands and wives spend a lot of time together working side by side; weeding, the most onerous of horticultural tasks, is shared equally. Married couples spend extended periods off by themselves living in bush houses, starting new gardens, or hunting and foraging in the forest, and men are equally at home minding children. Although public displays of affection do not occur between men and women, husbands and wives reveal their real affection for each other in private and in small domestic scenes only rarely glimpsed by the outsider.

Lineages

The lineages described earlier in this chapter have territorial tendencies but among the *am-nakai* Miyanmin they are submerged in the corporate parish. Lineage territorial sentiments are expressed in the context of minor disputes between fellow parish members who happen to be members of different lineages, but such sentiments are honored only in the short run and only to the extent that it is said that individuals who don't get along would do well not to live near each other. Parish solidarity seems to win out over lineage solidarity in resolving or at least mitigating such disputes in most cases, and harmony within the parish is a value commonly expressed. Fuyariten, a West Miyanmin parish notorious for a high level of internal conflict, is derisively referred to as *nema-morupsel,* that is, "lineage of cockatoos." According to Gardner, this is characteristic of *sa-nakai* groups.

In the long run, however, parish fission and the adhesion of small groups to other parishes occur along lineage lines; and in the low-altitude, low population density areas of the north and west, lineages appear to be more territorial. Gardner (1981) also suggests that patrilineal lineages are more important than parishes as residential and corporate units.[6] The core of the Usaliten segment (referred to in table 7-ll as Usaliten II) living on the Abe River is such a lineage. It has increasingly assumed many of the corporate attributes of a parish, including the possession of its own ceremonial buildings.

Variation in the degree of localization of lineages follows similar geographical lines. Lineages in the south are only cyclically localized because

Table 7-8. Marital Status and History of Kome Men (1968)

Status	f.	%	Total	Percent
Men without wives			26	49.0
a. never married	21	40.0		
b. widowers	5	9.0		
Men with one wife			22	42.0
a. married to one woman	19	36.0		
b. polygynous, widowed, one remains	1	2.0		
c. widowed, remarried	2	4.0		
Men with two wives			5	9.0
a. married to two women	4	7.0		
b. multiple series, two remain	1	2.0		
			53	100.0

* Nineteen are "young bachelors"; hence 2 are "perennial bachelors."

Table 7-9. Marital Status and History of Kome Women (1968)

Status	f.	%	Total	Percent
Women without husbands			11	26.0
a. never married	9	21.0		
b. widows	2	5.0		
Married women			32	74.0
a. married to one man	27	62.0		
b. widowed, remarried	5	12	43	

Table 7-10. Number of Marriages of Kome Residents (1968)

	0		1		2		3		4		Total People
	f.	%	f.	%	f.	%	f.	%	f.	%	
Men	21*	39.7	25	47.2	6	11.4	0	0.0	1	1.9	53
Women	9	21.0	29	67.5	5	11.7	0	0.0	0	0.0	43
TOTAL	0		54		22		0		4		80/96

Chi-Squared = 7.20   d.f.= 4   p.< 0.10

of the dual residence pattern. In the north hamlets are more dispersed and a cluster of dispersed hamlets may be associated with a particular lineage. The geographical divide for lineage territoriality and localization occurs on the east-west axis marked by the Fiak and Urame rivers in the eastern Miyanmin area. In the west according to Gardner (1981), only the Kariten resemble the *am-nakai* of the east.

As indicated earlier, each of the larger southern parishes can identify four of these lineages. Some of these are described as growing or declining ("all but finished"). Emigration, uxorilocal marriage and distant residence are symptomatic of decline. Most nonresident Kome are members of a single lineage, called Druban, which can be so characterized (chapter 10).

The Local Population

Another type of group differentiated by the Miyanmin is a regional cluster identified with an important drainage system and settlement area. These groups carry the name of the river involved and the suffix -*tamansel*, meaning "river valley people" (e.g., Haktamansel, for the Hak Valley people). I call these clusters "local populations" in the ecological sense. Following Rappaport (1968), a "local population" is "a unit composed of an aggregate of organisms having in common certain distinctive means whereby they maintain a set of shared trophic relations with other living and non-living components of the [ecosystem] in which they exist together" (225). The importance of the "local population" as a unit of demographic analysis was discussed earlier in this chapter.

In the Miyanmin case, a local population may consist of a single intact parish, a large parish segment, a parish and a segment of another parish, or two parishes. Some of these alignments (involving the "special relationship," or alliance, invoked earlier in this chapter in connection with variable parish exogamy) are relatively enduring, but the relationship in not obvious on the surface because individual parish identity is maintained. The reality of the phenomenon becomes clear only when one collects and analyses a corpus of genealogical data, oral traditions, and settlement histories. I have done this only for the Kome-Temse and Soka-Wame alliances.

In addition to a higher rate of intermarriage, alliances involve cooperation in the use of a particular occupation area that, while not as great as that within a parish, is greater than the degree of cooperation with other neighboring parishes. I am describing a scale of cooperation, particularly with respect to the articulation of settlement patterns, that diminishes with distance, an attribute that will become clearer when we look at movement per se.

The cooperative relationship between such units persists despite the fact that small parishes or segments attached to larger parishes are in a politically subordinate position characterized by a certain amount of tension and distrust, particularly with respect to women and interparish affinal relations in general. It will be recalled that although sister exchange, with no bride price, is the ideal for all marriages, within the parish it is not rigidly adhered to. In marriages between parishes, however, even parishes paired in a special relationship, the only possibilities are either sister exchange, delayed reciprocity, or uxorilocality (or elopement with retribution).

It might be argued, but be difficult to prove, that this kind of arrangement facilitates the tailoring of a local population to fit a particular area. For example, under population pressure, the smaller, less powerful segment (or a declining lineage, for that matter), or a part of it, would be the first to pick up and settle elsewhere. This seems to have been the situation in the relationship of Kometen and Temseten with which I am most familiar. This relationship has existed for at least a century with Temseten or a segment of it (as at the present time) always clinging to the "left flank" of the largely Kome settlement pattern. When, in the 1950s, Kome shifted back into the Hak-Uk area it had occupied jointly with Temseten 50 years before, a large Temse segment detached itself to join Hoten in the Usake River area and a smaller number of individuals settled with Usaliten I. (Note that the proximate cause was a dispute.) It is conceivable that Kome had a smaller population during the earlier occupation than it does now.

I speculate also that in certain contexts larger populations are more viable than smaller ones. There is the political problem of coping with the larger Telefol groups to the south (see chapter 10), as well as the question of demographic viability arising from the sex imbalance discussed earlier in this chapter. Figure 7-5, a population pyramid for the combined Kome-Temsak local population, shows the demographic side of close cooperation between parishes. It is much more balanced and stable in appearance than the age-sex structures for either of the two parishes considered separately in figures 7-2(a) and (b).

In table 7-11, eight local populations in the eastern Miyanmin area are identified. More time spent with some of the other groups might have allowed me to refine this to a certain degree. For example, I do have some evidence of a high degree of cooperation between Wameten and Sokaten, but I also have a feeling that this is a shadow left over from before Sokaten was displaced from the western side of the May River by Kometen 50 years ago (chapter 10) when both groups were much smaller.

Figure 7-5.   Population Pyramid for the Kome-Temsak Local
Population of the Hak Valley (1969)

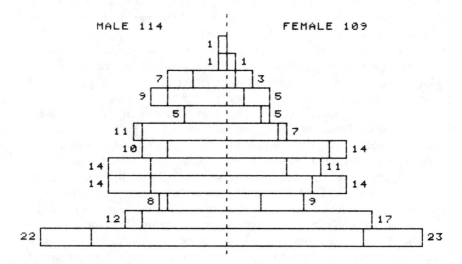

The Hamlet

The hamlet, designated by the suffix -*bip*, is a unit of residence, labor and food sharing, and hospitality. Its size varies, ranging from two or three family houses (*unangam*, literally "woman house") and a men's house (*timan*), to a single long house (*itam*) with 15 hearths, or a large centralized village with 12 or more family houses and a men's house. With the exception of bush houses that require from 3 to 10 people-hours to construct, Miyanmin houses are substantial, built on posts, with raised bark and palm wood floors, floor level clay hearths, lined bark and split timber walls and durable sago or pandanus and tree leaf roofs. Family houses and men's houses require between 600 and 900 people-hours to build. Thus hamlets represent a considerable investment of labor, and the apparent fluidity which characterizes their founding, use, and abandonment, to be described below, must be viewed against this background.

The average size of hamlets changes with the phase of the settlement cycle, with larger, more centralized villages, a tight cluster of smaller hamlets, or a long house, associated with the early phase of the cycle, and numerous smaller, more dispersed hamlets in the later phases of the cycle (the quantitative aspect of this is presented in chapter 9). Moreover, this change occurs as the overall number of domiciles (as measured by hearth frequencies in figure 9-3) increases. Applying the "rules" that "every married woman is entitled to her own hearth" and "every elementary family maintains houses in two hamlets," the expected frequency of hearths for Kome parish would be

Table 7-11. Population and Territory of East Miyanmin Parishes and
Local Populations

Parish Name	Location of Popula- tion	Population Males	Population Females	Sub- tot.	Local Pop.	Territory Area	Raw Density
Kometen	Hak River	86	73	159			
Temseten	San-Hak	28	36	64*	223	38.00	5.87
Usaliten I	San-Wamu	53	54	107	107	27.37	3.90
Usaliten II	Abe River	44	34	78	78	37.75	2.05
Sokaten	May River	87	71	158	158	26.19	6.08
Wameten	Wandagu R.	52	52	104	104	17.78	5.77
Amaloten	Ulame R.	29	24	53	53	76.00	0.697
Hoten+	Usake R.	42	30	72+	72	76.62	0.935
Boblikten+	Thurnwald Range	64	56	120+	120	14.06	8.57
TOTAL East Miyanmin		485	430	915	915	313.77#	2.91

* Kometen and Temseten parishes are lumped together for purposes of calculating territory and raw population density because, although the ownership of certain parcels of land can be established unequivocally, the actual boundaries between these units of what is essentially a single land-using group are actually very fuzzy. The common territory is referred to by the Miyanmin as *Kome-Temseri Betan* (map 3).

Omitted is a tract of indeterminate size in the Hoten area seized from Miyanten several generations ago which all groups claim. It includes part of the Frieda mine prospect.

+ Population figures for these groups are estimates based on raw administration census material.

twice the number of married women, 64, plus one hearth per men's house or eight (for the first half of 1969), a total of 72. In fact the maximum observed frequency for this period is 44, from which must be subtracted the eight hamlet men's house hearths to give 36 family house hearths. This discrepancy is readily explained.

In the earliest phase of settlement, mature, productive families are the first to establish houses and gardens in new locations. Younger families follow them, and also lag behind in house construction and full participation in the pattern of dual residence. In addition, the elderly are less involved. In other words, the familial developmental cycle status of a particular elementary or polygynous extended joint family is a good indicator of participation in settlement building. New, "immature" families are undercapitalized and underproductive in many respects (chapter 5); and, as they participate in dual residence, are likely to share houses with older agnates and affines. The quantitative effect of this is that the total number of domiciles is not consistent with the number of married women or elementary families, even in the third phase of the settlement cycle when an asymptote is apparently reached.

This general picture of hamlet location and growth is further complicated by ecological zonation, especially the north-south altitudinal gradient. The highest frequency of functioning long houses and dispersed settlement is characteristic of lower altitudes and flatter topography (mostly in the north and west) with larger centralized villages or hamlet clusters (two or three small hamlets within a few minutes' walking distance of each other) and somewhat tighter settlement patterns characteristic of higher altitudes and relief. These differences are related to the distribution of regularly exploited food resources in these settings as well as to the ease of getting to them. *Sa-nakai* groups of the lower altitudes, such as the Hoten, Amaloten, and Usaliten II local populations, depend more on sago and, although it is abundant in natural stands, mature palms are more patchily distributed. The *am-nakai* groups of the higher altitudes, exemplified by Sokaten and the Kome-Temsak local populations, depend on their taro gardens, which represent points of homogenization in an otherwise patchy environment. Also, as is argued in chapter 6, wild pigs are at times distributed in the same way.

Hamlets are located on scalped ridges or spurs, or on the banks of normally placid small rivers, the latter a stated preference but less possible in areas of high relief. On this level, there are two sets of parameters determining hamlet location. One set, to be dealt with in chapter 9, places hamlet location in the context of a cyclical movement strategy. I argue that the cycle determines the general location. The other set of parameters has to do with the distribution of suitable horticultural land. As discussed in chapter 5, gardens are usually made on the natural benches, and the steeper slopes between them, which are characteristic of the lower slopes of mountains and the divides between the lesser tributaries of rivers. These are accessible from the smaller rivers that provide natural walking paths. Gardens are also made in the hollows between spurs higher up the mountainside. In the absence of a riverbed to walk on, hamlets are connected with gardens and with each other by numerous narrow tracks.

Among the lower-altitude *sa-nakai* Miyanmin groups in the north, such as Amaloten and Hoten, hamlets and gardens are characteristically on the banks and terraces immediately adjacent to rivers, with small hamlets of only one or two houses set in the middle of large gardens a normal pattern. Here too, the patrilineages (*morupsel*) associated with the hamlets are more localized—not submerged in a more nucleated parish structure as in the south.

8

Ritual Dimensions

Afek of the Miyanmin

In ancient times, two women came to the upper Sepik from the east. They were Fitipkanip and her younger sister Dimoson.[1]

Bearing a huge *bilum* filled with plants and animals, Dimoson turned north into the valley of the Yuwa (May) River. There she approached Mekil (Mount Stolle) and asked him to wed but, due to the powerful odor emanating from both her *bilum* and her person, he refused. Continuing northward, she courted Kasa Mountain in turn and he also turned her down. Finally, near the Abe (right May) River, she proposed to Mount Weya and he accepted her offer.

Dimoson almost dropped her *bilum* in surprise and leaned back quickly to set it on the ground and avoid a fall. In doing so, she placed all her weight on one leg, impressing a footprint in the stone on which she stood. It can be seen to this day at a place called Misawe.[2] The contents of her *bilum* escaped into the bush, swamps and watercourses of the area; sago shoots, cane grass, possums, fish, turtles, birds, and wild pigs. This accounts for the bountiful resources for which the region is renowned.

Dimoson bore a son and daughter with Weya. Later, when her son was full grown, he tracked a cassowary to the north and there married a woman from a local riverine group. They had many (four or more) children who were the progenitors of the several Miyanmin parishes.

While Dimoson went north, her sister Fitipkanip remained at Blesobip near the head of the Hak (Fak) River. She made a garden and grew taro there. One day, she harvested taro and gathered stones, intending to cook it in a leaf oven. As she labored, some men appeared and announced that her little sister lay near death.[3] She rushed to Dimoson's side and told her what she had to do.

"When your descendants die, they will be eaten by dogs and other animals. To prevent this, you must precede them and break a path that they can follow after death. I, myself, will also follow you."

So, after her death, Dimoson cleared a new track, known as *bekeldep*, leading to two populated areas, Hawagan and Kwerogan that she had also founded. This is the land of the dead or spirit world.

Meanwhile, Fitipkanip returned to Blesobip. In a rage of grief she destroyed her taro and the leaf oven she had started.

She then set out down the Hak, crossing and recrossing it until she reached its junction with the Teken (Sepik) River. Moving downstream to the west, she sought a site suitable for a bridge, for in those days the river was broader than it is today. She paused at Gogotem to build a bridge. First she narrowed the gap with immense boulders that she transported gripped in her vulva. She bridged the remaining gap with parts of her labia that she held in place with smaller stones. The bridge known as Gogotemtrum was built in this way. She built similar bridges further west known as Dekaiyumtrum or Fitimtrum (at Atbalmin) and Sisimtrum. The boulders she employed are still visible on the Teken.

Fitipkanip then founded Urapmin to the south of the Teken by building the *kwoisam* at Nengrebip. As her labor neared completion she happened to glance up and observe smoke over the Ilam Valley. She followed it quickly and discovered a man, whom she killed. She returned with his body to Urapmin and entered the *kwoisam* to celebrate her victory.

She next took a piece of liana cane and journeyed to Kelefolbip (Telefolip) to build another *kwoisam*. A sago palm and a *semai* tree grew on the site she selected. She felled both and constructed a building with two rooms. She placed the hearth of one room on the base of the sago palm and said, "This hearth is for cooking taro (*imentul*)." The hearth of the other room she placed on the stump of the *simai* tree and said, "This hearth is for cooking arrows (*antul* or *awatul;* arrow hearth or combat hearth)."[4]

As she surveyed her work, Fitipkanip trod on sago bark and injured her foot on a thorn. Hence, she gathered a large quantity of fine white sand to cover the bark and the surrounding area. The results of this can be seen in the Ifitaman to the present day.

She glanced up and once again saw smoke rising, this time over the Feramin Valley. She followed it and discovered a man in an *isop* tree eating fruit. She killed him with her fighting club and bore the carcass back to Kelefolbip. There she butchered it, gathered taro, and prepared to cook in a leaf oven. She started a fire to heat stones and placed near it leaves in which she had collected blood drained from the body. As she gathered up the viscera to wash in the Difai River, she turned to Rat, Bird, and Frog, who lurked nearby, and said, "Keep watch on my place."

She completed this chore and looked up in time to see the three animal-kind fleeing. Then she noticed that the building was aflame. Discarding the viscera, she rushed to the village. During her brief absence, the fire had spread from the stone-fire to the leaves holding the coagulating blood and thence to the *kwoisam*. She attempted to put the fire out but it was by now a conflagration and soon spread to the surrounding bush. She rushed with her fighting club to Afekdafap, a peak in the Mittag Mountains at the northern end of the valley. There she made a stand, declaring, "This fire will not injure my people in the Eliptaman." She successfully contained the fire with her club.

Returning to Kelefolbip, she quickly restored it and set about creating all the other Kelefolmin villages. She also went hunting and assembled a quantity of animal young which she raised to be the people of the valley.

Many years later, Fitipkanip was attacked by a wild dog which copulated with her. Observing the act, a local man named Sarimin declared, "You cannot do that kind of thing." And with that he killed Fitipkanip with an arrow to the base of the skull. The dog turned and devoured her vulva before fleeing to the bush. She was buried by local women and later her remains were partially disinterred in order that the cranium could be recovered. This was placed above a hearth in the Kelefolbip *kwoisam* where it remains to the present day.

The role of ritual and belief in the ecological relations of the Miyanmin is not a major focus of this work although there are grounds for entitling it "Pigs *from* the Ancestors" (cf. Rappaport 1967, 1968). There are also good reasons for including an extended discussion of Miyanmin religious belief and practice. In accordance with Rappaport's discovery, I do not believe that religious belief and practice can be relegated to an "ideological superstructure" remote from the practical problems of everyday life.

The most important issues involving Miyanmin religion include the following:

1. Rituals are an integral part of responses to environmental problems with the fear and fact of death a particularly critical linkage.
2. A number of critical decisions having ecological consequences are made or promulgated in a ritual context.
3. Initiation instills "loyalty" and hence inhibits certain individual options.
4. Ritual performances are involved in the distribution of important segments of the population and workforce.
5. Ceremonies open to regional participation help to articulate the settlement patterns of different local populations and provide a test of the political relations between them.

In sum, certain ritual and ceremonial events are equilibrational or escalatory and have direct measurable effects on individual people, on the local human population itself, and on its relations with other human and nonhuman populations in its environment. The beliefs, the rituals, and the understandings of the social actors involved, insofar as these have such demonstrable material effects, are part of the human adaptation.

This chapter describes Miyanmin supernatural beliefs and outlines the kinds of rituals and ceremonies that are a part of the overall strategy. In particular, two complementary frameworks are suggested for examining the ritual and religious dimensions of Miyanmin adaptive behavior. The first focuses particularly on the behavior of individuals, including its context, costs, and benefits, and is based on the R. J. Lifton's model of the "survivor syndrome." The other framework involves a ceremonial cycle which is part of the settlement cycle presented in my systems model (chapter 3). I aim to pursue a model of ritual behavior in both of these and have three principal concerns: (1) How do religious conventions and idioms shape people's perceptions of problems and other changes?; (2) How do these, in turn, contribute to equilibrating, escalatory, and flexibility-restoring responses in such spheres as agriculture, hunting, movement, and warfare (the latter a species of movement)?; and (3) What are the temporal properties of these responses?

Both traditional and modern Miyanmin understandings and behavior are permeated by religious belief and ritual performance. Accordingly, the religious field is not easily compartmentalized and this is done here only in adherence to ethnographic convention. The modern period brings with it the additional complication of the widespread adoption of Christianity. This occurred with a certain suddenness in the 1960s, especially in the east, and superficially appears as a radical change. I speculate, however, that certain axioms of traditional belief are concordant with Christian tenets (e.g., the sacrifice of Oiyap [chapter I] and of Jesus). Moreover, the abandonment of certain responses that were laden with ritual meaning awaited the extinction of the conditions that otherwise elicited them (e.g., high mortality). An additional problem associated with the adoption of Christianity is that, to the best of my knowledge, no outsider ever witnessed any rituals in the male initiation cycle, although I have witnessed other kinds of traditional rites.

The Afterlife and Its Inhabitants

As the myth that began this chapter indicates, the Miyanmin attribute the creation of the known world, including the land of the dead, to two culture heroes. The inhabitants of the afterlife are *bekel* spirits (or ghosts), including the spirits of the dead who reside in the land of the dead uxorilocally, and the "full" members of Dimoson's lineage. Like anyone else. the latter have names (known to *kinkan* shamans) and are able to move to the fringes of their territory and beyond. For example, large boulders of volcanic conglomerate (*tom-goye*) found in the southern part of Miyanmin country are inhabited by this kind of spirit and are entrances to the spirit road. The spirits of both male and female dead of the various parishes, also *bekel*, marry into Demoson's line. Children are born and are regarded as the half-siblings of the living offspring of the dead. Although the spirits of the dead can intercede in human affairs almost from the time of death, they cannot physically return to the world of the living along the spirit road until offspring in the spirit world are mature. Then, one of these children may accompany their parent and be introduced to their kinsmen among the living. Such a reunion is the method of recruiting new shamans, a relatively rare and remarkable event indeed, for most parishes have only one, at most two, *kinkan*.

How Spirits Behave

It is one thing to have kin relations with a wide circle of persons, and another thing to exercise them. In effect, *kinkan* are able to establish relations with the matrikin of their spirit half-siblings who are *bekel* of Dimoson's line. These spirits are among the instruments of the shaman's vocation. It is with their assistance that the shaman performs rituals for the good of his community: curing, fight magic, and sorcery against other groups. A man learns to see death, for that is the derivation of the term *kinkan*,[5] through the agency of his "little brother" and is thus, in a sense, the creature of the spirit world.

The spirits of the dead normally act in aid of their own groups. A person who had died a happy contented member of a group will so act as a *bekel*. At the time of death, however, considerable anxiety is expressed on this issue. Did the person die with anger in his guts? Was he killed by sorcery? By what group? How shall we avenge him? Are *they* trying to wipe us out? Will he join our ancestors or will he abandon us? Can we kill a pig in aid of his journey to the afterlife (the smell of pork is attractive to *bekel* and will distract the dogs and other animals which will otherwise eat him)? All of these questions are expressed in public rituals which help people cope with grief, reassure people on these issues, and provide guides to action in a number of spheres. There is an equation here between discord, sorcery, and death. This is expressed on a group level in discrete acts of vengeance or compensation, conflict, or movement (even flight) and social change. I return to this equation shortly in connection with what I refer to as "death ritual."

There are numerous signs and events which indicate that the worst fears about the disposition of a particular person's spirit have been realized—that, minimally, a spirit cannot be counted on to aid the living, or the worst, that the spirit of their dead friend or relative is acting powerfully against them.

In June 1969, Idakep, a young man of about 20 years, was killed by a wild pig. He was hunting with a group of other Temse men in deep forest on the north side of the Hak River. A pig that had been driven toward a line of men waiting in ambush was wounded and attacked part of the line. The men scattered, abandoning their weapons and rapidly climbing small trees or the vines that cling to the trunks of larger ones. Idakep was wearing a pair of short pants at the time and had just pulled himself off the ground when the pig went after him. One of its feet slipped into a pants pocket, and the young man was borne to the ground and gored to death. The pig continued to maul the body and other men rushed to shoot at it. It was hit several times but many arrows missed, and the pig couldn't be killed. When their arrows were exhausted, some beat the pig with clubs while others attempted to drag the body away. The pig escaped, but was later hunted down and killed when enough undamaged arrows had been retrieved to resume the hunt.

Plate 12. A Sokaten Woman Grieves for Her Kin at Wameten, Where
People Are Attempting to Flee into the Afterlife

Plate 13. A Recent Widow Wearing a Distinctive Necklace and Arm
            Fringes
            She stands outside her house, which was the scene of a
            dramatic post-interment ritual.

Ultimately it was determined that the pig had been under the control of the spirit of a Temse man who had died by sorcery several months before. The latter had, in previous years, been cuckolded. The adulterer was beaten and fled his group, taking refuge with a Temse segment at the mouth of the Fiak River. This man, it was agreed, had sorcerized his fellow parish member, the husband of his ex-paramour. The latter died angry and unavenged and now sought to injure his own group.

Sorcery and Disease

It is axiomatic that sorcery is the cause of all adult nonviolent deaths or alternatively, that all deaths are violent. The case just presented is unusual in that sorcery is only indirectly implicated in the death, but here again, death by misadventure has mystical causes. In the 1960s adult deaths in Kome parish were attributed to the Telefol living in the Elip Valley to the south. Kometen is the closest Miyanmin parish to the Telefol enemy. Temseten divided its accusations between the same Telefolmin and a breakaway Temse segment. Among Miyanmin groups to the north, sorcery accusations were directed at neighboring Miyanmin groups. Wameten on the May River suffered six adult deaths during a very brief period of 1968 due to upper respiratory infections and their complications (see the earlier discussion of postcontact disease patterns in chapter 7). Wameten, however, accused the same refugee adulterer residing in the Temse-Usali hamlet on the Fiak River cited earlier.

The distinction between sickness and death is an important one. The causes of sickness are varied, but only persons who have been subjected to sorcery die. Among the agents of sickness (hence curable and cured) are *unimin* or "demons." Demons are not individually named the way *bekel* are named, but several kinds are distinguished. All are capable of taking people or objects temporarily in their grip. They are heard and felt but not seen, and operate mainly in the dark of night. Particular kinds of demons are associated with waterways, certain trees and shrubs (like the betel nut tree, *Canarium sp.*), habitats (low wet areas), and the like. Some demons have a dual nature, providing sanctions for taboos, guarding certain wild and domestic fauna, helping to effect certain of the mechanical aspects of the hunt, but these are also capable of causing illness.

In most curing ceremonies, the *kinkan*, aided by men and women of the community, diagnoses and either kills or "casts out" the demon implicated. For example, the *kinkan* may use a bamboo smoking tube to search for foreign matter (sometimes described as "dust") in the victims's body. He then uses the same tube with smoke to remove the condition. This may also be accompanied by the killing and preparation of a pig or some other animal (fish, snakes, lizards, or crabs) prescribed for curing the illness or the collection and use of special plants, such as betel, ginger, tangit, or fern tips, along with public singing and dancing. There is usually a food distribution, with the patient receiving a portion as part of the ritual formula (cf. Rappaport 1968:82–87). Women also have special curing rituals that they conduct in secret.

Other illnesses are attributable to taboo violations (eating restricted foods, eating pork raised by one's own daughter, revealing ritual knowledge, and the like), menstrual blood (affecting mostly children and livestock, but hazardous to others), and worms (apparently parasitic and found in meat). I have only limited knowledge of the range of herbs and other therapies: blood-letting for head pain, stinging nettle for the relief of pain and fever, inhalation of steam made with the aromatic root of *Homalomena sp.*, and several *tinea* remedies, including one made from the caustic sap of the tree *Semecarpis sp.* which appears to be efficacious but extremely painful.

The Miyanmin identify two varieties of lethal sorcery, one a Telefolmin patent, the other practiced among the Miyanmin themselves. The Telefolmin type, which the Miyanmin call *usem*, is widely reported in New Guinea and Australia and resembles felonious assault. Typically, the male or female victim is ambushed alone in some isolated bush location, wrestled or beaten to the ground, and held while bamboo or (now) steel needles are driven into the body. The victim returns home with no memory of the attack, sickens, and dies. The determination of cause of death is accomplished through mediumship at the end of the funeral (see below). To my knowledge a more empirical post mortem determination has not been conducted.[6] Nevertheless, an adult death in a southern Miyanmin parish sets off a hysteria of phantom Telefolmin sightings, and numerous suspected sorcery attempts are brought to public notice.

I participated in this phenomenon in July of 1968 early in my first year of fieldwork with the Miyanmin. The atmosphere was very compelling. It was set off by the death of a Kome man living uxorilocally at Sokaten. His death was attributed to *usem* sorcery and the details followed the outline given above very closely. Several days after his death, but before the news had widely diffused, a party of young Telefolmin did indeed appear in Kome territory from the direction of Sokaten, participating in the *Pax Australiana*. I met them in a hamlet on top of the Hak-Uk divide, spoke with several who were pidgin speakers, and was told that they had been trading with Miyanmin groups on the May. Shortly after they departed for Eliptaman, the news of the death and the logical connection between the two events was made by all into a good circumstantial case. A few days later another incident occurred involving the old Kome fight leader. He had constructed a blind for shooting birds on the upper Uk River fairly distant from any hamlet. He used it one day, missed the next day, and returned to it on the third. Then he detected many footprints around the base of the tree and inferred that a party of Telefolmin, bent on sorcerizing him, had surrounded the tree in the belief that he was occupying the blind. He made for the hamlet which housed most of the young men of the parish, "turning out the guard," so to speak, and went off hunting Telefolmin. None were found. I discovered later that the "bird blind motif" was a common one in sorcery stories.

The same month, I was walking from the Hak to my house on the Uk accompanied by an informant. At the point where the track first meets the Uk, we were met by a very agitated woman. While working in a garden further up the Uk, she and several other women had seen a Telefolmin watching them from beside a dead tree in an abandoned garden across the river. My companion and I rushed to the scene but there was nothing to see. My speed in getting there was certainly fueled by my own involvement in the hysteria accompanying the relatively mild influenza epidemic that was abroad in the community.[7]

A reportedly common type of Miyanmin sorcery is called *fae* and employs a *bekel*, summoned through the use of ancestral relics, to accomplish the homicide. In addition to the ancestral skulls and mandibles prominently displayed in the *kwoisam*, there are numerous smaller ancestral relics and charms of mixed provenance preserved in small bark cloth wrappings which have been smoked over the *kwoisam* hearth. For *fae*, eyebrow, chest, and belly hair are removed from a bundle and enclosed in a small bamboo tube with a piece of bark cloth. In the course of an otherwise public visit, the tube is brought to a main settlement of the group against which the sorcery is intended. A small hole is secretly dug in the ground along a well-traveled path or at a cross path and the tube is buried under a small flat stone. Any person chancing to pass over the charm will be shot with a spirit-arrow by a *bekel* that rises out of the ground. The victim will die a slow death with symptoms reminiscent of pneumonia, swollen glands and septicemia, and then his group will be swept by an epidemic.

Other charms and relics in the *kwoisam* and the sacred plants surrounding it are employed to aid in battle, gardening, and hunting. Among the items taken into battle were ancestral crania and the smoked relic of a unique snake said to be responsible for human aggression (described in chapter 10). Fight arrows were smoked over a fire that included the skin of a sacred snake.

Also possessing special properties are sacred plants taken from the *kwoisam* compound, including *kesak* ("tangit," *Cordyline sp. blasta (Cordiaeum variegatum), wenam-idem* and *wenam-namen* (respectively, red and yellow varieties of *Coleus sp.*), the latter referred to as in the "flower of the taro." All of these colorful plants are transplanted from the *kwoisam* compound to gardens that are doing poorly. The few female relics preserved are used to involve an honored ancestress in the well-being of children as well as gardens. Another charm to protect taro is the *imegebe*, a packet of finger bones and hair. Among the paraphernalia for hunting magic, crocodile (*Crocodilus novaguinea*?) bones from far down the May River are highly valued. The crocodile bone, with an incised groove encircling it, is stroked with a special vine, *dafino* (*Lygodim vertegii*) while the hopeful hunter thinks about his prey. There are also more local practices of hunting magic such as a rite carried out at the site of Dimoson's footprint on the May River. Here, a leaf is placed in the footprint while the hunter thinks about his aspirations (Morren 1981c).

Death Ritual

My concept of "death ritual" was first suggested by Lifton's *History and Human Survival* (1971). Here, and in other works (1968), Lifton's concern is the behavior of individuals under extreme conditions. By "extreme conditions" he seems to mean conditions of sufficient intensity and duration to result in high levels of mortality and a massive threat of imminent death to survivors. His first case was a study of the survivors of the Hiroshima nuclear bombing. Subsequently, he applied the framework, which he labeled the "survivor syndrome," to Nazi extermination camp inmates and to American P.O.W.'s of the Korean War. Originally Lifton thought that he had discovered a phenomenon peculiar to modern "massive technological murder." The applicability of the framework has been gradually broadened and its most significant current application is in the study and treatment of people involved in natural and anthropogenic catastrophes.[8] It has also figured in litigation for damages in connection with such events and, possibly for this reason, been assigned a new and more portentous label, the posttraumatic stress syndrome.

Death is *the* universal human problem. From the standpoint of survivors, groups as well as individuals, it is highly variable in frequency and duration. Mortality varies from nation to nation and community to community, and— within these units—in time. The experience of individuals varies as well, as does their capacity to cope. Against this background of the universality of the problem, Lifton discovered certain universal features in the psychic responses of people to the death experience, responses transcending cultural tradition and the specific nature of the threatening condition.

In outline, Lifton describes a process of response in which survivors may pass through a series of stages depending on the intensity and duration of their experience of death. The stages are cast in the form of "death images" or "psychic themes" that symbolically link the dead to the living. His original version, based on the Hiroshima research, explicitly described four stages, although in discussing these he recognizes two others. The four basic "death images" are, "immersion in death," "invisible contamination," "A-Bomb disease," and "identification with the dead." The implied ones are "normal bereavement" and "bearing witness," which fall respectively at the beginning and the end of the basic continuum.

I should state at the outset that what interested me was the resemblance of Lifton's "death imagery" to commonly reported themes and symbols of traditional and millenarian religion in Melanesia and other world areas. In summarizing his argument, I will make passing reference to the points of resemblance and provide greater detail when I apply my elaboration of the framework to Miyanmin behavior.

Immersion in Death

This phase begins with the exposure of the survivors to the array of dead and frightfully injured immediately after the blast, or as a recurrent feature of the death camp environment. The immediate or initial experience of fright, fear of dying, and rote and ineffective behavior is succeeded by a sense of doom, darkness and quiet, succeeded in turn by the defense of psychic closing off. The latter involves the numbing of affect, symbolic isolation, and the withdrawal of psychic connection to external experience. The symbolism entering at this stage involves guilt regarding the dead: self-condemnation, with people questioning their own survival and recalling the requests of the dying. This imagery continues through other phases.

This resembles normal grief in all societies. Catastrophic circumstances may give rise to the most morbid responses described in the foregoing, but many of these (including the defense of psychic closing off) are also associated with what psychologists call "pathological grief" in our own society. Pathological grief may be the result of either the diminished capacity of an individual to cope, the failure or inadequacy of coping institutions, continued (extraordinary) mortality, or a combination of these factors. The issue then is whether or not an individual or the members of a group can return to a "normal" state. In short, what psychologists view as pathology is actually escalation due to the persistence of problems and ineffective coping. Clearly both conditions pertained in Hiroshima and in the death camps, where normal coping mechanisms were overwhelmed by the circumstances. But what is the situation in a high-mortality society, particularly when even greater mortality occurs as in an epidemic? I hypothesize that the themes Lifton and others associate with guilt become part of institutions and belief systems.

Invisible Contamination

For the survivors of Hiroshima, who obviously were being continuously exposed to toxic levels of radiation or developing symptoms from the initial emissions, this took the form of relating their unfamiliar symptoms to infectious disease or mysterious poison emanating from the bomb. Rumor piled upon rumor to the level of elaborate mythology concerning further attacks of exotic weapons and even more bizarre forms of death. The symbolism here is one of total contamination, powerlessness, ultimate corruption, and supernatural punishment or curse. In short, Lifton describes a species of mysticism that I believe resembles the escalating fears of sorcery observed in many New Guinea communities.

A-Bomb Disease

Years after the bombing, leukemia and other malignancies continue to develop. Even those survivors who do not display diagnosable physical ailments fall into a pattern of A-Bomb neurosis involving real incapacity and preoccupation with sickness and death. At best, all have serious doubts about their ultimate freedom from radiation effects. Lifton labels the symbolism associated with A-Bomb disease as "enduring taint." In effect, the curse of the previous stage becomes permanent, irreversible, and from a social standpoint, institutionalized. In translating this to my scheme below, I merge the two stages of invisible contamination and A-bomb disease.

Identification with the Dead

There are two complementary features of this phase, on the one hand, the sense of group identity as *hibakusha* or survivors, and on the other hand, a lifelong identification with the dead. The survivors are living dead who also possess the sense that because their survival was made possible by the deaths of others, theirs is a continuing obligation and relationship. A seemingly contradictory theme—observed strongly in death camp survivors as well—is what Lifton calls a "pseudo-affirmation of life," a denial of the pervasiveness of death by affirming the continuity of the two life-cycle statuses (life and death). This is the psychic root of the ancestral cult, the associated belief in an afterlife, and in spirits of the dead.

Bearing Witness

Although in the context of Lifton's argument there is no fifth phase, he nevertheless indicates the existence of a further phase that can emerge after a period of time. This involves the survivors' coming to terms with death by acquiring a sense of special mission. Symbolically it involves "a victory of the dead" and "sending a message to the future." The aim is to establish a new order, providing participants with "symbolic immortality." I link this to Melanesian and other manifestations of millenarianism and, by extension, to rebellion and revolutionary activities that integrate similar symbolic meanings with violence.

My scheme expands and modifies Lifton's somewhat. I merge "invisible contamination" and "A-Bomb disease," for example, although in most respects I keep close to his original descriptions of the symbolism involved. It is important, however, to extend the scheme beyond the level of individual psychic states and imagery to include institutionalized coping devices and responses that have larger environmental effects.

This scheme is founded on the following questions. What happens when mortality in a group changes, particularly when it increases? Are there important differences to be discovered by comparing societies with chronically high mortality and those that have experienced significant declining mortality, especially with respect to the institutional aspects of coping with death? If there is a degree of universality at the psychic or symbolic level are there significant correlates at the behavioral level, including the kinds of options diverse peoples may pursue under similar circumstances?

Figure 8-1 describes a pattern of escalatory and flexibility-restoring responses. Inspired by Lifton's social psychological model of the survivor syndrome, it is an attempt to make sense out of my own observations of and informants' statements about events and behavior. My analysis begins at the beginning, a not entirely hypothetical state of relative equilibrium and high flexibility that defines the "normal." Representing peace and security, this is the standard against which people measure their situations.

This happy state is perturbed by death in a group, i.e., the family or larger community, defined by kinship and co-residence. Adult deaths, including those that are the objective result of infectious disease, give rise to responses that depend in part on the general level of mortality, including infant mortality, and the duration of higher-than-normal levels of mortality. Just as mortality might serve the scientific observer as an index of general well-being in a group, it also serves as an index to individuals in a high-mortality society such as the Miyanmin.

People experience grief and guilt in the ordinary course of things and the larger community rallies to deal collectively with the problem through mortuary rites that may permit a return to a normal and secure state, "the rites of passage at death" (Salisbury 1965:62). This pattern does not pertain, however, when a group is already mobilized at a higher level of response. The objective fact that the Miyanmin and Telefolmin were locked in a deadly competition for resources and that all were also subject to high mortality was transformed by the Miyanmin to the perception of universal taint and doom. Among the Miyanmin this is signalled by the presence in a community of a pervasive fear of illness and dread of sorcery, the condition of the Miyanmin in the 1960s. As the previous section indicated, curing rituals were a

Figure 8-1.   Death Ritual—Individual and Group Responses to
              Changes in Mortality: Options to Change Location,
              Life-Style, or Engage in Warfare

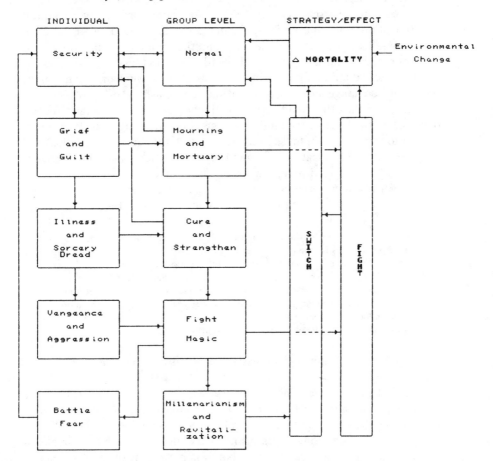

prominent feature of Miyanmin social life and these also have the potential for restoring a semblance of normalcy and security because they provide treatment to the group as well as to the patient. This effect also is not inevitable.

For a group that is already mobilized at a high response level, mortuary rites initiate a process that may entail changes in resource use, location, group cohesion, and relations with friendly groups, as well as a decision to seek retribution by engaging in warfare. I am arguing that there can be more to mortuary rituals than meets the eye. The elementary response in most societies is to hold a wake and funeral with the obvious goal of relieving grief and permitting a return to a normal state for some participants. But the content and effectiveness of such rituals varies cross-culturally, between closely related communities (e.g., Goody 1962), in the same community or cultural tradition at different time periods, and in individuals depending on the actual situations of the people concerned. Beyond the option of doing nothing (or little more than conducting a funeral), death provides the occasion or context in which individuals and groups may decide either to switch or to fight: on the one hand, to change location, group affiliation, or aspects of the life-support system or, on the other hand, to seek mitigation or redress through violence, or both. At the level of the individual, this is the meaning of the concept of population pressure employed as an explanatory tool by Boserup (1965) and Spooner (ed. 1972). Death in a community may initiate or sustain a series of escalatory responses, although this is not inevitable.

Meggitt (1965b:114) appears to have a similar escalatory pattern in mind as he describes mortuary ritual practice among the Mae Enga:

> Sometimes, however, misfortunes injure a clan parish as a whole. These may include military defeats costing many lives or leading to the loss of clan territory, a sudden rise in the death rate of children or pigs, a series of deaths of important men, a noticeable increase in the incidence of diseases such as leprosy or yaws, or a clan-wide failure of crops.
>
> Individual families at first deal with these circumstances at the domestic level and kill pigs to placate particular ghosts. But as the events recur and affect more and more people, clansmen look to the whole body of clan ancestral ghosts as the source of the calamity and turn for guidance to the older and important men.

Frequently, though not inevitably, the results involve a decision to pursue "blood revenge" (see also Meggitt 1977).

As indicated earlier, the threat of disease and death was real for the Miyanmin, and in the 1960s seemed to be a source of chronic anxiety. Then, all adult deaths were viewed as political acts carried out by an enemy. Thus a death initiates a day-long series of mortuary rites marked by outbreaks of symbolic and real violence, the latter barely contained by the cooler heads of the elders of a group. The woman's house of the deceased is brought under mock attack by arriving parties of male visitors. The deceased is eulogized spontaneously in song by individual men as women keen from their houses. Brandishing weapons, close kin of the deceased threaten other community members or possibly affines visiting from another group thought to have offended the deceased in the past. The targets of this aggression may be women as well as men. These acts may themselves escalate to brawls with the aggressors wrestled to the ground, their arrows broken; or the victims of the assault may be truly beaten, possibly to retreat from the site bearing permanent enmity.

Through the daylight hours men congregate in the principal men's house, filling it to bursting, and vigorously debate the implications of the death and possible courses of action. They reach no firm public conclusion, however. Near dusk, after the deceased has been interred, everyone in the community is barricaded in their houses with fires extinguished. The nearest kin retire with the shaman to the deceased's house, the entrance barred with arrows and thin poles. The shaman commences a litany, invoking the name of the deceased and exhaustively cataloging possible causes and remedies. Suddenly the poles and arrows barring the door shatter into many pieces and pandemonium descends as people hurl themselves from the houses. Some light torches to retrieve the wood and arrow fragments or to search the ground around the hamlet for other signs. The point where the litany has been interrupted signifies to the shaman and his congregation the responsibility for the death and which further escalating actions to pursue.

The minimal action is to gradually abandon the hamlet in which the death occurred, an integral part of the settlement cycle and system presented in chapters 3 and 9. More rapid abandonment, extending even to the uprooting and transplanting of growing gardens, may also occur. This is in addition to the destruction of a portion of the deceased's taro stock and simulates the behavior of war refugees. In addition, blame for the death is assigned. As stated earlier, it was typical of my area to affix responsibility to one of the Telefolmin groups in the Eliptaman to the south. Groups to the north might blame other Miyanmin neighbors. Traditionally, the highest level of response involved either retaliatory attacks or flight, depending on the circumstances.

While I was in the field in 1968 Wameten attempted to flee into the spirit world through ritual means after a viral epidemic killed six adults in the space of several weeks. In addition, established dissension within a local group or between closely aligned ones may come to a head in the course of a mortuary brawl. This can lead to a segment—a lineage group, typically—choosing to reside in another place where it has established ties. Individual nuclear and and extended families can choose not to abandon the hamlet and gardens in question.

The decision to engage in warfare is a perilous one which provokes anxiety and excitement among prospective participants. This is anticipated in fight magic which in some forms shapes battle plans, strengthens the resolve of a majority of participants, or advises others of their vulnerability. These seem to be the implications of a ritual that was carried out the night before an offensive engagement. In a camp set up within striking distance of an enemy settlement, the shaman withdraws from the other men of the force and privately summons a spirit. The spirit is instructed and then sent forward to the enemy village. It returns from its errand bearing human flesh, which is consumed by the shaman. The shaman then returns to the other men and predicts the course of the next day's combat in some detail. He may also warn those who are in jeopardy, and they can chose to withdraw. Informants state that a shaman is never wrong. I believe that this can be so only if, in some sense, they shape the conduct of the battle under the guise of prophesy. This is so whether they themselves author the plan or promulgate a consensus arrived at previously. Their authority and reputation is also reinforced by the gratitude of those who, forewarned, avoid injury and death. In this too they cannot fail.

If higher mortality persists people may then consider solutions involving radical changes in life-style. Among the Miyanmin of the east this was accompanied at its inception by the emergence of unusual political features involving supralocal cooperation and leadership. Our conventional label for this is millenarianism (or revolution, if innovation is linked to violence). With this framework we can at least partly understand the wide adoption by many Miyanmin of a modernization package which included Christianity.

Through the 1970s the Miyanmin of the east experienced a significant decline in mortality, including infant mortality (at the same time that some groups in the west were subject to a worsening situation). The eastern Miyanmin have perceived this improvement to be of a piece with other benefits achieved in the modern period, including reliable access to minimal medical services, a community school, modest cash incomes, and goods to purchase. Their response conforms to my model: not only has the dread of sorcery been extinguished in these groups, but under the guise of a pan-regional religious movement known as *Rabaibal,* peace has broken out between the Miyanmin and all of their former enemies in the south, and *natim-dowal* festivals have become routine (see below), a sure indication of security, optimism, and low mortality. I take a closer look at these and other modern developments in chapter 11.

Ritual Structures

When I catalogued the corporate attributes of the parish in chapter 7, I included the possession of certain important ceremonial and secular buildings. Unique to the Miyanmin is the *itam,* a large dance house. It was mentioned earlier in connection with marriage. As we shall see, the *itam* is normally built to start a settlement cycle in pioneering areas and, separate from its ceremonial use, it serves as a long house for several years. The *itam* is also the site of the first event in a long ceremonial cycle described later in this chapter.

Another special building is the *kwoisam,* or ancestral shrine—a small building similar in appearance to a village men's house—but located in a separate compound. It is the normal repository of ancestral relics, hunting trophies, and other ritual and magical paraphernalia. It also is the site of many ceremonies in the ritual cycle. The *yominam* is a large house with a roof approaching that of the *itam* in size because of its overhang. The central room has four hearths. A second wall under the eaves creates a narrow corridor on three sides, called the *fofolam*, that houses young male initiates during a period of rigorous isolation. The *yominam/fofolam* is always separated from its associated residential hamlet, either in the *kwoisam* compound or in a precinct of its own.

When I began my fieldwork among the Miyanmin in 1968 *kwoisam* were still extant for most of the groups I visited. The Kome temple collapsed in 1969 and, although it was never rebuilt, some relics were hidden in a rock shelter. I do not believe that any survive today either in East or West Mianmin.

In the first detailed publication regarding the male cult usages of any of the Mountain Ok peoples,[9] Fredrik Barth (1971) outlined the general characteristics of their ritual forms:

> Religious cult throughout the area takes the form of secret male rituals directed at growth and garden fertility, and is associated with ancestral sacrae. Crucial formal variations in this cult are found in the organization of male initiations and the constitution of different cult houses and their associated rituals. (179)

In terms of formal resemblance, the Miyanmin conform closely to the outline, falling roughly between the subtypes Barth identifies for "Enkaiakmin-Baktamin" and the "Southeast including Kwelmin" (185). It is difficult to draw the lines of resemblance too closely because Barth's essay was not intended as a particularistic description of a cult or cults. Thus the operational application of the term "permanent" in relation to cult centers and buildings in Barth's work is not entirely clear. In my usage, "permanent" will mean that most parishes will possess the "permanent" type of building most of the time; but that cult houses succeed each other in different locations for each parish, and that there are hiatuses (such as when a *kwoisam* is lacking and sacrae are stored in small caves). The applicability of my notion of "death ritual" to the interpretation of cult and noncult ritual activity among other Mountain Ok groups is even more difficult to assess.

Two of the permanent ceremonial structures (as noted), the *kwoisam* and the *yominam,* are associated with reverence for the male dead and ritual to interest the latter in, and ensure the welfare of, the living. In particular, the *yominam* is concerned with the transmission of knowledge of the supernatural to the younger generation. Some of the rituals are part of a graded male initiation cycle which is, literally and symbolically, a progression to the afterlife. This is, in turn, embedded in a more general ceremonial cycle to the extent that, for my purposes, it doesn't appear to be useful to distinguish between initiation rituals and noninitiation rituals. As the parish is the proprietor of the ceremonial structures, so it is a ceremonial unit or "congregation" (Rappaport 1968:1), an aggregate "of individuals who regard their collective well-being to be dependent on a common body of ritual performance." Among the sacrae displayed prominently in the *kwoisam* are simply decorated ancestral bones, mainly crania and mandibles belonging for the most part to deceased male parish members, with prominent (remembered) more remote cognates also represented.

In 1968, an informant succinctly summarized the outlook in this matter:

> Our ancestors' skulls take care of our taro and our meat. They take care of us. They give us our food. We go and get their bones and place them in the *kwoisam*, but we don't believe the spirit is in the bone. No, we just sleep with the bones and hunt and our ancestors think of us and we will be able to kill a wild pig.
>
> Often we take the blood of wild pigs we have killed after a father or brother has died and paint it on their skulls. But the decorations you see there on the wild pig jaws have no meaning, they are for thinking and remembering (e.g., "relics").
>
> We kill pigs after our father's death because his spirit will help us. This is a good thing because then (if successful) we know that he is with all our ancestral spirits. This is the reason for giving pork while our fathers and brothers are still living, for then, after they die, they will give us pork. If after the death of our father or brother we cannot find a wild pig, we think that he has aligned himself with (the ancestors of) another parish. And spirits belonging to other parishes cannot help us to hunt.

The Isolation of a Ritual Cycle

Earlier in this chapter, I referred to the extensive research on the male cult among many other Mountain Ok peoples. I also cited the problem of definition in drawing comparisons within the culture area, and this applies as well to the present discussion of ritual and initiation cycles. There are two questions I will attempt to frame in this section. First, how many levels of initiation do the Miyanmin possess? Second, do the Miyanmin possess a ritual cycle with ecological functions in any way comparable to that of the Maring analyzed by Rappaport (1966, 1968, 1984)? The former question may at first glance seem to be of interest only to those who have done research in the Mountain Ok area, but it is connected to the framing of the second question which has broader import; the two cannot be approached piecemeal. It is a methodological problem rather than an empirical one.

Barth (1971:191) has stated that the Faiwolmin cannot "be fitted to the pattern of ritual-ecologic programming analyzed for the Maring." In the narrowest comparative sense, this is so. There are other possibilities, however. Rappaport (1968) recognizes some in discussing similar ritual elements among other highland New Guinea peoples. He argues that although the arrangement of common elements may vary, "ritual regulation may be widespread in New Guinea" (231). He also suggests, "that as variables and the relations among them change so do the mechanisms that regulate them"(231). Logically, the next step is to suggest that a constructive approach to the question hangs, not on the identification of a set of similar ritual elements,[10] but on an analysis of particular systems (which is, of course, what Rappaport did). Many of the variables in the Miyanmin system, and possibly the Faiwol system too, are different from the variables in the Maring system. As we have seen, and as the Miyanmin see it, the ancestors give pigs; they received them in life. The system of a hunting people will be very different from that of pig herders, and we should expect that the mechanisms regulating the system will be different too. Nevertheless, the Faiwolmin apparently do sacrifice pigs to the ancestors (Barth 1975:194).

One reason why these possibilities were overlooked by Barth (1971, 1975) is that he focused on the communications aspect of cult activities. He does not present a detailed analysis of human ecology and has virtually nothing to say about "ritual regulation" beyond the statement cited.

A second reason is the treatment of the initiation cycle in isolation from the temporal context of other ceremonial events. If one is interested in studying initiation, and nothing else, focusing only on rituals which change the status of exclusive groups of people (Allen 1967:5ff.) is justified, but this does not confer ontological status on the category of initiation ritual. The methodological consequence of this criticism is that an investigation of regulatory functions of a ritual cycle must identify those rituals which are part of a serial or process irrespective of their structural or communicational objectives, but in contradistinction to rituals which occur irregularly or situationally. Some obvious examples of irregular ones are mortuary rites, curing rituals, and the performance of sorcery. As is argued earlier, even these are part of a process having equilibrating and homeostatic properties. Here, however, the issue is cyclicality; and the concurrent task is to isolate attributes of the adaptive routine of a group that also has a cyclical character.

As a comment on other work in the area, this discussion has most to do with how ethnographic information is employed to reach general or hypothetical conclusions. The underlying pattern of the initiation cycle that Barth described applies to the Miyanmin:

> ... progressively deeper religious secrets are rationed out in steps and the vast majority of the congregation participates to various degrees in a cult, the total structure of which is known only to a small core. This core, like the lower grades, is maintained through cumulative initiation (1971:187).

Initiation and the Ritual Cycle

The reasons for considering initiation and noninitiation rituals and ceremonies together are not just methodological ones.[11] Many Miyanmin rituals have multiple objectives: rituals intended to strengthen the initiates against demons that cause illness, cure; ceremonies that convey sacred knowledge to initiates, fatten pigs or aid the taro. Moreover, the Miyanmin justify the active participation of women in some ceremonies on the grounds of these multiple objectives. Feasts and ceremonies with wider social and political purposes are also linked to the more public aspects of rites of initiation.

There is also some variation between individuals (including informants) regarding participation in all the rituals in the initiation sequence, partly reflecting whether their group or a convenient neighbor has held them within a given time frame. There is also variation in content between different performances of the same named rituals. Gardner (1981) presents a more detailed description of Miyanmin initiation rituals and particularly emphasizes variation between the practices of the *am-nakai* and *sa-nakai* groups.

There are four progressive grades of initiation status, designated *unangamin, yominten, dil,* and *awel.* The *unangamin* are the "children of the women's house" and have been more or less passive participants in a special public ritual held for them in the *kwoisam* compound (see *memeyominam,* below). The *yominten,* "children of the (bark cloth) relic bundle," are subject to a long series of initiatory rites, starting around puberty and extending into the late teens. A given cohort will include a fairly wide spread of ages. The *dil,* the "first" or "prime," are the mature, active fraction of the male group in their early twenties to late forties with new and growing families.

The *awel,* who are "sacred" or "taboo," are the tiny core of ritually competent and sufficient men in their fifties and sixties. They are no longer particularly active in production or reproduction and, like ancestral spirits ready to temporarily visit the world of the living, have seen their children reach maturity before they can venture along the spirit road. They are the masters and keepers of the *kwoisam* and its contents, and one or more of the *awel* always sleeps in it. An *awel* has an extraordinary presence when he appears in a settlement in which he does not ordinarily reside, a presence which seems to derive from his involvement in the welfare of his own group and from his literal closeness to the source of this welfare (not the *kwoisam,* but the afterlife itself). When such a man visits a hamlet, he does not approach the men's house or a particular women's house as any other person would do. Rather, he tours the hamlet, stopping and looking in each house in turn under the watchful eyes of the residents, and the normal village noises are stilled. He, himself, appears to be watchful, but with some other sense. Such a scene is about the most dramatic, if subtle, of all the images of individual social action that have remained with me. The *awel* is supposed to die, everyone knows it, and good consequences are anticipated. The testament of the Wameten *awel*, Oiyap, recounted at the beginning of the book, is perhaps an extreme example of this.[12]

Such legendary accounts, in combination with more sacred testaments such as the myth of Fitipkanip and Dimoson, are part of the world view of the *awel* and the older *dil* who have experienced them as hearers and tellers in the *kwoisam* and bear witness to their continued relevance in Miyanmin affairs. In a sense, they formulate two ends of a continuum: the genesis of important elements in the world of the living, the end of all in the afterlife, as well as the movement of people, objects, and ideas along the continuum and through time. An *awel* has, of course, seen more of this than most, and has come to make it his philosophical specialty.

Just as the Miyanmin are not stingy with material possessions, *awel* are not stingy with sacred knowledge. However, there is a clear sense of the fitness of a person to understand and use it. Although a number of *awel* of various parishes[13] were generous and communicative, I am also convinced that they never went beyond a level appropriate for my age and status. You do not take a child hunting wild pig, and when I was taken hunting I was told to stand near a tree which I knew I could climb. Accordingly, I do not consider myself to be well informed on matters pertaining to the highest degrees of initiation and the esoteric knowledge associated with them[14] (like the details of the rituals practiced by the older *dil* and *awel*) beyond the fact that these are very secret and of small scale. In addition, no outsider has directly observed any Miyanmin initiation ceremony. My ignorance in these regards should not seriously affect the isolation of the ritual cycle possessing the properties I specified. It would appear that only the rituals associated with the lower degrees of initiation possess these properties in terms of their material attributes of scale and periodicity that facilitate decision making, relocating people, and articulating the settlement patterns of different local populations.

A number of students of the ancestral cult of Mountain Ok groups have discussed its possible role in supralocal politics and areal integration (Barth 1975, Jorgensen 1981a, Morren 1974, Gardner 1981, Brumbaugh 1980, Poole 1982). The initiation cycle has been of particular interest because, while it forges local identity among initiands, it also fosters a degree of intergroup amity and cooperation that is otherwise (or at other times) absent in the region. The former has been more or less taken for granted as the basis of intracommunity male solidarity and cohesion. The fact of extreme variability of adherence to the ritual pattern within a single cultural group, underscored by Gardner's (1981) work in West Mianmin, points to the need to examine what certain rituals actually do and what their decline or attenuation may actually signal. Using some perspectives from political economy and social psychology, I attempt to answer these questions in chapter 9 because I believe that the critical context involves patterns of movement, particularly of individuals.

Outline of the Ritual Cycle

The ritual cycle isolated here consists of as many as 12 named ceremonies, 10 of which are predominately initiatory in nature, with others having recognized initiatory implications. Apparently not all of the ceremonies are obligatory. The duration of the cycle and, hence, the number of rituals, is partly dependent on the length of the settlement cycle. This helps to explain the attenuated initiation cycle of *sa-nakai* groups reported by Gardner (1981).

The settlement cycle will be briefly described here (it is presented in detail in chapters 3 and 9). The start of the settlement cycle occurs at the point when a local population invades a pristine or recovered and topographically distinct area such as a divide between two small rivers. During this initial phase the settlement pattern is highly nucleated, but in the second phase a progressive expansion of the distance between hamlets occurs. Finally, in the third phase there is a unidirectional movement of the entire chain of hamlets. This continues until a geographical or political boundary is approached, with the duration of such cycles of settlement ranging from eight to twelve years. The ritual cycle conforms to this progression of settlement phases and to the seasonal flux of the pattern of dual residence. It motivates individuals to participate in key settlement changes. The articulation between ritual and settlement for a cycle is described in figure 8-2.

The succeeding description of the events making up the ritual cycle includes a consideration of their objectives, the objects and buildings employed, the social definition of participation, the food taboos and other behavioral restrictions associated with the rite or the pertinent initiation status, as well as the features of the event having important ecological consequences.

Natim

When a limit or boundary is approached during the third phase of settlement, a settlement shift to a new area is initiated. The shift begins with the establishment of new gardens. Confirmation of the intended move is signalled by the absence of an adult death during the succeeding seasonal turn. Then an *itam* is built in the pioneer area which first serves as the site of a regional dance and feast and then as a long house for the nucleated local population.

The interior layout of the *itam* was described earlier (in chapter 7). Each of its 15 hearths is assigned to a young married couple. In fact, the 15 men

Figure 8-2. The Cycle of Ritual and Settlement

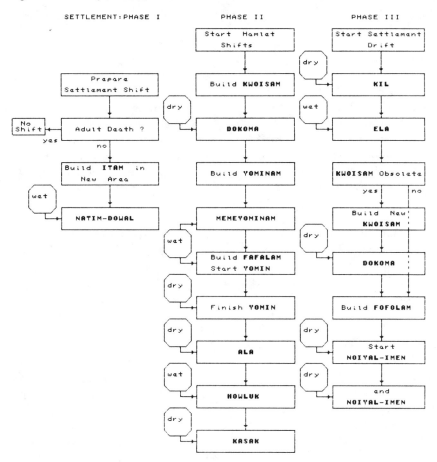

involved are the newest *dil* of the parish or local population; and one of the objectives of the *natim* is to accord public recognition and confirmation of their full ritual and social status. The *awel* and the oldest *dil* do not occupy hearths in the *itam*, and by the time another *natim* is held, a new cohort of *dil* will have succeeded the present hearth holders.

The *natim* itself is a festival of all-night dancing, drumming, and singing that may last more than a week. The performers are segregated by sex. Some men wear grossly exaggerated gourd phallocrypts that bob up and down as they dance, while women wear a special skirt with a long tassle hanging down from the buttocks which they flip as they dance. Otherwise, male and female participants wear similar ornaments and finery: bird of paradise plumes (lesser bird of paradise, king bird of paradise), jangling bangles of freshwater mussel shells (*kwal*), *giri-giri* and "job's tears" (*Coix lacryma*) headbands, necklaces of pig's tusk, animal, and human teeth, and miniscule amounts of marine shell.

Dowal

The *dowal* (vegetable food feast) occurs concurrently with *natim*. Small parties of mostly male visitors arrive before and during *natim* and, although no pigs are killed, visitors are provided with huge amounts of taro both during the dances and at larger feasts during the day. Such sharing of food is supposed to be an assurance of good will and peaceful intentions between the host parish and visitors' parishes, but the legendary record is not so reassuring: attendance at *natim-dowal* festivities and other food sharing occasions have been employed in the past to plant *fae* sorcery and to cover surprise attacks against the hosts.

In addition to eating a lot, visitors participate in the *natim* of their hosts, both dancing in their own groups and joining mass dancing. Much of the singing and dancing has a spontaneous character, with different parties and even individuals rising to entertain the rest of the assembly with songs recalling leaders and events of the recent past, regional history, joint adventures, and the realization of group strength and gardening and hunting bounty. The arrival of another party of visitors is an occasion for renewing or extending the festival for additional nights.

The *natim-dowal* has an important communications role in the region because it confirms that a course of action has been initiated: the settlement shift and cycle of a specific local population in a new area. By this time it is all but irreversible and other local populations must ultimately accommodate it. Like other forms of large-scale seasonal visiting (see chapter 9), it reinforces pan-regional male solidarity, and has often, in the past, provided the occasion for the initial preparations for an attack on an enemy group.

Dokoma

The second phase of settlement in a new area is marked when the dual residence pattern is established and most families have two houses and sets of gardens. Then a new *kwoisam* is built in or near a larger nucleated villages. The old *kwoisam* may already be far away, or in an advanced state of disrepair, and parish relics may be temporarily placed in a cave or rock shelter. *Kwoisam* are always replaced completely, never repaired piecemeal. Moreover, *dokoma*, the act of building a *kwoisam* together with the accompanying dedication ritual, may occur more than once in a settlement cycle which exceeds eight or so years.

The appropriate time for *dokoma* is the season associated with the fruiting of certain forest trees which attracts pigs. This is when their hunting is particularly favorable, and ancestral spirits are most likely to return. In this (as in other) ritual situation, wild pigs should be available when they are needed.

During the construction of the *kwoisam*, even the usual female tasks of clay hearth making and roof leaf gathering are done by men and boys, and hunting and consumption of all the important staples such as pork, taro, and bananas is banned. The ban on the vegetable foods is lifted when the building is finished and relics installed. The latter task is carried out in the dark of night to reduce the risk of women observing sacred objects. Hunting, particularly of pig, is then started; and the wild pigs (other animals may be substituted) that result from this are ritually consumed in three stages.

The first wild pig killed is the *el-awem-el*, or sacred pig. It is consumed by the *awel* and a few of the oldest (most advanced) *dil* privately in the new *kwoisam*—where sacred information is also transmitted—amidst singing and dancing outside the building. This apparently also makes the *dil* who participate inside into *awel*.

The second wild pig killed is the *el-kwiyam-unim*, the phallanger demon pig, which is ritually consumed by the rest of the *dil* and the *yominten* in the new *kwoisam*. The ritual accompanying this is a curing ceremony aimed at the demon type *tofinunim*, which guides arrows in flight but which can also cause illness. (When performed only as a curing ceremony it is called *el-wisam*.) The third pig killed is the *unang-el*, the women's pig, eaten by the women and children in the village.

Yomin

Other neighboring East Mianmin parishes are invited to participate in this initiation rite, the first of the series of rituals for adolescent and near-adolescent boys which continues for many years. It is held during the rainy season, which occurs from January to April (chapter 4).

The host parish provides the setting and hospitality for the event. Otherwise, all men, local and visitor alike, collectively organize the ritual and agree on the details of the testaments to be given to the boys. Then all of the participants, including the *unangamin* to be initiated, work to forage building materials and construct the *fofolam*. Three or four domestic pigs are slaughtered and cooked together with taro and other foods in a leaf oven. This food is eaten by everyone—residents, visitors, initiates, and women. After this meal, two *dil* and two *afok* (old women) stand beside the entrance to the *fofolam*, which has been decorated with flowers and colorful leaves. While other men and women drum and sing, the *unangamin* are lead by several *dil* between these four people and into the *fofolam*. The boys are seated inside and subjected to mild tricks and feats of legerdemain.

This commences an extended period of seclusion for the boys during which time the consumption of water, pandanus, certain birds, lizards, breadfruit, sago, and pork is forbidden. (The boys are supplied with other foods and allowed outside for brief periods.) They are rigorously disciplined and exhorted to be strong. This lasts for two or three weeks. The end of seclusion is marked by the slaughter of several pigs. The legs of the pigs are used as clubs to raze the *fofolam* as the boys are brought outside. The pork is cooked and the boys are teased with the meat, but finally allowed to eat it, amid drumming, singing, and dancing.

Meanwhile, a *no-kwiyam* (*Phallanger gymnotis*, "terrestrial cuscus") has been caught alive and secreted in the hamlet's *timan* (men's house). In the evening, the boys are taken into the *yominam*. Here the *kwiyam* is produced and, amid singing and drumming, it is dragged over the boys' heads and shoulders, scratching them, in order to give them strength. At this time a taboo on the eating of this animal is imposed; as *unangamin* they could eat it, but it is tabooed to *yominten* and *dil*. The taboo will not be lifted until they are *awel*. Then an ancestral mandible is produced and tapped lightly on the boys' heads, also to strengthen them. The boys remain in the *yominam* all night and at dawn are taken outside where they are painted with black (for night) and red (for the sunrise) pigments. They are then paraded in the hamlet to the *timan* and are allowed to sleep into the afternoon. When they are roused, the taboo on water is lifted and the initiates have become *yominten*. The *yominam* becomes their place of residence during the drier part of the year.

Although a given parish may only conduct *yomin* once a generation (or once a settlement cycle) other parishes will also be conducting such ceremonies from time to time, and boys of appropriate age whose male kin are anxious for them to enter the progression, are readily incorporated into the "class" of a neighboring parish for this, the most important of *yominten*-level rituals. Only some of the six or seven subsequent *yominten* rituals are considered to be essential; and only one or two of these is likely to involve substantial multiparish participation, permitting outside boys the opportunity to maintain their progress. The residual rituals, for the most part, do not require elaborate preparations or large numbers of initiates and thus can be conducted ad hoc in any parish. Nevertheless, it is not unusual for a young man who is the issue of an interparish marriage to complete the *yominten* series in his mother's parish if he is too old to wait for his home parish to start the round of ceremonies.

Ala

The *ala* "food" ceremony abrogates the rest of the temporary restrictions imposed at the *yomin*. It is likely to be held in the initiates' home parish toward the end of a subsequent dry season. On the morning before the ceremony, the *yominten* are sent to the bush and the women and children are also sent out of the hamlet which is to be the site. *Dil* collect food—including the items temporarily tabooed in the *yomin* such as pandanus and certain birds and lizards—and cook them with a wild pig. The cooked pandanus is placed on the track leading into the hamlet where the initiates, summoned by singing and drumming, discover and eat it. They then enter the hamlet and go into the men's house where the other foods are eaten and the taboos lifted.

Howluk

As in the *yomin*, other parishes are invited to participate in the *howluk*, an initiatory and curing rite for the *yominten*. Participants from other parishes are required to contribute "exotic fauna"—animals not normally found in the range of the host parish, but which figure in the stories related in the ritual. Items cited by Kome informants included *no-sumul* (*Thylogale sp.*), *no-kiyok* (*Echymipera clara*), *tim-sebaribo* (a lizard), and *map-mefomo* (a turtle). For the *howluk* (fern leaf cooking bundle) the *yominten* are isolated in the men's house and women and children sent away from the hamlet, while the competent male participants complete their preparations. This mainly involves cooking the previously collected food in leaf bundles on hot stones in the *kwoisam*. When the meat is cooked, the bundles are carefully opened and the meat separated from the leaves. The fern tips (*Alsophila sp.*?) are retained with the meat and it is placed back in the hearth and covered with some of the remaining leaves. The *yominten* are summoned and lined up in their birth order before being brought into the *kwoisam*. There they sit facing the hearth, the leaves are removed from the meat, and each item is displayed and its ritual name conveyed. The use of the *howluk* in curing is explained by one of the keepers of the *kwoisam*. For such purposes, the patient is placed on a platform over the hearth while the meat is cooked, the aroma of the meat being the important element in getting the attention of the demon type *tofinunim*. The meat is then eaten by all participants including the *yominten*. After the ceremony they are free to go about their business except that they must stay away from women so that the women will not smell the meat. In addition, all participants will avoid the gardens the following day.

Kasak

The object of the *kasak*, or *tangit* (*Cordyline sp.*), ceremony is to provide the initiates with ritual knowledge to protect them from dangerous "hot" and "cold"[15] spirits. It is a single parish event held during a dry season succeeding the last *howluk*. In preparation, a wild sow is killed and hidden in the *kwoisam* where it is painted with white clay. The *yominten* are assembled in the building. They are given the secret name of the tangit and told about the hidden role of Fitipkanip in making it red. Other secrets are also conveyed at this time. The initiates are then stood up and directed to contemplate the wild pig mandibles assembled along one wall of the *kwoisam*. They are also told to look at the ancestral skulls and mandibles which line the floor and periphery of the *kwoisam*, but the origin of these is not revealed and the initiates are fearful.

The painted wild sow is then suspended by ropes over the door of the *kwoisam;* the rope is the *boliet* made from the inner bark of the *boliyam* tree (*Gnetum sp.*). The *yominten* cluster outside the *kwoisam*, on the small landing by the door, and on the ground immediately in front of it. They all reach and take hold of the *boliet* supporting the weight of the pig and are told to lose their fear of its spirit which embodies coldness, dampness, and softness. The *yominten* are then sent forth to gather leaves and firewood. The pig is cooked in the *kwoisam* compound. When the leaf oven is breached and the aroma of the pork rises, the tangit demon is present and hopefully pacified. The *yominten* and *dil* eat the pork; the *awel* abstain out of fear of the *kasak* demon (the symptoms of the illnesses caused by this demon seem to be those particularly found in old people). After the ritual the *yominten* must, as usual, avoid contact with women and all participants refrain from garden work for a day.

Kil

The *kil* ritual, like the *kasak*, is an event of the dry season held in the *kwoisam* to transmit further ritual knowledge to the *yominten*. While preparations are made in the *kwoisam* and its compound, the *yominten* are assembled in the men's house. A wild sow and various small mammals previously killed are cooked outside in a leaf oven and then removed to the *kwoisam* proper and covered with leaves. The *yominten* are brought to the *kwoisam* and, as in the *kasak*, eat the meal with the *dil*. The "basic" myth regarding the activities of the culture heroine Fitipkanip is then related, reserving such further mysteries as the founding of the afterworld (related earlier in this chapter) for later rituals in the progression. This is followed by a pandanus feast outside the *kwoisam* compound which serves to mask the more important ritual meal that has been taken in secrecy. The normal prohibitions on contact with women and working in gardens pertain.

Ela

The *ela* (pig) ceremony is a parish event held during the rainy season with the intention of ensuring the health and growth of domestic pigs. The public hamlet phase of the ritual and feast involves the full participation of women (because they raise the pigs), with the final phase involving the secret transmission of further ritual knowledge to the *yominten*.

To prepare for *ela*, men gather yellow marita (*em-nameng*) and a special swamp plant (*kokep*) and women hunt the lizard *tim-sangrom*. The women then stake as many as five domestic pigs and the men slaughter them with bow and arrow and dress the carcasses, all in the usual manner (chapter 5). Others have undertaken the normal cooking preparations, collecting firewood and leaves for the oven; and the women have also taken and cleaned the pigs' intestines and hung them over the fires in their houses. The pork and other items are then cooked in the leaf oven. When the oven is opened the *yominten* are assembled in the *timan*. The food is more or less equally apportioned between the men and women, with men taking a portion of the pig intestine which is normally women's food, and the women getting a portion of the *sangrom* lizard which is normally tabooed to them. The men take their share to the *timan* where it is consumed by the *dil* and the *yominten* (the *awel* refrain). Episodes of the Fitipkanip myth concerned with yellow marita, the *kokep*, and the *sangrom* are then related to the *yominten*. The usual restrictions on the following day's activities apply.

Noiyal-Imen

As stated earlier, the number and timing of events in the cycle depends in part on the duration of the settlement cycle. In the normal progression of ritual events, it is at this point, perhaps in the eighth or ninth year of the cycle, that another *dokoma* must be held if it becomes necessary to replace the parish *kwoisam*. This structure is required for the traditional final initiation rite for the *yominten*, the *noiyal-imen*. A substitute "accelerated" graduation which was apparently introduced during a period of sustained warfare, will be described following this account.

The phases of the *noiyal-imen,* or "bandicoot-taro," ceremony actually bridge a seasonal turn. It starts towards the end of the dry season, is suspended during the subsequent rainy season, and is renewed in the next dry season.

This is because one of the key elements in the rite is the creation of a ritual garden for and by the *yominten*, the growth of which requires a minimum of nine months. The intervention of a rainy season provides optimal conditions.

To prepare for *noiyal-imen*, a special garden plot is cleared by the whole community, including women who are said to have a special interest in the outcome of the ritual. Close female kin also present the taro stalks from which will be selected those used in the ritual garden. On the appointed day, the *yominten* are assembled in the *kwoisam*. There the taboo on eating *noiyal* (*Echymipera kalubu*) is abrogated and other temporary taboos are imposed, including dietary ones on eating pig bones, rotten pork, and liver and other internal organs. There is also a prohibition on sex. A special paint is made from burnt bandicoot fur and the juice of the fruit of the *ablan* tree. This is painted on the taro stalks which are hidden underneath the *kwoisam,* out of the sight of women. The next day the *yominten* carry the stalks to the garden prepared for them. One of the *dil* plants the first stalk, using for a digging stick the handle of a hafted stone adze. Then the *yominten* plant the remaining stalks. As this is being carried out it is said, "Let the paint make the taro large and hard; let the taro make the boys large and hard." The *yominten* are then secluded, either in the *yominam* (if it is extant) or in a new *fofolam* built for the purpose, for the week or so it takes for the new taros to put out roots and display the proper complement of leaves. The *yominten* are then decorated with ornaments of bark twine made for them by women. Included is a conical wooden bangle suspended from the top of the head and hanging between the shoulder blades. They are free to go about their business during the subsequent months, but must avoid contact with women and be avoided in their turn. During this period they are responsible for the maintenance of the ritual garden and weed it after four or five months. After nine months or so the taros will be mature. The *yominten* are assembled in the garden at sunrise. The taro is harvested and examined by the participating *dil* for signs of rot. Such signs portend illness and death for the *yominten* who originally planted it. The person in jeopardy is tapped on the arm with a healthy taro to strengthen him. The harvested taro is first carried back to a principal hamlet where it is shown to the women who are anxious about the findings, and then to the *kwoisam* and left to rot under the floor near the hearth. The taboos associated with this ritual and the *yominten* grade are removed and the *yominten* become *dil*.[16]

Noiyal-imen, or its substitute, is the usual culmination of the ritual cycle. A new cycle is initiated when the perquisites for a large-scale settlement shift have been fulfilled. Any breakdown in the trajectory of the settlement cycle will entail the disruption of the ritual cycle. Such perturbations have been occasioned by warfare and, more recently, contact with white institutions.

With the growing adoption of Christianity, most of the rituals and ceremonies described in the foregoing have been abandoned, secularized, or absorbed into the routines of churches. In other words, the form of Christianity that has emerged in East Mianmin is necessarily based on traditional social patterns. The *natim-dowal* continues as a secular entertainment and a regional political event that often begins with a prayer. The initiation cycle has been superseded by bible school and ritual offices and statuses in the church. The integrative functions previously performed by the initiation cycle have also been superseded by bible school, and widened to the extent that formerly belligerent Mountain Ok groups are developing a "pan-Min" consciousness. *Kwoisam* have given way to churches, *yominam/ fofolam* to bush schoolhouses.

Obviously, one set of scripture has supplanted another but this still leaves open the possibility of variation in interpretation and emphasis. The topic of syncretism merits more attention than it has been given here. I will turn to some of the larger associated issues in my concluding chapter.

9

Movement

This chapter is the realization of the claim (in chapter 1) regarding the theoretical importance of the *movement* concept. Here, I attempt to provide empirical support for my hypothetical systems model (chapter 3) which linked movement to environmental change, thus grasping the central issue of the book: *how* the Miyanmin move around, in order to support the description of equilibrating movements embodied in the model of *why* they move around a lot.

In the introductory chapter I presented a theory stating that the field of human adaptive responses can be categorized in four basic types that possess cultural-evolutionary significance: movement, environmental modification, areal integration, and industrialization. Although I have chosen to isolate movement for analysis, in the 1980s all four types of response could be observed among the Miyanmin. Indeed, while their regional reputation in the early contact period was based on apparent expansiveness and bellicosity, their current renown stems from successful industrialization of movement responses. Their innovation is to make bush airstrips the centerpiece of modernization. Other mobile groups in the district send delegations to observe the pattern and seek technical assistance. Admittedly I am more concerned with the traditional pattern. However, I will return to the modern situation in the last chapter because the old and the new are inextricably related.

Group Behavior and the Individual

It is unrealistic to take consent and conformity for granted in analyzing movements of aggregates of people, especially when the objective is to understand how such group behaviors occur. The variability represented by the *sa-nakai* and the *am-nakai* Miyanmin (e.g., individual mobility versus group movements, thin versus rigorous initiation) also shows that we cannot fall back on a cultural deterministic explanation (or even on a "subcultural" one), since there is significant interpenetration between groups of different types. In particular, many members of *sa-nakai* have migrated from *am-nakai* groups.

The issue, then, is how it comes to be that members of *am-nakai* groups tend to stay with their groups through thick and thin rather than migrating at the drop of a *mulul.* In chapter 7 it was indicated that we might address these and related issues using a framework suggested by the political economist A. O. Hirschman (1970). The variable role of initiation looms as an important issue.

As was suggested in the previous chapter, a function of initiation rites which is often taken as a given without detailed discussion is what Hirschman refers to as *loyalty.* The function and meaning of loyalty can only be understood in relation to the two general social options open to members of a group, *exit* and *voice.*

The quality of performance of any organization changes continually for unspecified or uncontrollable reasons as well as for systematic and determined ones. This is reflected in the quality of service provided to members, or in their perception of it. They may respond either by leaving (exit) or grieving (voice). The big issue for any group is whether exit will prevail over voice or voice over exit. If the former is dominant, then the organization will not persist.

In these terms, the essential feature of a segmentary organization is the relative coexistence of the exit and voice options available to members. Exit and voice are nevertheless variables; and the balance between them is a function of other factors that foster voice or inhibit exit. According to Hirschman (1970:77), the function of loyalty is to foster "that special attachment to an organization" such that members willingly trade off the option to quit against the prospect of improving their situations by influencing the organization. Of particular significance to the persistence and long-term success of a group, loyalty "can neutralize within certain limits the tendency of the most quality-conscious [members] to be the first to exit" (79). In other words, it is of lesser importance if malcontents and *rabisman* pick up and leave. The overall capacity of the organization to cope is crippled irreversibly, however, when people of unusual competence do so. Thus, loyalty acts through these the most effective, creative, and innovative members; and an organization that is deteriorating due to random causes is more able to recuperate.

Loyalty and other barriers to exit are most useful in those situations where available substitutes are close at hand. According to Hirschman (1970:81), this produces a seeming paradox, "that loyalty is at its most functional when it looks most irrational, when loyalty means strong attachment to an organization that does not seem to warrant such attachment because it is so much like another one that is also available."

In noting that the barriers to exit are finite, Hirschman cites several approaches to ensuring loyalty or inhibiting exit in various arenas. These include high fees for entry or stiff penalties for exit, protective tariffs, complicated divorce procedures, and rigorous and seemingly silly doctrines in religious sects, political parties, and other voluntary associations. This also provides a basis for understanding the adaptive significance of both death ritual and initiation among the Miyanmin. Death ritual institutionalizes voice and defers exit; initiation fosters the prerequisite of loyalty.[1]

Hirschman takes us a step further. In collaboration with social psychologists[2] (and with the support of their experimental data), he presents the following propositions:

1. The more severe the initiation, the higher the degree of self-deception in a member's evaluation of the value of a group (here, self-deception is a permutation of loyalty and acts to inhibit exit).
2. After being complacent and passive initially, members who have undergone severe initiation will display more initiative and will be more activist than members who have not.
3. The threat to exit on the part of a severe initiation member is itself an effective method of giving voice.
4. Members who exit late are more likely to work to subvert the group from the outside than those who exit early.

These propositions go a long way toward making sense out of the differences observed between the *am-nakai* and *sa-nakai* Miyanmin. They also shed light on the discussion in chapter 7 of "scrambling" and "queuing." The prevalence of exit over voice and the absence of loyalty in *sa-nakai* groups is correlated to scrambling, opportunism, and intragroup violence in a relatively unconstrained environment. Contrastingly, the movement patterns of the *am-nakai* that are described below are queuing procedures that depend on voice for their operation. Voice, or "corrective innovation," in turn, depends on higher loyalty, the product of more severe initiation.

Movement Types

Nine kinds of movements are identified and placed on a rough continuum of scale, cost, and temporal patterning. They are (1) diurnal movement, (2) intergroup visiting, (3) dual residence, (4) hamlet shifts/settlement cycle, (5) settlement shifts, (6) warfare, (7) refuging and resettlement, (8) expansion, and (9) migration. Because they are not part of my hypothetical system, I discuss separately number (1) in relation to labor in relevant chapters and numbers (6) through (9) in chapter 10.

Scale refers to unit of response (see chapter 7 concerning groups), including its size and distance. In practice, I use distance in three senses: absolutely, as in distance between hamlets in a settlement; relatively, as in a shift from one valley to another in variable topographical space; and socially, as in a move from one group to another. Similarly, *cost* can refer to an additive cost such as the expenditure of a resource or a fractionating cost such as the loss of flexibility. *Temporal patterning* involves rhythmicity and order. There should be some relationship between the temporal properties of environmental changes and of responses. Certain control segments involving diurnal (1) and seasonal (2 and 3) movements are essentially of the open sequence type (chapter 2). Equilibrating movements, such as those of the settlement cycle (4), have an expected—though not inevitable—rhythmicity due to lags between environmental change, measurement and perception, response, and environmental effect. Temporal order is particularly concerned with responses that involve patterns of escalation and reversal. Reversibility implies a means of returning to the status quo and, hence, restoring flexibility and the ability to equilibrate.

In addition to scale, cost, and temporal patterning, we need also to be concerned about the contingencies incident to responses, their constraints and effects, and the larger issue of effectiveness. I use the term contingency loosely to include proximate causes, the perception and measurement of change, and the nature of choice and decision making (to the extent that these are matters of public behavior or self-reporting). Some movement responses depend on people's perceptions of problems and assessments of alternatives that, while possibly differing from the observer's view, nevertheless contribute to individual decisions: exit, voice, consensus, and action.

A constraint is a negative contingency—a limit, perennial or transitory, that pertains at a given place and time. The most common constraints to movement are physical factors, political boundaries, the spatial relationship between resources, and security. The *effect* of a movement response is to alter the distribution of activity and its impact in time and space. I discuss effects and attempt to assess effectiveness at the end of this chapter.

I am not the first to call attention to the importance of mobility or to attempt to distinguish types of movements. For example, Ackerman and Cavalli-Sforza (1971) emphasize the importance of small-scale, regular, incremental movements because they may have long-term cumulative effects comparable to those resulting from migration. Hill (1969) develops a tentative typology of nonseasonal movements in order to link them to "ecological pressures." Some of his terms are used below. Students of pastoral societies (e.g., Gulliver 1955; Barth 1959-60; Dyson-Hudson 1971) have of necessity pioneered the study of the features of movement, attempting especially to move beyond the concept of nomadism, just as I try here to go beyond the concept of shifting cultivation. Dyson-Hudson, for example, suggests that in the study of spatial mobility, "a preliminary ordering of elements could be achieved. . . . by asking whether movement is with or without households, within or between occupations, with or without capital resources, and so on" (1971:24).

In his monograph on the Raiapu Enga, Waddel (1972:67) uses the features of scale and duration to distinguish two types of movement:

> . . . first, short term movements involving absences from the residence of anything from a few minutes to a few weeks where there is no change in the location of agricultural activity or of residence, and second, long-term movements involving the explicit relocation of interests outside the group territory.

Waddel's two types correspond, in a general way, to the extremes of the range presented earlier. Note, however, that I substitute the concept of reversibility for Waddel's term "duration." Elsewhere, in his study of responses to the frost hazard among Outer Enga, Waddel (1975, 1983) describes an escalatory pattern involving environmental modification and several types of movement. He emphasizes the feature of reversibility, particularly with regard to refuging, the largest-scale and most costly response.

Diurnal Movements

Diurnal movements are the daily moves of individual people between residence (or temporary habitation) and work site or range. Agricultural and related work patterns are described in chapter 5, and hunting and foraging in chapter 6.

As prosaic as it may seem, people's daily activity patterns of work, feeding, sociality, and rest epitomize normalcy and set a perceptual standard of well-being. People need to account and compensate for deviations from this standard that are, over time, otherwise difficult to endure. Thus, I am concerned with a class of activities that do not feature positive contingencies, but which are surrounded by potential constraints. People do their daily work unless they are prevented by a constraint or upheaval, or lured by an unusual opportunity or prospect of compensation. The most ordinary constraint is weather: people do not normally leave their habitations on a rainy day. Others include illness, survivorship, required maintenance of personal or familial equipment and group infrastructure, preparation for feasts and ceremonies, and involvement in other kinds of movement.

Intergroup Visiting

Although these movements are temporary and individualistic, they provide for the conduct of intergroup politics. Young single men are the most numerous participants, with smaller numbers of older men also represented. Such visits involve the exercise of personal kinship rights and obligations in connection with funerals, prestations, regional dances, or certain economic activities such as hunting, trading, and collecting raw materials. Dances and economic activities in particular appear to possess a seasonal component. Young single men are likely participants because, more than any other segment of the population, they are free of the kinds of regular, daily work requirements that are characteristic of married men and women. Bachelors were formerly concentrated by the initiation cycle in pioneering areas of the settlement where their energies contributed to extensive garden clearing, construction, and pig drives in deep forest areas. Here again, the distribution of bachelors, as well as of other components of the population, was related to seasonality.

The Miyanmin recognize two seasons. The first is identified with the fruiting of particular trees (*Pasania sp.* and *Leca sp.*) when deep forest hunting, particularly of wild pigs, is favored. As is noted in chapter 7, since ancestral spirits are abroad, it is the appropriate time for constructing ancestral shrines (*kwoisam*) because the taking of a series of ritually important wild pigs is required to consecrate them. It is also the time when mourning restrictions may be removed for agnates by killing a wild pig with the assistance of the spirit of the recently deceased. This confirms that the ghost is friendly and has chosen to remain with his own group in the afterlife rather than exiting and working against it. It is also during this period that bachelors and young and mature families are grouped in the forward part of the settlement near large areas of forest.

Contrasting with this season of good, more reliable hunting is the period starting around January and extending to April, when rainfall is most abundant and deep forest hunting of wild pigs is difficult. The wild foods preferred by feral pigs are not available in the forest so they increasingly appear in gardens. As a result, hunting is diffused around and even within the periphery of the settlement and it tends to be less successful. Bachelors and active household heads (who are involved in this) are more dispersed too, with bachelors visiting and working with older agnates and matrikin of all the hamlets in the area.

This period is also characterized by regional dances sponsored by particular parishes (usually one per season for the eastern Miyanmin area) and other kinds of long-range expeditions that are aimed at the temporary exploitation of the resources of other zones. For the Kome of the Hak Valley, visits are organized for hunting in the May River valley to the north where wild pigs are very abundant, possibly associated with natural sago stands. Men are absent for two or three months and return home with 50 or 60 pounds of meat apiece, including smoked pork, crocodile, kangaroo, and exotica such as large live snapping turtles. Expeditions also were aimed at replenishing nonsubsistence items that are not available locally, such as palm wood varieties for bows and arrow parts, cane for arrow shafts and (before the introduction of steel tools) stone for the manufacture of adzes. For the latter, the Miyanmin in the past had their own quarry on the Seneya River in what is now Hoten territory which had been captured from the Yanfaten early in this century.

Seasonal pan-regional movements were an important organizational feature of predatory warfare (chapter 10). The gathering of parties of men from many different local groups provided either the manpower for an immediate small-scale raid, or the means for recruiting more men from visitors' home groups for larger, more organized attacks and campaigns. This was instrumental in the northward expansion of the Miyanmin and, in the short run, provided for the exploitation of another source of high-quality protein, human flesh.

I have mentioned work demands and seasonality as having a contingent role with respect to this kind of movement. There is also a set of political and communicational constraints. The "language" of the situation involves interparish marriage, marital irregularity, sorcery accusations, and milder distrust between intergroup affines. Because of the endogamous character of most marriages and the nonlocal or ambilocal nature of the lineages that regulate it, marriage (with exceptions to be noted) does not appear to be as important a vehicle for geographic or social mobility as it is in other societies. Interparish marriages tend to cancel each other out in terms of number and direction. I have already shed light on the few discrepancies (see table 7-5). Interparish marriages do provide a vehicle for movement outside of the parish circle. Aside from cases in which delayed reciprocity or uxorilocality have been agreed to, the discrepancies that do occur in the statistics are the proximate causes of the breakdown of interparish cooperation, or are otherwise connected with conflict between parishes. As noted above, conflict is often a matter of marital irregularity, interparish elopements without reconciliation, adultery between members of different parishes, the disposition of widows and their children, the flight or refuging of adulterers, and captured women. The failure to reconcile such discrepancies serves to limit movement, particularly visiting, across parish lines; and, before pacification, lack of compensation could trigger interparish fights.

Beyond this, on the occasion of an adult death, even amicable ties provide a perceptual test of interparish relations. If the deceased is a full parish member, affines and friends from other parishes who attend the funeral may be attacked and beaten in the course of a mortuary brawl (as I have previously described). The ostensible reason for this is the suspicion that they have killed their affine through sorcery; or that they have caused him to die angry, thus interfering with his willingness to perform as a beneficient ancestral ghost. The aggrieved visitors return to their home groups in a very angry state. Their home parish may make preparations for a fight, but in most cases compensation will then be paid by the parish of the deceased, and regular visiting will be resumed. A sub-case of this involves the death of an uxorilocally residing male. Kinsmen in his natal parish will accuse his affines' parish of either sorcerizing him or failing to see to his well-being (e.g., protecting him from *others*). Again, it is a matter of either compensation and the resumption of friendship and visiting, or a fight.

The absolute frequency of interparish marriage is low (see figure 7-5) with "irregularities" also infrequent, though not readily measurable, over the eastern Miyanmin area. Both kinds of events are much more common between social units sharing a "special relationship" and, to a somewhat lesser degree, are characteristic boundary phenomena.

Dual Residence

Grouped in this category are the more or less biannual movements in which elementary and joint families shift between the hamlets where they maintain houses and gardens. The proximate cause for shifts is the exhaustion of gardens associated with one hamlet and knowledge that the gardens associated with the alternate hamlet are maturing. The period of residence in a particular hamlet ranges from five to seven months. In addition, sometime after the midpoint of a period of residence, a family makes a visit of approximately one week's duration to its alternate hamlet to weed maturing gardens. Weeding visits are brief because food is in short supply (chapter 5). People subsist on bananas from old gardens and more quickly maturing sweet potatoes in the newer gardens. They can also depend on modest amounts of food from more sedentary (usually older) hamlet mates if any are in residence.

Adherence to the dual residence pattern depends on life- or developmental-cycle status. Thus, bachelors are sporadic participants, young newly married families are more engaged (although they often lack a full set of houses or sufficient taro planting stock), more mature families (with household head between 25 and 40) are fully engaged, and senescent or otherwise disabled families have dropped out and become more sedentary. Like visiting, dual residence movements are seasonal. Tabulation of a small sample of hamlet residence data has shown that these moves also possess the same kind of seasonal rhythmicity as that ascribed to "visiting" in the previous section. From the standpoint of dual residence, this means that during the dry season, when deep forest hunting is most appropriate, mature men with families as well as bachelors are grouped in those parts of the settlement which are most accessible to undisturbed forest. During the rainy season, however, when wild pigs are likely to resort for food to the gardens around the periphery of the settlement, such men in their "prime," as well as young bachelors, will be more evenly distributed throughout the settlement. The timing of events in the ceremonial cycle, described in the previous chapter, reinforces this effect. It also increases the area which is readily accessible for exploitation at any given time and is the means by which somewhat larger-scale moves, hamlet shifts of the settlement cycle and settlement shifts, are accomplished.

Hamlet Shift / Settlement Cycle

The seasonal pattern of concentration and dispersion described in connection with "visiting" and "dual residence" seems to be another instance of the kind of spatial organization that Richard Lee views as "basic to the hunting and gathering adaptation" (1972a). In this section, however, I describe another pattern of movement, the "settlement cycle," which is also characterized by concentration and dispersion. It is not seasonal, but rather unfolds over a much longer run of time, perhaps eight to twelve years. Here the adaptation is to the cumulative effect of human activity on resources in restricted areas over time. This corresponds to what Hill (1969:53), following ecologists such as Dice (1952), refers to as "range drift": the population follows a biotic zone, that is, "drifting" because of overuse of resources or a similar change in the distribution of resources.

The basic mechanism of the settlement cycle is the "hamlet shift," which refers to the process by which hamlets are being continuously founded and abandoned. The founding of a new hamlet is gradual, since a prerequisite for it is the maturation of a set of gardens near the site. (A lead time of eight to nine months is required under ordinary circumstances.) There are also extraordinary circumstances, when the abandonment of a hamlet is sudden. The proximate cause is the death of an adult, usually male. Miyanmin funerals have already been described. It will be recalled that a shaman invokes the spirit of the deceased and attempts to determine the cause of death and an appropriate course of action. This may involve the precipitous or gradual abandonment of the hamlet in which the death took place. The shaman is apparently the key figure in what ensues—a conscious practitioner of political economy or of consensus politics (or both) as he promulgates decisions about movement.

The decision indicates the extent and direction of the move, if such is to be the case (as it usually is). A movement usually involves the kind of preparation already described. But if the circumstances of the death are particularly aggravated and threatening, as in a series of deaths connected with an epidemic, more extreme measures may be undertaken. For example, it is possible to uproot immature taros and establish them in new, perhaps distant gardens, an action simulating evacuation and resettlement under emergency conditions (chapter 10). Distances involved in such moves are variable, ranging from a half-kilometer (little more than a quarter mile) to eight kilometers (or five miles), the higher figure observed only in the north. Moreover, the solidarity of the hamlet is not maintained absolutely since some hamlet members may elect to establish themselves in an existing hamlet rather than participating in the founding of a new one. This is particularly true of a widow and her children. At the hamlet level it has an idiosyncratic appearance; the regularities pertain to the level of the local population or parish.

As indicated in maps 4 through 10, over time there is a progressive expansion of the distance between hamlets as well as a steady movement of the center of the whole settlement in a particular direction. One constraint on the expansion of the settlement, especially on the interface between settlement and forest, is competition of wild pigs for garden produce. Although during the rainy season gardens are bait to put the hunter in contact with his prey, this is a mixed blessing. If gardens and hamlets are too dispersed, the gardens will not be subject to frequent observation, and remote gardens have been completely destroyed. The Miyanmin rarely fence their gardens, doing so only when the settlement is very new (that is, right after a pristine area has been invaded). Of course, village pigs present just the opposite problem. When the settlement is young and nucleated, garden invasions by domestic pigs are frequent occurrences, but this falls off rapidly with the expansion of the settlement as the distances between gardens and hamlets increase.

The direction of movement of the settlement is constrained topographically and politically as well as by the existence of nonportable capital. Within a particular settlement cycle, movement is with the grain of the land, and seems to average about a kilometer and a half (about one mile) laterally per year for large local populations in the higher-altitude south. As this movement progresses, such resources as marita pandanus plantations are rendered more and more inaccessible. A two-day round trip for a harvesting party appears to be a practical limit on regular use. Such orchards tend to be almost completely obliterated when an area is resettled after many years.

Settlement Shift

What I refer to as "settlement shift" typically occurs when a topographic or political boundary is approached, and marks the end of an old settlement cycle and the start of a new one. Settlement shifts are across the grain of the land—across rivers or divides—and are initiated by the establishment of a set of gardens and bush houses. The Miyanmin maintain that they must wait through a seasonal turn without an adult death before the intended shift can be confirmed by building a dance house/long house (*itam*) and holding a regional festival (*natim/dowal*). The long house becomes the residence of the bulk of the local population for the rest of the rainy season, during which time an additional set of gardens is established to provide food during the next rainy season.

The Miyanmin consciously view these longer-range shifts as a necessary response to the reduction of game animals and to the exhaustion of prime agricultural land and building materials. This makes sense as an outcome of the overall impact of human activity, particularly gardening activity, on the restricted area which has been the location of the completed settlement cycle. Miyanmin history has been a continuous serial of such shifts; and their legends, such as the one that opens the first chapter of this book, often recall the most intrepid ones.

The Environmental Effects of Movement

Most of this chapter has been devoted to describing patterns of movement, the means by which human activities and their effects are distributed in space and time. In this section I focus on the effects themselves, consequences of the various kinds of movements, particularly those having an impact on animals in their habitats. These have been divided into three categories: horticultural, village and settlement, and hunting.

Horticultural Effects

Agriculture provides the most striking examples of the disruption of local ecosystems by people (see Bulmer 1968:313). Although Miyanmin gardening does not promote complete deforestation (chapter 5) and the grass-dominated climaxes characteristic of many true highland areas in New Guinea are lacking, short-run local changes have an extensive impact on the forest community, including the faunal component. In the long run, the only irreversible changes that occur are land slips associated with garden clearing on very steep ground that alter natural drainage patterns (chapter 4).

Garden clearing leaves some large trees standing, and others are stunned or slowly killed by burning their roots. However, many are felled, and the characteristic canopy of the rainforest is thus breeched. Low scrub and underbrush is removed and only ground litter and humus remain. Consequently, most of the animal life that lives above the surface is driven off, including insects and reptiles that are food for some birds and mammals (Wiens 1962:407; Trevis 1956). Some of these, as well as new populations, will reinvade a given site at some point during its succession as a garden, abandoned field, and second growth tract; but an approximation of the original association will not be achieved for a very long time, and in some instances not at all.

Planting does not materially affect this picture, but the progressive drying of the garden as the cover slowly dies, affects the subterranean fauna (such as crabs, worms, and certain insects), as well as the surface fauna, populations of some trophic importance to many animals. The ensuing growth of weeds and grasses changes the characteristic surface insect life from coleoptera to orthoptera.

In addition, the reduction of forest floor moisture levels concurrent with reduced forest cover in a gardening area, has a negative effect on forest floor animals, even in interspersial tracts not actually cleared or gardened (see Gentry et al. 1968). Recovery and repopulation of such areas by forest floor animals is apparently more dependent on the renewal of cover than on the reconstruction of complete food webs (Cook 1959). Accordingly, not only the direct disruption of the food web, but also the changes attendant on the breaking of the forest canopy, leads to the disappearance of most of the forest fauna from the immediate area.

In the early stages of the garden, the invaders of the site are animals that can exploit human cultigens, especially taro, sweet potato, curcurbits, and later, banana and papaya. They include certain burrowing rats that eat taro and other cultigens and establish nests in the area—grassland types that are attracted to weedy or recently abandoned gardens, and edge dwellers (see chapter 6 for discussions of specific animals). Also, certain possums feed on bananas in older gardens. The abandonment of a garden, involving a floral transition to seed-producing annuals, should foster a faunal transition to seed-eating animals and, perhaps, to insectivorous ones as well. Consequently, some animals will be fostered.

A secondary effect of horticultural activity is the creation of extensive tracts of secondary forest and other disturbed areas in the wake of shifting settlements. Some authorities assert that feral pigs favor such areas over deep primary forest (Bulmer 1968a:313), but this requires extensive qualification (chapter 6). It is also true that certain other browsing mammals, as well as certain birds, may be similarly encouraged in montane zones. In any event, it may be easier to hunt certain quarry in secondary forest.

Village and Settlement Effects

The changes accompanying agriculture involve relatively short-term effects limited to narrow areas. A different perspective is gained by focusing on wider areas and longer runs of time. Miyanmin horticulture only needs to exploit a small proporation of the total accessible area at a given time. It is further limited to land suitable for the application of existing technology. Thus extensive tracts of primary and old secondary forest are left untouched. Yet the abundance of wildlife of the whole area encompassed by a string of hamlets is, nevertheless, affected. Apparently, a balance of broad scope is upset over a fairly extensive area and game declines at a rate greater than that attributable to harvesting alone. Some of this may be related to factors such as moisture balance described above. But it is also conceivable that such human artifacts as noise, smoke and marauding village dogs and pigs, and the daily comings and goings of people along the tracks between hamlets and between hamlets and gardens, drives shier animals away.

The Miyanmin consciously and explicitly limit the orbit of this disturbance by circumscribing it. The areas to which all settlements and gardens are confined are marked off and separated by rivers from relatively accessible areas reserved exclusively for hunting. Normally, such settlement areas are imposed on a single divide or a ridge descending from a higher mountain, with both sides of the drainage being used for gardens and hamlets. Across one of the rivers will be a pristine area which initially contains an undisturbed faunal community. Across the other river will be an area which has been disrupted during the previous occupation period, and which contains a full range of second growth tracts in various stages of succession. These two areas will be exploited in a manner consistent with their differing characteristics, perhaps on a seasonal basis (as described earlier). Moreover, the pristine hunting area is potentially the settlement area for the next succeeding settlement cycle.

The importance of this pattern is reflected in the fact that the political relations of territorial groups maintain the required spacing. Facilitated by the ritual cycle previously described, the settlements of territorial groups are interlocked regionally, and groups may be restricted in establishing settlements within their own territories by the previous moves of adjacent groups. Thus ephemeral borders and shifting (but effective) buffers are maintained in a manner reminiscent of other hunting peoples such as the Chippewa and eastern Sioux of North America (Hickerson 1965).

In 1968 Sokaten parish occupied the southwestern slopes of Mount Stolle, but desired to shift across the upper May River to occupy the divide between it and the Uk River. This would have allowed them to exploit both the May and the Uk fall of the range, a disposition that the group had not assumed since about 1910. The move, however, would have brought them within a few hours of the Kometen settlements then expanding to the east on the divide between the Uk and the Fak Rivers. Because their prime hunting area would have been affected, Kometen successfully opposed the move. Sokaten shifted instead to another area further west which had previously been reserved for hunting. This new area was in fact separated only by a river from Kometen territory that had not been occupied for some 20 years and was not likely to be reoccupied by them in the near future.

It is more difficult to assess the impact on the fauna of such human activities as the systematic utilization of the wild food plants of the rain forest, the felling of sago palms, and the maintenance of extensive red pandanus (*Pandanus conoideus*) plantations both near to and very distant from occupied areas (see Bulmer 1968a:313).

Hunting Effects

The disturbance of natural ecosystems by hunting is not as dramatic, in time or extent, as that associated with horticulture. The focus of human predation is widely diffused by the dispersal of settlements and the necessity to travel out from them to hunt. For example, the Miyanmin do not employ any of the hunting techniques, such as fire or mass drives, that lead to the simultaneous killing of large numbers of animals. Under traditional conditions, few species face even local extinction, but over time, the abundance of most mammals is reduced. Certain slow-breeding tropical species (Harrison 1955) are affected most dramatically in local areas, and quickly become rare from the hunter's point of view once an area is subject to regular exploitation. But, in terms of whole group territories, the existence of large pockets of unexploited ground, between and surrounding human population nuclei, and also areas which are beyond the range of regular human exploitation, insures the existence of a reservoir of animals that can slowly repopulate depleted areas.

The distinction between local areas and group territories needs to be emphasized. The local area is land suitable for exploitation by a group for a relatively short but variable period. During that time, it is seriously disturbed by human activity. The group territory, in contrast, includes the total area that will be exploited by a local human population over a very long run of time before a return is made to the exploitation of a hypothetical starting point. Human activity does not have a serious impact on the group territory as a whole. This is a basis for my assumption, in the absence of a long run of data, that a high level of sustained yield is maintained over a very long period and that the management routine followed by the Miyanmin to accomplish this is achieved primarily by dispersal mechanisms and secondarily by varying the intensity of hunting or prey selection. The latter are the kinds of mechanisms cited by resource management scientists like Kenneth Watt (see chapter 2). In Darling's (1956:778) terms, the persistence of the Miyanmin as a hunting people "depends upon not becoming an ecological dominant," not on destroying their total habitat, but rather on their migrating away from disrupted local areas.

Similarly, the built-in rhythmicity that is characteristic of all productive (predation) systems (Watt 1962:195) is present, but is only partly connected with a seasonal climatic cycle and its concomitants, and seems to involve variation in location rather than in the intensity of activity.

Some Model Predictions and Empirical Support

Because of the complexity of the system presented in chapter 3 and the strictures on verification, I can only hope to convince the reader of its general plausibility by selecting a portion of the system to analyze. I can make my best case with settlement variables that reflect movement patterns. I will also take up game animals, but I cannot do much with them for want of a long run of data.

I will adhere to the following procedure. First, based on my model I will predict the behavior of settlement variables over time. These predictions should be consistent with the verbal account rendered earlier, but I will present them in tabular and graphic form. Second, I will go to my settlement data for an appropriate time period and plot it in a similar way. We should then be able to assess the model. This may also suggest possibilities for verifying other portions of the system. Although I do not claim to have adhered to "physical science" standards of verification, I do think that this exercise will make a contribution. What I claim is that during a particular period of observation, the settlement pattern of a specific Miyanmin local population behaved as predicted by the model.

Settlement Variables

The specific variables I examine here are the "nucleation index" (X_{13}), "disturbed area" (X_{17}), and "accessible forest area" (X_{16}), along with a combination of the latter two, here referred to as "deep forest as a proportion of total area" $[X_{16}/(X_7 + X_{16})]$. These will be plotted against "settlement years" (X_{12}), and the two nonseasonal phases of settlement. The scale assigned to the main variables and the vertical axis in the graphs is an implicit variable which depends on such parameters as altitude and population size. Given this proposition—and consistent with the practice adhered to in the earlier verbal account of the operation of the system—I have assigned the values low, medium, and high. Thus, the range of values assumed by a particular variable is also the subject of empirical determination. This procedure seems justifiable insofar as it increases the generality of the model: we can assign different scales to different local populations, depending on the parameters specified. The relative values assigned to settlement variables are presented in table 9-1 and represented graphically in figure 9-1. In the latter graphs I have taken the

Table 9-1.   Model Predictions concerning Settlement by Phase

Phase	Years	Index of Nucleation	Disturbed Area	Forest Area	Forest Percent
I	2-3	Low	Low-Medium	Low	50
II	2-4	Med.- High	Medium	High	50
III	4-6	High	Med.-High	High-Med.	50

Figure 9-1.   Model Predictions for Settlement Variables

A. Index of Nucleation X_{13}

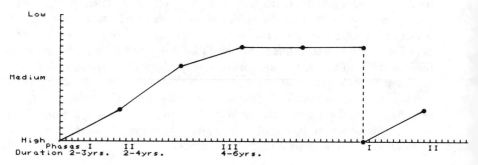

B. Disturbed Area X_{17}

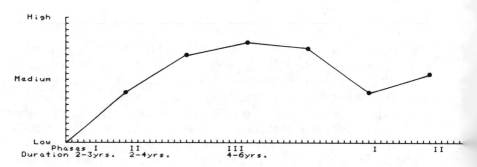

C.   Accessible Forest Area X_{16}

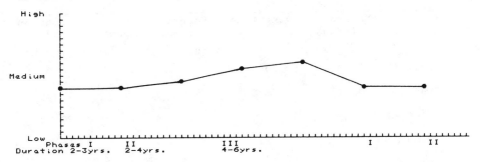

D.   Deep Forest as a Proportion of Total Area

$$\frac{X_{16}}{X_{28}}$$

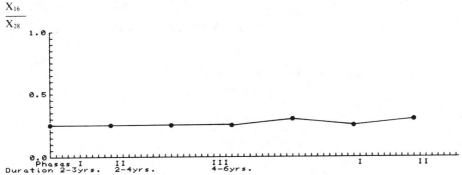

liberty of entering hypothetical data points representing the average values that would result from performing the specified operations on a sample of settlement cycles for several local populations.

The data presented in table 9-2 and plotted in figure 9-2 refer to one complete settlement cycle (between approximately 1959–60 and 1965–66) and parts of two others for the Kome-Temsak local population. The raw data is presented in maps 4 through 10. The curves should be compared to the model predictions in figure 9-1. When this comparison is carried out, a number of points emerge. In general, my predictions about the behavior of the variables in question are supported; and this extends support to other portions of the system that I cannot test directly.

It is clear that the area of disturbed vegetation (X_{17}) is an artifact of the nucleation index (X_{13}) and that this is also true of the total accessible area (X_{16} + X_{17}). On the other hand, the accessible forest area (X_{11}) is not. This dimension increases steadily throughout the cycle to compensate for reduced prey density resulting from human activity. A settlement shift is triggered when a limit on movement is approached and dispersal can no longer increase but, in fact, begins to decline.

Table 9-2.   Kome Settlement, 1957–70

Period	Nucleation Index	Disturbed Area	Forest Area	Forest Percent	Occupation Area
1957-58	1.64	10.0	10.5	51	20.5
1959-60	0.51	6.5	8.0	55	14.5
1961-62	1.87	12.0	8.5	41	20.5
1963-64	1.23	12.0	9.0	43	21.0
1965-66	0.79	8.0	10.5	57	18.5
1967-68	1.09	13.0	9.5	42	22.5
1969-70	1.49	16.0	12.0	43	28.0

Figure 9-2.   Kome Settlement Variables, 1957–70

A.   Index of Nucleation X_{13}

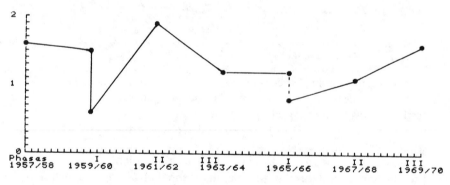

B.   Disturbed Area X_{17}

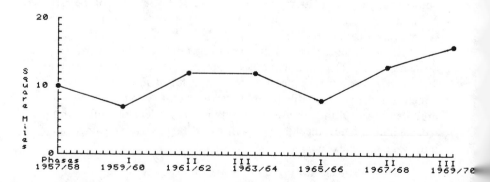

C. Accessible Forest Area X_{16}

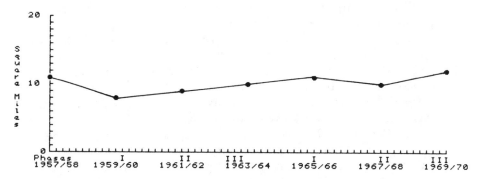

D. Deep Forest as a Proportion of Total Area

$$\frac{X_{16}}{X_{28}}$$

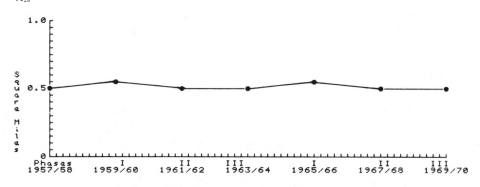

The variable "deep forest as a proportion of total area" $[X_{17}/(X_{16}+X_{17})]$ was calculated because it shows the effect of strong regulatory forces. It illustrates that, in the face of variation in the total accessible area $(X_{16}+X_{17})$ over the span of the cycle, the relative proportion of the two kinds of habitats is maintained in a steady state. As with other variables, the scale will vary with altitude and population. In the high-altitude areas (where the largest populations are also found) the proportion appears to be approximately 0.5. At lower altitudes (or perhaps with smaller groups), the proportion may be smaller, say, 0.3. I speculate that this function is particularly important to the operation of seasonal phases because they respectively focus on the two types of habitats. Note that if the settlement were static, then the proportion of disturbed vegetation would increase (which in reality it does only temporarily).

Visual examination of the curves reveals a number of apparent deviations from the model predictions that require discussion, although this will be inconclusive. The 61/62 nucleation data point attracts attention because it is too great. A plausible explanation for this is that it is a mistake—for example, I assigned a particular hamlet to the wrong time period. A review of the pertinent data, however, did not develop any information that I felt would justify changing it. If, however, I were to drop the westernmost hamlet in the settlement (map 6), the point would fall within the predicted range of values. Of course, the model suggests other possibilities. If I assume that the data point is accurate, that the constellation of hamlets was actually in the state indicated, then I can try to explain it. This data point refers to a settlement cycle carried out in the Uk River Valley on the southern fall of the Thurnwald range. The chain of hamlets making up the settlement at this time was apparently stretched out over some 13 or 14 kms (8 or 9 mi) of the valley. Such an attenuated settlement pattern might be related to the narrowness of the occupation area and/or to the fact that the boundary with Sokaten lays on the ridge between the Uk and the May. The main point is that with a longer run of settlement data, individual deviations would have little systematic meaning.

Another apparent discrepancy is that data points from comparable times in different settlement cycles differ from each other for all three of the primary variables. This is because the scale changes for every occupation area, probably because of topographic variability or other constraints.

Movement Variables

I can extend additional empirical support to my hypothetical system by focusing on a key movement pattern, hamlet shifts. In this case I see no utility in making a formal model prediction, but instead I present a reasonable proposition: from the founding of the settlement and extending through the first and second phases, the number of domiciles will increase lineally until an asymptote is achieved in the third phase of settlement. This will occur as a result of the founding, growth, decline, and abandonment of individual hamlets—the "hamlet shift" mechanism.

In this presentation the measure of number of domiciles is the number of hearths. This is appropriate because of the "rule" stated in chapter 7 (where these data were discussed from a sociological standpoint) that every married women has her own hearth. In figure 9-3, data on hearth frequencies are grouped by long house (*itam*), hamlet cluster, or hamlet, and are plotted against time. The resulting curve shows (1) the progressive increase in the number of domiciles as predicted, (2) the "hamlet shift" mechanism as it operates to shape the settlement in accordance with the model, and (3) the steplike character of the overall hearth curve which shows the three phases of settlement quite distinctly.

In this figure, the origin of each hamlet plot is its recorded or inferred founding date. Then the construction date (recorded or inferred) of each

Figure 9-3.   Kome Settlement Growth, 1965–70

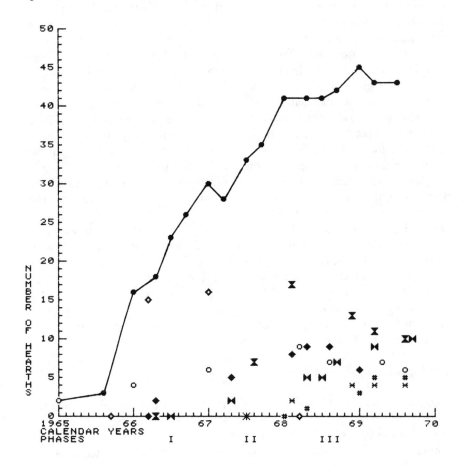

Data Points:
● Average Hearth Count
○ Ukdabip II
◇ Tebabip
◆ Sokabip Cluster
✗ Klemklutgolimbip Cluster
◣ Deptabip
✕ Ukbebip
Amitbip
Points on Horizontal Axis Indicate Founding.

residential structure, together with the number of hearths (domiciles) it encloses, can be plotted as a summation of the hearths in the hamlet. Thus, we can observe the growth and decline of each hamlet as it occurred during the time accessible to me. I have then taken the liberty of summing the curves rather than the data points to produce the total hearth curve. This seems justified, since the straight lines connecting a particular pair of data points are, at any point along them, mean hearth frequencies for the period of time in question. Thus, the summation represents growth of the hamlet means.

I attribute deviations in this curve, such as those at the beginning of 1967 and 1969, to the fact that I could only rarely establish any absolute time of abandonment for a particular house. For example, the declining curve for the *itam* is an estimate, inferred from the fact that two families were still living in the long house when I first visited the Miyanmin early in 1968, and that the structure collapsed and was burned early in 1969. Note also that all the declining curves refer to hamlets in the rear of the settlement. Another departure from the model is the curve labeled "Ukda II." The fact that its origin preceded the founding of the long house can be attributed to a small natural disaster. The two hearths marking its origin are the relic of an earlier attempt to shift to the south side of the Uk River in 1963–64 (map 7). At that time a long house was built on the site along with several family houses, but a flood destroyed most of it before the festival (*ita*) could be held. One family house with two hearths was spared, but most people stayed on the north side of the Uk for a few more years (map 8).

Settlement and Game Animals

I cannot present similar support for the model with a long run of data at the faunal level. Yet this is potentially one of the most interesting, even original, aspects of my model. Nevertheless, even without the required data, it is important to make some predictions about the faunal harvest based on the model, because they can guide future ecological and anthropological research in New Guinea (including my own) and may have possible implications for the work of archaeologists.

These predictions, concerning numbers of animals harvested by faunal class, are summarized in table 9-3 and represented graphically in figure 9-4. In conformity with the practice I followed earlier, a low-medium-high scale of relative values is employed for this purpose, and an attempt will be made below to suggest possible numerical values for this scale by reference to my limited observations.

The predictions suggest that the faunal classes succeed each other through the settlement cycle with respect to their relative prominence in the hunter's bag. The order of this succession of faunal classes is IIIa (Most

Table 9-3.   Model Predictions concerning Faunal Harvest

```
---------------------------------------------------------------------------
Settlement  Years of    Faunal Harvest
Phase       Settlement  Class IIIa    Ib         IV          V
---------------------------------------------------------------------------

I.          2-3         Med.-High     Medium     Low         Low

II.         2-4         High-Med.     Med.-High  Low-Med.    Med.-High

III.        4-6         Med.-Low      High-Med.  High        Medium
```

Rapidly Reduced), V (Domestic Pigs), IIIb (Reduced; Wild Pigs), and IV (Fostered), with the duration and scale of each stage variable in terms similar to those described previously for other levels.

For comparison and to convey some feeling for the scale that might be involved, table 9-4 presents the hunting bag for one three-week period in February, 1968. The sample of 157 individual animals represents a high proportion of all animals taken by residents of Kome parish during this period. The fauna have been grouped by class, with quantity, average weight, and undressed weight indicated by species, and with the resulting accessible protein tabulated by faunal class only.

Figure 9-4.   Model Predictions concerning Animal Harvest by Class

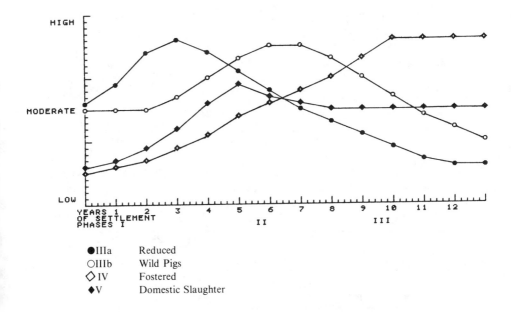

●IIIa   Reduced
OIIIb   Wild Pigs
◇IV   Fostered
◆V   Domestic Slaughter

Table 9-4. Kome Parish Faunal Harvest for Three-Week Period, February, 1969; Estimated Nutritional Value

CLASS/Species	Quantity	Average Weight	Data Source	Total Undressed Weight	Accessible Protein @
I.& II. RARE OR RELICT					
Perorhyctes raffrayana	2	1,224.0	3,+	2,448.0	
Hyomys goliath	1	1,279.0	3,+	1,279.0	
various	6			16,147.0	
subtotals	9			19,874.0	2,782.36
III. REDUCED					
Melomys lorentzi	2	95.7	4	191.4	
Uromys caudimaculatus	1	626.0	1,*	626.0	
Casuarius bennettii	2	22,600.0	4	45,200.0	
Sus scrofa (wild)	2	60,781.0	4	121,562.0	
subtotals	7			167,579.4	23461.12
IV. FOSTERED					
Echimipera kalubu	35	1377.0	3,+	48,195.0	
Phallanger gymnotis	7	2613.0	2,3,*	18,291.0	
P. orientalis	4	1930.0	1,2,3,*	7,720.0	
Dactylopsila trivigata	1	459.0	3,+	459.0	
Melomys spp.	50	63.8	1,2,3*#	3,190.0	
Rattus ruber	39	63.8	1,2,3*#	2,488.0	
subtotals	135			80,343.0	11,248.02
V. DOMESTICATED					
Sus scrofa (dom.)	0	54,432.0	4	0.0	0.0
subtotals	0			0.0	0.0
GRAND TOTAL	151			267,796.4	37,491.5

Data source of average weights: 1-Tate (1952) 2-Lidecker & Ziegler (1968) 3-Van Deusen (1972) 4-Own Data
Quality of Avg. Wt. Data:

* mean or weighted means from source indicated
+ .9 of maximum given by source
# Rattus and Melomys weights from sources averaged
Other Calculations: @ Accessible Protein = .14 x Undressed Weight
.14 = .8 (usable meat) x .18 (protein/gram) x .95 (digestibility)

The distribution of kills by class in this table can be related to the predicted distribution in figure 9-4 only in a general way. The data pertain to the transitional period between the the second and third phases of settlement. The distribution also reflects rainy season residence with reduced animals, including wild pigs, underrepresented and fostered animals overrepresented. To really test the system and assess the effects of the interaction between seasonal and nonseasonal strategies, I would need this kind of data for four such periods per year and for a run of perhaps 10 years or more.

In table 9-4 I have also calculated the amount of high-quality protein represented by the harvest.[3] I have totaled this by faunal class in order to show the importance of regularly exploiting many different prey. For example, other reduced fauna contributed more than 60 percent as much as wild pigs, while the fostered animals contributed more than 40 percent of the latter. The fostered animals are particularly important because their harvest (and dietary contributions) are so regular and evenly distributed after the initial settlement phase. This arrangement of the data also suggests the kinds of dietary losses that are entailed in the evolution of subsistence systems in New Guinea. It is clear that the reduced fauna (Class III) and their nutritional potential will drop out as agriculture intensifies.

If the Kome parish population is broken down by age and biomass and these figures are used to calculate dietary protein requirements, as in table 9-5, people were meeting approximately 50 percent of their requirements from game. This does not include dietary protein from other animal sources such as eggs, fish, birds, snakes, insects, and the like, as well as vegetable foods

Table 9-5.   Estimated Kome Parish Protein Requirements

Age Group	Average Weight (kgs)	Daily Requirements Group Member	Population in Age Category	Daily Requirements Category
0-5	10	7.1	32	227.2
6-10	20	14.3	20	184.0
11-15	30	21.3	11	234.3
16-20	50	35.5	19	674.5
20+	55	39.1	78	3049.9

Total Daily Protein Requirements   4369.8

including the staple taro, known to be the best protein source among the root crops. Although this is not a study of diet, I present these calculations to support the conclusion that the system works, and works well.

In this chapter I have presented a typology of movement responses, along with a specification of the relevant units of population involved in these strategies. This was necessary in order to flesh out the temporal and spatial aspects of the interactions between people and the faunal community. The final section of this chapter was an attempt to specify the important features of this interface. This is the basis I used in chapter 6 for isolating pertinent characteristics of the most important fauna involved in this relationship. In the following chapter I will take up the escalatory types of movements, expansion, warfare, and migration.

10

Expansion, Warfare, and Migration

The Curse of the Gururam

We have never actually seen it, but have only been told about it—the snake called Gururam.

In ancient times, a lone Telefolmin hunter saw it on Amawemam Mountain [in the Donner range] near the Hak River. It was of enormous size and of many colors; its anal region was swollen and crimson, its neck was bloated and white, the rest of its body was green and its tail was forked. It was a maneater.

The hunter shot the snake with a barbed fighting arrow (*fiyami*) and, so that the snake would hear him, yodeled for assistance. Men from many tribes and lines in the area came with shields and other weapons and they killed the snake with arrows and clubs. In its death throes, the arrows that had penetrated the snake were broken.

The snake was butchered and apportioned on the spot; men from Telefolmin, and Atbalmin, and the Om River tribes, as well as the several Miyanmin parishes, all received portions and bore them away to their home villages. There the snake relics were wrapped in leaves of antarctic beech and casarina [an unusual procedure] and smoked to preserve them.

The flesh of the Gururam was not eaten. Rather, the pieces were carefully wrapped in bark cloth and placed in small net bags decorated with wild pigs' tails. These were kept hidden from women and children in a *timan* or *kwoisam*.

Ever since then the Gururam has entered the bellies of men and made their gorge rise so that they fight perennially and everywhere; and their fellow men are fought and butchered and cooked and eaten as enemies; killed, quartered, baked, and consumed; slain, carved up, garnished and devoured, for ever and ever until all of them are dead and gone.

This myth, which the Miyanmin share in broad outline with neighboring groups (Brumbaugh 1980), accounts for their own bellicosity as well as that of other peoples known to them. It is, in effect, a theory of innate human aggression (cf. Lorenz, Ardrey, et al.) with explicit pessimism for the future of our kind.

Within the framework used to discuss other movements in the previous chapter, warfare, expansion, refuging and resettlement, and migration belong to the high, escalatory end of the continuum. They tend toward larger scale in distance and size of groups, and greater cost, especially in terms of potential irreversibility. Because they are essentially escalatory, they determine the parameters of equilibrational movements. Hence, my concern here is with gains and losses of territory and opportunity as well as with gains and losses of personnel, a high-stakes game for individuals and groups.

Warfare and expansion are intertwined. It is all very well to speak of "range expansion" and "range budding" (Hill, 1969) in the abstract but, without the boundary changes resulting from a martial victory, there may be no place for those crowded, displaced, or extruded people to go. I therefore separate my consideration of warfare among the Miyanmin, which appears to have accelerated markedly in this century, from my analysis of expansion and migration that occur at least partly in a context determined by warfare. I argue that, in a real way, expansion and migration follow the more fundamental act or pattern of acts involving intergroup aggression and violence.

Warfare on the Fringe

Elsewhere (Morren 1984:179) it is argued that warfare on the highland fringe of New Guinea has a distinctive character, contrasting with patterns found in highland and lowland core areas. Warfare strategy on the fringe involves maintaining extensive territories for hunting by aggressively staving off expansive neighbors, facilitating access to new territory through extensive and often unilateral raiding and genocide, and meeting certain specific needs through plunder, abduction, and cannibalism. Fringe groups such as the Miyanmin, Kukukuku, Biyami, and Jalé are locked in a continuous cycle of defensive warfare with their higher-altitude core group neighbors, while also engaging in sporadic, diffused, and smaller-scale predatory warfare against obviously weaker neighbors. As is argued elsewhere (Dornstreich and Morren 1974), exocannibalism is a fringe specialty. Having stated these general characteristics, it is also important to emphasize that there is a lot of variability among fringe groups with regard to patterns of warfare. Some— like the high-altitude Maring (Vayda 1971, Rappaport 1968)—resemble true highlanders. Others—like Kukukuku (Blackwood 1940) and Miyanmin— resemble lowlanders in their extensiveness, terrorism, and mobility. Yet others—such as the Gadio Enga (Dornstreich 1973) and lower-altitude Maring (Clark 1971)—are relatively pacific or participate in the wars of others as individuals. I believe that proximity to a highland population center is the determinant in these regards.

Historically, fringe groups have tended to be pushed to lower and lower altitudes, or to be extinguished unless (like the Miyanmin) they have successfully resisted by means of superior readiness, tactics, organization, military skills, and terror.

Miyanmin warfare, including beliefs and individual motives, can only be understood in the wider context of patterns of expansion. Accordingly, the account which follows is a composite of the history of expansion, warfare, and resettlement in the Mountain Ok region and on its northern margin.

While this context (and, for that matter, the myth) provides a general framework, particular conflicts have more specific explanations. In some cases a familiar story of feud and revenge was told: a parish member had been killed through the actual or putative actions of members of another group and this had to be avenged. In other cases, Miyanmin hunters or hunting parties, ranging over the less well-known or infrequently visited boundary areas of their domain, stumbled across evidence of alien human activity and this was provocation enough for a raid to be organized. In others, the enemy's surprise attack was discovered and successfully countered. In still other cases it was stated bluntly that the objective of a particular raid was nothing less than the acquisition of human flesh and the abduction of women or children. Whatever the proximate cause of particular Miyanmin engagements, an overall pattern can be discerned which requires that the source of population pressure and competition in the area be exposed.

Range Expansion in the Mountain Ok: The Telefolmin

There is ample evidence that the geographical arrangement of tribes and subgroups within the Mountain Ok region has been subject to continuous reshuffling over a long period of time. According to the linguist Alan Healey (cited in B. Craig 1969) the most distant likely relationships of the Ok family of languages (relationships on the order of 5000 to 10,000 years) are with languages to the south and west of the region. This is consistent with my own picture of Ok expansion in the more recent past, with the Miyanmin forming the vanguard of the northern line of advance (and interacting with the lowland region centered in the Abau groups of the upper Sepik).

One center of expansion within the Mountain Ok region is the Ifitaman Valley and within that valley perhaps Kialikmin parish of the Telefolmin. Up to 300 years ago the Telefol speakers apparently were confined to this valley. By one account, the Telefolmin displaced the Nukokmin from the Oksimin area to the east, the Nukokmin taking refuge to the west in the Ilam Valley. The Telefols who settled at Oksimin became the present day Feramin tribe speaking a Telefol dialect, whereas the Nukokmin apparently are the ancestors of the Tifalmin presently in the Ilam. Summarizing traditions of tribal origin and conquest for the Faiwolmin area, Barth (1971:132) sees "a consistent picture of eastward and southward movement" (see also Wheatcroft 1975:32–33; Hyndman 1980:54–56). Healey sees the "headwaters of the Sepik River around Telefomin" as the "obvious center of dispersal" for the Mountain Ok subfamily to which the Miyanmin language belongs and believes that the Miyanmin have been in the Fak (Mi:Hak) River area for at least 3000 years.

A century ago the disposition of the Miyanmin, living to the north of the Telefolmin, also was different. Those parishes which I have previously identified as forming the eastern Miyanmin group were compressed into perhaps half the territory they now control, but conceivably their populations were smaller than at present. Occupying the Hak Valley on the northern fall of the Donner range were the ancestors of the present-day Kometen and Temseten, even then closely aligned. Further west, at the end of the low divide between the Hak and Uk rivers, was the parish identified as Usaliten. Wameten was on the southwest side of the Yuwa (May) River, and closely aligned with Sokaten which (further east) straddled the so-called Mianmin Divide, with hamlets on the Uk as well as on the May. The now-extinct Miyanten parish was at the head of the May and Amaloten on the western slopes of Mount Stolle. The Miyanmin insist that there was also a non-Mountain Ok-speaking group (conceivably related to Duranmin of the Om River) called Siasrome living at the head of the Uk. ("Their speech was like the twittering of birds.") There were also apparently non-Miyanmin, possibly Iwam, groups on the eastern and northeastern slopes of Stolle in the Nia (Frieda) River headwaters and the upper Usake. The western Miyanmin groups were in the western Thurnwald Mountains and the headwaters of the August River system. Legend also states that Ivikten, now on the east side of the Sepik River south of the Schultze Anabranch, split from Kometen more than a century ago, moving to its present location via the Fiak-Aki Divide.

Interposed between the Miyanmin and the Ifitaman Telefolmin at this time were the Ilikimin in the Eliptaman. The Ilikimin, a Mountain Ok group, were occasional Miyanmin enemies, although the Miyanmin appear to have intermarried with them as well as with more distant groups such as Sowamin from across the Om Divide in the Fu River area. An elder Miyanmin informant provides an account of a set of reciprocal fights between Kome-Temsak and the Ilikimin while the former were living beneath the Donners on the south side of the Hak:

> The Ilikiten came and raided in the Hak Valley, attacking Yepminimbip. There they killed three brothers, Temiya, Olmitam, and Hapsalam. At that time an Iliki man, Hakdan, was living with Kome-Temsak. Anawesep, a surviving brother of the three killed, went and attacked Hakdan. Hakdan held him off saying, "If you kill me, you will not be able to avenge your brothers." Warily, Anawesep demanded, "Is that the truth or are you trying to trick me?" Hakdan replied, "I'm telling the truth, for I have a plan. I will go and lure the Ilikiten who will listen to me."

Anawesep was willing to discuss the plan and finally agreed to it. Then Hakdan went to the Elip Valley and spoke to the Ilikiten, "Now is the time to come and attack Kome-Temsak. There are nothing but women left in the village. My cock is sore from fucking. You must come and fuck them too!"

Meanwhile, Anawesep sent word to neighboring allies to assemble at Griangriangbip. Women went along the track leading to the village painting tree trunks with red ochre. This was to induce the Iliki to think of women as they approached the village and thus be incautious.

An ambush was established at a point previously agreed upon; Anawesep had told Hakdan that a cut *boliyam* (*Ficus sp.*) tree would mark the site. When the Iliki line reached this point, Hakdan turned and held the man nearest him, immobilizing his weapons. Anawesep stepped from his hiding place and shot the man held by Hakdan. The fight proceeded.

One Iliki man attempted to escape and, crossing the Hak, climbed the ridge to the north. There he was ambushed and killed by a party of Siasrome.

The entire Iliki party was killed and eaten. Anawesep subsequently gave Hakdan one of the brothers' widows and shot a pregnant domestic sow in his honor.

The Ilikimin were dire enemies of the Ifitaman Telefolmin. Ultimately the Telefolmin drove the Ilikimin out of the Elip Valley. According to B. Craig (1969:95) this occurred around 1870. Apparently many Iliki were slaughtered outright while some women and children were absorbed. Remnants of them, according to the Miyanmin, founded the present Telefolmin settlements at the head of the Nia (Frieda) River (Tl:Ninataman; Mi:Niataman). Settlers from Ifitaman established themselves in the Eliptaman and took over the old Iliki ritual centers as well.

A period of relative peace and friendship ensued between the Telefolmin and the Miyanmin. This was expressed in intermarriage, visiting, trade, and Telefol participation in Miyanmin fights in the upper May River area and, perhaps, Miyanmin participation in Eliptaman Telefolmin fights against the Om River tribes to the east. A number of Telefol women married into Kometen at this time through sister exchange. Barry Craig (Personal Communication) reports a Telefolmin trading expedition to Miyanmin which included both Ifitaman and Eliptaman Telefolmin.

This took place about 50 years ago when he [Kongsep, Craig's elderly Kialikmin informant in the 1960s] was a young lad. Many of the Telefolmin parishes were represented and the group was quite large. They went to Temovip (Mi:Kimobip) of Timelmin (Mi:Kometen) parish on the Fak (Mi:Hak) River and stayed for two months. They took mainly tobacco and exchanged it for net bags, *giri-giri*, and bows.

According to the Miyanmin, Telefol allies also assisted them in driving the "original" (because it lent its name to the entire ethnolinguistic group in modern times) Miyanmin parish out of the May Valley; and some Telefols actually settled in the May headwater area vacated by Miyanten. They assisted Sokaten, Wameten, and Amaloten in further attacks on Miyanten in the Nia River area, and also undertook independent attacks against Miyanten, launched from the Elip across the Hak headwater area. Apparently even at that time the Telefolmin could not always count on victory against a Miyanmin enemy due to their lack of caution:

Miyanten was then living in two hamlets on the southern side of the Yuwa River at its head; Kakamitbip to the east, and Wesinonbip to the west. Two brothers, Idambaep and Waeyak, were the leaders of the two hamlets, respectively.

A *kinkan* anticipated the impending raid by the Telefolmin and, to assure a successful defense, instructed the two brothers. Thus Idambaep and Waeyak took their aged mother into the bush and beat her to death with a club (*suldediya*). They then inserted lengths of the magical vine *tek-dafino* (*Lygodium versteggi*) in her nose. The objective was to make the Telefolmin weak and incautious.

"The Kelefoten must not tarry, but come quickly."

The *suldediya* club was carried to Wesinonbip by Waeyak, Idambaep returning separately to his own hamlet. That evening, a very large rain cloud came and hovered over the area, and after dark the people in both hamlets sealed themselves in their houses without hearth fires [a common practice for many rituals involving communication with the ancestral ghosts].

In the early morning, while the people were still sleeping, the old woman who had been sacrificed by her sons rose up and made her way to Kakamitbip. There she killed one of her pigs and tied it to the base of a tree. A bird alighted on the branch of the tree and began to sing. The woman called to her son Idambaep, "Come quickly and kill the bird!"

It was then that the Telefolmin appeared as a line of shield-bearing men on the slope above the hamlet. Advancing, they seized the old woman, and killed her. The residents remained quietly in their houses, undiscovered. Some Telefolmin advanced further into the hamlet, passing the seemingly deserted *timan* and *kwoisam* at the upper end.

The men then fell upon the Telefolmin from their houses, trapping them in the hamlet and killing all. Then they turned and fought those on the slope, killing more, and forcing the rest to flee.

Meanwhile, the people of Wesinonbip heard the clamor of fighting and regretted having missed it. However, the retreating Telefolmin had established a line of battle, setting shields edge to edge, not too distant from the hamlet. This was observed by some boys who ran to Wesinonbip with the report. The men said, "We will go and break the shields!"

They took their *suldediya*, attacked the Telefolmin, and broke their shields. Many of the Telefolmin were beaten and shot before they were dispersed.

Later, Waeyak took his dog and went to hunt giant rat and to gather rattan for a new bow string. He discovered the tracks of some Telefolmin stragglers. He returned quickly to Wesinonbip to get his club and gave chase alone. He finally sighted the men, one of them with a wounded leg. Waeyak pursued them to the head of the Uk and managed to overtake the wounded man and beat him to death with his club, although the other escaped.

Waeyak took flesh from his victim's abdomen and fastened it to his club, leaving the body beside the river. Thus he came back to Wesinonbip and, dancing and singing in triumph, told everyone to go the head of the Uk, "I have killed some bananas and you should go and retrieve them!"

Someone said, "You're tricking us. I saw the meat on your club."

But they went to retrieve the meat anyway and brought it back.

The leader of the Telefolmin settlement on the May was identified by the Miyanmin as Nenesenal, known to Ruth and Barry Craig (Personal Communication) as an Ifitaman leader of the period. Moreover, the Miyanten finally defeated the Telefolmin in the Nia headwater area, killing Nenesenal and leaving the survivors to be lead southward by another identifiable war leader, Brusanening.

Miyanten continued to move along the eastern side of Mount Stolle, and subsequently fought an Iwam group called Seneyaboten. Miyanten was assisted by some Hoten people (at that time the latter was little more than a lineage of hunter-gatherers with sporadic contact with larger groups to the south, a stereotypical *sa-nakai* group). The Seneya River area at the head of the Usake was thus occupied by Miyanmin people, who obtained a fine quarry which was subsequently the only source of stone for the eastern Miyanmin.

Although the Miyanmin situation vis-à-vis the Telefolmin was at this time an open one, with only Miyanten a consistent enemy of Telefolmin, the general outline of the influence of Telefol expansiveness on the movement of Miyanmin groups to the north and west already can be discerned. Accordingly it is appropriate to focus on the Telefolmin, particularly on the Ifitaman Valley, in order to speculate about the causes of this expansiveness.

The Roots of Telefol Expansion

There are at least three possible, but not mutually exclusive, factors underlying the historic expansion of the Telefolmin: (1) differential population growth of the Ifitaman population relative to surrounding populations; (2) limiting factors coming into play; and (3) the implementation by the Telefolmin of solutions to the first and second kinds of problem.

The great highland valleys contain the largest and most densely settled fraction of the population of the New Guinea land mass. Although Ifitaman is populated sparsely in comparison to the population centers of the highlands to the east and west, it does share certain characteristics with them. The most important is altitude in relation to the aboriginal distribution of malaria. The floor of the Ifitaman Valley averages 1660 m (5000 ft). Below this altitude, malaria parasites constitute an extreme limiting factor which increases in effect as an inverse function of altitude. This means that—in the absence of other extreme limiting factors—a highland population such as that of the Ifitaman would be able to expand exponentially whereas lower-altitude areas (because of their lower rate of natural increase) would function as population sinks. A long run of appropriate demographic data to support this statement is not available, but there is other less direct evidence that is suggestive.

According to Barry Craig (1969:92), "For a period of over 120 years, the Kialikmin (which is the core Ifitaman Telefolmin parish) have split into first two, then four, villages, from an original village, and the shifts have occurred at intervals between 15 and 40 years with an average of 25 years spent at each site." Given the fact that the Telefolmin maintain a pattern of permanent centralized villages (rather than the variable hamlets of the Miyanmin), this likely represents real growth. The contemporary (mid-1960s) population structure of Kialikmin also presents a more balanced picture than that of the Miyanmin: with a total population of 312, there are 85 men, 89 women, and 138 children (R. Craig 1969:177). There are a total of 3767 Telefol speakers of whom only 1000 are in the Ifitaman itself. The settlement by conquest of the three additional valleys of Oksimin, Eliptaman, and Ninataman has occurred within the past 300 years.

There is substantial evidence of extensive degradation and disclimax in the Ifitaman Valley. The Telefolmin attribute their longstanding food problem to the coming of whites. It is difficult to sustain this allegation, as the problem appears to be connected with deforestation and dryness, with the grassland ascending the mountains more every year (especially in the south and east). A lot of the valley, including some of the surrounding mountainside, is in grass. Agriculture is carried out largely in deep ravines below the valley floor and in portions of the slopes that remain forested, up to 2330 m (7000 ft). The most extensive forested areas appear to be on the slopes of the Mittag Mountains to the north, but this small range is extremely steep and, except for the western end, agricultural activity is slight.

Destruction of forest at this altitude has led to the loss or destruction of the habitats of forest animals, including wild pigs, in all but fringe areas. Grassland fauna are present but severely reduced. Instead of hunting locally, the Telefolmin practice intensive pig husbandry, intensive even when compared with the practices of more densely populated peoples in other parts of New Guinea. The most distinctive feature is the keeping of boars to impregnate sows. There has not been a wild pig sighting in the central Ifitaman in years. Accordingly, it is impossible to depend on wild boars for impregnation, which is the practice everywhere else in the Mountain Ok region and among other highland fringe groups such as the Maring (Rappaport 1968).

According to Ruth Craig (1969:193n.), domestic pigs among the Kialikmin average three per family, with a range of one to eleven. Although this number is inadequate if pigs serve as virtually the only source of complete protein, it is between four and five times the number of domestic pigs kept by Miyanmin family units in the 1960s. Of course, the ability of the Telefolmin to keep pigs in such numbers is based on their ability to feed them with garden produce. This necessity has magnified their land problem, a concomitant of human population growth, by an exponential factor (see Morren 1977). On the other hand, it may well be the case that the adoption of more intensive pig husbandry in the past solved a problem, leading to the growth of population already described until a new limit was encountered.

The people of Ifitaman have experienced food shortages and famine in the past. An extreme instance occurred between 70 and 100 years ago, before the first white man (Thurnwald) appeared. It was due to a prolonged drought, a hot sun in a cloudless sky baking the earth to a hard crust. Gardens were destroyed; and there was widespread hunger, with people dying of starvation. It was also a time of strife, with food theft and retaliation common. Extraordinary measures were taken. For example, taro was planted in swamps and gardens were guarded. A man fearful of thieves is said to have tied a thin string to all his taros and secured it to his wrist so that he would be alerted if a thief visited his garden as he slept.

Ivan Champion (1966:192), who visited the Ifitaman Valley in 1928, reported, "Always our first cry was for food, and always they promised it to us, but all of their offerings told the same tale, there was famine in the mountains." Of course this experience could have been the result of the stinginess for which the Telefolmin are notorious among their neighbors, but this stinginess could, in turn, be the result of a long experience of food shortages. In either case, the situation is unique in the region.[1] Ruth and Barry Craig confirm the sporadic occurrence of famine in the Ifitaman (Personal Communication).

Since the invasion of the Eliptaman by Ifitaman Telefolmin 100 years ago, the population of that area has risen to exceed that of the Ifitaman itself (by 1700 versus 1000). This total undoubtedly includes the descendants of some Ilikimin survivors, as well as the descendants of Telefolmin settlers and later migrants. However, Telefol expansiveness did not stop at this point. The Ifitaman Telefolmin invaded and occupied the Ninipil area of Feramin territory around 1916. During the same period the Eliptaman Telefols, with Ifitaman help, attempted to invade the Hak Valley territory of the Miyanmin. This resulted in tactical, although not strategic, success—at least according to Miyanmin accounts.

The Telefolmin-Miyanmin Wars

The 30 or 40 years of peace between the Miyanmin and the Telefolmin following the conquest of the Ilikimin ended between 1910 and 1920. As related by the Miyanmin, the proximate cause was an outgrowth of those peaceful relations: a dispute about women ending with a Telefolmin man, their father, being killed by some Usali-Miyanmin! Although there is not universal agreement, the following is a composite account of the events surrounding the breach. One informant summarized the situation as follows: "A long time ago we weren't enemies. My mother came from Kialikmin and married here. Later some Temanmin came from the Eliptaman to get some women [back?]. We were angry and there was a fight." Another informant provided particulars, "An Usaliten man named Keptema eloped with two Misinmin sisters, Watrop and Kokom. Their father, Fasanim, a very tall man, came to retrieve his daughters. He and Keptema fought and Fasanim was held from behind and stabbed with a bamboo knife." The women had apparently been taken from a Misinmin bush hamlet at Wengtaman on the lower Hak River, quite close to the main Usali settlement.

The Telefolmin retaliated with a raid on Usaliten with participants from Temanmin, Misinmin, Yokrimin, Sekrimin, Karikmin, and Ilikimin. The people of the Kome-Temsak settlements further east heard the fighting at Usaliten and, after sending women and children to safety in the Thurnwald range to the north, went to their assistance. One Temse man, Tasim, had just made a new arrow and went and killed a Telefolmin straightaway. Three Usaliten were killed. The initial skirmish stopped when Kome-Temsak killed a pig and gave it to the Telefolmin raiders. They took it to Bamabip, an Usaliten hamlet near the Hak-Uk junction, to cook and eat it. While they were away harvesting taro to cook with it, the Miyanmin ambushed them and killed another Telefolmin. The Miyanmin retreated eastward to Kome territory, but the Telefolmin pursued and fighting continued sporadically for several days as the Miyanmin withdrew northward into the May Valley or westward into the August Valley. In addition to the initial Usali dead, apparently Temseten suffered five killed, Kometen had no losses, with the Telefolmin suffering several more killed.

Initially Kometen took refuge with Ivikten far to the west, Usaliten moved into the San Valley, and Temseten settled on the divide between the Wamu and Fiak Rivers in the May Valley. Kome people were able to return to the Hak to salvage planting material from their gardens, although the Telefolmin had burned their houses and damaged gardens and plantations extensively.

The Telefolmin attempted to settle in the Hak Valley after this, but were only successful at the very head of the Hak where a small settlement of probable Ilikimin survivors was already established. In succeeding years, until a patrol post was established at Telefolmin, the Eliptaman Telefolmin also fought the Om River tribes, such as Sekanmin, Duranmin, Muduanmin, and Sisimin. During this period various Miyanmin parishes received refugees from Telefolmin displacements in the Om area, particularly from the Fu River, where Telefols increasingly hunted and gardened. In one such account, a displaced or extinguished group from the Fu called Daknanukmin is identified as Miyanmin. (It is particularly remembered as the source of a very rare and beautiful arrow foreshaft design, transmitted through the chance meeting of long-range hunting parties a century ago.) The group is said to have been wiped out by the Telefolmin 50 years ago, with a handful of refugees settling with the most southern Miyanmin groups.

The Miyanmin consider the Eliptaman Valley to be a poor, unsuitable, even dangerous place to fight in, let alone to inhabit. Informants attributed the attempts of the Telefolmin to settle in the Haktaman to this situation: "Misinmin is a bad place. The ground broke at Misinmin and the whole place fell into the Elip. This is why the Misinmin left and came over the mountain and made gardens on the Dak. Then we went and killed them." Or: "Because Misinmin ground was bad, we stopped fighting there and went further down the Elip and fought Temanmin. After that we fought at the head of the Hak. When Misinmin came to the Dak we fought there."

As indicated earlier, the geology of the Donner range is unstable. It consists of siltstone, sandstone, and rotten shale that, when exposed by erosion promoted by too much horticultural activity, break under the characteristically heavy rainfall. In many places, the Eliptaman landscape resembles a black desert in which large sections of the valley wall have slipped away. Geologically, the Eliptaman and Haktaman valleys appear to be similar; but until recently, the Haktaman has been subjected to the gardening activity of at most 200 Miyanmin, whereas the Eliptaman has been ravaged by horticultural activity in support of 1700. According to Patrol Officer Booth, who did the second census in the Eliptaman in 1952, only 4 out of the 13 Eliptaman villages depended solely on gardens in that valley, the other 9 gardening also in the Hak, Fu, Kwep, Om, and Mi valleys.

Miyanmin practice in the face of this expansiveness becomes more explicable, if no less remarkable. During the 30 or 40 years following the displacement of the Haktaman Miyanmin groups and until the pacification of the eastern Miyanmin in the late 1950s, there were at least 24 distinct raids against the Telefolmin. The highest frequency was in the 1940s and early 1950s, as Kometen shifted back into the Hak-Uk drainage area from the north. During the same period only five Telefolmin raids on Miyanmin groups can be documented, none of which appears to have been very successful even though the Miyanmin suffered losses. The Miyanmin raids documented are not of uniform scale. Many involved the mere ambushing of a small Telefolmin hunting party on the northern slopes of the Donners, killing or chasing them and stealing their bag. But others involved more than 100 men, as in the case of the raids which were being carried out in the Eliptaman when the administration was attempting to extend its influence in the early 1950s. Miyanmin raiding was reported in the Eliptaman at the same time that a government patrol was in the valley in 1954 (Jones, 1954). Earlier, in 1952, Colin Simpson (1953) had visited the Telefomin Patrol Post. Based on information provided by the Telefolmin, he styled the Miyanmin the "Kukukukus of the West" (1953:216), and cited a patrol officer in describing a recent raid conducted by the Miyanmin:

> In recent months they have killed, in a village of the Aliptamin [*sic*] people, two men, a woman, and three children, cut up the bodies and, leaving the entrails[2] in the center of the village, carried away the rest of the flesh which was roasted [*sic*] and eaten by men, women, and children alike. They had also abducted some women.

Around the same time a patrol officer estimated Miyanmin killing of Eliptaman Telefolmin at 138 for the previous 11-year period (Rogers 1950, cited in Neville 1956).

Although 24 raids may not seem like too many in 30 or 40 years, note that there were some reciprocal raids by the Telefolmin, and that many of the same Miyanmin were participating in raids on Atbalmin groups across the Sepik and on the various May River (Iwam and Arai) groups. This is described below in connection with Miyanmin expansiveness.

The lack of success of the Telefolmin is harder to understand. They could draw on a population base of 1700 in the Eliptaman and 1000 in the Ifitaman, as well as casual allies from other areas. The population of the Miyanmin involved was less than 1000 and was extremely dispersed. Much has been made of the political potential of the Telefolmin ancestral cult for organizing many diverse groups. This possibility was first promoted by Quinlaven (1954) and later by Fredrik Barth (1971:190), who was apparently deceived by the success of government officers, including Quinlaven, in covering up official wrongdoing[3] at Telefomin.

> It is intriguing that a hint of the socio-political potential of this organization should also have had occasion to assert itself before its eclipse of further development. After a brief and unhappy exposure to external contact, the Telefomin people in 1953 made a unique and concerted uprising. If the published account is adequate at this point (Quinlaven, 1954), the coordination and effectuation of this action depended precisely on this one characteristically regional organization in existence: the myth and temple at Telefolip.

Barth's speculation is poorly grounded factually because the example he cited of the simultaneous attack on two administration patrols in the Eliptaman in 1953 is incomplete. Indeed, the case testifies more to the strength of the human spirit in the face of extraordinary oppression than to the potential of Telefol politico-religious institutions. Moreover, the phase of the uprising that was supposed to occur in the Ifitaman, the location of the temple at Telefolip, never took place. But the most telling point is that the Miyanmin, although possessing only a shadow of the institution cited by Barth, could and did organize a dispersed group of allies to attack the Telefolmin at will, virtually without fear of reprisal.

My understanding of the situation is that the Miyanmin got much further than the Telefolmin in terms of political organization with far less "ritual effort." This was a consequence of their spatial adaptation to the diverse ecological situation into which Telefolmin expansiveness had forced them. The phase of Miyanmin adaptation involved is the seasonal long-distance "intergroup visiting" described in the previous chapter and elsewhere (Morren, 1980a). An important element of this involved widespread participation in regional ceremonies, some cult-centered and others not. Dance festivals seem to have attracted the largest numbers of external participants (see chapter 8). The scale of participation is an important attribute because it provides a model for other kinds of pan-regional cooperation, including that required for warfare. This cooperation is mediated by local big men and elders who enjoy high prestige but narrow competence in fields such as curing, the men's cult, hunting, politics, and warfare. Parties of visitors to other groups are centered on such men; and hospitality follows their personal networks of kin and friendship.

In addition, the Miyanmin possessed excellent tactics and the Telefolmin did not. According to the Miyanmin, the Telefolmin were incautious ("made to come quickly"), and the Miyanmin often were forewarned. After their strategic retreat to and resettlement in the May River Valley, the southern groups began to place scouts in the Thurnwald range to watch to the south and detect evidence of enemy movement (such as smoke from campfires). The practice succeeded; and it is reminiscent of the required hunting practice that emphasizes knowing where to look for prey. It also explains the only attack the Miyanmin ever made on whites, that against the famous Taylor-Black or "Hagen-Sepik" Patrol in 1938 (Taylor 1971; Morren 1981a). The patrol came from the south over the Donner range and across the Hak Valley and was dealt with as a typically incautious Telefolmin foray (until the gunfire commenced). By virtue of sighting the campfires of the Taylor-Black Patrol, the Miyanmin gained a day's warning and were able to muster upwards of 200 men for a first light attack on the patrol's camp in the San Valley a day and half later. According to Champion (1966), "one of Taylor's men received an arrow through the chest killing him, and almost killing Taylor, and four others were wounded" (214). According to the Miyanmin, they lost two men in this initial encounter and fourteen more in subsequent clashes with this patrol.

The establishment of these precautionary measures was provoked by a series of Telefolmin raids in the May River Valley in the 1920s. The earliest was against a joint Wameten-Sokaten settlement near the mouth of the Wandagu. The Telefolmin party came from the Ninataman (Frieda River) settlement via the Yuwa River headwaters and the western slope of Mekil (Mount Stolle). Early in the morning they laid an ambush on a track leading from the village of Kasowubip on a spur. Two women left the village to go to their gardens. The Telefolmin shot and captured one of them but the other escaped and warned the village. At dusk two men, Tom and Kekerabe, left the village to track the enemy party. Several miles from the village they discovered them building a bush shelter for the night. Holding their weapons in readiness, the two men waited until dark for the Telefolmin to light a fire. When the time came, they both shot and hit the same man and, amid the pandemonium, withdrew to the village. On their return, torches were lit and messengers sent to other villages in the neighborhood, including the main Sokaten village at Bantanteman and the Kome-Temsak settlements on the Kaemo. Sufficient numbers had assembled by morning for a pursuit, and there was one indecisive skirmish before the Telefolmin escaped to Eliptaman.

Around the same time a Soka hamlet near the Dekewake River was burned by Telefolmin raiders. It was almost deserted at the time, but one man was killed. His wife escaped to give warning and an unsuccessful pursuit was organized.

Around 1930, warning of another Telefolmin raid in the May was provided by two Soka hunters. A large Miyanmin force assembled and the two groups met on the southeast side of Mekil. Tom, one of the leaders, was well in advance of the main body which had moved into a rock shelter to escape a cloudburst. Tom blundered into the Telefolmin force, was attacked, but escaped with the Telefolmin in hot pursuit. The men in the rock shelter heard the tumult and called for Tom to lead his pursuers towards them. Five men, two with shields, barred the track. As the Telefolmin encountered them and stopped to regroup, the main Miyanmin force charged down a slope and attacked, driving them into the river. At least three Telefolmin were killed in close fighting near and in the water. The remaining Telefolmin retreated in disorder to the south with many wounded. Miyanmin casualties included one man shot in the back of the knee and the side, one man shot in the shoulder blade, and one man shot through the anus with the arrow exiting his groin. All but the latter survived.

Later, in the early 1940s, a joint party of perhaps 40 Miyanmin had come from the May River to the Uk. They slept in bush houses at the head of the Kaemo and, moving east the next morning, approached Kara Creek where someone climbed a tree to scout. From his vantage, he saw a small group of Telefolmin come to the water to bathe. The scout passed the word and the Telefolmin were surrounded. One wandered away from his fellows and was shot by Drifuf, a Kome fight leader (who died in 1963). At this the Telefolmin fled with the Miyanmin in pursuit. The Miyanmin were thus led to a larger body of Telefolmin and a confused melee developed at close quarters. Drifuf was shot, the arrow penetrating his nose and palate, but he survived. The Telefolmin party retreated, with a few individuals falling in the pursuit. The Miyanmin collected some of the meat and made a camp at Horonbip on

Mokim Creek where some of it was cooked and eaten. They slept there that night and returned to their various home settlements the next day.

The last known attempt by the Telefolmin to launch an attack into Miyanmin country occurred in the late 1940s, after the Allied Forces glider operation at Telefomin (Elsmore 1945), but before the government station was established there (Champion 1966). (The Miyanmin say that many of the Telefolmin were equipped with steel axes.) Esakiyap, a Kome big man, had made gardens at the head of the Gaga River on the Uk side of the Thurnwalds; and an *itam* had been built to commence the shift out of the May Valley (a clear indication that they viewed the threat of the Telefolmin to be nullified). Esakiyap and a few others were in Karkobip starting the fires to heat cooking stones, while others—including some Temse—were in the gardens harvesting taro for the feast. Esakiyap saw the shields of the Telefolmin party where the track was exposed on a bald spur. There was time to summon those in the gardens and they hurried back to get their weapons. The defenders went up the same track they expected the Telefolmin to take in attacking the village. The force was then divided, one squad taking to the bush to get at the Telefolmin rear. The fight developed as the Telefolmin and Miyanmin main bodies met on the track. Several Miyanmin women accompanying the force collected spent arrows for their men. When the Telefolmin attempted to retreat and regroup, they were struck from the rear by the other Miyanmin formation. In all, three Telefolmin were killed, the others escaping. The men then called back to the village for women to bring poles to carry the bodies of the slain Telefolmin. The fires already were alight.

At this level the possession of tactical superiority is adaptive. The Miyanmin practice appears to possess many of those attributes upon which Turney-High (1971:30) predicates the operational identification of "true war": tactics, command and control, the ability to conduct a campaign, and an adequate supply. Here, as in Turney-High's survey, the problem of ethnographic reporting is critical to such a determination.

An example is the question of whether or not the Miyanmin have "battle plans," this related to command and control. While still in the field I did not believe that the Miyanmin had battle plans, but I now attribute this oversight to my own narrow, ethnocentric view of the meaning of "plan." Earlier, in chapter 8, I described the singular role of the *kinkan* in decision making, including his participation in war. A plausible interpretation of the latter is that he is at least promulgating, if not formulating, a battle plan. According to a number of experienced informants (including the traditional fight leader of Kometen parish), a shaman is never wrong. It seems to me that they cannot be wrong if, in some sense, they shape the conduct of the battle under the guise of prophecy. As is argued earlier, this is so whether they themselves author the plan or merely reflect a consensus. Moreover, their authority will be reinforced by the dependence of those who, forewarned, avoid wounding and death. In this, too, the shaman cannot fail.

Refuging and Resettlement

The large-scale evacuation of an area under emergency conditions is an extremely costly response because, in many instances, it totally disrupts the life-supporting routine of members of a group and it is difficult to reverse. Yet it occurs in situations in which the only alternative, perceived or real, is widespread injury and death.

In an earlier section of this chapter I described the circumstances surrounding the displacement of Usaliten, Temseten, and Kometen from the Hak Valley and their early refuge experience. A singular feature of refuging among the Miyanmin is the convention that permits defeated groups to salvage taro planting stock. Its significance lies in the fact that planting stock is the single factor that cannot be replaced or substituted for in a timely way if people are to restore a semblance of normalcy. In other words, it represents reversibility, a feature of responses I have referred to previously.

Even with this feature, normalcy is a long time coming, as the resettlement process entails increased competition for resources, intra- and intergroup conflict, a ramifying pattern of displacement, and the emergence of a new set of alternative responses. This period of eastern Miyanmin history is worth examining in detail.

In the foregoing section, I described Telefolmin expansion and showed that, despite initial tactical success, they never actually settled Miyanmin territory. Nevertheless, three Miyanmin local groups were displaced from the Haktaman Valley; and, although the valley was being reoccupied by one of these groups at the time of pacification, a wave of displacement and expansion had been triggered within Miyanmin country and on its northern border. This involved numerous attacks on weaker Iwam and Arai peoples of the lower May River and perhaps a higher level of intra-Miyanmin conflict. It is to the latter subject that I wish to turn first.

The initial places of refuge for the Miyanmin groups displaced from the Haktaman have already been noted: Kometen to Ivikten, Usaliten to the San, and Temseten to Usali ground north of the Wamu River. There ensued a series of realignments of groups and reallocations of land, some peaceful and others involving force. The mechanisms involved in this can be described briefly.

Peaceful acquisition of land was accomplished between Kometen and Wameten by a Kome big man named Druban in the 1940s. A contributing element was that Druban had married a Wametan widow, and later married her daughter as well. A Kometen lineage thus gained an area of approximately three square miles on a low divide between the Makare Creek and the Ulame

River with Druban paying compensation of one domestic pig. The area is still occupied part-time by members of the lineage now bearing Druban's name who have also intermarried with Wameten (see table 10-1). In a similar arrangement, Temseten gained a small tract on the Kaemo Creek in the San Valley from Usaliten after pacification in the early 1960s.

In rare instances (in an intra-Miyanmin transaction), land has been taken by the outright annihilation or displacement of a group without subsequent compensation. The remnant of Miyanten parish was so annihilated perhaps forty years ago in the Usake area. Similarly, Mabweten was driven out of the Fiak valley around the same time, with the area being divided among Kome, Temse, and Usali parishes. (Mabweten moved back to the Fiak from the Aki River area only after pacification.) Among normally friendly parishes (i.e., those allied for a long time), when land was taken by force compensation was then paid for lost assets and the displaced group was permitted to retrieve certain capital such as taro stalks. This was the case in the 1920s when, after having been displaced from the Hak Valley by the Telefolmin, Kometen displaced Sokaten and Wameten from the western side of the Yuwa (May) River valley (see below). Grants of land involving compensation but not force are more characteristic of postpacification times, with the Wameten case being atypical for the reason cited. One source of bias in the present account is that much of my information on these affairs was gained from Kome informants, Kometen being one of the largest and possibly the most belligerent and confident of all Miyanmin parishes.

Kometen suffered its stay with Ivikten at the cost of several ancestral relics coveted by them and then, over a period of about five years, moved in with Temseten north of the Wamu. Mabweten was just over the range to the north from this growing settlement. The relations between the two groups were initially peaceful and a number of interparish marriages occurred. To the south was Wameten-Sokaten jointly occupying the Kaemo River area.

A dispute arose between the latter population and Kometen. A Kome named Fiteng was accused of adultery with a Soka matron. Tom, a big man whose earlier exploits I have recounted, shot Fiteng in the leg, a common sanction for this offense and not intentionally lethal. Fiteng died of the wound, however, and Kometen attacked the Wame-Soka settlement, killing one man, routing the inhabitants, and burning their houses. They were allowed to recover their taro and other portable capital and, as previously described, were also compensated for the loss of sago, pandanus and other permanent plantings. Kometen occupied this general area, along with other sites I will describe, until it returned to the Hak-Uk area in the 1940s. The group they displaced subsequently split along parish lines, Wameten settling on the Wandagu River, and Sokaten on the Upper Yuwa in an area previously reserved for hunting called Noiyalbil or "bandicoot ridge."[4]

Subsequently, a dispute arose between Temseten and Mabweten. It was provoked by a homely exchange of insults over a garden barrier between a Temse woman and a Mabwe man, the latter said to be morose over the loss of a favorite hunting dog. The woman upbraided him, casting doubt on the value of the dog and on his masculinity. He shot her. Temseten, supported by Kometen, immediately retaliated and Mabweten suffered very heavy losses—at least 15 dead were named by Mabwe informants—and was driven over the divide at the head of the Fiak River, whence they settled on the Aki (upper August). The Mabwe dead were eaten by the victors. Later still, Usaliten attributed several Temse deaths to Mabweten sorcery and provoked a further attack on Mabweten in the Aki Valley. It was later established that Usaliten sorcery had been responsible for the deaths. The story had been circulated by Usaliten for its own purposes and Usaliten occupied some of the Fiak territory. The latter area later served as the line of departure for the Usali seizure of ground from the non-Miyanmin Soriten on the Abe River (see below).

During this period, more Miyanmin were packed into less territory than had ever previously been the case, with the following consequences: (1) the area in which the settlement cycle could be carried out was reduced, (2) the settlement cycle accelerated, (3) local fauna were rapidly depleted, (4) a higher level of intra-Miyanmin conflict was fostered, (5) Miyanmin northward expansion was fueled, and (6) cannibalism became a significant subsistence activity.

I can describe other disputes in support of point (4), above. In one, the Miyanten (who were jointly occupying the Usake area with Hoten) was eradicated by their erstwhile partners with the support of the other East Mianmin groups. The proximate cause was a sorcery accusation against Miyanten by Hoten. A Kome woman (whose older children are now in their thirties) accompanied the attackers and killed a Miyan woman with an adze. The only known Miyan survivor was in his forties in the late 1960s and living uxorilocally at Sokaten; he had been captured and adopted by a Kome man during the fight. All of the parishes which participated in the event now share territory in the area (which includes a portion of the Frieda mining prospect) in addition to tracts taken from the Iwam Yanfaten. Hoten incorporates migrants from these parishes (see table 10-1) and provides hospitality to others who come to temporarily exercise their territorial rights. Hoten subsequently became a common point of departure for eastern Miyanmin raids on both sides of the lower May.

Another dispute, between the closely aligned Kometen and Temseten, occurred in the 1940s and is often cited as the motivation behind the breakaway Temse segment which has remained settled on the middle May River. The proximate cause was adultery between a Kome man and a Temse woman. The residents of a small Kome hamlet near the Urame (close to the site of the 1960s Amalo hamlet Awabip) were surprised by a shower of arrows as they prepared a leaf oven. A party of angry Temse men had gathered on a small rise near the hamlet and, after the initial volley, exchanged angry rhetoric. A Kome named Wawito became impatient and rushed a Temse orator named Webtidap who was standing on a boulder, shooting him dead.[5] The Temse party fled and, although there was no further violence, the hostility between this Temse segment and the Kome and Temse local population in the Hak Valley persists to the present.

Gardner (1981) has reported a comparably high level of violence among *sa-nakai* Miyanmin of the west. Thus I speculate that those groups consist of many unsettled recent arrivals and refugees fom past disputes and other groups.

My description of the somewhat chaotic resettlement of the Hak river groups on the May is the context for turning to the topic of warfare against various Iwam and Arai tribes on the lower May River and its tributaries. Northern expansion looks like a logical outcome of the set of circumstances I have posited, but for various reasons, it appears not to have been successful in ecological terms. Thus, it will be necessary for this discussion to return to the southern frontier, shared by the Miyanmin with the Telefolmin and Atbalmin, for this is what many of the eastern Miyanmin came to do historically.

The fivefold distinction the Miyanmin make between their non-Miyanmin neighbors in the lower May River area (map 3) corresponds to real tribal (sociopolitical and linguistic) divisions of the Iwam and Arai speakers (Chodkiewicz, Personal Communication; Laycock 1965b; Conrad et al. 1975) in the area. Included are the people of Brumai, called Wanifoten by the Miyanmin, on the west bank of the May below the confluence of the right May. The Wanifo were the only non-Miyanmin neighbor with whom the Miyanmin did not fight, and over the 30 years or so preceeding contact, they were the only trade source for marine shell. In immediate contact with the Miyanmin east of the May some 50 years ago were the hapless Yanfaten, whom they believed (until recently) had been destroyed. They appear to have been the first May River group against which the Miyanmin directed their campaign. They were probably the owners of the quarry on the Seneya River taken by Hoten and Miyanten, which became the only source of stone adzes (Mi:*bankli*) for the Miyanmin after their earlier source of a different and perhaps superior type called *fubi* was cut off by hostilities with the Telefolmin. Apparently, the campaign against the Yanfa was initiated sometime in the 1920s when a party of Soka hunters, operating far outside of the normal range, were attacked by the Yanfa and suffered several casualties. The raids that followed succeeded in clearing far more ground of Yanfa than ever could be occupied, although some of it is still claimed by Hoten and Kometen and used for hunting.

Many informants who participated in raids on the Yanfa told me that their purpose was the acquisition of human flesh. Certainly the participation of men from the most southern Miyanmin groups in this predation resembled the pattern of northern visiting for hunting and other purposes to be observed at the present time. This participation was seasonal, lasted for several months at a time, and resulted in "man-loads" of fresh and smoked meat, including human flesh, along with male and female children and other kinds of booty being brought back to the home communities of the principals. Raids against other May River groups, including Yawaten (also to the east of the May but further north than Yanfa), and such right May River (Arai) groups as Soriten (studied by J. L. Chodkiewicz), and Yasuten, had a similar character.

The frequency of such raids seems to have been on the order of two or three per year, with the highest numbers occurring in the 1930s and 40s. The Usaliten segment living on the Abe River occupies territory taken from Soriten and, according to Chodkiewicz (Personal Communication), the Miyanmin took virtually all of the Sori's women in the 1940s. According to Gardner (1981:14), West Mianmin groups have been moving down the valleys of the Aki and Tabo (headwater tributaries of the August River) for the last three or four generations, probably at the expense of Abau.

During the rainy season the Miyanmin raiding parties built rafts and, steering them with a rough plank held in a forked timber, floated themselves down river to make their attacks. Afterwards, they would walk back in a body southward through the open riverine forest.

In all this history there is no account of the May River peoples aggressively raiding the Miyanmin. Of course, this might be attributable to Miyanmin "rewriting" of history, an activity commonly practiced by the keepers of social charters, but I do not think that this is the case. For one thing, the Miyanmin don't seem to have done this with respect to the Telefolmin. Moreover, accounts of Miyanmin raids on May River groups include references to Miyanmin casualties and successful defenses, as well as stories of extraordinary valor on the part of the enemy. It is related that when Miyanmin raiders surrounded an isolated house and attempted to bring its occupants into the open by setting flame to the roof with fire-arrows, the occupants jettisoned the roof with poles, and thereafter it was impossible to dislodge them. There are several accounts of Yanfa defenders meeting the Miyanmin raiders on a track leading to their settlement and, although causing casualties, still losing. Another story attributes the successful defense of a house in a well-cleared area to the valor of a single man with a seemingly inexhaustible supply of arrows.

Several hundred square kilometers of territory were effectively cleared by these campaigns in the north, but the figure does not have much meaning. This is because little of this land has been occupied and exploited, and because Miyanmin occupying these areas have been only moderately successful in relation to their higher-altitude relatives. Moreover, whatever success they have enjoyed has been to the extent that their resource management strategies have converged with those of their displaced enemies. Perhaps reflecting recalled experience as refugees, the attitude of the majority of members of the higher-altitude Miyanmin groups that have (in the past two generations) provided most of the colonizers of this area is similar to that of visitors to New York City from the Midwest: "It's a nice place to visit, but I wouldn't want to live there." Approximately 60 Kometen moved in with Hoten in the Usake River area in the late 1930s and early 1940s. Some of the participants in this experiment told of their failures. For one thing, they attempted to establish large taro gardens similar to those they make in higher-altitude zones. They were defeated by the successful competition of wild pigs. They fenced their gardens, which is done in the higher-altitude zones only under the unusual circumstances already described (chapter 5). The results were the same. As they said, the only answer was to watch the garden, but if you watch a growing garden you have nothing to eat. The other answer was unacceptable to most: not to worry as much about the taro, eat more sago, and watch the gardens only as a hunting tactic. A different adaptation or approach to resources was involved, and only a small segment of any population has the cognitive orientation to be good colonizers, particularly when they do not have to be. Hoten is the subject of jokes among older Kome men who participated in the abortive resettlement; e.g., Hoten people abandon their houses as fast as they can build them.

Beyond these practical difficulties—not unusual for refugees attempting to adapt to a new environment—is the problem of endemic and epidemic malaria. Mortality, especially of infants, is high, and lowland groups on the fringe of the highlands barely hold their own demographically (cf. Lowman 1980). The alternative to expanding and colonizing the northern frontier is the pattern of seasonal visiting described earlier (and elsewhere, Morren 1980a). This can be seen as a progressive innovation because a large and ecologically diverse area has been integrated in a manner that may be without precedent before the present century of Miyanmin history. Many men exploit part-time the abundant wild pig and other game, the most attractive feature of the low-altitude zone, but a smaller number from various groups continue to settle with Hoten permanently. Moreover, the majority of East Mianmin children are removed from this zone of high risk while still benefitting from it nutritionally. I will return to the subject of migration in the next section.

Around the same time that the Kome colony at Hoten was abandoned, other Kome leaders were taking the first steps upon which a return to the Haktaman Valley depended. Gardens were established, a dance house constructed, a Telefolmin attack repulsed, and a new settlement cycle initiated. As long as the Telefolmin competitive threat was credible, the pressure to shift northward, as expressed in the Hoten colony, was effective. The removal of this pressure was effected by offensive tactics and later confirmed by the coming of the white man to Telefomin. The shift to the south by Kometen, which was followed by a Temseten segment, constituted a return to an approximation of the original conditions for the performance of conservative Miyanmin resource management. In short, normalcy and flexibility were restored after many decades as virtual refugees.

This also shifted the center of Miyanmin population southward and, although raids against the May River peoples continued, the involvement of Kometen, Temseten, and Usaliten in them was reduced. The increased intensity of raids on the Eliptaman Telefolmin during this period has already been described. With this, the involvement of other southern Miyanmin groups grew, particularly Boblikten and its western neighbor Kaliten, a West Mianmin parish of the Thurnwald range between the Sepik and the San rivers. Boblikten had been linked to the rest of the East Mianmin groups through its proximity to Usaliten in the San Valley. There is some evidence of close relations with Kometen in the past, in particular the record of several marriages in each of the past two generations. At the time of the return of Kome to the Hak there was only one Boblik man residing with them uxorilocally, and he did not return to his natal group until he was widowed a year or so before I started by fieldwork with the Miyanmin in 1968.

Despite these connections, Boblikten does not seem to have been involved in any large degree in the affairs of the eastern Miyanmin that have been discussed. Its concern, in alliance with other western Miyanmin groups such as Kaliten, was the Atbalmin (Mi:*Nemayeten*) across the Sepik to the south and southwest, with whom there had been longstanding enmity. The genesis of this is not known to me in any detail. I have no evidence of my own, one way or the other, of attempts by either Miyanmin or Atbalmin to cross the Sepik and displace groups in order to occupy territory. The accessible records regarding this matter begin just before pacification when the picture differs little from that for Miyanmin relations with Telefolmin. According to Gardner (1981:8), however, Atbalmin raiding across the Sepik was aggressive enough to have caused West Mianmin groups to leave the southern slopes of Three Pinnacles Mountain in the Thurnwalds and may account for some of the northerly expansion reported for West Mianmin groups. Yet around the time of pacification, Miyanmin raiding was relentless and there seems to have been no real reciprocity by Altalmin groups in later times. However, an Albalmin group did kill four Miyanmin when, early in the pacification period, two of them attempted to visit their affines in groups from which their wives had been captured.

Expansion and Migration

Expansion following victory in war corresponds to what Hill (1969) calls "range expansion" and "range budding," the latter conforming to our usual notion of migration under population pressure and/or competition. In the short run, or from the standpoint of one or two local populations in a small area, we see a picture of modest local migration activity, with proximate causes of an idiosyncratic nature (internal disputes, postmarital residence options, and the like) which reveal no apparent systematic cause and effect. The population units involved may be individuals, lineages containing 30 to 50 people, or local populations embracing 50 to 200 people. The point is that, as in the preceeding discussion, the problem has to be entered at different levels, viewing the small-scale movements in the context of population growth and expansion over very extensive areas and long runs of time. According to Ackerman and Cavalli-Sforza (1971):

> It has been shown mathematically that if such an increase in population coincides with modest local migration activity, random in direction (comparable to Brownian motion), a wave of population expansion will set in and progress at a constant rate. . . . [T]he model of a population wave of advance would be one of slow continuous expansion, involving the frequent formation of new settlements at short distances in those areas where the advance is taking place. (687)

In the Mountain Ok region, Miyanmin country is one of "those areas." This means that the contribution of local movements to the northerly expansion of the Miyanmin can only be viewed against the general background of warfare, expansion, and migration of the other Mountain Ok peoples. Local movement is the principal vehicle of expansion.

In view of the foregoing it should be apparent that the largest numbers of people have been distributed over the land in groups, a phenomenon better described under the rubric of expansion. Individual migration as a strategy is more progressive because it implies integration of a sort only beginning to be developed among the Miyanmin. In a segmentary system, however, it may betoken local decline.

If a migrant is identified as a person residing permanently away from his or her parish/local population of birth (rather than place of birth), I have recorded 143 migrants in table 10-1 (excluding war captives, for whom my data is incomplete) among the 915 people residing in the East Mianmin area. As noted, the cumulative effect of this migration is less than the effect of group territorial expansion and movement, but the results are consistent with the latter. The bulk of this individual migration, 86.2 percent, has been northward and the difference in direction of migration on a parish-by-parish basis is at the 0.001 level of significance. Moreover, most of the northward migrants are men (58.3 percent), whereas the majority of the southward migrants (81.0 percent) are women. The addition of war captives, most of whom are women and from the north, would only serve to increase this proportion. In addition, the majority of migrants (82.5 percent) have moved to groups at or north of the Fiak/Urame axis, the point at which the lower-altitude biotic associations and human adaptational strategies give way to mid-altitude patterns.

Table 10-1. The Magnitude and Direction of Migration by Sex and Birth Parish of Migrant (Including Postmarital Residence)

Parish of Birth	Host Parish	Males f.	%	Females f.	%	Sub-total f.	%	Direction	Parish Totals f.	%	Distance
Kometen	Hoten	6	75.0	2	25.0	8		North			25
	Wameten	7	63.7	4	36.4	11	82.6	North	19	14.4	8
	Temseten	0	0.0	4	100.0	4	17.4	West	4	19.1	8
	Usaliten	5	62.5	3	37.5	8		North			8
Temseten	Hoten	7	53.9	6	46.2	13	77.7	North	21	16.0	28
	Kometen	1	16.7	5	83.3	6	22.3	East	6	28.6	8
Usaliten	Usaliten II	44	56.5	34	43.6	78	98.7	North	78	59.1	13
	Temseten	0	0.0	1	100.0	1	1.3	South	1	4.8	6
Sokaten	Wameten	1	50.0	1	50.0	2	40.0	North	2	1.6	5

Wameten	Koneten	1	33.3	2	66.6	South	3	60.0	3	14.3	5
	Amaloten	1	50.0	1	50.0	North	2	33.3	2	1.6	6
	Sokaten	1	33.3	2	66.6	South	3				5
Amaloten	Koneten	0	0.0	1	100.0	South	1	66.6	4	19.1	5
	Hoten	6	60.0	4	40.0	North	10	83.3	10	7.6	15
	Waneten	1	50.0	1	50.0	South	2	16.7	2	9.6	6
Hoten	Koneten	0	0.0	1	100.0	South	1	100.0	1	4.8	25
Grand Total	North	77	96.3	55	76.6	North	132			86.2	
	South	4	3.7	17	23.4	South	21			13.8	

Chi-Squared = 41.88   d.f. = 6   p < 0.001
for the direction portion of the table.

NOTE: The migration data in this table are grouped and tabulated by direction for each of the seven parishes of birth (origin) in the sample. The direction frequencies and proportions are in the right-hand columns of the table where the relative distance is also presented for purposes of reference. The male/female proportions in this table are row percentages for each parish of destination. The Grand Totals at the bottom of the table are the summations of the individual parish frequencies and break the total sample down by sex of migrant and cumulative direction of migration.

The most important donor groups to this migration have been Usaliten I (in part through fission) and Temseten, and the effects on population structure are characteristic. Again, most of the migrants are young males, and donor populations to northward migration do not appear to suffer from greatly reduced fertility. There is a tendency for immigrants in a group to cluster in hamlet communities and maintain their old group (parish-lineage) identities in opposition to the identity of the host group.

Where migration has occurred in the context of group fission, there is usually hostility between the migrant group and the main segment of the original parish. As is the case with the Temse migrants on the Fiak in opposition to the main Temse segment residing with Kometen, sorcery accusations are the medium of expression and the level of tension is renewed every time an adult in either group dies. Several instances of this were cited earlier in this chapter and elsewhere in the book. In some cases, sorcery accusations are the initial proximate cause of fission.

Any environmental disturbance which directly or indirectly contributes to an increase in the death rate over an area will increase the likelihood of this kind of response. Such disturbances are diverse, including the exposure of the population to new disease organisms (as with remote contact or certain kinds of range expansion), the results of intergroup competition and displacement on nutritional levels, and the like.

Looking at the migration situation on the ground within the wider context already described, it would appear appropriate to apply an "intervening opportunities" model (Stoufer 1940 and Zelinski 1971 cite more recent literature on this subject) to individual migration among the eastern Miyanmin. In fact, my attempt to do this failed to confirm the model. This is because we are not dealing with an areally integrated, central place situation. The groups from which people migrate are themselves moving and it has been shown that the dynamic of movement is more significant. For example, many of the Kome migrants to Hoten moved at the time Kome was still on the May River. In fact, some remained at Hoten when the experimental colony was abandoned. Moreover, the Druban lineage area near the Ulame was founded before this, and many northward migrants have filtered through it. Now that the main Kome segment has shifted to the south, the intervening points of opportunity have been further obscured. Thus the identification of migrants as northward or southward in table 10-1 is a convention having to do with relative direction and cumulative effect, rather than absolute direction or actual movement. If the bulk of Kome moves south and one member stays put, that person is a northern migrant.

11

History and Modern Times

We were living on the May River when we first encountered white skins. I was perhaps eight years old at the time. We called them *sebrip*, which means "different smell" or "smell of soap" because their skins or clothing had a distinctive odor. You could smell them at great distances so people could run away and hide. We really did not know what this meant. We suspected that the black policemen might be our younger half-brothers born in the afterlife, but we were very frightened.

Later, some Miyanmin went to Atbalmin over there. The little girl who came on the plane with you is from the very village. The Miyanmin went and killed them. I too went to the fight. The *kiap* came and caught us and took us by force to Wewak. We were there for about six months. Then the present aid post orderly, another young man who died a long time ago who also became an APO [aid post orderly], and two more who have since died, both carpenters, and I myself—five together—we all went to Madang. The older men stayed [in jail] in Wewak and the government sent the five of us to the Lutheran Mission in Madang... 1957... the 17th of September.

I was around 20 years of age after three years at Madang—so I was 17 when this all happened. And after three years we came back to Telefomin [in 1961]. We went to the Baptist Mission to work, attend bible school, and I was in charge of the store at the same time. You know the PASUWE store there now; I worked at the old one and then it got very large.

Before we went to Wewak I underwent initiation in the spirit house... I'm not sure when it was. There were five distinct times [rituals], but I did not do the sixth and last. We were taken into the spirit house and told the lore of adult men—women couldn't hear these things. The reason for [initiation] is like this: if the adults don't take us into the spirit house then we could never grow up to be true adults ourselves—we would be of no account—that is what we thought.

One reason for this—there are some game animals—they aren't sacred now—we can eat them freely. But formerly some game was taboo, like the possum *kwiyam*, certain snakes, other animals we couldn't eat; one kind of wild fowel with red legs *sena*, the fish with whiskers *fini*, these things were for adult men. If you hadn't been initiated you couldn't eat these things. So you had to be initiated.

But my son won't be initiated because we have heard of the new ways. School is somewhat a substitute. Although there are many customs we will keep, we will loose that one [of initiation].

I started to think about things in Madang. I thought about bringing the word of God to everyone, about peace, about not being afraid of the white man, and about the good ways of the white skins, about schools and what I had been taught. We couldn't fight anymore and we didn't have good things of our own. So we had to go and build an airstrip because we did not have good roads for cars—so the airstrip was the most important thing.

In Madang we saw everything of the white man—ships and cars and all the activities there were. The mission took us to see everything in the town and all the livestock the *didiman* were raising. And we saw the hospital and its work. And we traveled by ship to the Rae Coast, Lae, the Markham River and we came back. And this started me to thinking.

Nothing happened quickly, all has come slowly. The first thing was the big speech [announcement] and teaching some of the young men *tokpisin*—teaching about God and *tokpisin* were the first steps. Second was teaching young men to write. Then I thought about building the airstrip—around 1965. Then we thought about persuading authorities to start a primary school. Everything very slowly.

We would wait until the *kiap* came to conduct the census and we would talk about it and it took us something like four years to do it. The school started in 1974—before independence.

Since then we have been thinking about ways of supporting kids in school. That's next and we are "out of breath" . . . some kind of business in the village or some other way of getting the money. It won't come quickly, it's hard—six months, a year, two years. If it doesn't come quickly we'll wait years.

For my own kids, I want them to go to school to gain knowledge. We'll see what happens after that. You have to take things one step at a time. I admire a lot of things in the white man's way and I like a lot of our own good ways too, but some white skin ways and some of our ways are not good.

Some of the people working for the government have done good things for us; they too believe that the community should be improved. I've seen business people, people from different government departments—*didiman*—and if they try to help us I admire them. There are good people and bad people with us too. (Amusep, April, 1981)

This is a capsule history of the Hak River Miyanmin in modern times and of one man's role, in his own words. Amusep is the man who, in the absence of success, would be a mere cargo prophet. By dint of an authentic vision, indeed one that might do credit to a development specialist, the Miyanmin have enjoyed a degree of success in joining the modern world both in their own terms and in the eyes of their neighbors. Particularly intriguing is that national independence, which occurred in 1974, had real meaning for this most remote Papua New Guinea village.

In our science, every ethnographer must grapple with both the ethnographic present and present reality. Morgan and Lowie alike believed that their subjects stood for something enduring, ancient or primitive; and I, too, wonder about the essentials of Miyanmin-ness signalled by the use of such words as "traditional" and "precontact." With only a synchronic data base at our disposal, this has been a convenient axiom because we will only see what we will see within a narrow slice of time. The reality is that all of our research has been carried out in a maelstrom of change, change so rapid that it reinforced our illusions of primordial stability. Ultimately our confusion is reflected in attitudes toward modernization, which are conflicting at best and tempered both by romanticism and by the historic sensitivity that, although inevitable, little good can come of it.

I have been fortunate in pursuing a research problem that is fluid, dynamic, and inherently diachronic: patterns of movement that I believe have been characteristic of Miyanmin groups for a long time and that, although influenced by altered circumstances, will persist in the future. I also had the favorable subjective experience of identifying with my Miyanmin friends and neighbors, understanding their aspirations, and giving in to their pressure to be involved. It was always difficult to sustain a "cultural preservationist" stance in the face of their drive and optimism and my growing realization that they were critical and selective in their approach to the ways of the "white skins." Perhaps it is easier for an ecological anthropologist than for a student of ritual to be a pragmatist in the face of the kinds of changes that have occurred. I know that Gardner and I have different views on personalities (such as Amusep), institutions, and Miyanmin history.

Contact and Conquest

While I am unwilling to attribute long-term stability to the Miyanmin, there is no doubt that in the past they were relatively isolated even within their region, at least by Melanesian standards. I particularly have in mind the sporadic nature of their trading contacts. This isolation changed only slowly with the gradual onset of contact with whites. Richard Thurnwald reached the Ifitaman Valley and the Telefolmin people in 1914 (Craig 1969) but no whites appeared in Miyanmin country until 1927. Even then, I have no evidence that Karius and Champion made direct contact with Miyanmin people during their epic exploration of the Fly and Sepik drainages (Champion 1966). Champion was the first to record the name of the Miyanmin, elicited from a Telefolmin informant along with names of other neighboring groups (Champion 1966:140,172). When Karius and Champion left the grassy floor of the Ifitaman, they followed the narrow course of the upper Sepik, crossing its junction with the Elip and Hak rivers. From there they laboriously journeyed along the southern fall of the Thurnwalds, clearly Miyanmin country. They do not report contacts with the people but crossed the Sepik opposite Three Pinnacles Mountain using a suspension bridge built either by the Miyanmin or the Atbalmin (see chapter 10).

Direct contact was made with the Miyanmin in 1936. Then, a group of prospectors led by the American Ward Williams built a crude airstrip in the Ifitaman and set about collecting geological samples in every direction (PIM 1943, 1954). Helpful Telefolmin deterred the prospectors from going north. As the pilot Campbell put it, "our friends of the upper Sepik told us that in this direction, at the head of the May, we would encounter the savage and hostile Mianmin. Our way must lie down the Sepik..." (Campbell 1938:242). Campbell flew the group in his amphibian to a landing site down the Sepik past the Hoffungs River junction. But their caution was for nought, as the party—consisting of three whites and fourteen carriers—set out on foot to the northeast, reaching the May Valley in February 1937. They seem to have encountered initially hostile Miyanmin in the vicinity of the Aki (August)-Fiak Divide but there was no conflict and some trading was actually conducted. There was further contact with Miyanmin at the head of the right May River according to informants who described to me the tracks made by the undercarriage of the aircraft on the river bank and the variety of discarded material they salvaged.

The Williams party may have been lucky to have entered Miyanmin country from the west, since the next group of aliens came from the south and was mistaken for an incautious Telefolmin raiding party (Morren 1981a). This was the legendary Hagen-Sepik patrol of 1938-39. Led by J.L. Taylor and John Black, it was attacked by a large body of Miyanmin in the San Valley (Taylor 1971), suffering one dead and four wounded while also killing as many as sixteen Miyanmin in the course of the encounter.

The next meeting with whites occurred in May, 1942 when a group of refugees, fleeing the Japanese invasion of the north coast of New Guinea, journeyed up the May Valley en route to Daru on the south coast via Telefomin (PIM 1944; Champion 1966; Allied Geographical Section 1943). Led by the prospector Jack Thurston, it consisted of eight whites and 80 police and carriers. On chronological grounds, this is probably the encounter Amusep recalled from his childhood in the statement opening this chapter. This party came from the north and contact seems also to have been peaceful.

An indirect encounter with whites occurred when the Miyanmin were "bombed." In the 1940s people discovered two large iron objects near the right May River, one of which had broken into shards. Likening them to the structure of a *kundu* type drum, my informants corroborated the story by their possession of two crude iron adze blades they had fashioned by pounding

Plate 14. A Participant in the 1938 Attack on the Hagen-Sepik Patrol
Tells the Tale

and grinding. The bombs had probably been jettisoned unarmed by an American war plane returning from an aborted bombing run against the Japanese on the north coast. In any event, the war made significant quantities of steel tools available in the region for the first time. The Telefolmin had a few manufactured tools as a result of Thurnwald's visit in 1914 (R. and B. Craig, Personal Communication) and these were revered as sacred objects. They gained a few more from later visitors such as Karius and Champion. In 1944 the Allies carried out a glider landing in the Ifitaman in order to construct an emergency landing strip. Local Telefolmin people were employed as laborers and were paid in trade goods including steel tools. Miyanmin gained access to these as a by-product of their increasing aggressiveness (chapter 10). Informants said that initially they saw strange-looking axe cuts in the vicinity of Telefolmin hunting camps on the north fall of the Donners in the Hak Valley. Later they were able to capture modest numbers of axes in the course of raids on such camps. They did not gain consistent access to these valuable tools (chapter 5) until the onset of adminstration patrols in the 1950s.

The most important impacts of the events of this protracted early contact period can be briefly summarized. The most traumatic effects were the result of introduced contagious diseases, especially respiratory ones (chapter 7). Disease killed many people and probably fueled elevated levels of intergroup violence (Morren 1984; see also chapter 8). Others, of course, had been killed in the clash with the Hagen-Sepik patrol. It is too easy for an outsider such as myself to view these events as unmitigated tragedies, resulting in some cases from official behavior that was evil, unlawful, and immoral . . . and leave it at that. Only partly reflected in Amusep's statement, the Miyanmin view in retrospect is quite different, reflecting their characteristic pragmatism, optimism, and opportunism.

When I first lived with the Miyanmin in the late 1960s and discussed these events and subsequent developments with them, most people were neither rancorous nor frustrated in their vision of the new life opening up to them. They recognized the clash with Taylor's patrol as of a piece with their own practices. They also quickly recognized the superiority of white weapons, medicine, and other utilities and were better prepared when whites penetrated their sovereignty permanently in later years: much of the novelty had been removed. These early events were revelations, provoking intense curiosity, hope, fear, caution, enthusiasm, even boldness, rather than aloofness and bitterness at whites. The Telefolmin people did not fare nearly as well.

Administration patrols from the new station at Telefomin visited the Miyanmin in 1950 and 1953, but regular patrols with the explicit mission of pacification did not really start until 1955. The necessary resources were only made available to this remote area because of the 1953 Telefolmin rebellion in which two patrol officers and two constables were assassinated.

The journalist Colin Simpson visited Telefomin on the eve of that rebellion and was put up by the man most responsible for provoking it. Simpson's function in this era seems to have been to popularize a kind of malignant "Alice in Wonderland" image of New Guinea peoples which nevertheless reflected official thought well into the 1970s. He did not invent it but rather credulously recorded the views of local whites.

Simpson (1953:215) used the phrase "Murderous Miyanmins" in a chapter heading and thus continued the "bad press" the Miyanmin had suffered almost from the beginning of contact. He then went on to describe their regional reputation, undoubtedly filtered through the impressions of the Telefolmin and the incumbent patrol officer.

> The Miyanmin are by way of being the Kukukukus of the west. In fact, though they are a much smaller group than the Kukukuku, their pacification may well prove a proportionately tougher proposition. They are a small group who, many years ago, were driven off the plateau [*sic*] and into the rugged mountains. Fiercely resenting that they have to live there, they war incessantly with their neighbors with the idea that if they can kill of enough of the other tribesmen they can move back to the better land.
>
> The present difficulties of peaceful penetration of the Miyanmin Mountains are (i) the inaccessibility of the country itself, (ii) the difficulty of recruiting carriers to go into the region of a people of whom they stand in dread, (iii) only maximum strength patrols can go in (216).

Reading this characterization after a year or so of residence in Miyanmin country, I might have laughed if only it had not remained the prevalent view of high administration officials. While I was in the field in 1969 the West Sepik district commissioner ordered his assistant at Telefomin to make an emergency patrol into East Mianmin to "prevent another [*sic*] Mianmin uprising." This had been provoked when some river people discovered the body of a Miyanmin woman floating in the May River. East Sepik district officials conducted a preliminary investigation of the matter which determined that the woman had been killed by her husband who, returning from plantation labor, found her living with another man. These results were conveyed to West Sepik authorities who duly issued the order quoted above. Certainly by the late 1960s mission and administration personnel at Telefomin had a more favorable and accurate view of the Miyanmin. Hence, the patrol officer made a quick visit to the most southern Miyanmin group to request that the message be passed on for the suspect to come into the station. He did.

After the Telefolmin rebellion the administration intensified its pacification efforts in the subdistrict. During one patrol aimed at restoring administration influence in the Eliptaman where the assassinations had actually occurred, the Miyanmin actually carried out raids in the same valley. It was undoubtedly a coincidence but was taken by authorities as a deliberate affront.

Patrols to Miyanmin in the early 1950s were effective in spreading the administration's message. As each new community was reached in its turn, the patrol officer gave away trade goods, purchased and executed by firing squad a local pig and disseminated the details of the *Pax Australiana*. The message was heard and believed so faithfully that a series of tragic events ensued. Two men from Boblikten whose wives had previously been captured from the Atbalmin decided to give peace a chance. Accompanied by two friends they set out to visit their Atbalmin affines according to the routine pattern described in chapter 7. They were massacred. Subsequently, a joint East Mianmin force retaliated and killed four Atbalmin.

Reports of this exchange reached Telefomin and simultaneous patrols were dispatched to persuade each side that a balance had been struck and that hostilities should cease. Within days of the return of these patrols to the station the Miyanmin mounted yet another raid. This is the one Amusep speaks of in his statement. Although he was but a teenager he had a key role in the action which ensued. As the force approached an enemy village, Amusep paused along the track to urinate. He heard voices. Peering through the thick vegetation he detected a group of Atbalmin working in a garden. The force quickly surrounded them, killing 16 men, women, and children.

The administration responded promptly and forcefully. Two patrols lead by Assistant District Officer Ron Neville combed the area, and after several skirmishes in which some Miyanmin were shot, detained 40 men for questioning. Later, 25 were tried before a bewigged Australian judge (Gore 1965:179–82); 24 were convicted and sentenced to death, a sentence later commuted to four years of imprisonment to be served at Wewak on the north coast. Of that group, the five youngest were taken in hand by Neville himself and sent to the Lutheran Mission vocational school in Madang. Amusep was among this group and he described the experiences they shared in the account at the beginning of this chapter. In addition, I knew and interviewed three others of this group of whom only Amusep and Yatamanap, an aid post orderly, survive today.

By their own account, the experience was exciting and favorable for these youths as well as for the younger men in jail. They witnessed the everyday rhythms of alien life made up of events prosaic to us but extremely exotic to them. These are some of the things they cited to me. The first happening was, of course, the long march back to the station at Telefomin, the homeland of their longstanding enemies, where the pretrial investigation was conducted. Then there was the flight to Wewak in a DC 3 aircraft and the view of the wide ocean and the immense village itself. During their stay in Wewak they saw a ship burning in the harbor with white people killed and injured and a child struck and killed by a truck on the Wewak-Boram Road. Undoubtedly they were occupied in the common chore of the *kalabus*, cutting grass along roadsides and around other public facilities such as airstrips, excellent points of observation. They ate exotic foods, rice and canned meat and fish, wore clothing, received medical treatment, and learned *tokpisin*. The boys at Madang acquired literacy, saw strange domestic animals such as cows, sheep, and horses, received vocational training in either carpentry or elementary medicine and arithmetic, and were converted to Christianity.

Peace and Optimism

All of the foregoing formed an overwhelming impression and belief that their people would receive a package consisting of all these new things: the goods, the institutions, peace, medicine, education, air travel, and the Christian faith, which they see as forming an integrated whole. Upon their repatriation in 1961 they expected their homeland to already have been transformed. Of course, it was not and many of them found instead wives, parents, siblings and friends dead, pitifully few children born, and the rest of life unchanged.

Amusep quickly emerged as the leader, planner, and visionary in the quest for the new life. As the prophet of the new times, however, he is constrained by Miyanmin egalitarianism, deals in consensus, and remains one of several men in his community who possess exceptional influence but narrow competence. In short, he is a rising *kamok* (or big man) in a traditional mold, although pursuing modern goals. The new dimension he brings to the role is an attempt to extend authority beyond his own locality. This has been successful only to the extent that almost from the beginning he attracted and trained young men from other communities who have since risen to prominence at home. Several years ago he stood for a seat in the Sandaun (West Sepik) Provincial Parliament in competition with a West Mianmin man and a Tifalmin. The latter won, perhaps because the Miyanmin vote was split.

The first thing Amusep did after his "big speech" was to organize a school. In many respects it resembled a traditional *yominam* and it was built with the assistance of the same cohort of youths who might otherwise be facing the rituals of the second initiation grade. They would also constitute the student body. The curriculum was devoted to bible study, reading and writing *tokpisin*, and arithmetic, and quickly began to attract boys from other East Mianmin parishes.

Focusing on this cohort was important for structural reasons as well as situational ones. The elder of those jailed were not so committed to the "package." Some were shocked by their experience, rancorous, or literally bereft. The last official *kwoisam* was built at Kometen (Amusep's and my home parish) under the direction of some of these elders with many of the same youths participating who were involved in the school. The ability to mobilize this group of young men is a matter of authority, but widely diffused, shifting and ad hoc. So Amusep was only one participant in an established structure as he directed some of this labor to innovative projects or added new wrinkles to the established flow.

The next major step was the construction of an airstrip, which commenced in 1965. Amusep selected the site and directed the project to its completion, which was accomplished with no outside support or even consultation until after it was in use. Imagine finding a large tract of flat land in such rugged terrain at the foot of the Donner Mountains and then clearing it of primary forest and grading it with hand labor. It was a political-economic as well as a technical feat, notwithstanding its resemblance to "cargo cult." Almost from the beginning, what prevented outsiders from so classifying these activities was that they have been effective.

A routine administration patrol stumbled over the airstrip. The patrol officer assumed that it was an authorized mission undertaking and reported to the mission that it was nearing completion. After evincing surprise, the missionary arranged to inspect it from the air with members of the Missionary Aviation Fellowship. They were impressed enough to attempt a landing and have been returning regularly ever since 1966, bringing good-quality medical service, stock for a store, a modest payroll, occasional trips to Telefomin and beyond, as well as mission doctrine.

This airstrip has become the centerpiece and model for local development in the region. Even in the late 1960s, other Miyanmin groups coveted it and one local population, Mabweten and a Temseten segment, started their own near the junction of the Fiak with the May River. While in the area in 1968, I was pressed to inspect the site and, after some hesitation, did so. I feared that if I so much as blinked approvingly the forest would ring with the concussion of axe blows. Subsequently, the mission surveyed the area from the air and decided that since a sufficiently large population was accessible they should directly aid the project. Later, a missionary, who happened to be a former pilot, visited the area with a chain saw and considerable progress was made before a low ridge was discovered which would make using the prospective airstrip hazardous. Later still, the project was shifted further down the May and was almost finished in 1981.

In the meantime, several other airstrips had been built in Miyanmin country. Yapsiei in West Mianmin was built by the government between 1972 and 1973. Located in the August River headwaters, it is part of the border security system and therefore quickly achieved the status of district office with a permanent staff of police, a clerk and an A.P.O. According to Gardner (1981:32–35), this facility was a mixed blessing, fueling people's optimism about participating in the modern world but also contributing to serious health problems and a population crash of around 11 percent between 1973 and 1976 (see also Morren 1981). Yet another airstrip, Hotmin at the right May-May junction, was built by local people with mission support in the late 1970s.

People view these airstrips, Miyanmin, Yapsiei, Hotmin and the prospective one named Fiak, as extremely important to their present and future well-being—an attitude established by Amusep when he led the first such project. This outlook has been reinforced by success, the Miyanmin airstrip on the Hak River leading the way. When I left in 1969 it only possessed a small timber shed serving as a mission clinic and store. In subsequent years it gained an aid post (the one Yatamanap founded in the San Valley upon his return from detention in 1961 was shifted to the Hak when *his* Temseten segment shifted there), a community school staffed by four teachers, a metal-sheathed child and maternal welfare clinic building, a cooperative store and water tank, a steel cable suspension bridge, and a gasoline lawn mower!

Groups in the area have responded to these attractions by building what is by Miyanmin standards an immense village around the airstrip, with houses for a majority of the members of Kome and Temse parishes, as well as for smaller numbers of Soka, Usali, Kali, and some Telefolmin. Beginning in 1980, a modest fruit and vegetable business was slowly gaining a market based on the two mining projects in the region, Ok Tedi and Frieda. Moreover, labor mobility, which had begun in the 1960s, was firmly established, with several Kome men even achieving supervisory positions with enterprises in the highlands.

Yapsiei has also built up with an aid post, a community school, a bible school, a store and, in 1977, a billet for a patrol officer (Gardner 1981:29–32). There, as of the late seventies, opportunities to earn cash remained very slim. This was graphically illustrated by the amount of Australian currency that was turned in for conversion to the new national tender of Papua New Guinea. "The entire cash holding of the West Mianmin, a sizable portion of the Atbalmin population, and a few Abaus amounted to just over eight hundred dollars" (Gardner 1981:32). I take this to represent something like 50 cents per capita!

The situation of Hotmin on the middle May River is also mixed. With the disappearance of white traders on the Sepik and its tributaries certain local opportunities such as crocodile hunting and access to imported commodities have declined. Crocodile skins must actually be marketed through Department of Primary Industry representatives at Telefomin. Labor mobility has been significant in this area since the 1960s and is probably the principal, virtually the sole source of cash. Aside from an aid post and a mission clinic staffed part-time from Telefomin, the Hotmin strip has not yet done much to validate local optimism.

In 1981 I found people at Hotmin exploring their own alternatives. Several men had pooled their earnings from contract labor and purchased an outboard motor with which, it was hoped, communications could be established with Ambunti. The Hoi had already become "canoe people," although continuing also to use traditional rafts (Morren 1982). There was also talk of rebuilding the airstrip at a new location east of the May which would be more convenient to currently exploited resource areas. Certainly from the standpoint of highly mobile Miyanmin groups this looks like a realistic approach to the problem, but undoubtedly the Department of Civil Aviation would resist. The Hoi population finds itself politically isolated in any event, possibly the only Mountain Ok community in East Sepik Province. I understand that there has been some consideration given to adjusting the border between East and West Sepik.

Regional employment opportunities are in prospect only, represented by the development of the mines at Ok Tedi and Frieda. The latter, which is partly in Miyanmin territory, has already employed small numbers of local people, paid occupation fees to one group erroneously assumed to own the land, begun local purchases of food supplies, and helped to finance education in the area. The latter has included assistance to families of prospective high-school students who face expenses approaching U.S. $200 per annum and support for the new high school at Telefomin. Many questions regarding the impacts of these big projects and the quality of local participation remain to be answered (Jackson 1982; Morren 1982b). And as of 1985 both projects are in serious jeopardy, Ok Tedi due to a series of environmental and political disasters, and both due to low gold and copper prices.

Rabaibal and Regional Integration

The prospect of the mining projects has stimulated intense interest and change among local people and there has emerged a pan-Min movement which seriously advocates the creation of a Min Province out of northern Western Province (including Ok Tedi) and southern Sandaun (West Sepik) Province (including the Frieda site). Although the Miyanmin are not caught up in the movement *per se*, they are involved in more localized political development which is, at this late date, a realization of the *Pax Australiana*. Returning to the Miyanmin in 1981, I was certainly astonished by my first sight from the air of the village around the Mianmin Airstrip. But I was bewildered by my discovery that there were Telefolmin living in it. I was suffering a 1960s mentality: the pervasive fear of sorcery and incipient violence against the Telefolmin in the 1960s (chapter 8) has vanished. How this has occurred is a long story which I will condense here.

Sometime in the mid- to late 1970s a religious movement, now referred to as the Baptist Revival or *Rabaibal*, surfaced in the Telefomin area.[1] Initially, the wives of some local pastors experienced shaking fits and seizures. These were attributed to possession by the Holy Spirit who, in this way, revealed plans for the Telefolmin people and ultimately for all the peoples of the region. The plans include mass conversion to Christianity, abandonment of traditional beliefs and practices including the male cult and initiation cycle, confession of sins, equality of the sexes, the priority of the nuclear family over wider obligations of kin and community, and integration of the larger regional population.

Although the movement may have been triggered by the experiences of women, leadership has been in the hands of an established male pastor named, appropriately, Dios. As a youngster, Dios had served as houseboy to the wife of an early Baptist missionary and was particularly well-versed in the basics of white domesticity. Dios is a native of Eliptaman to the north of the home Telefolmin valley of Ifitaman and has maternal ties to Duranmin in the Om Valley to the south which was partially conquered by the Telefolmin earlier in this century (chapter 10). He does not appear to possess unusual charisma but is nevertheless a successful leader and executive.

Rabaibal spread quickly among the Telefolmin people of several valleys and resulted in the destruction or conversion to church use of traditional temples in a dozen villages. It also provided justification for shifting to a cash economy, involving not just market-oriented cash crops and goods but also the privatization of basic subsistence items of vegetables and pork within communities.

Initially Dios and *Rabaibal* were accorded only grudging recognition by the mission, but ultimately they jumped on the bandwagon. An early accommodation was to accept Dios's decision to establish a bible college at Duranmin. The new airstrip associated with it has been a liability ever since due to its tendency to slip into the Om River. *Rabaibal* also energized intensive evangelism by Telefol pastors in remote parts of the district such as Atbalmin, where it has a definite coercive character in isolated communities whose members are able to offer little resistance. Moreover, at a mass meeting at Telefomin in 1978 it was decided that the great temple of Telefolip, the traditional ritual center for many Mountain Ok or Min groups over thousands of square miles, would have to be discarded. This, however, has been resisted successfully by the traditionalist custodians of the temple and the government has extended protection to the center.

In my view, *Rabaibal* among the Telefolmin is an attempt to respond to the opportunities perceived in mine development, deal with other longstanding problems such as resource scarcity (chapter 10), and resolve some of the consequences of the failed rebellion of 1953. The latter were still visible when I first visited Telefomin in 1968, 15 years after the event that resulted in the assassination of two white patrol officers and two police, and the subsequent trial and imprisonment for 10 years of a large number of Telefolmin. Many people I met in Ifitaman and Eliptaman still seemed to be overwhelmed by their powerlessness: demoralized, unfriendly, withdrawn in demeanor, distrustful, inhospitable, or overtly hostile.

Though opportunities for cash employment were sparse, Telefomin station had some amenities to offer local people in the late 1960s. A primary school had been in operation since the early 1960s and some Telefol children (and one Miyanmin, Amusep's youngest brother) were already in high school on the coast. There was a medical facility, and the mission's child and maternal welfare clinic and nursing school, operated by the redoubtable Sister Betty Crouch of Baiyer River fame, already had had a profound effect on infant and maternal mortality. On the negative side, as it had since before the rebellion, Telefomin served as a "punishment post" for marginal or unstable patrol officers. There was also a very large contingent of police and warders for the local jail and young *kiaps* took up their posts with a certain stereotype of the Telefolmin and the Miyanmin. When I first approached the authorities at district headquarters in Vanimo in 1967 about the possibility of doing field research with the Miyanmin, the police there urged me to take a gun.

I found significant changes at Telefomin when I returned in 1980. Most important were the people themselves, who were marked by optimism, friendliness, and aggressive pursuit of opportunities. An excellent example is the Telefomin High School now (as of this writing in 1985) entering its fifth year though, according to correspondents, still controversial. When I passed through Port Moresby (the national capital) in 1980, officials of the department responsible for mining development were bemoaning the decision of provincial authorities to locate their only new high school in Vanimo, the provincial capital, rather than at Telefomin. When I arrived in Telefomin the then–district commissioner skeptically described how the local member of the national parliament was poking around the station looking at condemned buildings and unused land to site the new Telefomin High School. When I got out to Miyanmin country, people were gearing up to send their second high-school class out to Aitape on the coast. Word soon came that the children should wait because the Telefomin High School would shortly open to receive them for that year. And indeed it did open, although several months behind other high schools in the country. It took a while for people living in the vicinity of the station to throw together the buildings out of local materials and for a staff to be assembled. It has remained the subject of conflict between the national and provincial governments: the latter consider the school to be the creature of the former and refuse to support it. Yet I agree with national officials that it is an essential component of any plan to foster local participation in mining development and associated enterprises.

Thus *Rabaibal* is more than "indigenization of Christianity" (Jorgensen 1982). More significantly, it is an assertion of local power over institutions dominated by outsiders. The prophet of *Rabaibal* stole the show from the

Baptists, sited the new bible college against their better judgment, and was successful in the very area where the mission had failed among the Telefolmin people, gaining converts. *Rabaibal* is also a force for integration in the Mountain Ok area, although this is expressed in a variety of ways in different places. It is involved in the pan-Min movement (referred to earlier) which is attempting to promote the identity and common interests of all the Mountain Ok peoples in such matters as the development of mineral resources. It is a vehicle for Telefolmin expansiveness (see below). Finally, it is related to the changed atmosphere at Telefomin described above, involving both self-image and the perception of outsiders. An index of this change is the remarkable fact that in 1981 there were periods when Telefomin station had only *one* policeman assigned.

The Miyanmin present another variation. In the 1960s, when I found the Telefolmin demoralized, hostile, and resisting conversion to Christianity, the Miyanmin were optimistic and ambitious (though hostile to the Telefolmin) and already beginning to realize some of the fruits of their pursuit of modernization. It will be recalled that this also had been stimulated by a mass trial and imprisonment. By the time *Rabaibal* spread to the Miyanmin, the men's cult and initiation cycle had been defunct for up to 10 years in some communities. It had been displaced by the locally developed modernization package which, like *Rabaibal,* included Christianity but had as its principal feature the airstrip as the center of local civic and material advancement— health, education, and enterprise. Although parts of this were in operation in the late 1960s, it only really occurred to me in the course of my 1980–81 field work why it was particularly appropriate to the Miyanmin and possibly other groups in the region with similar life-support systems requiring dispersed settlement and mobility for hunting and extensive shifting cultivation. People can maintain their dispersion and mobility while exploiting the resources of the airstrip only intermittently, just as they exploit other resources.

The elements *Rabaibal* added to this already established complex among the Miyanmin were security, regional integration, and the spread of the modernization package itself to other Miyanmin and non-Miyanmin groups. As indicated in earlier chapters, in the 1960s and early 70s the Miyanmin were still living in fear of Telefolmin sorcery and the threat of violence seemed very near the surface. Jorgensen (1982:62) notes that this perception was reciprocated by the Telefolmin. And between communities of the two groups there also lay a dispute over the boundaries of lands in the Donner range. As a mater of fact, while I was in the field in 1968 the adminstration initiated a land investigation, completed the field phase (I was informally advised that the Miyanmin had "won"), and then failed to conclude the process due to the fact that the investigating patrol officer was drafted for service with Australian forces in Viet Nam.

Thus, the background to my wonder at finding Telefolmin people in residence at the Mianmin Airstrip. Local people had designated land for a *quartier étranger* to facilitate access to the community school, aid post, and air strip. "Strangers" were allowed land for gardening and the larger boundary question had been settled as well. In addition, kin ties based on marriages between Miyanmin and Telefolmin going back more than five generations have been revived and the groups have been exchanging sing-sing invitations for several years now. The ideology of *Rabaibal* is cited as the root of all of this.

Prospects

I am not predicting entirely happy consequences for the Miyanmin from these arrangements. In the short run, there have been accusations against Telefolmin neighbors of theft of produce and planting stock, and other frictions are likely to emerge. In 1981 the climate on both sides remained very positive. The expanding Telefol community on their own land in the upper Hak River, about three hours away (by foot) from the airstrip, withdrew from the Telefomin Local Government Council and nominated a *tultul* who would be subordinate to the longstanding Miyanmin *luluai* in the valley. In the long run, however, I see this as a "Trojan horse" comparable to *Rabaibal*'s invasion of Duranmin, with the Telefolmin expanding in peace as they never could in war.

For me the test of adaptation in some of these changes is reversibility, whereas others themselves represent reversal. The latter refers particularly to the innovations that have fostered peace and security. The development of a cash-oriented agricultural sector, an original part of their modernization package, has proceeded very slowly with many false starts (such as pineapple in the 1960s and coffee and chiles in the 1970s). While pineapple plantings were fairly extensive, none of these trials were ever large enough to significantly deflect subsistence production and by 1981 all were overgrown or uprooted. The market-oriented fruit and vegetable business referred to earlier in this chapter constitutes a mixed blessing since it does involve selling part of one's subsistence. Yet the staple taro is not in demand (a drug on the market throughout the Mountain Ok region), sweet potato and cassava are easy to expand or contract and, at the very worst, if the market for a commodity dries up one can always eat the crop. The same cannot be said of other commercial crops that have caught on elsewhere in Papua New Guinea.

Big projects within the region or elsewhere in the country remain a major threat. The state of planning is such that local people are likely to be swamped by outsiders in their own territories who will tend to fill the quality jobs and gobble up the ancillary enterprises. Many Miyanmin view education as a possible remedy to this and disdain World Bank-sponsored vocational programs aimed at supposed village needs (Morren 1982b). Labor mobility, stimulated by development in other parts of the country, poses the ultimate threat of depopulation. So far, this has assumed a "boom and bust" pattern with groups of men going out and returning together followed by a "quiet" period. This is not a credible threat in Miyanmin eyes and therein lies an important aspect of their self-image and perhaps their future.

When I returned to the Miyanmin in 1981 I expected some kind of reaction from people and from myself. I remember my first night in the bush after friends had left my house, leaning back and feeling as if I had never left in the first place. I also felt mildly disappointed that there had been no hubbub surrounding my return, just matter of fact greetings from friends of the 1960s. I finally realized that they took my return for granted just as they expect any other member of the community to return. And this is because they believe that their society offers such immense satisfaction and comfort that it could not be otherwise.

Maps

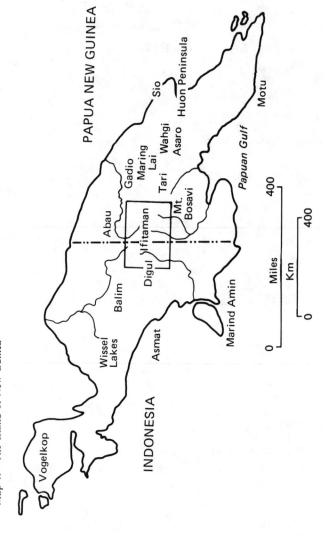

Map I. The Island of New Guinea

Map 2. The Mountain Ok Region

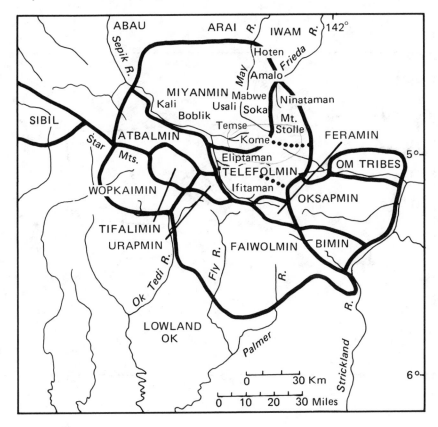

Map 3.   East Miyanmin: Territorial and Ethnic Groups

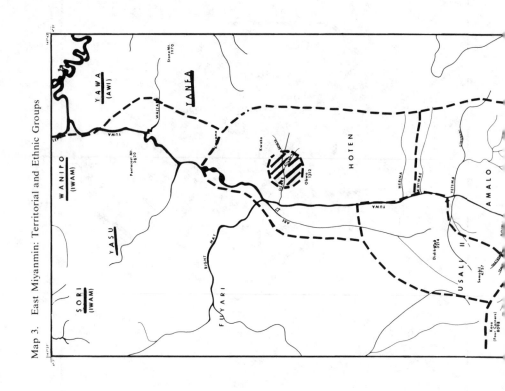

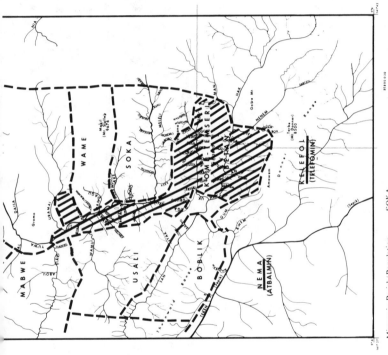

Miyanmin Parish/ Population .....SOKA

Ethnic Group: Mi. Name.........SORI

Official Name ....(IWAM)

Boundary ....

River ....YUWA

Creek ....Klemklut

Mission Airstrip .... ◇

Mountain: Elevation in Feet ....Kasa 8098

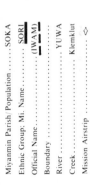

NOTES: 1. Ground claimed by the
          Kometen–Temseten local
          population.

        2. Mabweten, a non-East
          Mianmin parish.

        3. Fuyariten, a non-East
          Mianmin parish.

Map 4.   Hak River Settlement, 1957–58

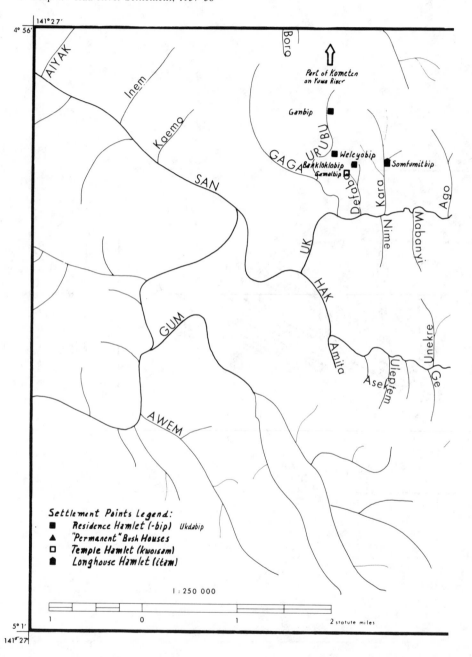

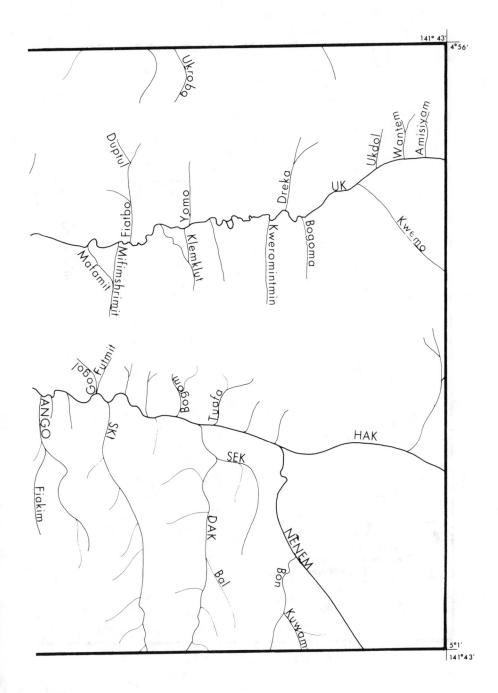

141° 43'

4° 56'

Ukrobo

Duptul

Wantem

Amisiyam

Ukdol

UK

Dreka

Yomo

Klemklut

Kweromintmin

Bogoma

Kwemo

Fiatbo

Mifimshrimit

Matamit

Futmit

Gogol

Bogoma

Twafa

HAK

ANGO

SKI

SEK

Fiakim

DAK

Bal

NENEM

Bon

Kuwam

5° 1'

141° 43'

Map 5.   Hak River Settlement, 1959–60

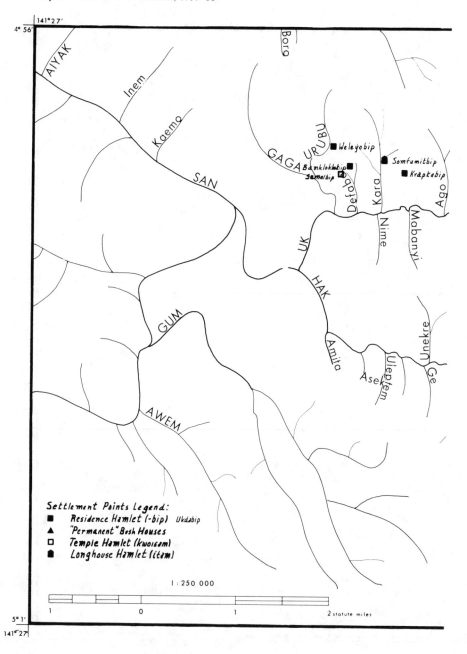

141°27'
4° 56'

AIYAK

Inem

Kaemo

SAN

Boro

URUBU
GAGA

■ Weleyabip
Banklokbabip■
Samalbip□
Defabu
Kara
Nime
Mabanyi
Ago

■ Somfumitbip
■ Krapkabip

UK

HAK

Amila

Aselem

Uleptem

Unekre

Ge

GUM

AWEM

Settlement Points Legend:
■   Residence Hamlet (-bip)   Ukdabip
▲   "Permanent" Bush Houses
□   Temple Hamlet (kwoisam)
⬟   Longhouse Hamlet (itam)

1 : 250 000

1   0   1   2 statute miles

5° 1'
141°27'

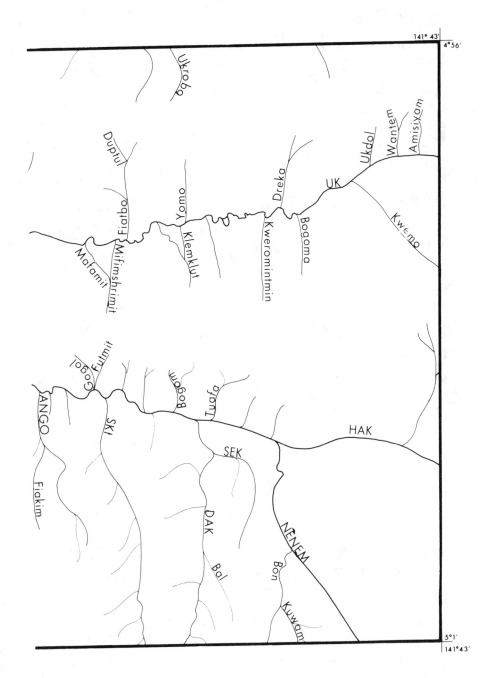

Map 6.   Hak River Settlement, 1961–62

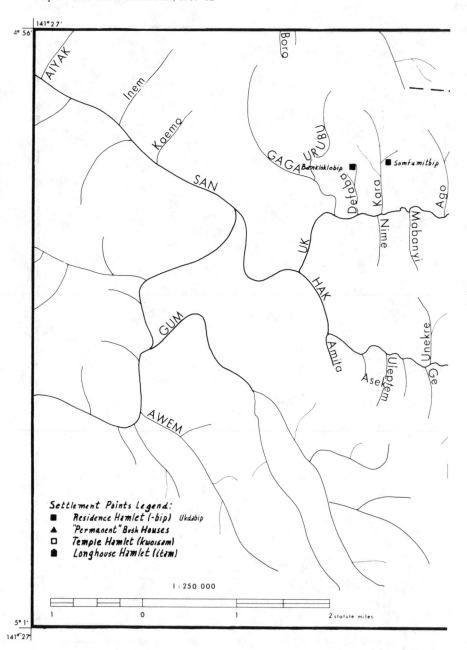

141°27'
4° 56'

AIYAK

Inem

Boro

Kaemo

URUBU

GAGA   Bamkloklobip ■   ■ Somfumitbip

SAN

Defabaa

Kara

Nime

Mabanyi

Ago

UK

HAK

GUM

Amita

Aselem

Ulepfem

Unekre

Ge

AWEM

Settlement Points Legend:
■   Residence Hamlet (-bip)   Ukdabip
▲   "Permanent" Bush Houses
□   Temple Hamlet (kwoisam)
⬠   Longhouse Hamlet (itam)

1 : 250 000

1   0   1   2 statute miles

5° 1'
141° 27'

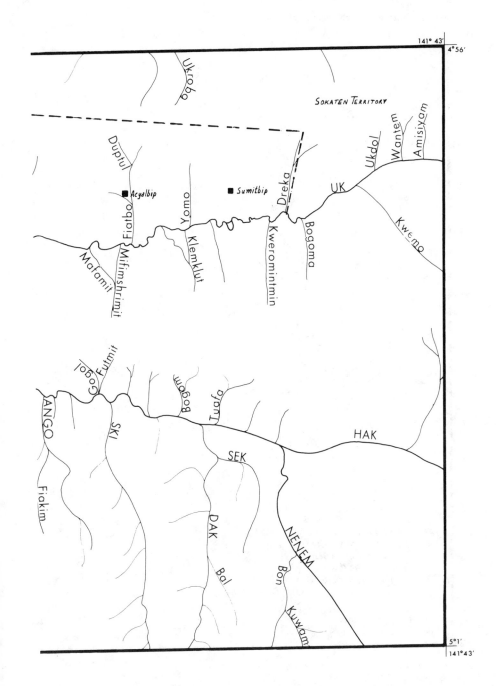

Map 7.   Hak River Settlement, 1963-64

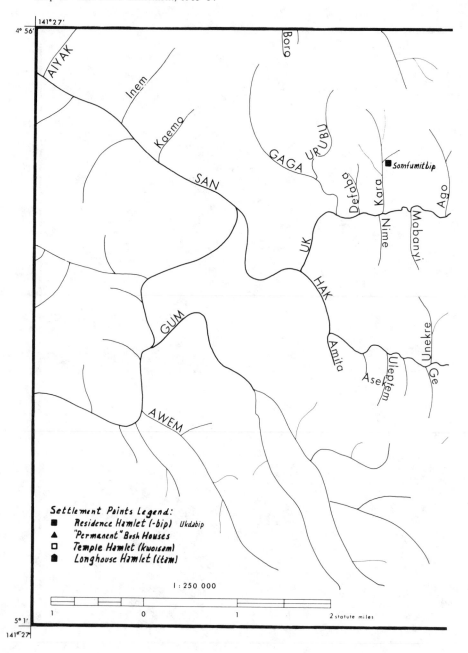

141°27'
4° 56'

AIYAK

Inem

Boro

Kaemo

SAN

GAGA

URUBU

Defata

Kara

■ Somfumitbip

Nime

Ago

Mabanyi

UK

HAK

GUM

Amia

Asekm

Uleplem

Unekre

Ge

AWEM

Settlement Points Legend:

■   *Residence Hamlet (-bip)* Ukdabip
▲   *"Permanent" Bush Houses*
□   *Temple Hamlet (kwoisam)*
⬟   *Longhouse Hamlet (itam)*

1 : 250 000

1   0   1   2 statute miles

5° 1'
141°27'

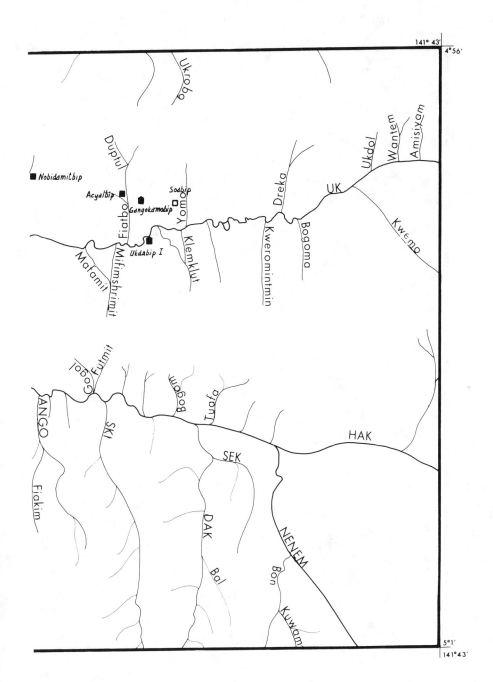

141° 43'

4°56'

Ukrobo

Duptul

Nobidamitbip

Acyalbip

Soabip

Yomo

Fiatbo

Gangokamobip

Ukdabip I

Klemklut

Mafamit

Mifimshrimit

Dreka

Kweromintmin

Bogoma

UK

Ukdol

Wantem

Amisiyam

Kwemo

Gogo

Futmit

Bogom

Tjafa

ANGO

SKI

Fiakim

HAK

SEK

DAK

Bal

NENEM

Bon

Kuwam

5°1'

141° 43'

Map 8. Hak River Settlement, 1965-66

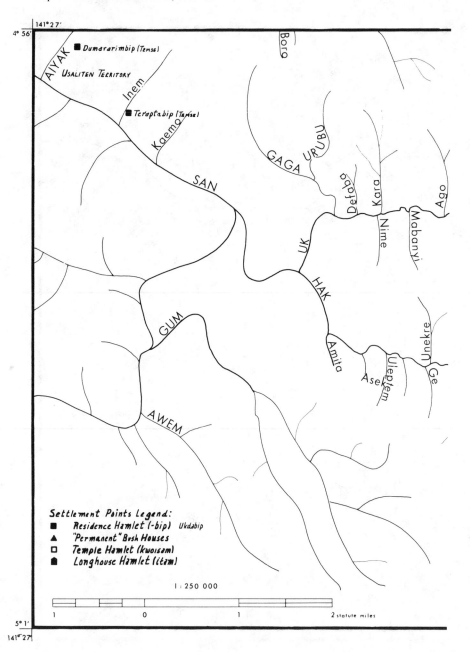

Settlement Points Legend:
■ Residence Hamlet (-bip) Ukdabip
▲ "Permanent" Bush Houses
□ Temple Hamlet (kwoisam)
⬟ Longhouse Hamlet (itam)

1 : 250 000

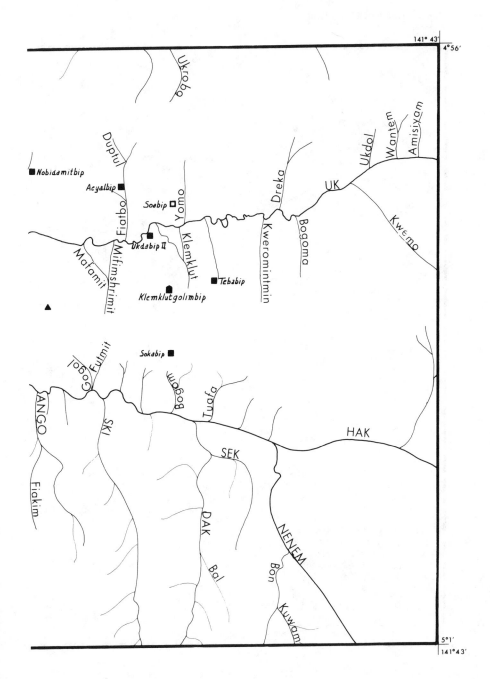

141° 43'

4°56'

Ukrobo

Wantem
Amisiyam

Duptul

Ukdol

Dreka

UK

■Nobidamitbip

Acyalbip ■

Soabip □

Yomo

Kwema

Fialobu

Kwer;mintmin

Bogoma

Ukdabip Ⅱ ■

Klemklut

Mifimshrimit

Mafamit

▲

Tebabip ■

Klemklutgolimbip ⬟

Sokabip ■

Futmit

Gogol

Bogom

Tuafa

HAK

ANGO

SKI

SEK

Fiakim

DAK

NENEM

Bal

Bon

Kuwam

5°1'

141°43'

Map 9.   Hak River Settlement, 1967–68

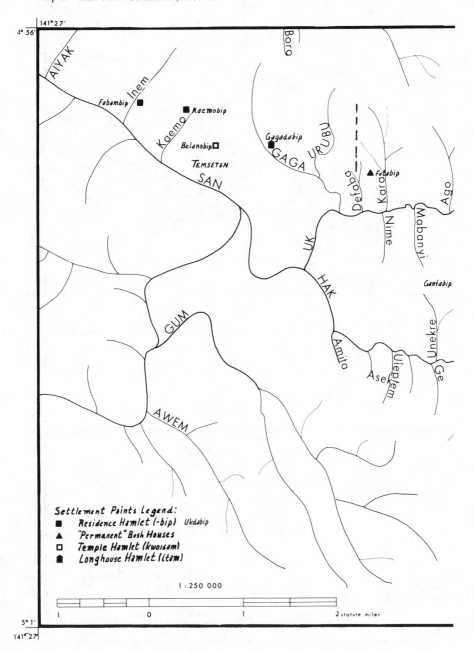

Settlement Points Legend:
■   Residence Hamlet (-bip)   Ukdabip
▲   "Permanent" Bush Houses
□   Temple Hamlet (kwoisam)
⬟   Longhouse Hamlet (itam)

1 : 250 000

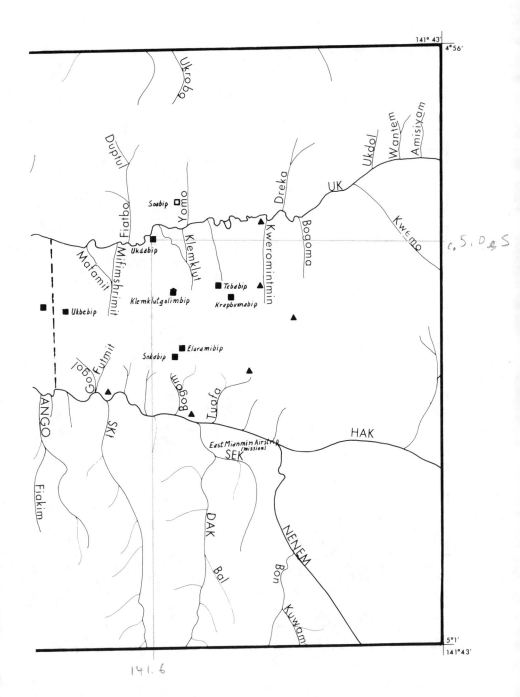

141° 43'
4°56'

Ukrobo

Duptul

Ukdol
Wantem
Amisiyam

Fiatal
Mifimshrimit
Mafamit

Soabip

Yomo
Klemklut

Dreka
Bogoma

UK

Kwemo

c. 5. 0 ₅ S

Ukdabip

Kweromintmin

Klemklutgolimbip

Tebabip

Krapbumabip

Ukbebip

Eluramibip

Gogol
Futmit

Sokabip

Bogoma
Tuafa

ANGO

SKI

East Mianmin Airstrip
(mission)

SEK

HAK

Fiakim

DAK

Bal

NENEM

Bon

Kuwam

5°1'
141° 43'

141. 6

Map 10.   Hak River Settlement, 1969–70

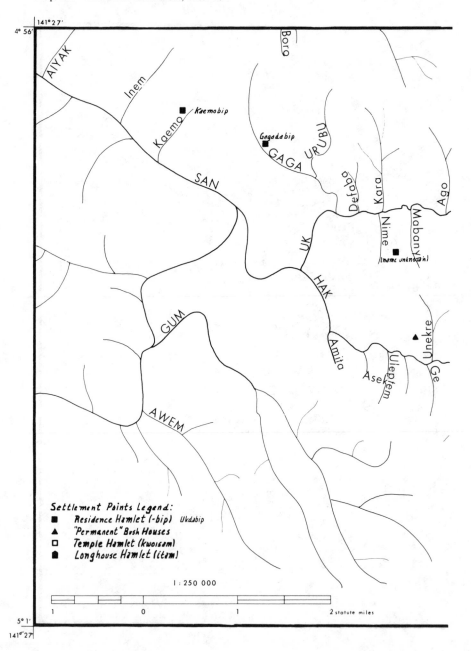

141°27'
4° 56'

AIYAK

Inem

Kaemo

■ *Kaemobip*

SAN

GAGA URUBU

Gegadabip ■

Boro

Defaba

Kara

Nime

Mobanyi

Ago

■
(name unknown)

UK

HAK

GUM

Amita

Asekem

Ulepem

▲
Unekre

Ge

AWEM

Settlement Points Legend:
■   *Residence Hamlet (-bip)*   *Ukdabip*
▲   *"Permanent" Bush Houses*
□   *Temple Hamlet (kwoisam)*
⬟   *Longhouse Hamlet (itam)*

1 : 250 000

1   0   1   2 statute miles

5° 1'
141°27'

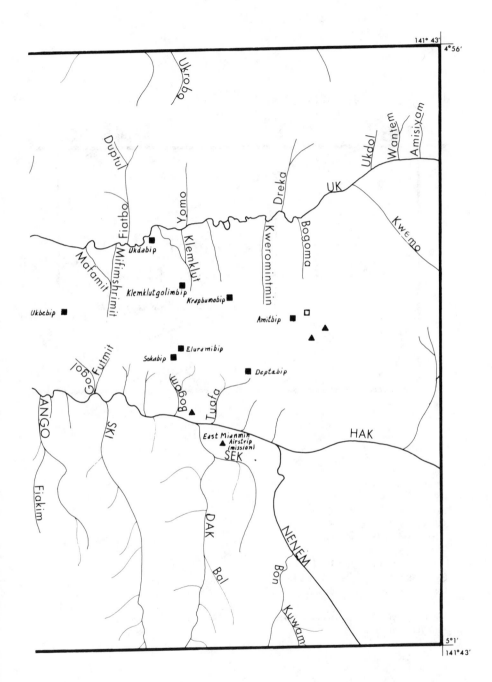

Location Map (maps 4-10)

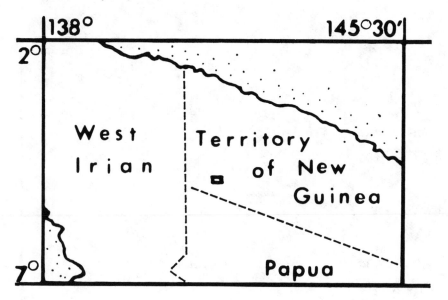

SOURCE (maps 3-10):

Royal Australian Survey Corp.
Edition 1-AAS Series T 504
AHQ/B1-4/2648, 2649; 1966.

Air survey by Kennecott Explorations
(Australia) Pty. Ltd. Pa's 85 and 102
Geology and Sample Results; 1969.

Field Data compiled by George Morren;
1967 through 1969.

Construction and design of maps
by Susan Naughton, 1972.

Notes

Chapter 1

1. For a review of the dimensions of problems and hazards see Barton (1969) and Burton and Hewitt (1974), and chapter 2.

2. Excluded are classes of responses that have indirect effects such as demographic responses. Put another way, people can respond to problems by changing the way they interact with the environment or by changing themselves (for example, population control, physiological acclimation, etc.).

3. I have borrowed the phrase from Schwartz (1962).

Chapter 2

1. Scientists and scholars employing one or another systems approach include mathematicians such as Weiner (1948) and Ashby (1952, 1956); economists such as Murphy (1965), Dunn (1971), and the Meadowses (D. Meadows et al. 1972); Jay Forrester (1968, 1971) an engineer-planner; sociologists and anthropologists such as Merton (1957), Frank Cancian (1960), Marris (1975), Marwick (1984), and Bateson (1958, 1963, 1972 1980); and biologists such as Quastler (1952), Margalief (1968), Watt (1968), and Slobodkin (1961, 1968).

Chapter 4

1. "Min" derives from the common, though not universal, suffix meaning "group" or (more narrowly) "children."

2. By one count these 11 valley systems are Airona-Aiyura, Goroka, Wahgi, Lai, Ialibu-Pangia, Mendi-Nipa-Lai, Lagaip, and Tari-Koroba, all in the east, Sibil-Ifitaman-Teken in the center of New Guinea, and Baliem and Paniai Lakes in the west. These valley systems are of particular importance because they are centers of population in the highlands (see Hyndman and Morren n.d.).

3. Although Oksapmin is not a member of the Ok Family of languages (or the Mountain Ok Subfamily) it has been included in the Mountain Ok culture area by Craig (1969) on cultural grounds and the Central (Mountain Ok) sphere by Hyndman and Morren (n.d.) on an ecological basis.

4. For aid in identifying plants I collected in Miyanmin country I am grateful to the staff of the Lae Herbarium of the Division of Botany, Office of Forests, Department of Primary Industry of Papua New Guinea and the former Territory of Papua and New Guinea. The late J.S. Womersley and E. E. Henty were particularly helpful in lending equipment and advice and responding to queries. The collections consist of 75 items gathered in 1968–69 and 200 items in 1981.

Chapter 6

1. For aid in identifying various animal collections I am grateful to James Menzies and Gerry Maynes, mammals; Fred Parker, lizards and frogs; and Michael Tylor, frogs. Other identifications I offer should not be confused with those provided by zoologists. In addition, Menzes and the late Hobart Van Deusen commented extensively and critically on earlier attempts (Morren 1974) to describe the fauna of the Miyanmin area. I have also benefitted immeasurably from discussions with Ralph Bulmer, David Hyndman, and Peter Dwyer. Maynes and Dwyer also loaned collecting equipment and technical advice. Since my departure from the field, the genus *Rattus* has been extensively revised and doubt has been cast on the status of the creature I (and others) refer to as *Rattus ruber* (Taylor, Callaby and VanDeusen 1982). Rats previously attributed to that species are now dispersed to five or so other species. Given this perhaps temporary confusion, I continue to use the traditional nomenclature until my own specimens can be reworked. I am, of course, responsible for this and any other errors that remain.

2. J. Menzies (Personal Communication) estimates that in the wider Miyanmin area referred to there would be some 30 species of marsupials and 25 to 30 rodents, a total of 50 to 60 species of mammals My collecting activity was largely confined to the Hak Valley where I was based rather than covering the wider Miyanmin area, although some lowland and mid- to upper-montane specimens were acquired by hunters I employed or by purchase.

3. We can also relish the argument that biological taxonomy, at least at the species level, is folk taxonomy to the extent that it is based on anatomical and behavioral characteristics. One need ponder (only for a moment) the outrageous, sometimes inaccurate, occasionally self-aggrandizing names that have, from time to time, been assigned to the creatures of nature. Until recently, the evolutionary relationships of genera and species could not be rigorously tested.

4. Obvious examples are the Bohr model of the atom and Mendel's discovery of genetics without chromosomes or statistics.

5. Excellent comparative material for another Mountain Ok society now exists in Hyndman's work among the Wopkaimin (1979, 1982).

6. Tertiary taxa exist in both the plant and animal domains, a fact I did not discover until 1981.

7. There are a number of interesting parallels between Miyanmin and the Karam ethnozoological taxonomy reported by Bulmer (1967). These include the assignment of cassowaries to a seperate taxon, the lumping together of birds and bats, and the assignment of dogs to a separate taxon.

8. According to my preliminary analysis of data gathered in 1981, in some instances terminal tertiary taxa refer to use, in others to morphological or ascribed habitat differences. It may therefore be related semantically if not syntactically to the consumption taxonomy presented here.

9. I am thinking of such cases as Indian sacred cattle (Harris 1966), New Guinea pig herding and feasts (Rappaport 1968; Vayda, Leeds and Smith 1960), West African cattle (Schneider 1957), Northwest Coast potlatching (Suttles 1960; Vayda 1961; Piddocke 1965), and New Guinea cannibalism (Dornstreich and Morren 1974).

10. I justify the low ranking of the quest category *kuruan*, involving relations with various edible insects, on the basis of the almost infinite number of related or similar creatures which are inedible or *misiyam*.

11. According to Hobart Van Deusen (Personal Communication, 1973), migration is not a characteristic of rain forest mammals. Reports on closely related Australian mammals are particularly misleading because they are fauna of semiarid lands.

12. I agree with Ian Hughes (1970) that there is little point in persisting in the use of the word "feral" to refer to an animal that has always run wild. I will use the term "wild" to refer to "nonvillage" Miyanmin pigs henceforth, but do not mean to imply any genetic differentation between "wild" and "village" pigs in New Guinea, at least not until the introduction of European stock.

13. Coon (1971), following Osgood's account (1936), describes a very similar tracking tactic for the Kitchin of North America. Coon states that it also is used by certain Australian Bushmen, and lower California Indian hunters (1971:85f.).

Chapter 7

1. One of the reasons for undertaking this exercise is to resolve or reduce discrepancies of choice and interpretation between Gardner's (1981) work among the Miyanmin and my own. Some of these differences are, however, based on real differences between the *sa-nakai*, Gardner's predominant subjects, and the *am-nakai* groups who were mine. Our disagreement extends to the spelling of the group name. He has adopted the "official" spelling, and I opt for a more phonetically accurate rendition in conformity with the Telefolmin (ethnographic)–Telefomin (official) difference.

2. Aspects of parish fission, fusion, and other ways of looking at groups are discussed below and in chapter 9.

3. As of 1969.

4. These are estimates based on relatively poor maps and inferred parish boundaries.

5. Due to their distinctive physical attractiveness, there was a stated preference for Nema (Atbalmin) women over women of other enemy groups. Kome men turn their noses up at May River women (they say because of endemin *tinea* [ringworm]). Women captured from these groups are more common in northern Miyanmin populations.

6. In the textbook *Anthropology Today* (Anon. 1971:446), there is a picture and caption, apparently provided by Theodore Schwartz, who briefly visited the most northerly Miyanmin on the May river in the early 1960s. The picture shows a family in front of a house. They are undoubtedly Miyanmin. The caption reads, "This family belongs to a newly contacted group in the hills of the May river area of New Guinea. This area, remote and sparsely populated, is characterized by small patrilineal descent groups. Marriage is frequently by sister-exchange."

Chapter 8

1. This is a composite account recorded from several informants. Fitipkanip is a secret name of the Telefolmin afek. The Miyanmin cognate of afek is *afok,* the kin term for "old woman" or "ancestress." Fitipkanip is widely accepted as the name of the elder of the two women, although Gardner (1981:206) reports alternatives Yabyobim and Wogwogim. Many alternate names for Dimoson turn up in renditions of the myth or portions of it, varying especially from place to place (cf. Gardner 1981; Morren 1981c; Jorgensen 1984:7–8). Alternate names include Abaninyap, Blangim, Aniyok, Kwison, Sel, and Fiyo. These names, along with those of several men who are identified from time to time (Amfiyap, Monitap), probably refer to the children and grandchildren of Dimoson who are sometimes cited as the progenitors of particular Miyanmin parishes. There is universal agreement among Miyanmin that "Fitipkanip is the mother of the Telefolmin (and peoples to the south)," and that "Dimoson is our mother." As such, Dimoson is the progenitrix of all Miyanmin, the disseminator of resources, and the savior of the people through her creation of the spirit world and the path to it. Compared to her elder sister she is a quiet culture heroine, a proponent of the family, and nonviolent. She admires lofty men and is sexually conservative, in short, an ideal woman and mother. For her part, Fitipkanip is the antithesis of her little sister: bossy, passionate, violent, blood-thirsty, and incautious in may of her endeavors, an entirely appropriate progenitrix for the Telefolmin.

2. Misawe is the site of the stone footpint and cave I have reported on elsewhere (Morren 1981c).

3. Versions of the myth collected in the Hak Valley and upper May say that Dimoson died at Kikibip on the Fu River (a tributary of the Om). Northern versions identify the place of her death as the Abe (Right May) River.

4. The purpose of the hearth is for conducting fight and hunting magic.

5. Gardner (1981:144) offers an alternate translation: "eye open."

6. Ruth and Barry Craig (Personal Communication) have told me of one instance of this kind of sorcery known to them in the Telefolmin Valley, an attempt made more in the spirit of experimentation than of malice. A group of Telefolmin chose a *rabisman,* no-account fellow villager as their subject. The victim belatedly escaped and, although badly frightened, survived.

7. I can remember thinking as I ran up the riverbed, "At last we are going to catch one of the bastards."

8. An excellent example of this application is the case of the Buffalo Creek dam burst and flood (Erikson 1976; Stern 1976).

9. Additional information on the male cults of other Ok peoples can be found in Quinlaven 1954; Pouwer 1964; Poole 1976; Craig 1968; Cranstone 1967; Wheatcroft 1976; Jorgensen 1978; Berkovitch 1980; Brumbaugh 1980.

10. Actually, a case could be made for the existence of common ritual elements between Mountain Ok peoples and the Maring, and between many other New Guinea cultures. One cited by Barth (1975:194) is the relationship between ancestors and marsupials and other game.

11. I am indebted to Barry Craig for his generous loan of detailed field notes on ritual collected from Miyanmin informants starting in 1963 that provoked my curiosity and lead me to the cycle described here.

12. The reader will have noted my intellectual debt to Gregory Bateson expressed throughout this work. I was thus startled to read in David Lipset's (1982) biography of Bateson that as he lay dying in 1980, Bateson "demanded that his son John beat him to death with a stick" (303). Is this "universal imagery" or a recollection from fieldwork among the Iatmul?

13. I am particularly grateful to Sawoiyap of Kometen whose attendance at my home hamlet I described, Mirimap of Temseten who could tell stories and also explain them, and Sipmap of Sokaten who was also a shaman. Other men of comparable age also provided information on these matters, but as they seemed not to be as "involved," so they failed to involve me, telling stories as if on a sight-seeing tour.

14. In this connection, Fredrik Barth spoke of being the beneficiary of the Faiwol's recognition of his "senior citizen" status, when we met briefly in Port Moresby in 1969.

15. In common with other New Guinea peoples, the Miyanmin describe a dialectic between the attributes of heat, dryness, light, and redness, on the one hand, and the attributes of cold, dampness, dark, and blackness on the other. The sexual connotations here are not predominant, but part of a larger set, i.e., male-female, highland-lowland, day-night, and the like.

16. Most *dil* are said to have participated in the *noiyal-imen* ritual to complete the *yominten* grade of initiation, but the *klem* or shield ritual appears to have been introduced in the 1940s during a period of escalating intergroup violence, particularly against the Telefolmin and Atbalmin enemies to the south (chapter 10). Only *dil* have the ritual strength to participate in battle. When there has been a protracted delay in commencing the *yomin* phase, and there are both *yominten* in their late teens who are anxious to fight and to exercise other adult prerogatives, as well as a need for fighting men, an abbreviated *yominten* sequence may be initiated—the Miyanmin version of the "Ninety-Day Wonder" program.

Under such circumstances the regular *yomin* ceremony is performed or parts of the series may be deferred or omitted. Older boys and young men who haven't completed the cycle are taken to the battle or raid as food bearers. They watch the fight from a secure position and then return home with the successful war party. Outside a main hamlet, shields are laid end to end and the men form a gauntlet on either side. They boys walk through this gauntlet and are beaten with the bloody limbs of the slain enemies. Victory songs are sung and, informants insist, the boys enter the hamlet as *dil*.

Chapter 9

1. It is suggestive that although the relatively low penalty for exit for men is balanced by initiation, the lack of initiation for women is balanced by a rather severe penalty for exit (see chapter 7).

2. The psychological reduction of Hirschman's (1970) model involves a modification of the theory of cognitive dissonance. This is extensively discussed in an appendix to the work prepared by the social psychologists Zimbardo and Snyder. See pp. 146–55 and p. 94, note 10 of Hirschman's (1970) work for a discussion of the relevant literature.

3. I have followed White's (1953) outline in making these calculations except that I disagree with his assumptions regarding "butchering efficiency." It is my impression that New Guinea butchers dress for consumption everything but the "oink" or the "squeak."

Chapter 10

1. At the end of my field work, in September, 1969, and after a short stay in the Ifitaman, I undertook to visit Wilson and Peggy Wheatcroft who were doing field work among the Tifalmin of the upper Ilam Valley. I was accompanied by two young Miyanmin friends and we spent our first night on the road at Ulapmin, a small non-Telefol tribe in the lower Ilam. As we left the village the next morning, some Ulapmin women gave us taro and sugarcane. My Miyanmin friends expressed their surprise, "Gee, they're just like us!"

2. Although "leaving the entrails" seems to be the thing that horrified Simpson the most, it is possibly an example of the "schlep effect." According to Pat Daly (1969:149), "The larger the animal and the farther from the point of consumption it is killed, the fewer of its bones will get 'schlepped' back to the camp, village or other area." I do not mean to dismiss the overall terroristic character of Miyanmin raids on the Telefolmin, however.

3. It would be very difficult for me to prove wrongdoing by Australian patrol officers in the years preceeding the aborted revolt of the Telefolmin in 1953. For one thing, I have little primary evidence of my own. The Miyanmin told me that they saw a policeman beat a Telefolmin carrier to death in the early 1950s. The pertinent patrol report states that a tree fell on the victim. I have heard second-hand accounts of other atrocities in the Ifitaman Valley. Morevoer, there has been some official recognition of wrongdoing, but no official public investigation. Ivan Champion (1966) alluded to the untold story in the postscript of a new edition of his book. Justice R. T. Gore, who presided at the trial of the Telefolmin rebels, apparently heard evidence put forward by the defense in mitigation and extenuation, and denied its relevance (Gore, 1965:164). He writes, "The complaints were subsequent excuses and not collectively the prior and actual motive." Even at the present time a fair-minded person who undertook to gain the confidence of the Telefolmin, could collect depositions from witnesses to the taking of women, the forced requisitioning of food, arbitrary beatings, murders, and house burnings by government officials. According to an informant in the public service in the 1960s, such an inquiry may actually exist. However, later rumors allege that the Moresby copy of the report has disappeared and that the Telefomin station copy was also misappropriated some years after independence. Even the ignorant and dishonest Gore admits to the possibility of "administratively wrong processes" (1965:164).

4. This is a name recorded by the Thurston party (Allied Geographical Section 1943) and subsequently noted on government maps as "Narbit."

5. This incident is often cited by informants as an example of Kome "style." I had occasion to question Kome informants about their reaction to Wameten's attempt in the late 1960s to evade sorcery by escaping into the afterlife (described in chapter 7). All agreed that under similar circumstances Kome would fight and not lose any time about it.

Chapter 11

1. Here I follow Jorgensen's (1982) account of events among the Telefolmin and am particularly grateful to him for personal communications on these and related matters.

Bibliography

Ackerman, A. J. and Cavalli-Sforza, L. L. 1971. The rate of spread of early farming in Europe. *Man* 6:674–88.

Alland, Alexander, Jr. 1970. *Adaptation in Cultural Evolution: An Approach to Medical Anthropology.* New York: Columbia University Press.

Allen, M.R. 1967. *Male Cults and Secret Initiations in Melanesia.* Melbourne: Melbourne University Press.

Allen, William. 1965. *The African Husbandman.* Edinburgh: Oliver and Boyd.

Allied Geographical Section (Southwest Pacific Area). 1943. *Area Study of the Sepik River District.* Terrain Study No. 65.

Anderson, Sydney and Jones, J. Knox. 1967. *Recent Mammals of the World.* New York: Ronald Press.

Annel, Bengt. 1960. *Hunting and Trapping Methods in Australia and Oceania.* Studia Ethnographica Upsaliensia 18.

Anthropology Today. Del Mar, Calif.: CRM Books, 1971.

Ashby, W. Ross. 1952. *Design for a Brain.* New York: Wiley.

———. 1956. *An Introduction to Cybernetics.* London: Chapman and Hall.

Audy, J. R. 1947. Scrub typhus as a study in ecology. *Nature* 159:295.

Baker, John R. 1929. *Man and Animals in the New Hebrides.* London: George Routledge and Sons.

Barnes, John A. 1962. African models in the New Guinea Highlands. *Man* 62:5–9.

———. 1967. Agnation among the Enga: a review article. *Oceania* 38:33–43.

Barrau, Jacques. 1958. *Subsistence Agriculture in Melanesia.* Bernice P. Bishop Museum Bulletin 219.

Barth, Fredrik. 1959–60. The land use patterns of the migratory tribes of South Persia. *Norsk Geografisk Tidsskrift Bind* 7:1–11.

———. 1971. Tribes and intertribal relations in the Fly headwaters. *Oceania* 31(3):171–91.

———. 1975. *Ritual and Knowledge among the Baktaman of New Guinea.* New Haven: Yale University Press.

Bartholomew, George A. and Hoel, Paul G. 1953. Reproductive behavior of the Alaska fur seal, Callorhinus ursinus. *Journal of Mammalogy* 34:417–36.

Barton, A. H. 1969. *Communities in Disaster: A Sociological Analysis of Collective Stress Situations.* New York: Doubleday.

Bates, Marston. 1952. *Where Winter Never Comes: A Study of Man and Nature in the Tropics.* New York: Scribners.

Bateson, Gregory. 1958. *Naven.* 2nd. Edition. Stanford: Stanford University Press.

———. 1963. The role of somatic change in evolution. *Evolution* 17:529–39.

———. 1972. *Steps to an Ecology of Mind.* New York: Ballantine.

———. 1979. The pattern which connects. *The CoEvolution Quarterly* (Summer):5–16.

———. 1980. *Mind and Nature: A Necessary Unity.* New York: Bantam.

Bawden, Richard J.; Macadem, R. D.; Packham, R. J.; and Valentine, I. O. 1984. Systems thinking and practices in the education of agriculturists. *Agricultural Systems* 13–205–25.

Bayliss-Smith, Timothy P. 1977. Energy use and economic development in Pacific communities. In: *Subsistence and Survival.* T. Bayliss-Smith and R. Feachem, eds. London: Academic Press. pp. 317–62.

Beehler, Bruce McP. 1978. *Upland Birds of Northeastern New Guinea.* Wau Ecology Institute Handbook No. 4.

Bennett, G. 1860. *Gatherings of a Naturalist in Australasia.* London: John van Voorst.

Benton, Allan H. and Werner, William E., Jr. 1966. *Field Biology and Ecology.* 2nd. Ed. New York: McGraw-Hill.

Berlinski, David J. 1976. *On Systems Analysis: An Essay Concerning the Limitations of Some Mathematical Models in the Social, Political and Biological Sciences.* Cambridge, Ma.: MIT Press.

Bicchieri, M.G. 1969. The differential use of identical features of physical habitat in connection with exploitative settlement and community pattern: the Mbuti. In: *Contributions to Anthropology: Ecological Essays.* D. Damas, ed. National Museum of Canada Bulletin 230, Anthropology Series 86.

Bik, M. J. 1967. Structural geomorphology and morphoclimatic zonation in the Central Highlands, Australian New Guinea. In: *Landform Studies from Australia and New Guinea.* Jennings and Mabbutt, eds. Canberra: Australian National University Press.

Blackwood, Beatrice. 1940. Use of plants among the Kukukuku of Southeast Central New Guinea. *Proceedings of the Sixth Pacific Science Congress* 6:111–26.

Booth, G. F. 1957. *Report of Patrol to Eliptamin* [sic]. Telefomin Patrol Report 3–56/57. Sepik District, Territory of Papua and New Guinea.

Boserup, Esther. 1965. *The Conditions of Agricultural Growth: The Economics of Agricultural Change under Population Pressure.* Chicago: Aldine.

Bridges, E. M. 1970. *World Soils.* Cambridge: Cambridge University Press.

Brongersma, L. D. 1958. *The Animal World of Netherlands New Guinea.* Groningen: J. B. Wolters.

Brookfield, Harold C. 1962. Local study and comparative method: an example from Central New Guinea. *Annals of the Association of American Geographers* 52:242–54.

———. 1964. The ecology of highland settlement: some suggestions. In: *New Guinea: The Central Highlands.* J.B. Watson, ed. *American Anthropologist* 66(4, Part II):20–39.

———. 1972. Intensification and disintensification in Pacific agriculture. *Pacific Viewpoint* 13(1):30–48.

———and Brown, Paula. 1963. *Struggle for Land: Agriculture and Group Territories among the Chimbu of the New Guinea Highlands.* Melbourne: Oxford University Press.

———and Hart, Doreen. 1966. *Rainfall in the Tropical Southwest Pacific.* Department of Geography Publication G/3. Canberra, Research School of Pacific Studies, Australian National University.

———. 1971. *Melanesia: A Geographical Interpretation of an Island World.* London: Methuen.

———and White, J.P. 1968. Revolution or evolution in the prehistory of the New Guinea highlands: a seminar report. *Ethnology* 7:43–52.

Brown, Paula. 1978. *Highland Peoples of New Guinea.* Cambridge: Cambridge University Press.

Brumbaugh, Robert. 1980. A Secret Cult in the West Sepik Highlands. Ph.D. Dissertation in Anthropology. Stonybrook, State University of New York.

Bulmer, Ralph N. H. 1967. Why is the cassowary not a bird? A problem of zoological taxonomy among the Karam of the New Guinea Highlands. *Man* (n.s.) 2(1):5–25.

_____. 1968a. The strategies of hunting in New Guinea. *Oceania* 38(4):302–18.

_____. 1968b. Worms that croak and other mysteries of Karam natural history. *Mankind* 6:621–39.

_____. 1968c. Which came first, the chicken or the egg-head? In: *Echanges et Communications.* J. Pouillon and P. Miranda, eds. Paris: Mouton. pp. 1069–91.

_____ and Menzies, J. I. 1972–73. Karam classification of marsupials and rodents. *Journal of the Polynesian Society* 81(4):473–99; 82(1):86–107.

_____; Menzies, J.I.; and Parker, F. 1975. Karam classification of reptiles and fishes. *Journal of the Polynesian Society* 77:333–85.

_____ and Tyler, M. J. 1968. Karam classification of frogs. *Journal of the Polynesian Society* 77:333–85.

Bunge, M. 1977. The GST challenge to the classical philosophies of science. *International Journal of General Systems* 4:322.

Burton, Ian and Hewitt, Kenneth. 1974. Ecological dimensions of environmental hazards. In: *Human Ecology.* F. Sargent, ed. Amsterdam: North Holland. pp. 253–83.

Burton, Maurice. 1962. *University Dictionary of Mammals of the World.* New York: Appollo Editions.

Calaby, J. H. 1966. *Mammals of the Upper Richmond and Clarence Rivers.* Division of Wildlife Resources Technical Paper No. 10, CSIRO (Australia).

Campbell, Stuart. 1938. The country between the headwaters of the Fly and Sepik Rivers in New Guinea. *Geographical Journal* 92(3):232–58.

Cancian, Francesca. 1960. Functional analysis of change. *American Sociological Review* 25(6):818–27.

Cancian, Frank. 1965. *Economics and Prestige in a Maya Community: The Religious Cargo System in Zinacantan.* Stanford: Stanford University Press.

Cape, Nicky. 1981. Agriculture. In: *Oksapmin: Development and Change.* S. Weeks, ed. Port Moresby: Educational Research Unit. pp. 149–90.

Carneiro, Robert. 1960. Slash and burn agriculture: a closer look at its implications for settlement patterns. In: *Men and Cultures.* A. F. C. Wallace, ed. Philadelphia: University of Pennsylvania Press. pp. 229–34.

_____. 1968. Slash and burn cultivation among the Kuikuru and its implications for cultural development in the Amazon basin. In: *Man and Adaptation: The Cultural Present.* Y. Cohen, ed. Chicago: Aldine.

Champion, Ivan F. 1966. *Across New Guinea from the Fly to the Sepik.* 2nd Ed. Melbourne: Lansdowne Press.

Chaplin, Raymond. 1969. The use of non-morphological criteria for the study of animal domestication from bones found in archaeological sites. In: *The Domestication and Exploitation of Plants and Animals.* P.J. Ucko and G.W. Dimbleby, eds. Chicago: Aldine.

Checkland, P. B. 1979. The shape of the systems movement. *Journal of Applied Systems Analysis* 6.

_____. 1981. *Systems Thinking: Systems Practice.* New York: Wiley.

Clark, Phillip J. and Evans, Frances C. 1954. Distance to nearest neighbor as a measure of spatial relationships in populations. *Ecology* 35(4):445–53.

Clarke, William C. 1966. From extensive to intensive shifting cultivation: a succession from New Guinea. *Ethnology* 5:347–59.

_____. 1971. *Place and People: An Ecology of a New Guinea People.* Berkeley: University of California Press.

Colinveaux, P. A. 1973. Introduction to Ecology. New York: Wiley.

Collins, Paul W. 1964. Towards a reconstruction of functionalism: the aim of functional analysis in anthropology. Paper presented at the 63rd Annual Meeting of the American Anthropological Association, November 19–22, Detroit, Michigan.

_____ and Vayda, A. P. 1969. Functional analysis and its aims. *Australian and New Zealand Journal of Sociology* 5(2):153–56.

Conklin, Harold C. 1957. *Hanunoo Agriculture: A Report on an Integral System of Shifting Cultivation in the Philippines.* FAO Forestry Development Paper No. 12. Rome: Food and Agriculture Organization of the United Nations.

_____. 1959. Population-land balance under systems of tropical forest agriculture. Proceedings of the Ninth Pacific Science Congress, Bangkok, Thailand, 1957. *Pacific Science Association,* Volume 7:63.

_____. 1961. The study of shifting cultivation. *Current Anthropology* 2:27–61.

Connel, J. 1978a. The death of taro: local response to a change of a subsistence crop in the Northern Solomons. *Mankind* 10.

_____. 1978b. *Taim Bilong Mani: The Evolution of Agriculture in a Solomon Island Society.* Development Studies Centre Monograph No. 12. Canberra: Australian National University.

Conrad, R.; Dye, W.; Thomason, N. P.; and Bruce, L. P., Jr. 1975. Some language relationships in the upper Sepik region of Papua New Guinea. *Papers in New Guinea Linguistics* No. 18. Canberra: Australian National University.

Cook, Sherburnes F. 1959. The effects of fire on a population of small rodents. *Ecology* 40:102–8.

Coon, Carlton S. 1971. *The Hunting Peoples.* Boston: Little Brown.

Craig, Barry. 1967. The houseboards of the Telefomin Sub-District, New Guinea. *Man* 2:260–73.

_____. 1968. Bark painting and rock art of the Mountain Ok. *Mankind* 6:595–97.

_____. 1969. The Art of the Mountain Ok. M.A. Thesis, Department of Anthropology, Sydney University, Australia.

Craig, Ruth. 1969. Marriage among the Telefomin. In: *Pigs, Pearlshells, and Women.* R. M. Glasse and M. J. Meggitt, eds. Englewood Cliffs, New Jersey: Prentice Hall. pp. 176–97.

Craighead, John J. and Craighead, Frank C. 1969. *Hawks, Owls and Wildlife.* New York: Dover.

Cranstone, B. A. L. 1967. Some boards from a New Guinea haus tamboran. *Man* (n.s.) 2(2).

Cremer, K. W. 1969. Browsing of mountain ash regeneration by wallaby and possum in Tasmania. *Australian Forestry* 33(3):201–10.

Cummings, Ralph W., Jr. and Wortman, Sterling. 1978. *To Feed This World: The Challenge and the Strategy.* Baltimore: The Johns Hopkins University Press.

Daly, Patricia. 1969. Approaches to faunal analysis in archaeology. *American Antiquity* 34(2):146–53.

Darling, F. Fraser. 1956. Man's ecological dominance through domesticated animals on wild lands. In: *Man's Role in Changing the Face of the Earth.* W. L. Thomas, ed. Chicago: University of Chicago Press. pp. 778–87.

Davis, David E. 1957. The use of food as a buffer in a predator-prey system. *Journal of Mammalogy* 38:466–72.

De Schlippe, Pierre. 1956. *Shifting Cultivation in Africa: The Zande System of Agriculture.* London: Routledge and Kegan Paul.

Diamond, Jared M. 1972. *Avifauna of the Eastern Highlands of New Guinea.* Publications of the Nuttall Ornithological Club No. 12. Cambridge: Harvard University, Museum of Comparative Zoology.

Dice, Lee R. 1952. *Natural Communities.* Ann Arbor: University of Michigan Press.

_____. 1955. *Man's Nature and Nature's Man: The Ecology of Human Communities.* Ann Arbor: University of Michigan Press.

Dornstreich, Mark D. 1973. An Ecological Study of Gadio Enga (New Guinea) Subsistence. Ph.D. Dissertation in Anthropology. New York: Columbia University.

_____. 1977. The ecological description and analysis of tropical subsistence patterns: an example from New Guinea. In: *Subsistence and Survival.* T. Bayliss-Smith and R. Feachem, eds. London: Academic Press. pp. 245–72.

______ and Morren, G. E. B., Jr. 1974. Does New Guinea cannibalism have nutritional value? *Human Ecology* 2(1):1–12.

Dunn, Edgar S., Jr. 1971. *Economic and Social Development: A Process of Social Learning.* Baltimore: Johns Hopkins Press.

Dwyer, Peter D. n.d. Edible waste ratios for some New Guinea mammals. MS.

______. 1974. The price of protein: 500 hours of hunting in the New Guinea highlands. *Oceania* 44:278–93.

______. 1975. Observations on the breeding biology of some New Guinea murid rodents. *Australian Wildlife Research* 2:33–45.

______. 1978. Rats, pigs and men: disturbance and diversity in the New Guinea highlands. *Australian Journal of Ecology* 3:213–32.

______. 1982a. Prey switching: a case study from New Guinea. *Journal of Animal Ecology* 51:529–42.

______. 1982b. Wildlife conservation and tradition in the highlands of Papua New Guinea. In: *Traditional Conservation in Papua New Guinea: Implications for Today.* L. Morauta, J. Pernetta, and W. Heaney, eds. Boroka: Institute of Applied Social and Economic Research. pp.173–90.

______. 1983. Etolo hunting performance and energetics. *Human Ecology* 11:145–73.

Dyson-Hudson, Neville. 1971. The study of nomads. *Journal of African and Asian Studies* 7(1–2):1–29.

Dyson-Hudson, Rada and Smith, Eric A. 1978. Human territoriality: an ecological reassessment. *American Anthropologist* 80:21–41.

Ellerman, J. R. 1966. *The Families and Genera of Living Rodents.* London: Whilton and Wesley.

Ellsmore, R. T. 1945. New Guinea mountain and swampland dwellers. *National Geographic Magazine* 88:670–94.

Elton, Charles. 1942. *Voles, Mice and Lemmings: Problems in Population Dynamics.* London: Oxford University Press.

Errington, Paul L. 1943. *An Analysis of Mink Predation upon Muskrats in North-Central United States.* Research Bulletin 320. Ames: Iowa Agricultural Experiment Station. pp. 797–924.

______. 1946. Predation and vertebrate populations. *Quarterly Review of Biology* 21:144–77; 221–45.

Flowers, N.; Gross, D.; Ritter, M.; and Werner, D. 1982. Variations in swidden practices in four central Brazilian Indian societies. *Human Ecology* 10:203–15.

Fonaroff, L. Schuyler. 1965. Was Huntington right about human nutrition? *Annals of the Association of American Geographers* 55:365–76.

Forrester, Jay W. 1968. *Principles of Systems.* 2nd Preliminary Edition. Cambridge, Mass.: Wright Allen.

______. 1971. *World Dynamics.* Cambridge, Mass.: Wright Allen.

Frauca, Harry. 1965. *The Book of Australian Wildlife.* London & Melbourne: Heineman.

Freeman, J. D. 1955. *Iban Agriculture.* Colonial Research Studies 18. London: H.M.S.O.

Friedman, Jonathan. 1974. Marxism, structuralism, and vulgar materialism. *Man* 9:444–69.

Frith, H. J. and Calaby, J. H. 1969. *Kangaroos.* New York: Humanities Press.

Gagne, W. C. 1982. Staple crops in subsistence agriculture. In: *Biogeography and Ecology in New Guinea.* J.L. Gressitt, ed. Vol. II. The Hague: W. Junk. pp. 229–62.

Gardner, Donald S. 1980. The determinants of Mianmin settlement and residential patterns: a reply [*sic*] to Morren. *Mankind* 12:215–25.

______. 1981. Cult Ritual and Social Organization among the Mianmin. Ph.D. Dissertation in Anthropology. Canberra: Australian National University.

______. 1983. Performativity in ritual: the Mianmin case. *Man* 18:346– 60.

Gausse, G. F. 1934. *The Struggle for Existence.* Baltimore: Williams and Wilkins.

Geertz, Clifford. 1963. *Agricultural Involution: The Processes of Ecological Change in Indonesia.* Berkeley: University of California Press.

Gentry, John B.; Odum, E. P.; Mason, M. O.; Nabholz, V.; Marsha, S.; and McGinnis, J. T. 1968. The effect of altitude and forest manipulation on relative abundance of small mammals. *Journal of Mammalogy* 49:539–41.

Gerlach, Luther P. and Hine, Virginia H. 1970. *People, Power, Change: Movements of Social Transformation.* Indianapolis: Bobbs-Merrill.

———. 1973. *Lifeway Leap.* Minneapolis: University of Minnesota Press.

Glasse, Robert M. and Meggitt, M. J., eds. 1969. *Pigs, Pearlshells, and Women: Marriage in the New Guinea Highlands.* Englewood Cliffs, New Jersey: Prentice Hall.

Godelier, M. 1971. Salt currency and the circulation of commodities among the Baruya of New Guinea. In: *Studies in Economic Anthropology.* G. Dalton, ed. Anthropological Studies No. 7. Washington: American Anthropological Association.

Golson, Jack and Hughes, P. J. 1976. The appearance of plant and animal domestication in New Guinea. In: *La Préhistoire Océanienne.* Congress of Pre- and Proto-Historic Sciences, Nice, September. Centre National de la Recherche Scientifique, Paris.

Goody, Jack. 1962a. *Death, Property, and the Ancestors.* Stanford: Stanford University Press.

Gore, R. T. 1965. *Justice Versus Sorcery.* Brisbane: Jacandra.

Griffiths, J. T. 1947. A further account of tsutsugamushi fever at Sansapor, Dutch New Guinea. *Journal of Parasitology* 33(4):367–73.

Griffiths, Mervyn. 1968. *Echidnas.* Oxford: Pergamon Press.

Gross, A. D. 1947. Cyclic invasion of the snowy owl and the migration of 1945–46. *Auk* 64:584–601.

Gross, Daniel R. 1975. Protein capture and cultural development in the Amazon Basin. *American Anthropologist* 77:526–49.

——— and Underwood, Barbara. 1971. Technological change and caloric costs: sisal agriculture in northeastern Brazil. *American Anthropologist* 73:725–40.

Guiler, Eric C. 1958. Observations on a population of small marsupials in Tasmania. *Journal of Mammalogy* 39(1):44.

Gulliver, P. H. 1955. *The Family Herds: A Study of Two Pastoral Tribes in East Africa, the Jie and the Turkana.* London: Routledge and Kegan Paul.

Hames, R. B. 1979. A comparison of the efficiency of the shotgun and the bow in neotropical forest hunting. *Human Ecology* 7:219–52.

——— and Vickers, W. T. 1982. Optimal diet breadth theory as a model to explain variability in Amazonian hunting. *American Ethnologist* 9:258–78.

Harris, L. Dale. 1961. *Introduction to Feedback Systems.* New York: Wiley.

Harris, Marvin. 1964. *The Nature of Cultural Things.* New York: Random House.

———. 1966. The cultural ecology of India's sacred cattle. *Current Anthropology* 7:51–66.

———. 1968. *The Rise of Anthropological Theory: A History of Theories of Culture.* New York: Thomas Y. Crowell.

———. 1971. *Culture, Man and Nature.* New York: Thomas Y. Crowell.

———. 1979. *Cultural Materialism: The Struggle for a Science of Culture.* New York: Random House.

Harrison, J. L. 1955. Reproduction data on some Malayan mammals. *Proceedings of the Zoological Society of London* 125:445–60.

———. 1957. Habitats of some Malayan rats. *Proceedings of the Zoological Society of London* 128:1–21.

———. 1958. Range of movement of some Malayan rats. *Journal of Mammalogy* 39:190–206.

———. 1959. Animal populations in rainforest. *Proceedings of the First All-India Congress of Zoology* 2:234–44.

_____. 1960. Faunal diversity in Australian tropical rainforest. *Australian Journal of Science* 22:424–26.

_____. 1962a. Mammals of Innisfail. *Australian Journal of Zoology* 10:45–83.

_____. 1962b. The distribution and feeding habits among mammals in a tropical rainforest. *Journal of Animal Ecology* 31:53–63.

_____. 1962c. Ecology of the forms of Rattus rattus in the Malay Peninsula. *Proceedings of the Ninth Pacific Science Congress,* Bangkok, Thailand, Vol. 10.

_____ and Traub, R. 1950. Rodents and insectivores from Selangor, Malaya. *Journal of Mammalogy* 31:337–46.

Hartman, Carl G. 1952. *Possums.* Austin: University of Texas Press.

Hawkes, K.; Hill, K.; and O'Connell, J. 1982. Why hunters gather: optimal foraging theory and the Ache of eastern Paraguay. *American Ethnologist* 9(2):379–98.

Healey, Alan. 1962. Linguistic aspects of Telefomin kinship terminology. *Anthropological Linguistics* 4(7):14–28.

_____. 1964. *A Survey of the Ok Family of Languages.* Canberra: Australian National University (Mimeo).

Heer, David M. 1969. *Society and Population.* Englewood Cliffs, New Jersey: Prentice Hall.

Hempel, Carl G. 1959. The logic of functional analysis. In: *Symposium on Sociological Theory.* L. Gross, ed. Evanston: Row Peterson.

Herdt, Gilbert H. 1981. *Guardians of the Flutes: Idioms of Masculinity.* New York: McGraw-Hill.

_____. 1982. Fetish and fantasy in Sambia initiation. In: *Rituals of Manhood in Papua New Guinea.* G. Herdt, ed. Berkeley: University of California Press, pp. 44–98.

Hickerson, Harold. 1965. The Virginia deer and intertribal buffer zones in the upper Mississippi Valley. In: *Man, Culture and Animals.* A. Leeds and A.P. Vayda, eds. Washington, D.C.: American Association for the Advancement of Science Publication No. 78.

Hide, Robin L. 1981. Aspects of Pig Production and Use in Colonial Sinasina, Papua New Guinea. Ph.D. Dissertation in Anthropology. New York: Columbia University.

Hill, James N. 1969. A processual analysis of non-seasonal population movement in man and other terrestrial mammals. *Anthropology U.C.L.A.* 1(1):49–59.

Hirschman, Albert O. 1970. *Exit, Voice, and Loyalty: Responses to Decline in Firms, Organizations and States.* Cambridge, Ma.: Harvard University Press.

Hitchcock, W. B. 1964. An introduction to the natural history of a New Guinea highland community. *Emu* 63(5):351–72.

Hogbin, H.I. and Wedgewood, Camilla. 1953. Local grouping in Melanesia. *Oceania* 23:241–76; 24:58–76.

Holling, C. S. 1959. The components of predation as revealed by a study of small mammal predation of the European pine sawfly. *Canadian Entomologist* 91:293–320.

_____. 1961. Principles of insect predation. *Annual Review of Entomology* 6:163–82.

_____ and Goldberg, M. A. 1971. Ecology and planning. *Journal of the American Institute of Planners* (July).

Howell, Nancy. 1979. *Demography of the Dobe Kung.* New York: Academic Press.

Hughs, Ian. 1970. Pigs, sago and limestone: the adaptive use of natural enclosures and planted sago in pig management. Paper presented to the 42nd Australia-New Zealand Association for the Advancement of Science Symposium on Agriculture in New Guinea. P. Moresby, Aug., 1970.

Husson, A. M. 1955. Notes on the mammals collected by the Swedish New Guinea Expedition, 1948–49. *Nova Guinea* (n.s.)6(2):283.

Huxley, Julian. 1964. *Evolution: The Modern Synthesis.* New York: Wiley.

Hyndman, David G. 1979. Wopkaimin Subsistence: Cultural Ecology in the New Guinea Highland Fringe. Ph.D. Dissertation in Anthropology. Brisbane: University of Queensland.

_____. 1982. Biotope gradient in a diversified New Guinea subsistence system. *Human Ecology* 10:219–59.

———. 1984a. Hunting and the classification of game animals among the Wopkaimin. *Oceania* 54:289–309.

———. 1984b. Ethnobotany of Wopkaimin Pandanus: a significant Papua New Guinea plant resource. *Economic Botany* 38(3):287–303.

———and Morren, George E. B., Jr. n.d. The human ecology of the Moutain Ok. Unpublished MS.

Jackson, Richard. 1982. *Ok Tedi: The Pot of Gold.* Port Moresby: University of Papua New Guinea.

Jacobs, Jane. 1967. *The Economy of Cities.* New York: Vintage.

Johns. R. J. 1982. Plant zonation. In: *Biogeography and Ecology of New Guinea.* J. L. Gressitt, ed. The Hague: W. Junk. pp. 309–30.

Jones, Barbara. 1980. Consuming Society: Food and Illness among the Faiwol. Ph.D. Dissertation in Anthropology. Charlottesville: University of Virginia.

Jones, F. D. 1954. Report of a Patrol to Eliptamin [*sic*]. Telefomin Patrol Report 3–54/55. Sepik District, Territory of Papua and New Guinea.

Jorgensen, Daniel. 1981a. Taro and Arrow. Ph.D. Dissertation in Anthropology. Vancouver: University of British Columbia.

———. 1981b. Life on the fringe: history and society in Telefomin. In: *The Plight of Peripheral People in Papua New Guinea.* Vol. I: *The Inland Situation.* R. Gordon, ed. Cambridge, Ma.: Cultural Survival. pp. 59–79.

———. 1984. *A Survey of "Min" People in the May River Area.* Report to the Telefomin District Development Agreement (April).

Kauie, Harry T. 1966. Foods of rodents in the Hamakua District, Hawaii. *Pacific Science* 20(3):367.

Keast, A.,; Crocker, R. L.; and Christian, C. S. 1959. *Biogeography and Ecology in Australia.* Monographia Biologicae 8. Den Haag: W. Junk.

Kelly, Raymond. 1977. *Etoro Social Organization.* Ann Arbor: University of Michigan Press.

Laughlin, William S. 1966. Hunting: an integrating biobehavior system and its evolutionary importance. In: *Man the Hunter.* R. B. Lee and I. DeVore, eds. Chicago: Aldine pp. 304–20.

Laurie, E. M. O. 1952. Mammals collected by Mr. Shaw Mayer in New Guinea, 1932–1940. *Bulletin of the British Museum (Natural History), Zoology* 1:269–318.

Laycock, D.C. 1965a. The Ndu Language Family (Sepik District, New Guinea). Canberra: Linguistic Circle of Canberra.

———. 1965b. Three upper Sepik phonologies. *Oceanic Linguistics* 4:113–18.

Lea, D.A.M. 1964. Abelam Land and Sustenance: Swidden Horticulture in an Area of High Population Density, Maprik, New Guinea. Ph.D. Dissertation, Australian National University, Canberra.

Leach, Edmund. 1954. *Political Systems of Highland Burma.* Boston: Beacon.

Lee, Richard B. 1969. !Kung Bushman subsistence: an input-output analysis. In: *Environment and Cultural Behavior.* A.P. Vayda, ed. Garden City, New York: Natural History Press. pp.47–79.

———. 1972a. !Kung spatial organization: an ecological and historical perspective. *Human Ecology* 1(2):125–48.

———. 1972b. Work effort, group structure, and land use in contemporary hunter-gatherers. In: *Man, Settlement, and Urbanism.* P.J. Ucko, R. Tringham, and G.W. Dimbleby, eds. London: Duckworth. pp. 177–85.

———and DeVore, Irvin. 1968. Introduction. In: *Man the Hunter.* R. B. Lee and I. DeVore, eds. Chicago: Aldine.

Levins, Richard. 1968. The strategy of model building in population biology. *American Scientist* 54(4):421.

Lidecker, William Z. and Ziegler, Alan C. 1968. *Report on a Collection of Mammals from Eastern New Guinea: Including Species Keys for Fourteen Genera.* Berkeley: University of California Publications in Zoology 87.

Lifton, Robert Jay. 1968. *Death in Life: Survivors of Hiroshima.* New York: Random House.

_____. 1971. *History and Human Survival: Essays on the Young and Old, Survivors and the Dead, Peace and War, and on Contemporary Psychohistory.* New York: Vintage.

Lindbloom, C.E. 1959. The science of muddling through. *Public Administration Review* (Spring):79–88.

Lipsett, David. 1982. *Gregory Bateson: Legacy of a Scientist.* Boston: Beacon.

Little, Michael A. and Morren, George E.B., Jr. 1973. *Ecology, Energetics, and Human Variability.* Dubuque: Wm. C. Brown.

Longman, C. J. and Walrond, H. 1967. *Archery.* New York: Frederick Ungar.

Lotka, A. J. 1925. *Elements of Physical Biology.* Baltimore: Williams and Wilkins.

Lowman, Cherry. 1980. Environment, Society and Health: Ecological Bases of Community Growth and Decline in the Maring Region of Papua New Guinea. Ph.D. Dissertation in Anthropology. New York: Columbia University.

MacArthur, R. H. and Wilson, E. O. 1967. *The Theory of Island Biogeography.* Princeton: Princeton University Press.

MacArthur, R. and Pianka, E. 1966. On the optimal use of a patchy environment. *American Naturalist* 100:603–19.

Maelzor, D. A. 1965. A discussion of components of environment in ecology. *Journal of Theoretical Ecology* 8:41–62.

Majnep, S. M. and Bulmer, Ralph. 1977. *Birds of My Kalam Country.* Auckland: Oxford University Press.

Margalef, Ramon. 1968. *Perspectives on Ecological Theory.* Chicago: University of Chicago Press.

Marris, Peter. 1975. *Loss and Change.* Garden City: Anchor.

Martin, J. 1983. Optimal foraging theory: a review of some models and their applications. *American Anthropologist* 85:612–29.

Maruyama, M. 1963. The second cybernetics: deviation-amplifying causal processes. *American Scientist* 51:164–79.

Marwick, Max. 1964. Witchcraft as a social strain gauge. *Australian Journal of Science* 26:263–68.

Mayr, Ernest. 1932. A tenderfoot explorer in New Guinea. *Natural History* 32:83–97.

McArthur, Margaret. 1977. Nutritional research in Melanesia: a second look at the Tsembaga. In: *Subsistence and survival.* T. Bayliss-Smith and R. Feachem, eds. London: Academic Press. pp. 91–128.

McCay, Bonnie J. 1981. Optimal foragers or political actors? Ecological analyses of a New Jersey fishery. *American Ethnologist* 8(2):356–82.

McHarg, Ian L. 1969. *Design with Nature.* Garden City: Natural History.

McNaughton, S. J. and Wolf, L. F. 1973. *General Ecology.* New York: Holt, Rinehart and Winston.

Meadows, Donella et al. 1972. *The Limits to Growth.* New York: Universe.

Meggers, Betty J. 1954. Environmental limitation in the development of culture. *American Anthropologist* 56(5).

_____. 1971. *Amazonia: Man and Culture in a Counterfeit Paradise.* Chicago: Aldine.

Meggitt, Mervyn J. 1965a. *The Lineage System of the Mae-Enga of New Guinea.* Edinburgh: Oliver and Boyd.

_____. 1965b. The Mae Enga of the Western Highlands. In: *Gods, Ghosts and Men in Melanesia.* P. Lawrence and M. J. Meggitt, eds. Melbourne: Oxford University Press, pp. 105–31.

_____. 1977. *Blood is Their Argument.* Palo Alto, Ca.: Mayfield.

Menzies, James I. and Dennis, Elizabeth. 1979. *Handbook of New Guinea Rodents.* Handbook No. 6. Wau Ecology Institute.

Merton, Robert K. 1957. *Social Theory and Social Structure.* Glencoe, Ill.: The Free Press.

Meur, R. L.; Blakelock, E. H.; and Hinomoto, H. 1965. Simulation of ecological relationships. *Behavioral Science* 9:67.

Middleton, John and Winter, E. H. 1963. *Witchcraft and Sorcery in East Africa.* London, Routledge and Kegan Paul.

Mitchell, Donald D. 1976. *Land and Agriculture in Nagovisi, Papua New Guinea.* Institute of Applied Social and Economic Research. Monograph No. 3. Boroko: Papua New Guinea.

Mohr, Carl O. 1947. Notes on chiggers, rats, and habitats on New Guinea and Luzon. *Ecology* 28(2):194–99.

———. 1956. Comparative infestations by ectoparasites of two native rats of Sansapor, New Guinea. *American Midland Naturalist* 55:382–92.

Moore, Omar Kayam. 1957. Divination—A new perspective. *American Anthropologist* 59:69–74.

Morren, George E. B., Jr. 1974. Settlements Strategies and Hunting in a New Guinea Society. Ph.D. Dissertation in Anthropology. New York: Columbia University.

———. 1977. From hunting to herding: pigs and the control of energy in montane New Guinea. In: *Subsistence and Survival.* T. Bayliss-Smith and E. Feachem, eds. London: Academic Press, pp. 273–316.

———. 1980a. Seasonality among the Miyanmin. *Mankind* 12:1–12.

———. 1980b. The rural ecology of the British drought of 1975–76. *Human Ecology* 8(1):33–63.

———. 1981a. A small footnote to the "Big Walk." *Oceania* 52:39–63.

———. 1981b. Cultural ecology, the Mianmin, and seasonality: A reply to Gardner. *Mankind* 14(2).

———. 1981c. Report of a visit to the Hotmin area, Middle May River, East Sepik, to investigate a human footprint in stone. *Oral History* 8(8):81–85.

———. 1983a. The Bushmen and the British: problems in the identification of drought and responses to drought. In: *Interpretations of Calamity.* K. Hewitt, ed. London: Allen & Unwin. pp. 44–66.

———. 1983b. A general approach to the identification of hazards and responses. In: *Interpretations of Calamity.* K. Hewitt, ed. London: Allen & Unwin, pp. 284–97.

———. 1984. Warfare on the highland fringe of New Guinea: the case of the Moutain Ok. In: *Warfare, Culture, and Environment.* B. Ferguson, ed. Orlando: Academic Press. pp. 169–207.

———. (In press). National and local development in Papua New Guinea: Another view from Telefomin District. In: *The Plight of Peripheral Peoples of Papua New Guinea.* Vol. II. Cambridge, Ma.: Cultural Survival.

Moylan, Thomas. 1979. *Identification of the Landowners in the Frieda River Area and Their Affiliations with Other Groups.* Papua New Guinea: Department of Minerals and Energy.

Murphy, Robert F. 1957. Intergroup hostility and social cohesion. *American Anthropologist* 59:1018–35.

Murphy, Roy E. 1965. *Adaptive Processes in Economic Systems.* New York: Academic Press.

Nagel, Ernest. 1956. A formalization of functionalism. In: *Logic without Metaphysics.* Glencoe: The Free Press. pp. 247–83.

Naughton, John. 1981. Theory and practice in systems research. *Journal of Applied Systems Analysis* 8:61–70.

Neville, Ron T. 1956. Report of a Patrol to the Mianmin. Telefomin Patrol Report 2–56/57. Sepik District, Territory of Papua and New Guinea.

Norgan, N. G.; Ferro-Luzzi, A.; and Durnin, J. V. G. A. 1974. The energy and nutrient intake and energy expenditure of 204 New Guinean Adults. In: *A Discussion of Human Adaptability.* G. Harrison and R. Walsh, eds. Philosophical Transactions of the Royal Society of London, B. *Biological Sciences,* 268(893):309–48.

Odum, Howard T. 1971. *Environment, Power and Society.* New York: Wiley-Interscience.

Oliver, Douglas V. 1955. *A Solomon Island Society: Kinship and Leadership among the Siuai of Bougainville.* Boston: Beacon.

Orlove, Benjamin S. 1977. *Cultural Ecology: A Critical Essay and Bibliography.* Institute of Ecology Publications No. 13. University of California, Davis.

Osgood, Cornelius. 1936. *Contributions to the Ethnography of the Kutchin.* Yale University Publications in Anthropology No. 14. New Haven: Yale University Press.

Pacific Islands Monthly (PIM). 1943. Explorer Bill Korn. 13(June):11.

_____. 1944. The Sepik tragedy: what really happened at Angoram in March 1942. 14(April):29–30.

_____. 1954. Ward Williams party saw Telefomin in 1936–37. 24 (March):22.

Pearson, M. and Thistleton, B. 1981. *Taro Diseases in the Hotmin Area, East Sepik Province, and the Telefomin Area, West Sepik Province: Report of a Field Visit, 1981.* Konedobu, Department of Primary Industry, Papua New Guinea.

Perey, Arnold. 1973. Oksapmin Society and World View. Ph.D. Dissertation in Anthropology. New York: Columbia University.

Peterson, J. T. 1981. Game, farming, and inter-ethnic relations in northeastern Luzon, Philippines. *Human Ecology* 9(1):1–22.

Piddocke, Stuart. 1965. The potlatch system of the southern Kwakiutl: A new perspective. *Southwestern Journal of Anthropology* 21:244–64.

Pitelka, F. A.; Tomich, P. Q.; and Treichel, G. W. 1955. Ecological relations of jaegers and owls as lemming predators near Barrow, Alaska. *Ecological Monographs* 25:85–117.

Poole, Fitz-John Porter. 1967. The Ais Am: An Introduction to Male Initiation Ritual among the Bimin-Kuskusmin of the West Sepik District, Papua New Guinea. Ph.D. Dissertation in Anthropology. Ithaca: Cornell University.

_____. 1981. Transforming "natural" woman: female ritual leaders and gender ideology among Bimin-Kuskusmin. In: *Sexual Meanings.* S. B. Ortner and H. Whitehead, eds. New York: Cambridge University Press.

_____. 1982. The ritual forging of identity: aspects of person and self in Bimin-Kuskusmin male initiation. In: *Rituals of Manhood: Male Initiation in Papua New Guinea.* G. H. Herdt, ed. Berkeley: University of California Press.

Pospisil, Leopold. 1963. *Kapauku Papuan Economy.* Yale University Publications in Anthropology 67. New Haven: Yale University Press.

Pouwer, J. 1964. A social system in the Star Mountains: toward a reorientation of the study of social systems. In: *New Guinea: The Central Highlands.* J. B. Watson, ed. *American Anthropologist* 66(4, Part II):133–61.

_____. 1966. Toward a configurational approach to society and culture in New Guinea. *Journal of the Polynesian Society* 75:267–86.

Pullar, E. M. 1950. The wild (feral) pigs of Australia and their role in the spread of infectious diseases. *Australian Veterinary Journal* (May):99–110.

_____. 1953. The wild (feral) pigs of Australia: Their origin, distribution and economic importance. Melbourne: Memoirs of the National Museum 18:17–23.

Quastler, Henry. 1952. Feedback mechanisms in cellular biology: In: *Cybernetics.* New York: Transactions of the Ninth Josiah Macy Foundation Conference.

Quinlaven, P. J. 1954. Afek of Telefomin: A fabulous story from New Guinea which led to a strange story. *Oceania* 25:17–22.

Rand, Austin L. 1937. Some original observations on the habits of Dactylopsila trivigata. *American Museum Novitates* No. 957.

_____ and Gilliard, E. Thomas. 1967. *Handbook of New Guinea Birds.* London: Weidenfeld and Nicolson.

Rappaport, Roy A. 1963. Aspects of man's influence upon island ecosystems: alteration and control. In: *Man's Place in the Island Ecosystem*. R. Fosberg, ed. Honolulu: Bishop Museum.

———. 1966. Ritual in the Ecology of a New Guinea People. Ph.D. Dissertation in Anthropology, Columbia University.

———. 1968. *Pigs for the Ancestors: Ritual in the Ecology of a New Guinea People*. New Haven: Yale University Press.

———. 1971a. Nature, culture, and ecological anthropology. In: *Man, Culture, and Society*. 2nd ed. H. Shapiro, ed. New York: Oxford.

———. 1971b. The flow of energy in an agricultural society. *Scientific American* 225(3):116–32.

———. 1979. *Ecology, Meaning and Religion*. Richmond, California: North Atlantic Books.

———. 1984. *Pigs for the Ancestors: Ritual in the Ecology of a New Guinea People*. 2nd Edition. New Haven: Yale University Press.

Rapport, D.J. and Turner, J.E. 1977. Economic models in ecology. *Science* 195:367–73.

Regan, Colm. 1983. Underdevelopment and hazards in historical perspective: an Irish case study. In: *Interpretations of Calamity*. K. Hewitt, ed. London: Allen & Unwin. pp. 98–120.

Reynders, J. J. 1962. Shifting cultivation in the Star Mountains area. *Nova Guinea* 10, Anthropology No. 3. Leiden: E. J. Brill.

Richards, Audrey I. 1948. *Hunger and Work in a Savage Tribe: A Functional Study of Nutrition among Southern Bantu*. Glencoe: The Free Press.

Ride, A.W.D.L. 1970. *A Guide to the Native Mammals of Australia*. Melbourne: Oxford University Press.

Ruddle, K.,; Johnson, D.; Townsend, P. K.; and Rees, J. D. 1978. *Palm Sago: A Tropical Starch from Marginal Lands*. Honolulu: University Press of Hawaii.

Rudner, Richard S. 1966. *Philosophy of Social Science*. Englewood Cliffs, New Jersey: Prentice Hall.

Rutgers, A. 1970. Text for "John Gould: Birds of New Guinea." London: Methuen.

Ruxton, B. P. 1967. Slopewash under primary rainforest in northern Papua. In: *Landford Studies from Australia and New Guinea*. Jennings and Mabutt, eds. Canberra: Australian National University Press.

Sahlins, Marshall. 1972. *Stone Age Economics*. Chicago: Aldine.

——— and Service, Elman R. 1960. *Evolution and Culture*. Ann Arbor: University of Michigan Press.

Sakagami, Shoichi F. 1961. An ecological perspective of Marcus Island with special reference to land animals. *Pacific Science* 15(1):82–104.

Salisbury, Richard F. 1962. *From Stone to Steel*. New York: Cambridge University Press.

———. 1965. The Siane of the eastern highlands. In: *Gods, Ghosts and Men in Melanesia*. P. Lawrence and M.J. Meggitt, eds. Melbourne: Oxford University Press, pp. 50–77.

Scheffler, Harold W. 1965. *Choiseul Island Social Structure*. Berkeley: University of California Press.

Schieffelin, Edward L. 1975. Felling the trees on top of the crop. *Oceania* 46(2).

———. 1976. *The Sorrow of the Lonely and the Burning of the Dancers*. New York: St. Martins.

Schneider, Harold K. 1957. The subsistence role of cattle among the Pakot and in East Africa. *American Anthropologist* 59:278–300.

Schwartz, Theodore. 1962. Systems of areal integration: some considerations based on the Admiralty Islands of northern Melanesia. *Anthropological Forum* 1:56–97.

Sharp, Lauriston. 1953. Steel axes for stone-age Australians. *Human Organization* 11:17–22.

Simon, Herbert. 1962. The architecture of complexity. *Proceedings of the American Philosophical Society* 106(6).

Simpson, Colin. 1953. *Adam with Arrows*. Sydney: Angus and Robertson.

Siskind, Janet. 1973. *To Hunt in the Morning*. New York: Oxford University Press.

Slobodkin, L. B. 1961. *The Growth and Regulation of Animal Populations*. New York: Holt, Rinehart and Winston.

———. 1968. Toward a predictive theory of evolution. In: *Population Biology and Evolution*. R. C. Lewontin, ed. Syracuse: Syracuse University Press. pp. 187–205.

Smith, Robert L. 1966. *Ecology and Field Biology*. New York: Harper and Row.

Spedding, C. R. W. 1979. *An Introduction to Agricultural Systems*. London: Applied Science.

Spooner, Brian, ed. 1972. *Population Growth: Anthropological Implications*. Cambridge, Ma.: MIT Press.

Steadman, L. 1975. Cannibal witches among the Hewa. *Oceania* 46:114–21.

Stenning, D. J. 1957. Transhumance, migration, and migratory drift. *Journal of the Royal Anthropological Institute* 87:57–73.

Stouffer, Samuel A. 1940. Intervening opportunities: a theory relating mobility and distance. *American Sociological Review* 5:845–67.

Street, John. 1969. An evaluation of the concept of carrying capacity. *Professional Geographer* 21:1104–7.

Suttles, Wayne. 1960. Affinal ties, subsistence, and prestige among the Coast Salish. *American Anthropologist* 62:296–305.

Swadling, Pamela. 1981. *Papua New Guinea's Prehistory: An Introduction*. Boroko: Papua New Guinea National Museum and Art Gallery.

Sweet, Louise E. 1965. Camel pastoralism in North Arabia and the minimal camping unit. In: *Man, Culture and Animals*. A. Leeds and A. P. Vayda, eds. Washington: American Association for the Advancement of Science Publication No. 78.

Tate, G. H. H. 1951. The rodents of Australia and New Guinea. *Bulletin of the American Museum of Natural History* 97(4):183–430.

———. 1952. Weights of Queensland mammals. *Journal of Mammalogy* 33(1):117–18.

Taylor, J. L. 1971 [1939]. Hagen-Sepik Patrol 1938–39: Interim Report. *New Guinea* 6(3):24–51.

Taylor, J. Mary and Homer, B. Elizabeth. 1973. Results of the Archbold Expeditions No. 98. Systematics of native Australian Rattus (Rodentia, Muridae). *Bulletin of the American Museum of Natural History* 150:1–130.

Tevis, L. 1956. The responses of small mammal populations to logging Douglas fur. *Journal of Mammalogy* 37:189–96.

Thomas, David. 1971. Cybernetic modeling of historic Shoshoni economic patterns. *Anthropological Papers* No. 1, University of Oregon.

Thomas, R. Brooke. 1973. *Human Adaptation to a High Andean Energy Flow System*. Occasional Papers in Anthropology No. 7. University Park: Pennsylvania State University.

Timbergen, N. 1960. The natural control of insects in pinewoods. I. Factors influencing the intensity of predation in songbirds. *Arch. Neerl. Zool.* 13:265–343.

Tisdell, C. A. 1982. *Wild Pigs: Environmental Pest or Economic Resource*. Sydney: Pergamon.

Toffler, Alvin. 1971. *Future Shock*. New York: Bantam.

Townsend, Patricia K. 1969. Subsistence and Social Organization in a New Guinea Society. Ph. D. Dissertation in Anthropology. Ann Arbor, Mi.: University of Michigan.

———; Liao, S-C; and Konlande, J. E. 1973. Nutritive contributions of sago ash used as a native salt in Papua New Guinea. *Ecology of Food and Nutrition* 2:91–97.

Troughton, Ellis. 1967a. *Furred Animals of Australia*. 9th Edition. Sydney: Angus and Robertson.

———. 1967b. Marsupials. In: *A Treasury of Australian Wildlife*. D. F. McMichael, ed. Sydney: Ure Smith.

Turnbull, Colin. 1968. The importance of flux in two hunting societies. In: *Man the Hunter*. R. B. Lee and I. DeVore, eds. Chicago: Aldine, pp. 132–37.

Turney-High, Harry Holbert. 1971. *Primitive War: Its Practice and Concepts*. 2nd Edition. Columbia: University of South Carolina Press.

Tustin, A. 1952. Feedback. *Scientific American* (September). *Scientific American Offprint* No. 327. Salt Lake City: W. H. Freeman.

Van Deusen, Hobart M. 1957. Results of the Archbold Expeditions No. 76. A new species of wallaby (Genus Dorcopsus) from Goodenough Island, Papua. American Museum Novitates 1826.

_____. 1960. Notes on the marsupial feather tailed glider of Australia. *Journal of Mammalogy* 41(2):263–64.

_____. 1966. Range and habitat of the bandicoot Echymipera clara in New Guinea. *Journal of Mammalogy* 47(4):721–23.

_____. 1971. Zaglossus, New Guinea's egg-laying anteater. *Fauna* 2(March/April):13–19.

_____. 1972. Some comments on the ecology of some highlands mammals. In: *Ol Tumbuna*. J. P. White. Terra Australis 2. Department of Prehistory, Research School of Pacific Studies, Australian National University, Canberra.

_____ and George, Graeme G. 1969. Results of the Archbold Expeditions No. 90. Notes on the echidnas (Mammalia, Tachyglossidae) of New Guinea. American Museum Novitates 2383.

Vayda, Andrew P. 1961. A re-examination of Northwest Coast economic systems. *Transactions of the New York Academy of Sciences, Ser. II*, 23:618–24.

_____. 1966. Diversity and uniformity in New Guinea. *Acta Ethnographica Academiae Scientarium Hungaricae*. Thomus 15.

_____. 1983. Progressive contextualization: methods for research in human ecology. *Human Ecology* 11(3):265–81.

_____ and Cook, Edwin A. 1964. Structural variability in the Bismarck Mountain cultures of New Guinea: a preliminary report. *Transactions of the New York Academy of Sciences, Ser. II*, 26:798–803.

_____; Leeds, A.; and Smith, D. 1961. The place of pigs in Melanesian subsistence. In: *Patterns of Land Utilization and Other Papers*. Proceedings of the 1961 Annual Spring Meeting of the American Ethnological Society. Viola Garfield, ed. Seattle: University of Washington Press.

_____ and McCay, Bonnie. 1975. New directions in ecology and ecological anthropology. *Annual Review of Anthropology* 4:293–306.

_____ and McCay, Bonnie. 1977. Problems in the identification of environmetal problems. In: *Subsistence and Survival*. T. Bayliss-Smith and R. Feachem, eds. London: Academic Press. pp. 411–18.

_____ and Rappaport, Roy. 1968. Ecology, cultural and non-cultural. In: *Introduction to Cultural Anthropology*. J. D. Clifton, ed. Boston: Houghton Mifflin.

Volterra, V. 1931. Variations and fluctuations in the number of individuals in cohabiting animal species. In: *Animal Ecology*. R. N. Chapman, ed. New York: McGraw-Hill.

Waddell, Eric. 1972. *The Mound Builders: Agricultural Practices, Environment and Society in the Central Highlands of New Guinea*. Seattle: University of Washington Press.

_____. 1975. How the Enga cope with frost: responses to climatic perturbations in the Central Highlands of New Guinea. *Human Ecology* 3:249–73.

_____. 1983. Coping with frosts, governments and disaster experts. In: *Interpretations of Calamity*. K. Hewitt, ed. London: Allen & Unwin. pp. 33–43.

Wagner, Roy. 1967. *The Curse of Souw: Principles of Daribi Clan Definition and Alliance in New Guinea*. Chicago: University of Chicago Press.

Wallace, A. R. 1962 [Original 1869]. *The Malay Archipelago*. New York: Dover.

Watson, J. B. 1965a. From hunting to horticulture in the New Guinea highlands. *Ethnology* 4:295–309.

_____. 1965b. The significance of recent ecological change in the Central Highlands of New Guinea. *Journal of the Polynesian Society* 74:438–50.

_____. 1977. Pigs, fodder and the Jones effect in post-ippomoean New Guinea. *Ethnology* 16:57–69.

Watt, Kenneth E. F. 1962. The conceptual formulation and mathematical solution of practical problems in population input-output dynamics. In: *The Exploitation of Natural Animal Populations.* LeCren and Holgate, eds. *Symposium of the British Ecological Society* 2:191–203.

———. 1964a. Computers and the evaluation of resource management strategies. *American Scientist* 52:408–18.

———. 1964b. The use of mathematics and computers to determine optimal strategy for a given insect pest control problem. *Canadian Entomologist* 96:202–20.

———. 1968. *Ecology and Resource Management.* New York: McGraw-Hill.

Watts, Michael. 1983. On the poverty of theory: natural hazards research in context. In: *Interpretations of Calamity.* K. Hewitt, ed. London: Allen & Unwin.

Weeks, Sheldon, ed. 1981. Introduction. In: *Oksapmin: Development and Change.* S. Weeks, ed. Port Moresby: Educational Research Unit, University of Papua New Guinea. pp. 13–33.

Weiner, Norbert. 1948. *Cybernetics: On Control and Communication in the Animal and in the Machine.* New York: Wiley.

Wheatcroft, Wilson. 1975. The Legacy of Afekan: Cultural Symbolic Interpretations of Religion among the Tifalmin of New Guinea. Ph.D. Dissertation in Anthropology. Chicago: University of Chicago.

White, J. Peter. 1972. *Ol Tumbuna: Archaeological Excavations in the Eastern Central Highlands, Papua New Guinea.* Terra Australis 2. Department of Prehistory, Research School of Pacific Studies, Australian National University, Canberra.

White, Leslie. 1959. *The Evolution of Culture.* New York: McGraw-Hill.

White, T. E. 1953. A method of calculating the dietary percentage of various food animals utilized by various aboriginal peoples. *American Antiquity* 18(4):396–98.

Wiens, Harold J. 1962. *Atoll Environment and Ecology.* New Haven: Yale University Press.

Wilmsen, Edwin N. 1973. Interaction, spacing behavior, and the organization of hunting bands. *Journal of Anthropological Research* 29:1–31.

Winter, J.W. 1966. Bird predation by the Australian marsupial squirrel glider. *Journal of Mammalogy* 47:530.

Winterhalder, B. and Smith, E. A., eds. 1981. *Hunter-Gatherer Foraging Strategies: Ethnographic and Archaeological Analyses.* Chicago: University of Chicago Press.

Womersley, John S., ed. 1978. *Handbook of the Flora of Papua New Guinea,* Vol. I. Melbourne: Melbourne University Press.

Wood, G. W. and Barrett, R. G. 1979. Status of wild pigs in the United States. *The Wildlife Society Bulletin* 7(4):237–46.

Wood, G. W. and Lynn, T. E. 1977. Wild hogs in southern forests. *Southern Journal of Applied Forestry* 1:2.

Woodham-Smith, C. 1962. *The Great Hunger.* London: Hamish Hamilton.

Wurm, S. A. 1964. Australian New Guinea highland languages and the distribution of their typological features. In: *New Guinea: The Central Highlands.* J. B. Watson, ed. *American Anthropologist* 66(4, Part II):77–97.

Wynne-Edwards, V. C. 1962. *Animal Dispersion in Relation to Social Behavior.* London: Haffner.

Zelinsky, Wilbur. 1971. The hypothesis of the mobility transition. *Geographical Review* 61(2):219–49.

Ziegler, A. C. 1972. *Rodents. Encyclopaedia of Papua and New Guinea.* Vol. II. Melbourne: Melbourne University Press. pp. 1017–20.

———. 1982. An ecological check-list of New Guinea recent mammals. In: *Biogeography and Ecology of New Guinea.* J. L. Gressitt, ed. The Hague: W. Junk. pp. 863–96.

Index

Abau, 282
Ackerman, A.J., 240
Afek, 203, 330
Afterlife. *See* Religion
Age: and activity, 242–43, 244–45; role of elderly, 2, 224
Agriculture: accessibility of economic trees, 246; and intensification 57; and modernization, 84, 109, 110; and topography, 67; and urbanization, 107, 108; change in, 102; clearing, 86; crop selection, 72, 73, 92, 93, 96, 97, 98, 108, 109, 111; crops: *abika,* 87; amaranthus, 73, 82; banana, 73, 82, 87; beans, 87; breadfruit, 72; cassava, 72, 106, 111; citrus, 72; coconut, 72; gourds, 82; green vegetables, 82; pandanus, 68, 76, 109; papaya, 87; pineapple, 304; pit-pit, 82, 87, 88; rungia, 72; sago, 71, 74, 76, 106; spinach, 82; sugar cane, 71, 82, 87; sweet potato, 56, 76, 82, 88, 92, 97, 101–12, 145, 152; taro, 64, 73, 74, 76, 80, 90–101, 106, 109, 110, 145, 152; tobacco, 73, 82; cultivation methods, 86–88; domestic pig herd size, 48; effect on environment, 37, 47, 247–48; erosion, 71; export crops, 108; fallow cycle, 106; flexibility in, 87, 88, 93; garden invasion by pigs, 48, 145–46, 246; garden types, 48, 82; growing conditions, 66; harvest, 80; labor requirements of, 86, 89–90, 101, 111; monoculture vs. polyculture, 74, 92–98, 110; ornamentals, 73; pests and pathogens, 96, 110–11; pig husbandry, 48, 49, 56, 88–89, 107, 145; pig slaughter, 50; planting, 86–88; productivity, 79, 87; rainfall, 66; resource pressure, 112; role of, 79; seasonality, 66; sexual division of labor in, 84–85; site selection, 86; soils, 67; sylvaculture (*see also* particular crops), 74; systems, metataxonomy of, 80; technology, 82–84,

87; technology: steel tools, 82–84, 292–94; stone tools, 82–83; Telefolmin pig husbandry, 270; weeding, 244
Alland, A., 7
Allen M., 223
Alliance. *See* Parish: alliance
Am-nakai Miyanmin, 54, 72, 97, 131, 160, 161, 162, 181, 198, 224, 238, 239; as house people, 76; identified, 202; lineages, 194; warfare, 54
Amaloten (Amaromin), 198, 201, 202, 266, 268, 281
Ancestral spirits. *See* Religion
Atbalmin, 61, 96, 164, 175, 178, 179–80, 192, 263, 289, 292, 296, 301
Aviation, 237, 290, 296, 298–300

Baker, J., 138
Bandicoot, 107, 113, 114, 125, 130, 151
Barnes, J., 159, 175
Barrau, J., 83
Barth, F., 62, 86, 221, 222, 223, 265, 274, 331
Bartholomew, G.A., 38
Bateson, G., 16, 19, 20, 162, 331
Bats, 113, 115, 126, 138
Behavior (*see also* Group behavior: and the individual): scrambling and queuing, 159, 239
Berlinski, D., 16, 17, 37
Bicchieri, M.G., 133
Big men, 2, 164
Bimin, 92, 96
Biological taxonomy: compared with ethnotaxonomy, 75, 124, 328
Bip (*see also* Hamlet), 75
Birds, 116, 117, 118, 126, 134, 135, 138, 154; cassowary, 107, 113, 116, 119, 126, 135, 143, 150, 151; cockatoo, 113, 119; hornbill, 113; pigeon (crown), 113; of paradise, 113, 118, 154
Biyami, 264